Women in the Peninsular War

Also by Charles J. Esdaile

The Spanish Army in the Revolutionary Era, 1788–1814 (Lancaster, UK, 1985)
The Spanish Army in the Peninsular War (Manchester and New York, 1988)
The Duke of Wellington and the Command of the Spanish Army, 1812–14 (Basingstoke, UK, and New York, 1990)
Spain in the Liberal Age: From Constitution to Civil War, 1808–1939 (Oxford, 2000)
The French Wars, 1792–1815 (London, 2001)
The Peninsular War: A New History (London, 2002; New York, 2003)
Fighting Napoleon: Guerrillas, Bandits, and Adventurers in Spain, 1808–1814 (New Haven, 2004)
Popular Resistance in the French Wars: Patriots, Partisans and Land Pirates (Basingstoke, UK, and New York, 2005)
Napoleon's Wars: An International History, 1803–1815 (London and New York, 2008)
Peninsular Eyewitnesses: The Experience of War in Spain and Portugal, 1808–1813 (Barnsley, UK, 2008)
Outpost of Empire: The Napoleonic Occupation of Andalucía, 1810–1812 (Norman, Okla., 2012)

Women in the Peninsular War

Charles J. Esdaile

University of Oklahoma Press : Norman

Library of Congress Cataloging-in-Publication Data

Esdaile, Charles J.
Women in the Peninsular War / Charles J. Esdaile.
pages cm
Includes bibliographical references and index.
ISBN 978-0-8061-4478-8 (hardcover) ISBN 978-0-8061-8569-9 (paper) 1. Peninsular War, 1807–1814—Participation, Female. 2. Peninsular War, 1807–1814—Women. I. Title.
DC231.E8343 2014
940.2'70820946—dc23
2013049516

The paper in this book meets the guidelines for permanence and durability of the Committee on Production Guidelines for Book Longevity of the Council on Library Resources, Inc. ∞

For all the women

Contents

Preface

This book is in the first instance the product of a historiographical anomaly. In brief, for the past thirty years or more, in line with the growth of a much wider interest in women's history in general, there has been a steady stream of publications dealing with, first, the role played by women in warfare in the period from 1650 to 1850; second, the manner in which women both experienced and reacted to the onset of armed conflict; and, third, the relationship which developed between women and the military estate in peace and war alike.[1] Many of them very sound, these works provide a good general grounding for anyone interested in the female dimensions of matters relating to the field of 'war and society', and they are certainly drawn to the attention of anyone who chooses to read the current study. That said, the coverage afforded by this literature is at best patchy, and sometimes surprisingly so. Thus, although the Napoleonic Wars were by far the bloodiest and most destructive conflict in the period under consideration, they have, for whatever reason, attracted only a limited amount of attention: there is a fair amount on Britain, France and various parts of modern-day Germany, but beyond that very little.[2] Nor is this an end to the problem. By far the most prolonged campaign of the entire period, and, with the possible exception of the Russian campaign of 1812, easily the most costly and destructive was the Peninsular War of 1808–14. Yet this figures scarcely at all in the English-language historiography: setting aside works that make some mention of it in the context of studies of the camp-followers of the British and French armies, the only ones that look at it as a topic in its own right are two short pieces by the American historian, John Tone. To make matters worse, these are for a number of reasons less than satisfactory, not least because Tone insists on, first, holding fast to the increasingly questionable line that the war against Napoleon enjoyed the unwavering support of the people, and, second, making the idea of active female participation in the war effort the centre piece of his argument.[3] Meanwhile, matters are scarcely improved if we turn to works in Spanish (in Portuguese, alas, there is nothing whatsoever). In recent years, certainly, the dated historiography of the nineteenth-century tradition—a tradition whose line is pretty much the same as the one advocated by Tone—has been augmented by the efforts of a variety of academic historians, the vast majority of them women.[4] Yet the value of this material, too, is open to question: like Tone, the dominant voices within this tendency proceed from an unquestioning acceptance of the idea that the struggle in Spain and Portugal was very much a people's war, while, like Tone again, proceeding from a very limited range of information, they are concerned to push the notion of the woman as combatant or, at least, participant, being so set on this that they completely fail to examine other ways in which women understood, experienced and responded to the conflict.[5]

These deficiencies, meanwhile, are accompanied by a further problem in that it is evident that no historian has ever attempted to assimilate the women who came to the war with the women to whom the war came. Thus, if Page's work on women in Wellington's army barely scrapes the surface in its mentions of the thousands of Spanish and Portuguese campfollowers who joined its ranks in the course of the war, Fernández García's *Mujeres en la Guerra de la Independencia* is all but devoid of any references to the British and French campfollowers who also participated in the struggle. Yet, as has been long since recognised in the wider historiography, camp-following was a central feature of the military experience of the period, and at the same time one which afforded important opportunities to the women who found themselves caught up in the conflict, including, not least, the chance to choose their own partners.

Quite clearly, then, there is a need for a study that goes some way towards filling the gap in the historiography which yawns before us. However, this is, perhaps, easier said than achieved. As is widely understood, the female voice is often absent from the sources, and all the more so in respect of the Spain and Portugal of 1808, a society, of course, in which the vast majority of women were either altogether illiterate or discouraged from informing themselves about the issues of the day, let alone expressing themselves upon them. To some limited extent, this problem can be addressed through the use of alternative sources such as folksong, but these present their own problems of interpretation. At the same time, while the contemporary press offers a rich vein of information (if also a somewhat intermittent one), the advertisements, lists of donors and court reports of which the bulk of the material concerned consists at best of mere 'snapshots' that are often as tantalising as they are revealing). As for the archives, these do contain some material, but it is both widely dispersed and for the most part extremely sparse. No apology, then, is made for relying heavily on the hundreds of journals, memoirs and collections of correspondence that have come down to us from British and French veterans of the conflict (one would wish, of course, to include here Spanish and Portuguese veterans of the conflict as well, but the fact is that the numerous differences that existed in the post-Napoleonic age between the societies of Britain and France and those of Spain and Portugal mean that very few of them left any written record of their experiences). To say that these sources are not perfect either is an understatement, but care has been taken to exclude or at least to challenge their most dubious elements, whilst the sheer volume of material that they offer means that it is possible to establish, for example, common patterns of behaviour. Clearly, very rarely can a guarantee ever be offered of this or that incident being true or even semi-true, but, taken in the round, they at the very least cannot be dismissed out of hand.[6]

Finally, some notes on the text. First of all, quotation: in transcribing original material, the author has had no hesitation in modernising spelling and punctuation alike and, where necessary, correcting place names, but, in doing so, he has taken care to ensure that no damage has been done to the passage's meaning. Second of all, usage: for the sake of simplicity, whilst it is recognised that some men and not a few children can be comprehended in its meaning, the term 'campfollowers' will be employed to refer to those women who marched with the baggage trains of one or other of the armies that fought in the conflict; equally, whilst it is recognised that the men which made it up included Germans, Frenchmen, Italians, Poles and even Spaniards, the term, 'British army' will be used to refer to all soldiers and military units in the employ of King George III; and, finally, while it is similarly recognised that the men which made it up included Belgians, Dutchmen, Germans, Italians and Poles, some of whom were serving in armies of one or other of the satellite states of the French empire, the term 'French army' will be used to refer to all soldiers and military units in the employ of Napoleon Bonaparte.[7] And third of all, Spanish and Portuguese surnames: for the sake of brevity, only patronyms have been employed except in those cases where they are so common—e.g., Fernández/Fernandes, Gómez/Gomes, Suárez/Soares—that to omit the matronym would cause inconvenience.

First of all, the mistakes and failings in this work are mine and mine alone. Second of all, as usual, my thanks are heartfelt and go out to many people: Chuck Rankin and his excellent (and very long-suffering) team at Oklahoma University Press; my agent, Bill Hamilton; the staff at all the libraries and archives that have figured in the elaboration of this project; my friends and colleagues, Alan Forrest, Louise Carter, Tom Cardoza and Michael J. Hughes (not to be confused with the other Michael J. Hughes, though he too is worthy of mention on account of many years of fellowship and good counsel), all of whom have read large portions of the manuscript and been most generous with comment and encouragement alike; Maria de Deus Duarte, whose kind invitation to give a seminar paper in Lisbon sowed the seeds that led to this book; the medical team that exactly one year ago today saved my life in a moment of dire medical emergency; the many Spanish friends who put up with my endless comings and goings with unfailing grace and generosity, and have in some instances—Arsenio García Fuertes, Alicia Laspra and Jesus Maroto are particularly good examples here—been most generous in terms of sharing material with me or keeping me up to date with the historiography; and, last but not least, Alison—truly the best and bravest campfollower of them all—and my *enfants du troupe,* Andrew, Helen, Maribel and Bernadette: as ever, I am sure that I have got more from all of them than they have ever got from me, but at least I can assure them that my days of—dare I say it?—womanising are at long last at an end!

University of Liverpool
28 August 2012

Women in the Peninsular War

1

Images

Let us begin with a paradox. In essence, this book is about the manner in which women experienced the Peninsular War of 1808–14 and the impact which the latter had upon their lives. As stated in the preface, this aspect of the struggle is one that has hitherto at best been treated in a very inadequate fashion. Yet the women of the Peninsular War are very far from being unknown, or, at least, unenvisaged. On the contrary, from 1814 onwards they have been imagined as experiencing the conflict in a wide variety of ways, some of them conventional and some of them less so, the greatest want of the historiography having been its failure to test out these images. In this book we shall try to remedy this situation, but, before doing so, it is first necessary to spend some time reviewing the images that have come down to us, and all the more so as we shall in the process discover a far greater breadth of historic memory than might at first be expected.

If we are looking for images of women, the logical place to begin is the art spawned by the conflict. For a long time interested only in high politics and operational military history, chroniclers of the war and the academic historians who succeeded them could happily expunge women from their works, but for artists this was much less easy: away from the actual battle lines, it was difficult to conceive of a world in which women were not part of the visual scene. At the same time, whereas women constituted a distraction from the narrative within which writers wished to operate, artists actually had many positive reasons to include women in their work. Thus, women could be used to add colour, to heighten emotion, or to stress some political point, whether it was the unity of the populace in the face of French aggression or the atrocities engaged in by one side or the other. In consequence, it is only a slight exaggeration to say that, other than in the set-piece battle scenes associated with such artists as Butler, Caton Woodville and Casado de Alisal, the women of Iberia were almost as present in the iconography of the Peninsular War as they were absent from its historiography. That said, whether the iconography of the war did very much to further historical understanding is another matter, for, as we shall see, it set in stone many myths which to this day continue to obstruct the study of the 'women's history' of the conflict (and not just that: Goya's famous *Desastres de la Guerra* are probably the images of the Peninsular War that are most frequently reproduced, and yet the view that they offer of the struggle is at best incomplete and, at worst, wildly misleading).

In so far as the iconography of the Peninsular War is concerned, the prints, paintings and engravings which constitute it fall into a relatively small number of categories. In brief, although the three groups are inclined to be a trifle blurred, we have the woman as heroine, the woman as victim and the woman as auxiliary in the patriotic struggle. In so far as the first category is concerned, the obvious place to begin is the image of Agustina de Aragón (more precisely, Agustina Zaragoza Domenech). The history of this woman—conceivably the most famous individual combatant of the Peninsular War—is detailed elsewhere, but in brief she came to fame when she rushed forward at a crucial moment during the first siege of Zaragoza in July 1808 and saved a key position by firing a cannon into the faces of some advancing French troops. Within weeks of this event having taken place, it was on its way to becoming *the* stock image of Spain's struggle against Napoleon. Determined to enhance his reputation by every means available, in the autumn of 1808 the Captain General and *de facto* dictator of Zaragoza, General José Palafox y Melci, summoned a trio of well-known artists from Madrid and commissioned them to create a visual record of both the city's defenders and the ruins left by the siege. Of the men concerned, the most famous—none other than Francisco de Goya—went his own way (see below), but the other two—Fernando Brambila and Juan Gálvez—proved more co-operative, and the result was the publication in 1812–13 of a set of engravings entitled *Las ruinas de Zaragoza* depicting, first, a series of ruined buildings; second, the main events of the siege; and, third, the chief defenders of the city. Prominent among these last, needless to say, was Agustina Zaragoza, the latter being depicted in a virago-like pose suggesting both anger and contempt for the enemy.[1]

Reproduced many times over in the course of the nineteenth century in print, painting and engraving, and more-or-less subtly adapted to reflect the views of the artist, the image of Domenech and her cannon became a metaphor for both the Spanish people's determination to resist Napoleon and the women of Spain's active participation in the struggle that resulted.[2] It is important to realize, however, that, Domenech was never short of sisters. On the contrary, in the very collection that first gave her image to the world, the image of the warrior woman is repeatedly revisited. Amongst the individual portraits, then, we have Casta Álvarez, a young peasant woman who is supposed to have armed herself with a musket and bayonet and helped defend the Puerta de Sancho, and the Condesa de Bureta, a female relative of Palafox's who placed her personal fortune at the service of the defenders and assisted with the provision of food and medical supplies. Meanwhile, in several of the battle scenes, women may be seen fighting in the front ranks and even taking on the French without any men being present at all. As the nineteenth century wore on, meanwhile, images of the woman in arms continued to proliferate. The Condesa de Bureta made a renewed appearance as an amazon at the hands of the Extremaduran painter, Nicolás Mejía, while a fresh addition to the iconography of Zaragoza's heroines appeared in the form of a painting of one Manuela Sancho that was produced by Fernando Jiménez Nicanor in 1887, Sancho being a woman of some means who was wounded whilst helping to defend the convent of San José in December 1808.[3] In addition to these images there appeared many paintings of the siege in which unknown women were very obvious foci of attention: in Vicente Palmoril's *Escena de los sitios de Zaragoza,* a woman stands poised with a musket above her head ready to kill the first French soldier brave enough to emerge from a hole that has just been blown in a wall, while in Maurice Orange's *Defenseurs de Zaragoza* (1893) another woman turns aside from a long column of emaciated survivors to harangue the French troops lining the street.[4] Meanwhile, it was not just the defence of Zaragoza that provided examples of women who had sprung to arms. Almost equally fruitful as a source was the rising of the Dos de Mayo, women appearing in several paintings of the defence of the artillery park of Monteleón.[5]

Thus far, we have seen the Peninsular War treated very much in terms of military glory. The second group of images that we must look at, however, are much darker (indeed, often quite literally so): consider, for instance, the alternative vision of the Dos de Mayo painted by Palmeroli which has the women of Madrid not battling the French to the death but rather wringing their hands over the bodies of menfolk killed by Murat's firing squads.[6] We come here to the idea of women as victim. Although there are a few other examples—in an engraving published in 1813 by the Portuguese artist, Domingos de Sequeira, we see a Lisbon street over-run with desperate female refugees, while successive depictions of the disaster that took place at Oporto in March 1809 when large numbers of fugitives who were trying to get across the River Douro were drowned when the pontoon bridge they were using gave way beneath them emphasise the fact that many of the victims were women[7]—the chief exponent of this position is Francisco de Goya. Though a participant in the visit to Zaragoza mentioned above, Goya was clearly unimpressed by Palafox's bluster, while his attitude towards the uprising remained distinctly ambivalent. Thus, at first sight the 'Dos de Mayo' and the 'Tres de Mayo' seem a hymn to popular heroism, but, especially when viewed in the light of the later 'Caprichos', they can just as easily be read as a condemnation of popular violence and stupidity. And consider, too, the relatively unknown 'Ataque sobre un campamento militar': painted in approximately 1809, this shows a group of civilians including a young woman cradling a baby flying in panic before some advancing troops without putting up the slightest resistance.[8] For Goya, then, neither the Spanish people in general, nor Spanish women in particular, were necessarily heroic, and it is therefore no coincidence that he remained aloof from Gálvez and Brambila and instead worked in secret on a parallel series of engravings that presented an extremely negative view of the war and was entitled 'The Fatal Consequences of Spain's Bloody War with Bonaparte and other Decided Caprices' (the title by which they are known today—'The Disasters of War'—was only given them when they appeared in print in 1863).[9]

Yet, denunciations of the Spanish struggle though they were, the effect of these engravings was rather to confirm belief in the War of Independence as a glorious epoch in Spanish history. In the first place, there were echoes of the myth of the female warrior. In the engraving entitled 'Que valor!' ('What courage!'), we see the slim figure of Domenech not just standing erect and defiant beside an enormous fieldpiece, but also symbolically shielding the observer from an unseen opponent. Nor, meanwhile, is this the only engraving in the series that projects the idea of the woman as combatant, albeit perhaps as a temporary one who takes up arms only in dire emergency. Thus, in 'Y son fieras' ('And they, too, are furies') a group of women who have obviously been taken by surprise by French troops—one of them is carrying a baby under her arm—are seen fighting desperately to defend themselves with a variety of improvised weapons. Less dramatic, but otherwise rather similar is 'Las mujeres dan valor' ('The women inspire courage') in which we see two women locked in combat with two French soldiers who have evidently been trying to rape them, and 'No quieren' ('This is not love') in which a French soldier grapples with a girl while an old woman—possibly her mother, perhaps—attempts to stab him in the back. However, striking though these four engravings are—engravings which, it should be stressed in no way imply that women were anything other than occasional combatants—on looking at the 'Disasters of War' as a whole, we generally see women rather as the helpless victims of man's inhumanity. In 'Tampoco' ('Nor this'), 'Ni por esas' ('Not even for these'), 'Amarga presencia' ('Bitter presence'), 'Ya no hay tiempo' ('There is no longer any time'), women are seen being raped; in 'No se puede mirar' ('One cannot look'), they figure in a mass execution; in 'Estragos de la guerra' ('War damage'), they are crushed in the wreckage of a collapsing building; in 'Escapan de las llamas' ('Escaping from the flames'), 'Yo lo vi' ('I saw this') and 'Y esto también' ('And this too'), they become fugitives and refugees; in 'Que alboroto es este?' ('What is all this row'?), they collapse in floods of tears on receiving news of the death or execution of a son or husband; and, finally in 'Cruel lástima' ('Cruel misfortune'), 'Caridad de una mujer' ('Charity of a woman'), 'Madre infeliz' ('Unhappy mother'), 'Gracias a la almorta' ('Thanks be to vetch'), 'No llegan a tiempo' ('They did not arrive in time'), 'Sanos y enfermos' ('Healthy and sick'), 'De que sirve una taza?' ('What is the use of a cup?') and 'Si son de otro linaje' ('If they are of other lineage'), they are seen begging in the streets or succumbing to famine and disease (be it noted that in one or two instances these images of women enduring the utmost misery also show women succouring the poor and starving, but this, of course, merely opens a door on yet another aspect of traditional ideas of how women become engaged with the experience of war). War, then, was horrible, but, precisely because the enemy appeared to be so terrible, the War of Independence in particular was a struggle that self-evidently had to be embarked upon and, indeed, had called forth the heroism of men and women alike.[10]

It is, alas, not just nineteenth-century Spaniards who have a tendency to read into the *Desastres de la Guerra* a message that their author never intended them to portray. Thus, Janis Tomlinson has suggested that a constant theme in the work of Francisco de Goya was the emergence of Spain's women from the reclusion typical of the 'Golden Age' to a new position of much greater visibility in which they were not only much more widely seen, but also much bolder in their general behaviour. In this development, there were two main 'types': the *petimetra*—the fashionable woman of good family who affected French fashions and considered herself the epitome of the new age of enlightenment—and the *maja*—the rough, tough harridan of street and market who rather stood unashamedly for the values of traditional Spain—and the two of them are certainly faithfully recorded by Goya. However, can we go further than that? Let us for the sake of argument agree with Tomlinson that women were indeed becoming more visible (though it is hard to imagine that the streets of Hapsburg Madrid were not just as teeming with women as that of its Bourbon counterpart: even if the women of the upper classes were kept locked away, economic necessity alone would have ensured that their poorer counterparts would still have been a constant presence). And, even if this is definitely a double-edged sword in terms of feminism, let us agree, too, that, as is sometimes claimed, Goya also celebrated both pregnancy and motherhood. But for Tomlinson all this was but the first step, the war bringing a new dimension that transformed the image of women in Spanish society. Thus:

> The women who populate *The Disasters of War* bring to a heroic conclusion the roles for women that emerged in Goya's earlier works. Like the *majas* who populate the tapestry cartoons, these are working-class women unafraid of confrontation; like the Duchess of Osuna or the expectant Countess of Chinchón, they are mothers whose mission is to protect their children and family.[11]

In short, Goya's women were not just champions of the cause of Spain, but also, however unconsciously, champions of the cause of women. This idea, meanwhile, is taken still further in the latest retelling of the tale of Agustina of Aragón. A garish strip cartoon, this repackages Zaragoza's heroine for a twenty-first century audience. In visual terms, this transforms her into a sex-object (or perhaps simply renders overt an aspect of the story that, though always present, has hitherto tended to lurk in the shadows), and yet the authors present her as the veritable epitome of female emancipation—'a warrior who . . . takes the lead instead of remaining in the background and is ready to fight rather than seek protection . . . a new type of woman who is not bound by the social conventions of the moment'.[12]

Moving on, we come to the third category of image that we have alluded to, namely that of the woman as patriotic auxiliary. In so far as this is concerned, we may here again cite *Las ruinas de Zaragoza,* for in several of the engravings—'Alarma en la Torre del Pino', 'Batería en la Puerta del Sancho', 'Batería de la Puerta del Carmen'—one may spot women who are evidently bearing food and water to the defenders. Rather more personalised, however, is James Armytage's 'The Wounded Guerrilla'. Dating from 1849, this shows a member of some irregular band slumped on the back of a mule arriving home in the custody of a priest and being greeted at his door by a plump matron who is waving her hands in the air in grief, and a younger woman who, more practically, is readying the means of his care.[13] Meanwhile, if women care for the wounded, they also encourage the soldiers to fresh feats of arms: in a print dating from the late 1840s entitled 'Wellington at Madrid', the illustrator Joseph Kronheim shows a crowd of young women strewing the British commander's way with flowers, whilst in 'Malasaña y su hija', Eugenio Álvarez Dumont shows the outraged father of a young Madrid embroideress named Manuela Malasaña who died in the course of the insurrection of the Dos de Mayo, hurling himself upon the French cavalryman who has seemingly just cut her down.[14]

Even the most 'élite' of these images being popularised by a host of cheap reproductions, not to mention the manner in which such themes as the defence of the artillery park of Monteleón was made use of in respect of commemorative items such as fans and packs of cards, the idea that Spanish women occupied an honoured place in the struggle against Napoleon became ever more entrenched.[15] Meanwhile, this development was reinforced still further by developments relating to the official commemoration of the war. For the oligarchy who dominated Iberian politics throughout the nineteenth century and beyond, their age was one of great fear, for, with Spain and, to a lesser extent, Portugal, repeatedly thrown into turmoil by rebellions, military coups and civil wars, the streets frequently erupted in violence. If the figure of the armed woman represented a frightening challenge to sexual norms, then, she was also strangely comforting: the fact that even women had fought the French suggesting that the nation as a whole was absolutely solid in its defiance of the invaders, Domenech and her fellow 'amazons' became a symbol of a class unity that seemed ever more desirable.[16] The consequence is still visible even today: all over Spain and Portugal the heroines of the war began to be remembered in the names of streets or even entire districts, while the monuments that it everywhere generated in many cases featured women, good examples being on show in Lisbon, Zaragoza, Bailén, Valdepeñas, Pontevedra and Segovia. With literacy slowly growing even in backward and poverty-stricken Spain and Portugal, the idea that women had played a significant part in the war was at the same reinforced by many works of literature, the obvious name to conjure with here being that of Spain's greatest nineteenth-century novelist, Bénito Pérez Galdós. Born in Las Palmas in May 1843, Galdós moved steadily leftwards, and as such became increasingly determined to rescue the Spanish people from the scorn in which it was held by the Spanish élite—the same scorn, indeed, that is so evident in the later works of Francisco de Goya—to achieve which object he wrote a series of historical novels—the so-called *episodios nacionales*—in which he sought to portray the populace as the real hero of modern Spanish history.[17]

For Galdós, however, the Spanish people was not just composed of men (like artists, novelists do not find it easy to ignore the female sex). On the contrary, amongst the characters who fill his pages are to be found many women, some of whom correspond to the stereotypes we have surveyed. For a good example, we have only to consult the first of the *episodios nacionales* that deals with the War of Independence. Entitled *El 19 de marzo y el 2 de mayo,* this centres on the insurrection that brought down the regime of King Charles IV and the subsequent revolt in Madrid. Thus, on the one hand we see La Primorosa, the tough and outspoken wife of a knife-grinder, and on the other, Inés, the poor seamstress of noble origins who becomes the lover of Galdós' hero, Gabriel Araceli. The climax of the novel being centred on the last stand at the artillery depot, this allows Galdós to highlight two of the three roles which have been outlined in the current chapter. On the one hand, La Primorosa, who throughout the novel is depicted as personifying the traditional values of the Spanish people, stiffening the morale of those around her and bullying her more timorous husband into adopting an appropriately bellicose attitude, ends her days manning a cannon and screaming abuse at the French.[18] In a house a few yards away a very different scene is being enacted in that a terrified Inés is hiding in Araceli's lodgings. Far from, say, demanding how many French soldiers he has killed, when her lover comes to check on her, she rather assails him with a barrage of lamentations and tells him that she had been so terrified that she had to hide under her bed.[19]

If Galdós was by far the most important Iberian novelist who addressed the role played by women in the Peninsular War, he was by no means the only one to do so. Thus, the theme was also being addressed in Portugal, and, what is more, in a way that was remarkably diverse. Featured personally, then, are two different types, these being represented by Camila do Lobos and Madalena Corveiro. The respective heroines of Arnaldo Gama's *Sargento-mor de Vilar* (1863) and Pinheiro Chagas' *Os guerrilheros da morte* (1872), the former is a girl of gentle birth who falls in love with a young man who enlists in the army and thereafter stays loyal to him through thick and thin while cheerfully and courageously enduring the travails of life in war-torn Portugal, and the latter a reluctant nun who seizes the opportunity constituted by the arrival of Junot's forces in 1807 to flee her convent and elope with an enemy officer. With still other examples of Portuguese women portrayed in Carlos Malheiro's tale of the invasion of 1809, *A vencida* (1907)—in particular, a young girl who sacrificed her life to lead some French troops into an ambush and the wife of a nobleman who secretly engineers a plot to blow up a French garrison and commits suicide in the wake of its eventual discovery—it is clear that in Portugal as much as Spain it was at the very least recognised that women could not be excluded from a consideration of the struggle.[20]

Whilst on the subject of the Portuguese novel of the Peninsular War, a further note is required to cover the somewhat anomalous case of Edward Quillinan. A member of the substantial British community that had grown up in Oporto in the course of the eighteenth century, Quillinan was among the many British residents who fled to England following the French invasion of 1807. Enlisting in the army, he then served in the Peninsular War as a cavalry officer. Drawn into literary circles in England on account of his pretensions as a poet, in 1841 he published a novel with the title *The Sisters of the Douro.* In this tale, however, women are not heroines, but rather victims, if only of their own naivety. Thus, as the title suggests, the book is about two sisters from the city of Oporto. When the French arrive in the city in March 1809, one of the two proceeds to fall for the affections of a dashing French officer only for him eventually to reveal that the man has a wife and family back in France. Very clearly, then, we see the other stereotype that is embraced by the stock image of the experiences of Iberian women: the heroine of the story is the epitome of the figure of the woman as tragic victim, indeed, of the woman as sex object.[21]

A further area to mention here is the theatre. As can easily be imagined, the struggle against Napoleon offered just as much material to the playwright as it did to the novelist. In Spain in particular, then, the Isabelline and Restoration periods saw the production of at least twenty-seven dramas on this subject. Given that the vast majority are essentially love stories in which history suddenly intrudes, women could not but figure strongly in these productions, whilst even those pieces which were more overtly historical—good examples are Francisco de Paula Martí's *El día dos de mayo de 1808 y muerte heroica de Daoiz y Velarde,* Joaquín Tomeo's *Zaragoza en 1808* and Juan Lombía's *El sitio de Zaragoza en 1808*—were based on episodes in which women were seen as having been prominent participants in the proceedings. In fairness, some of the plays show women as remaining aloof from the war effort or hesitating considerably before they joined the struggle, while, in one of the more ridiculous efforts on offer, a young girl even becomes the lover of a Napoleon Bonaparte who has travelled to Spain in disguise to spy out the lie of the land, but the theme of female heroism remains prominent: in Juan de la Coba's *Amor a la Patria* much of the action revolves around the attempts on the part of two women to rescue the lover of the one and the sister of the other from French captivity, while in *El día dos de mayo en Madrid* we see stage versions of La Primorosa fighting gallantly to the last bullet. Indeed, on occasion, Spain's women are even held up as being braver than Spain's men: in Manuel Tamayo's *Fernando el pescador de Málaga y los franceses,* the fisherman who is the hero of the story reacts to the arrival of the French in the city in February 1810 by trying to keep his head down, but his extremely bellicose patriot of a wife has no time for such a stance and spends the entire play castigating him for his cowardice and implicating him in one conspiracy against the invaders after another. What all this meant is another matter—for some of the authors concerned the object was to stress the conservative nature of resistance to the French, whilst for others the object was rather to damn the propertied classes and exalt the people—but the net result is clear enough: whatever the exact nature of the Spanish cause, Spain's women had been an integral part of the struggle.[22]

Given the poverty and illiteracy prevalent in the Iberian Peninsula until well into the twentieth century, the novel and the theatre remained forms of culture whose influence was restricted to a fairly narrow section of the populace. At this point, then, we would do well to look at other means by which the figure of the Iberian woman at war acquired a lasting purchase. One area that can certainly be explored in this connection was the form of popular opera known as *zarzuela* and another the Aragonese dance known as the *jota,* both these *genres* being closely connected with the depiction of the Spanish people as a simple race wedded to traditional values characteristic of the Restoration era. In 1879, for example, Zaragoza saw the first performance of Manuel Fernández Caballero's *La jota aragonesa,* a romantic tale set in the sieges of 1808–1809, while other *zarzuelas* that appeared over the years with a War-of-Independence theme included *Cádiz, El tambor de granaderos,* and *La Viejecita.* All these works featured the heroically anti-French *maja* to some extent or another, while in 1893 Justo Blasco published his *Gran Jota Agustina de Aragón.*[23] However, pride of place in this last respect should probably given to the traditional *Sitio de Zaragoza:*

> When Agustina fired her cannon,
> When Agustina fired her cannon,
> All the French forces who had entered the town,
> Took one look at her and turned and ran . . .
> With just three steps that took her to the fore,
> Agustina showed herself to be the bravest of us all.[24]

By the late nineteenth century, then, the women of Iberia were firmly entrenched in the historic memory of the Spanish War of Independence, if not of the Peninsular War as a whole. Meanwhile, despite the fact that it continued to be dominated by military narrative, women had also become embedded in the historiography. Indeed, they crop up here and there in most of the classic nineteenth-century accounts of the conflict. In this respect, let us look first of all at the Spanish sources. Thus, the liberal chronicler Toreno describes how the sobs and cries of women played a key role in whipping up the emotions of the crowd that gathered before the royal palace in Madrid to protest at the departure of the last members of the Bourbon family for Bayonne on the morning of 2 May 1808, whilst he also notes that women were in the forefront of the rioters who raised Zaragoza in revolt on 24 May, and that in Segovia it was a group of women who hacked to pieces the body of the murdered director of the artillery academy, Miguel de Cevallos.[25] Equally, the chronicler of the sieges of Zaragoza, Augustín Alcaide, laid much stress on the role that women—not just Agustina of Aragón, but many women—played in the defence of Zaragoza.[26] Finally, the republican, Enrique Rodríguez Solis, included a number of examples of women fighting in militias or guerrilla bands in his late nineteenth-century attempt at a 'people's history' of the struggle, one such being that of Susana Claretona, the wife of a commandant of the Catalan militia known as the *somatén,* who fought alongside her husband in various actions in 1809 before being badly wounded, the Junta Central—i.e. the provisional government formed in 1808—eventually granting her a commission in recognition of her valour.[27]

Similar examples can be found, meanwhile, in the English-language literature, and, in fact, were a feature of it from the very beginning, thanks in large part to the fact that one of the earliest accounts of the conflict to be published in England was written by a young British diplomat named Charles Vaughan who was presented to Agustina of Aragón when he visited Zaragoza in September 1808 and regaled with tales of her heroism. His text being the first reference that we have to the 'maid of Saragossa' in English, it is worth presenting here in full:

> The attack . . . seemed to be directed principally against the gate called Portillo . . . It is here that an act of heroism was performed . . . to which history scarcely affords a parallel. Agustina Zaragoza, about twenty-two years of age, a handsome woman of the lower class of the people, whilst performing her duty of carrying refreshment to the gates, arrived at the battery . . . at

> the very moment when the French fire had absolutely destroyed every person that was stationed in it. The citizens and soldiers for the moment hesitated to re-man the guns, [but] Agustina rushed forward . . . snatched a match from the hand of a dead artilleryman, and fired off a twenty-four pounder. Then, jumping upon the gun, [she] made a solemn vow never to quit it alive during the siege, and, having stimulated her fellow citizens by this daring intrepidity to fresh exertions, they instantly rushed into the battery, and again opened a tremendous fire upon the enemy.[28]

The story of female participation in the fighting having thus been sanctioned by something other than what most British historians of the war regarded as Spanish braggadocchio, it was therefore incorporated into the historiography in more-or-less the same manner as was the case on the other side of the Bay of Biscay. To take a number of examples at random, then, Southey claimed that during the assault of 20 June 1808 the women of Gerona 'regardless of danger, carried food and ammunition to their husbands and fathers and brothers and sons', while Oman had no hesitation in recounting the assertion that the governor later formed an all-female auxiliary corps known as the Companía de Santa Bárbara that went on to serve with great distinction in the siege of 1809.[29] Ever suspicious, if not downright, contemptuous of all things Spanish, Napier was less happy to accept stories of gallant heroines, but even he could not quite bring himself to deny them altogether. As he wrote of the first siege of Zaragoza, 'The current romantic tales of women rallying the troops and leading them forward at the most dangerous moments of this siege, I have not touched upon, and may, perhaps, be allowed to doubt, yet it is not unlikely that, when suddenly environed with horrors, the sensitiveness of women, driving them to a kind of frenzy, might produce actions above the heroism of men . . . wherefore I neither wholly believe, nor will deny, their exploits at Zaragoza, remarking only that, for a long time afterwards, Spain swarmed with heroines from that city, clothed in half uniforms and loaded with weapons'.[30]

There is, of course, an interesting question here in that women's heroism, if it exists at all, is deemed to be false: whereas an Agustín of Aragón would have manned a cannon out of resolution, an Agustina must have done so out of hysteria. However, setting that aside, it can be seen that, by the time the centenary of the Peninsular War came round in 1908, the figure of the Iberian woman at war had become extremely familiar. That said, even in the Peninsula, only in very recent years had a start been made upon the assimilation of women into the historiography as a topic in their own right. Appropriately enough, this had come from the pen of José Gómez de Arteche, the author of the official history of the war. However, champion of political conservatism as Arteche was, there was little hope that he would address the issue in a fashion that was anything other than platitudinous. Thus, the 1903 lecture that constituted his contribution to the debate operated on two levels, the one historical and the other political. To begin with the historical, it sought first of all to show that, ever characterised by the deepest patriotism and religious feeling imaginable, Spain's women had thrown themselves into the struggle. Yet, continued Arteche, if it was right and proper to remember the heroines of such episodes as the Dos de Mayo, Zaragoza, and Gerona, a thought should also be spared for the thousands of women who had served the cause of Spain in humbler ways, whether it was the women of Utrera who had sewn the uniforms worn by the volunteers who had fought at Bailén; the girls of Cádiz who had made fun of the huge projectiles fired by the special mortars constructed for the bombardment of the city; the hundreds, if not thousands, of women who had wandered the countryside in company with one or other of the guerrilla bands, encouraging their menfolk, looking after their needs and on occasion fighting and dying alongside them; and finally the myriads of ordinary women who had resisted every advance made by the French soldiers occupying their homes, whilst at all times maintaining an attitude that was as haughty as it was hostile.[31]

The women of Spain, then, been an integral, and, indeed, enthusiastic, part of the Spanish people's war. However, reading between the lines, it is clear that Arteche's paper was not just a reflection of what he perceived as a historical reality. Also present was a strong desire to apply the past to the present. At the time that the general was speaking, the political establishment was increasingly aware that republicanism, socialism, anarchism and Catalan nationalism were all on the march, and that the structure of society was gradually being transformed by urbanization. Faced by this situation, the oligarchs who dominated politics were increasingly dreaming of a 'revolution from above' in which the people would be mobilised in support of the old order in exactly the same way as was perceived to have happened in 1808. The prime exponent of this idea was the then prime minister, Antonio Maura, but it is clear that Arteche's lecture had a similar purpose in mind. In brief, this appears in the last paragraph. Thus, the women of 1808 are held up as models for the women of 1903, the latter being enjoined to show just as much courage and devotion in the political tasks that had fallen to their lot, of which the most important, or so it was implied, was the defence of the old order against the rising tide of reform and revolution:

> Worthy representatives of worthier mothers . . . in whose veins runs the blood of the famous warriors who triumphed at Bailén, Talavera y San Marcial . . . never renounce the most noble sentiments that move you. Above all, inspire your households and your children with that religious faith, that love of country, that generous scorn of rank and fortune . . . which . . . will always constitute the greatest glory of mankind.[32]

A century on from the Peninsular War, then, it was widely recognised that the struggle against Napoleon had not just been a male affair. Yet women never had more than an auxiliary role to play in the story, while, to the extent that they figured in it at all, it was in a fashion that was wholly stereotypical. The odd caveat aside, the women of Spain and Portugal had been gripped by patriotic enthusiasm and religious fervour in exactly the same fashion as their menfolk, whilst, within the limits imposed on them by their sex, they had rallied to the cause and done everything that they could to support the struggle, on occasion even displaying a capacity for genuine physical heroism. In the Spain of 1908 such a stance was entirely understandable, for it was consonant not just with the trumpeting of such figures as Arteche, but also with the more progressive analysis of the struggle that was sustained by Iberian republicanism. Since then, another century has passed, but in Spain at least the historiography has really only moved on very slightly. For a long time, of course, the field of the War of Independence was dominated by military historians of a deeply conservative stamp whose writings could hardly be expected to address any sort of revisionist agenda. Yet matters did not change very much as it was gradually penetrated by historians of a more progressive sort, few of those concerned being very interested in women's history.[33] This, however, was most unfortunate, the result being that the stereotypes of the nineteenth century continued to reign supreme. A good place to start here would be the film industry. As can be imagined, the struggle against Napoleon was an obvious subject for historical epics and costume dramas alike. However, as witness such works as *El Dos de Mayo* (1927), *Agustina de Aragón* (1928), *El tambor de Bruch* (1948), *Agustina de Aragón* (1950) and *El mensaje* (1953), the image of the women of Spain and Portugal that emerged from the cinema (and, later on, television) version of the years from 1808 to 1814 has often been stereotypical in the extreme. In short, women are seen fighting the French, urging the men of Spain to fight harder, caring for the sick and wounded and acting as spies or couriers, and, what is more, doing so in favour of a cause that is portrayed as being conservative and Catholic rather than progressive and liberal. From time to time, true, the importance of the love story introduced a degree of variety, *El verdugo* (1947), *Lola la Piconera* (1951) and *Carmen la de Ronda* (1959) all examining the idea of women forging relationships with enemy soldiers. In the end, however, such images are aberrant, the fact that the Spanish film industry's commemoration of the bicentenary of 1808—the multi-million-dollar *Sangre de mayo* (2008)—was in essence nothing more than a restaging of the Galdós novel on the subject being all too suggestive of the extent of its willingness to engage in serious debate.[34] In this last instance, perhaps, what predominated was no more than a desire to avoid controversy in an era of bitter political division—Galdos' novels are, after all, ambiguous enough to offer succour to both Left and Right—but, for the rest, we can hardly be surprised: the two main periods of film production—roughly speaking, 1927–28 and 1947–59—coincided with periods of military dictatorship in which every effort was being made to whip up popular nationalism and coerce the Spanish people into accepting the existing structure of Spanish society.[35]

If one popular medium through which images of the past may be transmitted is the cinema, another is the children's comic. In so far as Spain is concerned, this form of publication may be said to date from the appearance of the comic called *Chicos* in 1938, and this last is characteristic enough in its treatment of the subject to allow us to make use of it as a useful case study. A product of the Nationalist zone, *Chicos* naturally reflected the values of 'national-catholicism' and continued to do so throughout the years of its publication. In consequence, Spain's past was always a subject of great interest to it, and its writers therefore repeatedly featured it in their stories in the hope that the tales of grandeur and glory which they retailed would inspire the youth of Franquist Spain. For obvious reasons the chief focus tended to be the Reconquest and the Golden Age, but from time to time series did appear that featured the War of Independence. In these, the war was always portrayed very much as a people's struggle, and from this it followed that there was plenty of scope for introducing such figures as Agustina of Aragón. In time, *Chicos* disappeared, but the theme was periodically revisited, most notably by the colour magazine, *Trinca,* whose children's section ran a long running series called 'Los guerrilleros' in the 1970s. The style is very different—the tone, for example, is distinctly humoristic—but the message is the same: thus, the French oppressed the people and were defeated by the people, a people, moreover, in which women were well to the fore.[36]

Finally, there is the question of the novel. In contrast to the attention lavished on the war by British novelists from the late nineteenth century onwards, in Spain the treatment of the War of Independence remained extremely patchy (to the extent that it was looked at at all: after the publication of the last of the *episodios nacionales* to deal with the subject, no further novels were published about it until 1944). In fairness, coverage was less uni-dimensional than that of either the film or the comic—for example, Juan Antonio Vallejo-Naguera's 1985 novel, *Yo, el Rey,* was written from the point of view of none other than Joseph Bonaparte, whilst, published in 2003, Antonio Luis Martín Gómez's *Los Héroes de Bailén* is a careful account of the battle of Bailén that gives full weight to the role of the Spanish army—but, from Manuel Halcón's *Aventuras de Juan Lucas* (1944) through to Arturo Pérez-Reverte's *Día de cólera* (2007), the bulk of what has appeared can be defined as 'people's war, people's war, and still more people's war', this being an approach in which the role of women is all but pre-programmed. In fairness, there are exceptions. Set in the sieges of Zaragoza, for example, Jorge Casamayor's *Te Deum: victoria o muerte* (2006) not only displays a convincing range of female characters, but attempts to engage with the choices facing them in a far more reflective fashion than the one that has become the norm, but even in this work a defining moment is constituted by the heroic single-handed defence mounted by the poor seamstress, Enriqueta, of a house in the city against the repeated assaults of overwhelming numbers of French troops.[37] Yet, feature many women though it does, *Te Deum* is a work about the Spanish people at war rather than Spanish women at war. In so far as this last topic is concerned, the only place to go is Angeles de Irisarri's *La artillera: la lucha de España por la libertad* (Madrid, 2008), but this again is all too predictable in its approach in that the ten women, some real and others imaginary, who are Irisarri's central characters, all respond to the coming of the French by participating in the war effort in one way or another. In short, truly it is the least novel of novels.[38]

When academic historians finally began to look at the role of women—something that only happened in the first decade of the current century—they were therefore confronted by a solid wall of assumption that would at best have been hard to overcome. That said, however, the results have not been encouraging. Thus, the first articles and conference papers that we may refer to do little more than present women in their traditional guise as either victims or heroines. Speaking in 2002, for example, Lucienne Doumergue offered an analysis of *Los Desastres de la Guerra* that confined itself exactly to these parameters. Thus: 'Women did not just watch the bull-fight from behind the barrier, and, in consequence, paid an inflated price for their tickets'.[39] Meanwhile, setting aside one or two contributions that looked at the cases of one more-or-less mythologised heroine or another, other conferences in the period 2005–2008 saw speakers discuss a variety of forms of female participation in the Spanish war effort.[40] Progress was still slow—a thematically organised 'manual' of the War of Independence published in 2007 failed to include a chapter on the subject, for example[41]—but a rash of publications at the end of the decade may be said at last to have gained women their place at the table. Thus, in *Heroínas y patríotas: mujeres de 1808,* a group of largely female historians headed by the well-known specialist on Spanish liberalism in the first half of the nineteenth-century, Irene Castells, published a collection of essays covering many of the better known heroines of Spanish resistance as well as a number of other figures. At about the same time, meanwhile, Elena Fernández García produced a monograph entitled *Mujeres en la Guerra de la Independencia* in which she argued that the War of Independence not only saw the women of Spain align themselves with the rest of the nation in the war against Napoleon, but also acted as a catalyst that allowed them for the first time to become a visible element of the Spanish political firmament.[42] Embedded in these works, naturally enough, was a clear commitment to feminism, and, with it, an implicit critique of much of the traditional Spanish historiography, but in no case did this receive so sharp an expression as it did in the case of an article published by María José de la Pascua. Thus, as usual, women are enthusiastic participants in the struggle, but, if that was the case, it was not just because they were devoted to *Díos, Rey y Patria.* On the contrary, they wanted to find a greater sense of self-worth, to escape the trammels of domesticity and to assert themselves in the face of Spanish men. To quote the author, 'In this time of war there were other battles that were being fought out'.[43]

If Pascua probably stretches some of her evidence a little too far, there is much that one might agree with in this argument: as we shall see, for at least some women the War of Independence was indeed a time of rebellion. However, it is not really this theme that is predominant in the literature, the chief concern of this being rather to show that the women of Spain and Portugal embraced the patriotic struggle with the utmost fervour. Yet it cannot but be felt that there is a serious flaw at the heart of this earnest endeavour to swathe Spanish womenhood in colours of red and gold.[44] Thus, at the heart of all these monographs, articles and conference papers there is an unthinking acceptance of the idea, first, that the war against Napoleon was a popular crusade which had the united support of the nation, and, second, that the struggle took the form of a 'people's war' and therefore afforded greatly increased possibilities for female participation in the struggle. Unfortunately, however, there is considerable archival evidence which suggests either that there was no crusade in Spain at all or that the idea has at the very least been much exaggerated.[45] Yet, absorbed in visions, first, of women getting involved in the war effort, and, second, becoming ever more engaged in the fight to give Spain a liberal constitution, Castells and her followers seem blind to this development. Alternative patterns of behaviour are therefore discounted or even ignored, and that even when to do otherwise might well have flattered feminist sensitivities.[46]

What makes this all the more surprising is that the existence of a more complex reality has always been well understood. Present in a minor key even in the popular Iberian memorialization of the conflict, elsewhere it is a common theme. Let us begin here with the many British novels spawned by the Peninsular War. Of these perhaps the first was Alexander Dallas' *Felix Alvarez.* Published in London in 1818, this was the work of a commissary who had been stationed at Cádiz, and consists of a curious mixture of personal reminiscences and literary narrative, this last focusing on the adventures of Felix Álvarez, a young Spaniard who forms a guerrilla band in the wake of the massacre of his family. Through Álvarez we are introduced to the realities of life in occupied Andalucía, and in this fashion stumble across suggestions that there were Spanish women who neither tried to fight the French nor simply suffered the trials and tribulations of war in virtuous silence. Thus, at Puerto de Santa María Álvarez comes across two women who had been 'driven from their own home by the insolence of the French officers billeted in it' and taken refuge at the headquarters of the local French commander, Marshal Victor.[47] Whether the women encountered by Álvarez could be classified as collaborators is a moot point, but, evidently aware of the growing mass of memoir material that was so clearly being overlooked by the Peninsular War's successive chroniclers, British writers certainly picked up on the idea that many women had for one reason or another rallied to the occupying forces. In *The Bivouac, or Stories of the Peninsular War,* then, the Irish clergyman William Maxwell refers to 'nuns from Castile and ladies from Andalucía, mounted on horseback and attired *en militaire*' deserting 'convent and castle to follow the fortunes of some bold dragoon', while we also hear of 'the daughter of the collector of Almagro' being stabbed to death by some guerrilla 'for professing attachment to the usurper', and of 'the wife of the *alcalde* of Brihuega' being 'tarred and feathered, disgracefully exhibited in the public market place and . . . then put to death amid the execrations of her tormentors' after being detected as being in 'secret correspondence' with a French general.[48]

To women who were opponents of the French and women who were victims of the French, we must therefore now add women who were on one level or another involved with the French.[49] Why women should have made this choice was not explored in any depth, but such hints as we have suggest that such conduct was put down to the perceived weakness of 'the fair sex', whether physical or moral. What is not found, at least in overt form, is the idea that women's actions might be governed by some more positive motive. This more advanced stage in the re-evaluation of the female experience of the Peninsular War is not encountered until the works of the prolific Victorian novelist, G. A. Henty. The author of a long series of historical novels that attained great popularity, Henty first turned his attention to the Peninsular War with the publication of *The Young Buglers,* this being a tale of how two young British school boys enlist in the army as buglers and are eventually promoted to the rank of ensign, in which capacity they are dispatched from Portugal to liaise with the Spanish *guerrillas.* In so far as women appear in this story at all, however, they do so in fairly conventional guise—on the one hand we encounter the female inhabitants of a small village in the Cantabrian mountains providing food and shelter for the guerrilla band of one Núñez, and on the other the wife of a French general who the heroes of the novel save from execution at the hands of the self-same

Núñez[50]—and it is not until the much later *With Moore at Corunna* that Henty has something interesting to say on the matter.

The story of a young officer named Jack O'Connor, *With Moore at Corunna,* covers the period from August 1808 till May 1809. Very much a stereotypical Victorian hero, O'Connor is separated from his comrades during the battle of La Coruña, but manages to escape to Portugal. In the course of his adventures, however, he discovers that his cousin, Mary, who is half-Portuguese and had been brought up in the substantial British community in Oporto, had been forcibly incarcerated in a convent by her step-mother in an attempt to deprive her of her inheritance. In time, Jack contrives to rescue her, but the interesting thing here is that the girl is not just a passive player in the story. Thus, discovering that a party of British soldiers had entered Oporto in the wake of the battle of Roliça, she waits at a window until an officer happens to pass by and then throws him a letter begging for help, which eventually, by sheer luck, reaches O'Connor.[51]

Mary, then, is very enterprising, while she also turns out to be extremely brave: determined to break her will, the nuns with whom she is incarcerated put her on bread and water in solitary confinement, but she holds out for an entire year, and would doubtless have held out forever had succour failed to appear. But, then, of course, Mary is both British and Protestant and therefore inherently superior to her native cousins, these last, by contrast, being portrayed in a very different fashion. Sickened by the apathetic behaviour of the Spanish populace, O'Connor and his best friend, Ryan, decide to give the inhabitants of Salamanca a fright by spreading a rumour that the French are at the gates. This ruse succeeding even better than they had hoped, within a few minutes the whole city is in uproar, but on this occasion no amazon is at hand to rally the defenders. On the contrary, we have a very different picture: '"It was splendid . . . Did you ever see such a funk as the Spaniards were all in, and . . . didn't the women yell and howl?"'[52] Nor, meanwhile, is the situation any better when French troops actually put in an appearance: in Henty's description of the storm of Oporto in March 1809, the only mentions that we have of women refer to them either fleeing the city before the French launch their attack or running in panic through the streets once the enemy break through.[53]

A novelist who was imbued as Henty was, first, with the social conventions of the Victorian era, and, second, with the violently anti-Spanish attitude that coloured much British writing on the Peninsular War, is hardly likely to have had much capacity to empathise with the complex dilemmas that often faced the women of Spain and Portugal, whilst it has also to be said that, whether British, French, Portuguese or Spanish, his female characters are at best thinly depicted.[54] In fairness, other British novelists have dealt with the subject with greater empathy: in *Death to the French,* for example, C. S. Forester charts the misery endured by a group of women and children forced to flee their homes in the course of the third invasion of Portugal in some detail, while in *The Spanish Bride* Georgette Heyer retells the true story of Juana María Dolores de León, a young girl from Badajoz who, as we shall see, found refuge with an officer of Wellington's army following the sack of 1812.[55] However, to find something more satisfying, we really have to return to Pérez Galdós. As we have seen, Galdós played at least some part in the generation of the stereotype of the Spanish woman at war, but buried in his work can also be found examples of a greater sensitivity. A particularly good instance of this capacity to engage in more imaginative thinking occurs in *Cádiz.* Thus, one of the central characters is Asunción, a young girl who has been condemned to the convent to avoid the problem of having to provide her with a dowry. Trapped in a sterile existence of the most stultifying boredom in which she has no independence whatsoever, she allows herself to fall in love with—indeed, positively flings herself at—an exotic British visitor named Lord Gray. Sadly, the end of the story is not a happy one: having taken advantage of the unfortunate Asunción, Gray promptly abandons her, leaving her in a state of ruin. That said, however, what is imagined is a very different scenario to the one envisaged in *El 19 de marzo y el 2 de mayo.* For the group of young women on whom the story centres—Asunción; Asunción's sister, Presentación; and Araceli's beloved, Inés, who is currently living as a ward of Asunción's family and being groomed as a prospective wife for Asunción and Presentación's brother, Diego—the war comes as a liberating influence.

With the city gripped by all the excitement of war and political revolution, the controls to which they had habitually been subjected became all the more irksome while they were now surrounded by exciting figures of the same stamp of Lord Gray. In all sorts of ways, then, war came as an opportunity, and one that Asunción, at least, proves unable to withstand, a reaction, perhaps, that was strengthened by the fact that, outraged by an unauthorised excursion to visit the *cortes,* Asunción and Presentación's mother, Doña María, had imposed even tougher limitations on her charges. At all events, abandoned by her lover, Asunción responds with a mixture of anger and defiance:

> Oh Inés! You are perfectly familiar with the life that we lived in my mother's household; you know, all too well, its boredom, its depressing character, its dreadful loneliness . . . Forced to do so by mother's rigour, our hands worked, but not so our minds. Yet if our mouths prayed, our souls did not; equally, if we abated our eyes, we did not abate our spirits. The hundreds of prohibitions that shut us in on every side awoke ardent curiosities in our breasts. Wanting to know everything, we tried to find out all we could, and made everything an object of desire and speculation . . . Ever since we were little girls, mother has been pigeon-holing us in accordance with the position that we were to occupy in society . . . Neither our understanding nor our will was permitted to deviate in the slightest from the paths that had been marked out for us . . . We didn't dare either to say anything, to ask for anything, even to think of anything, that had not previously been ordained by mother. We barely breathed while we were in her presence, while her dictates and commands filled us with such fear that it was impossible for us to live.[56]

However, conscious though Asunción is of the need to seize the day, it seems that she is blind to wider issues. Thus, another matter that is discussed in *Cádiz* is the extent to which women were drawn into the new political process unleashed by the convocation of the *cortes* in Cádiz in 1810. With the city gripped by political debate, the leading ladies of the city take sides and fill their *tertulias* with guests who back the ideas they favour. On the one hand, then, Araceli's old patroness, Doña Flora, gathers round her men of a liberal persuasion, while on the other Doña María seeks rather to associate herself with the cause of reaction. Yet, when various combinations of the female characters featured in the novel pay visits to the *cortes,* the women regard the proceedings as a species of play or public spectacle and show absolutely no understanding of their political significance; so much, then, for the idea that the war plunged the women of Spain into some sort of political awakening.[57]

If the vision of the women of Spain and Portugal as so many amazons, virgin-martyrs or blue-stockings therefore seems likely to be sadly adrift of the reality, any discussion of the subject of women in the Peninsular War that looks at the women of Spain and Portugal alone is even more deficient. Thus, thousands of women from other countries also became caught up in the conflict. Who these women were and how they came to the Peninsula will be discussed elsewhere, what we are interested in here being rather their treatment in the historiography. Initially, their story was even more disregarded by historians of the war than their Spanish and Portuguese cousins: in all his thousands of pages of writing, for example, Sir Charles Oman could only manage a few hundred words on the women who accompanied Wellington's army, and even then only did so to dismiss them as 'impedimenta'.[58] Gradually, however, things changed. In this development the most important influence was the emergence from the 1960s onwards of the so-called 'new military history', an approach to the subject of armies and warfare that eschewed the narrow institutional and campaign history by which it had hitherto been characterised in favour of a much broader approach that made use of the methodologies of social history. Almost entirely absent from Spain and Portugal—countries where the survival of the Franco and Salazar dictatorships in effect rendered military history a taboo subject for anyone other than career soldiers—this new focus on 'war and society' empowered the historical community to introduce women into the study of matters military. Even then, progress was rather slow, but, as we have seen, a substantial corpus of material now exists that can be used as an introduction to the study of women at war in the so-called 'horse and musket' period.

Contained within this literature are several works that look at the experiences of British and French military women in the Napoleonic Wars in general, and yet as yet there is nothing on the campfollowers of the Peninsular War in particular. Once again, then, one is forced back on the imagination of various novelists. Based on the adventures of a British infantry officer of lowly origins, Bernard Cornwell's Sharpe novels offer numerous highly sympathetic vignettes of the wives of the rank and file, and even explore one or two of the more serious problems which they were likely to experience, such as blackmail and sexual harassment at the hands of corrupt non-commissioned officers.[59] However, generous though his words often are, Cornwell makes no attempt either to tell his stories through the female voice or to put much flesh on the bones of the campfollowers. Rather more arresting, then, is Arthur Eaglestone's *Forward the Baggage,* focusing as this does on the adventures of, first, a woman named Harriet Ffoulkes who insists on accompanying her officer husband to Spain in 1808 and takes part in the campaign of La Coruña, and, second, the same woman's long-suffering and resourceful maid-servant, Susan Thompson, it in fact being the latter who emerges as the heroine of the story. Interestingly, here, too, there is a hint of the opportunities offered by war: a lively and intelligent woman, Mrs Ffoulkes is bored of life in a country house, and determined not to let issues of class deny her the chance of adventure (or so she imagined it) offered to other women; as she says, indeed, 'I do not see why I should not take up what many women are doing and have done in the past'.[60] And worth noting, too, is R. F. Delderfield's 1964 work, *Too Few for Drums,* a story set in the course of the third invasion of Portugal in which a Welsh campfollower named Gwyneth plays a major part in saving a small party of British soldiers cut off by the advancing French from capture, what is particularly interesting here being the manner in which the girl is imagined as seeing her sexual favours as a means of steeling the successive men she attaches herself to to the horrors of war—of, indeed, making them men.[61]

Still more interesting as having been not only written by women, but also, one suspects, for women, are two more recent novels. First of all, there is the romantic novelist E. V. Thompson's *Cassie,* a work that makes no pretension to be anything other than the archetypal 'saga' which it is, and yet is researched in great detail and founded in an accurate knowledge of both army life and the Peninsular War. More to the point, meanwhile, the characters that it follows—Cassie, the Cornish fisherman's daughter who searches out her plough-boy lover when he runs off to join the army, marries him and travels with him to Portugal at the end of 1811; Sarah, the 'good-time girl' who chooses life with a soldier rather than face perpetual incarceration in a workhouse, and discovers both sexual adventure and professional satisfaction; and Josefa, the Spanish gypsy who finds a refuge in Wellington's army when her own family is scattered to the four winds—face problems that reflect the issues faced by many camp followers (including, not least, the complicated dynamics that operated within the little communities of women into which 'the baggage' broke down), whilst, unlike Mrs Ffoulkes and her maidservant, they are not in any way associated with the élite.[62] And, secondly, there is S. Tillyard's *Tides of War:* in this work, an alternative perspective that rather considers the women who were left back in Britain, the reader follows the fortunes of the Duchess of Wellington, who (most implausibly) is shown throwing herself into the world of financial investment, and Harriet Raven, a young girl married to an army officer whose interest in science leads her into an affair with a German entrepreneur, the suggestion being that war could act as a liberating force even on the home front. Thus, the women featured in the story are both betrayed by their husbands, as well as physically left behind by them, and yet they explore intellectual challenges and, in the case of Harriet Raven, exact a degree of sexual revenge.[63]

Finally, if no author has gone as far as Thompson, at least one work of a much earlier vintage makes a soldier's wife a central character. We come here to George Manville Fenn's *Our Soldier Boy.* A brief work published in 1898 by a prolific writer of boy's stories in the style of G. A. Henty, this work opens with a vignette of camp life in which a group of Wellington's infantrymen are sitting round a campfire at which a pot of stew is being tended by a corporal's wife known to one and all as 'Mother Beane'. There is no doubt as to the social class of this character—on the contrary, she is described as a 'big, rough, coarse woman'—but she is yet portrayed both as a loving wife who is within her limits clean and respectable—she wears a 'battered old straw bonnet cocked up as if it were a hat . . . [an] old scarlet uniform tail-coat . . . [and a] very clean cotton gown'—and a dutiful member of society who very much knows her place and is almost comically deferential in respect of authority. At the same time, she has the proverbial 'heart of gold': a soldier has only to tear a sleeve for her to offer to sew it up, while she endeavours to look after not only her husband, but also the men of his squad. When her husband discovers a small English boy who has mysteriously been left for dead in the ruins of a small Portuguese village, she therefore lavishes care upon him and loves him as if he were her own son. Needless to say, the tale ends in suitably happy fashion, but this is of no account: what matters is rather that women are seen to be anxious to conform to type and respect the proprieties of society even in the heart of war.[64]

Just as with the women to whom the war came, then, so the women who came to the war have provided novelists with plenty of food for their imagination. Meanwhile, there is one work of fiction in which the two strands are woven together with great success, this being Julian Rathbone's *Joseph.* Shortlisted for the Booker Prize, this purports to be a long letter from one Joseph Bosham, the illegitimate son of a village priest of Jacobite ancestry, to the Duke of Wellington, Bosham's purpose being to extract some money from him on the grounds, among other things, that he saved the life of his illegitimate son when the latter was abandoned as a baby on the battlefield of Vitoria. In practice, however, it is in effect a rather confused and disjointed memoir of Bosham's experiences in the Peninsular War. As a fictional portrait of Spain in the Napoleonic ear, it is unlikely ever to be bettered, but, more to the point, Bosham—a sometime student of the University of Salamanca who turns both pimp and a spy—spends much of his time in the company of a variety of women through whose eyes we experience many of the dangers, dilemmas and difficulties (and yet, with them, opportunities) that formed the lot of all the women caught up in the war, women, moreover, who are drawn from both sides of the divide delineated in this chapter. Flora Tweedie, for example, is the daughter of a penniless Irish officer who found herself marooned in Lisbon when her father died and was forced to attach herself to Wellington's army as a better sort of prostitute; Violeta Martín, a girl from Salamanca who marries a British officer named Reaney; and Anna la Granace, a madam who runs a travelling brothel.[65]

To conclude, then, women are not absent from the historiography of the Peninsular War. The women of Spain and Portugal—the women to whom the war came—were present in the heroic literature from the very beginning, and as a result were assimilated into the national myths that grew up in respect of the conflict, not to mention their more recent feminist counterparts. Meanwhile, the women of Britain and France—the women who came to the war—are looked at in a rather slender list of books that deals with the figure of the soldier's wife and the sutleress and draws upon a wider literature whose subject is the role and experience of women in the age of 'horse and musket' warfare. However, this material must on the whole be deemed to be distinctly unsatisfactory. In particular, there is a want of human detail. Thanks in large part to the availability of large numbers of soldiers' memoirs, the British and French material is rather better in this respect—as we shall see, it is possible to access the lives of those involved in considerable detail—but its Spanish and Portuguese counterpart relies very heavily on the discussion of a handful of highly mythologised individuals whose actions are held to be a pattern for that of the female populace as a whole. At the same time even the British and French material is very limited in that we generally only meet Spanish and Portuguese women when circumstances draw them into the orbit of the rival armies. For anything beyond, it is therefore necessary to fall back on the imaginings of a succession of novelists who open interesting windows on the subject, and yet in no case succeed in escaping the limitations of time, culture and language. Thus, Pérez Galdós and Henty both explore the concept of women seizing upon the war as a means of effecting a radical change in their circumstances, but the one fails to shake off his politically inspired exaltation of the Spanish people, while the latter remains in thrall to the prejudices imposed upon the British historiography by the violently anti-Spanish William Napier. Equally, if Thompson, Eaglestone and Cornwell incorporate much empirical research into their writing, their ability to expand their coverage of the subject to groups other than British campfollowers is limited by their want of French and Spanish. Even if such limitations were not present, meanwhile, what are even the best and most carefully researched of novels but exercises in representation that cannot be regarded as anything approaching historical sources? In short, what is needed is a study of the subject that will finally pull together all its various components and tell a more integrated story: such, at least, is the object of this book.

2

Matrons and Majas

To introduce this chapter, which will look at the position of women in Iberian society on the eve of the Peninsular War, we can do no better than summarise the first paragraphs of a seminal article that was published by María Victoria López-Cordón in 1982, and took as its starting point a classic description of the typical Spanish woman at the time of the Peninsular War that was published by the early Spanish feminist, Emilia Pardo, in 1890. In brief, as López-Cordón pointed out, this envisaged said woman as wearing traditional dress, never going out except to mass, occupying her time in such domestic tasks as needlework and embroidery, bringing up her children in the Christian faith, and not knowing any books other than the Order of Mass and the catechism. For many years, López-Cordón continued, this picture was taken as gospel, but, quite rightly, it was her opinion that in reality it was wildly misleading in that it captured the lifestyles of only a tiny minority of the female population. Thus, to one flank of the women concerned, there was a privileged band of noblewomen who enjoyed access to a lifestyle that was both infinitely more cosmopolitan and infinitely less circumscribed, whilst on the other there were the millions of lower-class women who lived out lives that were marked by endless drudgery and yet were by no means confined to the home. Meanwhile, at both extremes of the spectrum and probably in the middle as well, the submissive matron of Pardo Bazán's imagination existed alongside other women of a much more combative nature. *Pace* Pardo Bazán, then, the picture was far from homogeneous.[1]

Before going any further, however, we need first to look to examine the idealised norms which formed the basis of Pardo Bazán's vision of the typical Spanish woman. In so far as these are concerned, in the beginning was the word, and the word was 'Eve'. Herein lies the key to all. Thus, Eve had caused the Fall, and, with it, the corruption of creation. From this, meanwhile, three things followed: first, women could not resist temptation and were, by implication, inherently sinful; second, women were incapable of reason, for, had the reverse been true, sinful or not, Eve would never have listened to Satan; and, third, women, at least potentially, had great power over men and could therefore very easily lead them astray. It was, then, in the interests of all that women should be subjected to men, but this was not just the result of social necessity. On the contrary, women had been created as beings who were helpmeets to men, physically and mentally inferior to men, and, in a very literal sense, dependent on men, Eve having, after all, been created out of Adam's very being, whilst their menstruation was interpreted as both a manifestation of sin and divine punishment. To subject women to men was therefore but a just reflection of the social order and, by implication, an acceptance of the divine model.[2]

If the need to subjugate women is implicit in the creation story, as the numerous texts that make up the Bible accumulated, so the message was repeated over and over again until at length an absolute seal was put upon it by the epistles of Saint Paul. However, these writings had steadily been added to by a succession of ecclesiastical commentators, while they had been further reinforced by the emergence of a concept of manhood that measured a man by his honour, this last being a concept that was at least in part measured by his ability to control the women around him. Thus, at its most simple, honour was the respect that accrued to a man through the extent to which he lived up to certain standards that were considered to be inherent to—indeed, even definitive of—moral rectitude. A man of honour, then, was among other things responsible, strong, brave, upright, chivalrous, independent, generous and just. Implicit in this, however, was the idea that he both should and could control the women around him, for, if the women around him were out of control—if they were allowed to scold, fly into rages or fall prey to the unbridled sexual passions central to their sinful nature—a man could hardly be regarded as responsible and strong, whilst he was necessarily at risk of accusations of cowardice.[3]

Yet the issue was certainly not just the honour or self-respect of the individual man. In brief, the woman who was out of control in the sense that she was in nobody's tutelage must necessarily be out of control in the rather different sense of being unable to contain her instincts, emotions and passions, all of which were irredeemably base. To put this another way, women would not just be a danger to themselves, whether physically, emotionally or spiritually, but also a danger to others. In short, the issue was one that pertained to the whole of society. One way or another, women were in and of themselves a source of disorder, of corruption, even of evil, and to let them live free would therefore be to disrupt the natural order and spread crime and immorality, thereby risking divine wrath.[4]

From all this it followed, first, that women could on occasion expect the most savage treatment on the part of the law—in 1782, for example, a woman acting under what she claimed to have been divine instruction was burned at the stake in Seville for having seduced a series of ecclesiastics[5]—and, second, that women had over the centuries become subject to a whole system of social control. Most importantly, marriage was interpreted in such a way as to ensure that wives were totally subordinate. When they married, then, women perforce swore to obey their husbands (one of the results of this, of course, was actually to reinforce traditional stereotypes of women: because women could not hope to make their views prevail by force, they had no option but to resort to the very wiles and artifice that were deemed to make it so essential to subject them to male control). Yet, women being women, it was assumed that they would be incapable of knowing their place, nor still less of curbing their passions—passions that, in another self-fulfilling prophecy, were in at least some cases inflamed by the fact that family marriage diplomacy led to many upper-class women being handed over to husbands who were much older than themselves—the result being a tacit assumption that male authority needs must be backed up by force. Women who did not obey their husbands, betrayed their marriage vows, or even were simply not deemed to be sufficiently deferential and attentive, then, risked being locked up for days and beaten black and blue. In past centuries in certain circumstances they could simply have been murdered outright, but, although such times were now past, this was only because jurists and theologians were agreed, in the first place, that capital punishment had to be the preserve of law, and, in the second, that to murder someone was to take away their chance of confessing their sins and making their peace with God. Finally, it was not enough that women should obey their husbands and refrain from adultery: by convention, they were also barred from engaging in any action whatsoever without the express permission of their husbands, and expected to live up to an ideal of absolute perfection.[6]

In the most extreme cases wives did not even enjoy freedom of movement within their own homes. On the contrary, in many households it had been the custom for husbands to confine their wives to a special raised enclosure. Within these spaces, the unfortunate women concerned passed their time sitting on special thrones surrounded by their personal servants, the result being that they were quite literally transformed into ornaments. Moreover, even when such bounds were not imposed on them, women had to accept controls that had similar intent, including, most importantly, the expectation that they should at all times dress modestly and in dark colours, the aim being, of course, that they would both be curbed in their inherent inclination to engage in flirtation and waste money on fripperies and rendered less attractive in the eyes of other men.[7]

Female inferiority within marriage was reflected by the law. In theory, women could not be forced into marriage without their consent, and could marry whoever they chose: according to Canon Law, marriage could be entered into at will, the only restriction placed upon it being that the partners concerned should be joined to one another by their own free will in full knowledge of the consequences of what they were doing. However, whilst this might satisfy the Church, it did not satisfy society, and a variety of controls had therefore sprung up which in practice ensured that girls could not only be denied free choice, but also forced into marriage against their will.[8] Thus, according to the code of law promulgated by Philip II in 1567 that remained in force right up until 1808, couples who married without consent were both disinherited and banished on pain of death. Divorce, meanwhile, was non-existent and annulment almost impossible to obtain even for a woman of property, not least because her complaints were unlikely to be listened to. Finally, even separation was out of the question as wives had to live in the conjugal home, and could be subject to imprisonment if they failed to do so. As for protection, the one area in which women had any rights was in the field of property. In so far as this was concerned, it was admittedly true that a married woman could not buy, sell or administer property of any sort. However, wives did have the right to half-shares in any income or property that resulted from the marriage, whilst they both acquired the whole of the property concerned should the husband die before them and retained possession of everything they brought into the marriage (in effect, the dowry).[9]

The fact that brides were in effect obliged by law to be of economic benefit to their husbands might at first sight appear to be advantageous to women, but in reality nothing could be further from the truth. In one sense, certainly, dowries were vital to women's well-being, and yet at the same time they sapped their status still further: without a dowry, women could not get married and therefore risked falling into an even deeper servitude, whilst the size of the dowry was a direct measure of the woman's status, from which it followed that women had no intrinsic worth of their own. Still worse, the need to provide them with a dowry converted women into an economic burden, and all the more so as the value of the endowments had tended steadily to increase, and that despite a variety of laws that had tried to limit this process.[10]

However, arranging matters so as to ensure that marriage would institutionalise women's second-class status was insufficient: not all women could be married, whilst, even if they could be, their husbands could not be in attendance upon them all the time. There being no option but to recognise this fact, a secondary series of social controls had therefore evolved that related to married and unmarried women alike. No woman could become a priest, of course, but because of their unclean status, women—nuns included—were barred from the sacred enclosure marked in all churches by the communion rails. Except when attending church, women were expected to remain in the home at all times. And, finally, at no point in their lives were women permitted to be independent of patriarchal control. Thus, until they got married, women lived in the parental home, whilst they then switched to that of their husbands. Meanwhile, if they remained unmarried, they either eventually had pass from the control of their father to that of some other male—an uncle, a brother or a nephew (a process that very often reduced them to the status of an unpaid domestic)—or go into a convent, in which case they instantly became subject to the supervision of a chaplain, and, indeed, 'brides of Christ'. To *de facto* imprisonment and permanent subjugation, meanwhile, were added both ritual humiliation—whenever they were outside the home, for example, they were expected to cover their heads with a shawl known as a *mantilla* as a sign of their recognition of their sinful status, whilst at the same time being accompanied by an elderly female retainer known as a *dueña* (literally, in this sense, 'keeper'), the task of the latter being both to chaperone them and to keep them in order—and a species of mind control in that their leisure occupations were confined to a narrow range of activities that were seen as being suitably womanly and, assuming they could read at all, their reading matter to devotional works. Finally, as if this were not enough, they could also be expected to be continually spied upon by servants and other retainers.[11]

Mention of books and reading leads us on to the subject of education. Here we might begin with the French diplomat, Alexandre de Laborde: 'If the Spanish ladies are agreeable, if they are sometimes well-informed, they owe it only to themselves, and in no degree to their education, which is almost totally neglected. If their native qualities were polished and unfolded by a careful instruction, they would become but too seductive'.[12] This is, perhaps, a little too arch. Thus, if women were supposed to be kept from anything other than works of religion, it was not just because anything else was deemed likely to drive them into sin or encourage a degree of rebellion. Just as important was the idea that they were too unintelligent to be able to cope with anything else—even that trying to cope with anything else was likely to make them ill.[13] Whatever the precise reason, the result was one and the same. Traditionally, then, such instruction as women received was, first, delivered within the home by private tutors and, second, extremely limited.[14] One may presume, then, that for many women life was even more restrictive than it might have been, and all the more so as the general misogynism was solidly reflected in the culture of the era, many of the products of the golden age of Spanish drama ridiculing women and painting them in the blackest of colours.[15] Yet the fact was that all too many women *were* ignorant: over and over again, then, we find British officers who served in the Peninsula marvelling at the frivolity and lack even of the most basic general knowledge of the women they encountered.[16]

One may assume that for many women ignorance was not bliss—that they rather lived out their lives in a state of intense frustration.[17] Rebellion of any sort was difficult, however. Setting aside the savage punishments that might be inflicted within the conflicts of the home, fathers, husbands or guardians who had reason to be displeased with one or other of the women of their households could apply to the courts to have the offender imprisoned. Meanwhile, running away was likely simply to lead to the same fate given the numerous round-ups that the authorities conducted in an attempt to clear the streets of beggars and vagabonds. Found in many cities, the female jails in which offenders found themselves were primarily aimed at the reform of prostitutes, but accepted unruly wives and daughters as well. As López Barahona has pointed out, the records of the various female prisons in Madrid show many examples of women whose only crime was to have sought their freedom or rebelled against their servitude, not to mention the sexual abuse or physical violence that court records suggest to have been very common. For example, in 1780 a fourteen-year-old button-maker named Catalina García was imprisoned at the request of her widowed father after having tried to run away with her lover. In general, such cases were more frequent among married women, however. In 1783, then, one María Angela de Olmos was arrested in Madrid when a patrol discovered her in a tavern in the company of some soldiers, the interrogation that followed revealing that she was from Toledo and had just left her husband. Just as interesting, meanwhile, are three women named María Martínez, Felipa Redonda and Manuela Yecla, who fled their homes in Alcalá de Henares in 1771 only very soon to be arrested in Madrid as vagrants. Finally, among the women incarcerated in 1780 was a 29-year-old woman named María Fernández who had seemingly been put away by her husband after running away from him on various occasions.[18]

The issue of imprisonment is one to which we must return in due course, but for the time being let us simply reiterate the role which it played in helping husbands and fathers keep their houses in order.[19] Incarceration in a gaol of some sort was obviously a far greater likelihood for the woman of indigence than it was for the woman of substance. At the same time the latter was probably also unlikely to experience the sort of overt physical brutality recorded by such observers as Wellington's Judge-Advocate-General, Francis Larpent: 'On my way home I found a Portuguese half-drunk, killing his wife. He had . . . laid her head open with a large stone'.[20] On the other hand, the woman of substance was far more likely to face the sort of domestic incarceration written of by Pardo Bazán. To quote Lord Blayney, a British general who was captured by the French in October 1811 and left an amusing memoir of his subsequent journey into captivity:

> In my intercourse with Spanish families, I could not help remarking the listless indolence in which the females doze away their lives: never have I seen a book or a needle in their hands, and their sole occupation seems to be playing with pet animals, particularly cats and dogs. Besides a monkey, several parrots and some pigeons, my landlady [at Granada] had four little curs, whose barking and snarling made them complete nuisances; she had also a large and small cat, for each of which a proportionate sized hole was cut in the bottom of every door.[21]

For many women at the upper end of the scale, in short, life remained very rigid. However, that said, the absolute reclusion of earlier centuries was starting to break down. In brief, by 1808 the wives and daughters of the nobility had greater freedom to appear in public, greater opportunities to socialise both with each other and with members of the opposite sex, greater opportunities for personal gratification and even greater opportunities for education. To represent the age as being one of liberation would be absurd, yet the frontiers of the possible had shifted just a little. At the heart of this development lay two very different issues, of which the first was intellectual and the second societal. Thus, in the course of the Enlightenment, a number of writers—most notably, the leading polymath, Bénito Feijóo, and the Seville newspaper editor, José Clavijo—began to challenge the manner in which the female sex had been so rigidly stereotyped. Absolute equality was not championed by such figures, certainly, but they did at least demonstrate that, by virtue of the simple fact that women were as much human beings as men were, they were capable of reason, and, by extension, taking advantage of education to improve their knowledge and understanding. In short, they could be schooled to be better human beings, whilst it was obviously very much in society's interests that this should be done.[22]

The idea of trying to turn out better women making good sense in at least some heads, the period witnessed a modest expansion in female education. Most women of the propertied classes continued to receive private tutoring only—writing in the mid-1770s, for example, the English traveller, William Dalrymple, still had no hesitation in insisting that Spanish women had 'no other education but what they receive from their parents'[23]—but even here the influence of the Enlightenment was not without effect (see below). Meanwhile, in the larger towns and cities girls might instead attend one of the increasing number of private colleges that were set up in the course of the eighteenth century (in 1798 there were fifty such colleges with 2,745 students). At the same time there had been some advance in what was on offer: until the mid-eighteenth century, the emphasis had been on teaching religion and morals and such skills as embroidery, but a good wife now, as we shall see, increasingly being expected to be an accomplished person able to engage in polite conversation, the result was that literacy became *de rigueur* and with it French, drawing, music and even a little history and geography.[24] By 1808, then, even the most remote provincial cities numbered among their inhabitants women who were well educated and, not only that but in some cases passionately interested in the issues of the day.[25]

On the basis of this rather limited beginning, a number of women emerged as genuine intellectual figures. Of these, although dozens of women—one authority estimates that the total number who managed to get something published was as high as 180[26]—took an active part in the discussions of the period, by far the most prominent was Josefa Amar y Borbón.[27] Born in Zaragoza in 1749, Amar was the daughter of Philip VI's personal physician, and, as such, came from a background that was both highly privileged and highly cultured. Quickly emerging as a young woman of ferocious intelligence and insatiable curiosity, she used her leisured existence to read voraciously and teach herself many foreign languages, whilst in adulthood she graduated to translating numerous texts into Spanish and writing several tracts concerning the education of women. Perhaps influenced by the fact that she was, in archetypal fashion, married off to a man much older than herself, she also emerged as a champion of Spanish feminism as well as a fierce opponent of the institution of the convent.[28] Also very important, meanwhile, was María Rosa de Gálvez, a girl from Málaga whose privileged background—she was the adoptive daughter of a wealthy army officer—enabled her to indulge a very considerable literary talent that eventually earned her the patronage of Manuel de Godoy and resulted in the production of a series of plays that challenged established gender norms.[29]

It was not just (or even primarily) as writers that educated women were able to make their mark. Also important was the figure of the society hostess and patron of the arts. By the mid-eighteenth century, largely as a result of the massive changes in fashions brought by the substitution of the Bourbons for the Hapsburgs in 1700, the institution of the *tertulia* had become a central part of the Spanish upper classes' social lives. In brief, a gathering that mirrored the *salons* of eighteenth-century France, this phenomenon could not but offer new opportunities to Spanish women as it both broke down the isolation of their lives and created roles that allowed them the chance to wield a certain degree of influence, the net result being the emergence of such figures as the Condesa de Montijo. Like Josefa Amar, a product of the Aragonese nobility, the countess was not a major intellectual figure in her own right, but she was a patron of such figures as Jovellanos, and by 1800 had emerged as a champion of the reformist tendency within the Catholic Church known as Jansenism. Also important as a focus for the Spanish Enlightenment, however, was the *tertulia* of the Condesa-Duque de Benavente, an early patron of Francisco de Goya who did much to bring him to the attention of the court.[30]

As the eighteenth century wore on, so these developments could not but have some impact. Many of those in intellectual circles remained hostile, but the issue would not go away, and in 1775 it was revived by the formation of Real Sociedad Económica Matritense de Amigos del País—the Madrid branch of the aristocratic reform movement articulated through the so-called 'societies of the friends of the people'. From the beginning a number of members took an interest in the idea of women contributing more to economic well-being of society through such activities as cottage industry, while in 1786 a limited number of women (Josefa Amar and the Condesa de Montijo among them) were actually admitted to its ranks and allowed to form an autonomous section known as the Junta de Damas de Honor y Mérito.[31]

By the late eighteenth century, then, women had begun to make an impact in the discussions of the social élite. Yet very few women were directly affected by these developments. Much more important in this respect were changes in the patterns of sociability. We return here first of all to the *tertulia*.[32] Primarily a social gathering in which politics were sometimes discussed rather than a political gathering that was conducted in a social context—the English naturalist, John Dillon, specifically observed that talk of politics was banned[33]—the *tertulia* at the very least rendered it impossible for women to be kept in seclusion. Exactly what happened varied from house to house—in some cases, men and women mingled freely together, while in others they effectively remained segregated[34]—but, whatever the arrangement, women were now social beings, and, what is more, social beings who had a central role in proceedings: as is quite clear from the writings of foreign visitors, *tertulias* were identified by their hostesses and in large part revolved around them.[35] Meanwhile, on occasion, they were not just social beings, but also autonomous social beings: passing through Córdoba, for example, Dalrymple encountered what appears to have been an all-female *tertulia* at the house of the Condesa de Villa Nova.[36]

Nor was the end of female reclusion amongst the propertied classes restricted to the home. In the first place, by being allowed out into the open, élite women were empowered to act as emissaries for their families when it came to securing favours from the authorities, this being a process that under the notoriously lascivious Manuel de Godoy was to become a subject of public scandal: according to the Spanish dissident, Blanco White, he showed himself to be especially accommodating to 'those who appeared at his public levees attended by a handsome wife or blooming daughter'.[37] Meanwhile, female members of the élite began increasingly to appear at the three traditional mainstays of public sociability in Spain, namely the *paseo,* the bull-fight and the theatre, though on occasion they might still be subjected to a degree of segregation: in Córdoba and Granada alike, British travellers noted that women were restricted to particular sections of the cities' theatres.[38] One might well argue that this was a by-blow of changing patterns in men's behaviour—that all that had happened was that men had found new ways to pass their time and wanted to use them simply to show off their wives—but that is by-the-by: from the point of view of the women concerned, almost any change in their husbands' patterns of sociability was a change for the better. Meanwhile, whatever the causes of the phenomenon, as witness descriptions of the popular promenade known as the Prado, women had soon established themselves as a prominent presence in the public view.[39]

Even more extraordinarily—from what we know of the layout of such places, the bathers were barely shielded from the general view—we discover that women of the propertied classes also turned the public bath houses that had been established along the banks of the River Manzanares into places where women could meet one another and have fun together.[40] Meanwhile, to return from an excursion was no longer to return to the gloominess and austerity that had typified the homes of the propertied classes in Hapsburg Spain. Thanks to the influence of French fashion, the houses of the aristocracy, at least, were now furnished with comfortable furniture and decorated in the light and airy style typical of the eighteenth century, while those that were erected from scratch were now modelled not on the fortress-like dwellings of early-modern Spain, but rather the mansions that were currently springing up from Paris to Moscow.[41] With comfortable homes, meanwhile, came a wider range of personal pleasures, one fact that is, perhaps, particularly striking being that there appear to have been few prejudices in respect of women smoking.[42] Finally, clothing, too, was now very different—dresses became shorter, thereby revealing the feet and developing a need for attractive footwear, while even the *mantilla* lost its sting, evolving from a symbol of shame to one more item of attractive apparel.[43]

If the pursuit of pleasure and the consumption of luxuries had become central to the lives of the women of the upper classes, to a more limited extent they had also begun to be drawn into social and charitable work of various kinds that again widened their horizons. Thus, the Junta de Damas made the welfare of the female prisoners housed in the various jails of Madrid one of its special interests and, with the aid of a substantial royal grant, from 1788 onwards began to try to provide inmates with some schooling or, at least, training, as well as to increase their rations and improve their conditions, whilst by 1791 it was also superintending the handful of primary schools that had been set up in Madrid at the instance of Charles III.[44] Meanwhile, women were just as prominent in succouring the sick in Madrid's various hospitals, Fischer noting that the Hospital de la Pasión—an institution that, as it happened, catered entirely for women—were given 'the kindest attention' by 'many ladies of quality, especially old dowagers'.[45] Finally, here and there, there was also female involvement in charitable activity. As a British officer captured during the American War of Independence named Richard Croker noted of Arcos de la Frontera remembered, for example: 'Collections of money . . . are very frequent. In a procession of young women a few days since, a very beautiful girl indeed brought the charity box to the window of our messroom. This had the effect it was undoubtedly intended to produce—a very liberal contribution'.[46]

Amongst the propertied classes, then, by the late eighteenth century women had enjoyed a considerable advance in their situation, and, or so it was claimed, 'recovered a liberty by which they are, perhaps, less tempted to go astray than formerly, when their virtue was entrusted to locks and grates, and to a superintendence often faithless and easy to be corrupted'.[47] Accompanying this, meanwhile, was a development whose realities are impossible to judge, but which yet assumed considerable prominence. We come here to the *cortejo,* a man who may in brief be defined as the escort-cum-confidante of a married woman. Exactly how this phenomenon came into being is unknown, but what seems to have occurred is that, as the women of the upper classes came into ever greater contact with a wider social circle, so this inevitably increased intercourse between women and men from outside their immediate families. How, though, were such meetings to be managed? Etiquette called for men to take the leading role in bridging the gulf between the sexes—a gulf which clearly had somehow to be bridged—but, in so far as this was concerned, their only guide was the mediaeval idea of courtly love. At any *tertulia,* then, a woman was very likely to find one or more men—the majority of them probably married to other women—paying them extravagant compliments, and all the more so as they were very likely to have put considerable pains into their appearance: after all, was not part of the purpose of the *tertulia* the display of wealth, good taste and a sense of fashion? To these compliments the women in many instances responded warmly, even flirtatiously, and very soon acquaintances were pairing off with one another as *de facto* couples. Initially tolerated on the grounds that it was safer for women to have one male friend rather than a dozen (and more proper for a man to give his attention to one woman than to many), gradually the situation received the sanction of fashion until the point was reached that it was an absolute requirement, and all the more so as both sides found a certain advantage in its existence: on the one hand, often treated badly by their husbands, wives found comfort and emotional release in the attentions of a *cortejo,* while husbands were both spared the need to entertain their wives and relieved of some of the cost of providing the constant supply of new finery required by the social round (not that they had an real chance of putting a stop to matters even had they wanted to: any husband who tried such a thing would have been stigmatised as a backwoodsman).[48]

Exactly what the *cortejo* amounted to is unclear—it is, for example, by no means obvious that the men concerned necessarily enjoyed a sexual relationship with the woman they had given themselves over to[49]—but what is clear is that the position was a somewhat uncomfortable one. Thus, forced to accept the role by the dictates of fashion or, more cynically, hopeful that it would provide him with all the advantages of matrimony without incurring its responsibilities, the man then found himself unable to escape its clutches, for, whereas a wife could not divorce her husband, a mistress could very easily divorce her *cortejo,* subject only to the restriction that doing so too many times would be to incur such a reputation for flightiness that no man would again take up with her. For a gentleman of fashion to be jilted in such a fashion, however, was intolerable, and the net result was that the *cortejo* was absolutely under the thumb of his lady. Yet to throw the woman over was unthinkable as it did not sit well with the notion of honour, let alone that of the courtly lover, and so there was no way out. What this meant could be demanding, indeed: the *cortejo* would have to dance attendance upon his mistress morning, noon and night, endure her constant prattle about the doings of the servants, the behaviour of this or that lady of her acquaintance or the latest Paris fashions—unfortunately, it is clear that the *tertulia* did little to rescue most women from the limitations of their education[50]—sit through long sessions at the dressing table offering appropriate suggestions and compliments and, above all, ply the woman with a constant stream of presents. In short, they had to supply the companionship that was seemingly so utterly absent from most marriages, but with this came a corollary in that their mistresses could take out all the frustrations consequent upon their situation upon them, and even live out a fantasy of role reversal. In the words of the British commissary, Edward Buckham, then, the women concerned were 'the greatest tyrants in the world'.[51]

There is much to ponder here, particularly with respect to the cataclysm that was about to befall Spain and Portugal: in many different ways the women of the propertied classes were clearly kicking at the bonds that held them in check. More than that, indeed, with the help of the dictates of fashion, they had achieved a certain degree of personal freedom. However, even among the élite, it seems likely that this advance in the situation of women was at best patchy: strong in Madrid and some of the larger provincial cities, it is probable that it dwindled away almost to nothing in places that were more out of the way of the influence of foreign culture.[52] Here, for example, is Jean Oyon, a quartermaster-sergeant in the Fourth Dragoons who took part in the occupation of Lisbon in 1807, on the women of Estremoz:

> At Estremoz . . . the customs are still those of the Moors. . . . The women never once show their visages, wearing, as they do, a sort of shawl, or rather enormous wrap, of black wool that is gathered under the arms, thrown over the head, and finally tied at the waist. Often in some way attached to this garment, meanwhile, a skirt of the same material falls to their very feet. Attired in this bizarre fashion, maiden and widow alike are turned into shapeless bundles that would be impossible to take for women but for the sentinels that watch their every move.[53]

Away from Madrid and Lisbon, meanwhile, even women who aspired to some sophistication fell well short of the mark. Such at least was the opinion of Beresford's *aide-de*-camp, William Warre, of a group of young women he encountered at the village of Fornos de Algodres. Thus: 'At the general's . . . last quarters we had seven or eight grown-up young ladies . . . the most affected stupid misses I ever met with . . . They were never three miles from home, and ape notwithstanding from hearsay what they fancy great people should do'.[54] Still worse, even if all the women of the propertied classes had managed fully to participate in all of the changes that we have discussed, it would have made no difference in respect of the position of the women of Iberia as a whole: if absolutely every woman of, for want of a better term, 'good family' had attended a *tertulia* or acquired a *cortejo,* there would probably still have been one hundred who never had any contact with such circles. In short, then, we must now shift our focus to the mass of the population.[55]

In so far as this is concerned, the picture is very different, the first thing to say being that for the vast majority of women education was non-existent: there were almost no girls' schools whatsoever, whilst the tiny handful that did exist offered little more than the catechism and such practical skills as spinning and weaving.[56] Meanwhile, even had there been a better provision for lower-class girls, there were very few careers to which they could aspire: the odd midwife or woman teacher was to be found here or there, but that was about all.[57] That said, if they were illiterate, they were scarcely idle. On the contrary, what lay at the heart of their existence was not leisure but labour. For most women, of course, what this meant was that they contributed in whatever way they could to the family economy, and that this role continued even after they got married. Beginning with the countryside, the evidence here is extremely sparse, but such anecdotal evidence as we have suggests that in the north of Spain women engaged in most agricultural tasks alongside men, and even instead of men (the eighteenth-century writer, Larruga y Boneta, complained that in some areas of Castile the women were all to be found in the fields and the men to be found in the taverns and plazas!): in the Basque country it has been argued that the fact that ploughing was carried out, not with the aid of ox-drawn ploughs, but rather primitive hand-held diggers known as *layas* encouraged the employment of women in this capacity, but, be this as it may, elsewhere the key issue was rather the fact that much of the male population had to seek work as migrant labourers, the women therefore having no option but to look after family smallholdings themselves. In general, indeed, women who worked on the land did so in the context of such plots, but there were also cases of women (especially widows and unmarried girls) finding paid work as labourers, shepherds or goat or swine herds (it is significant here that the word *zagala* means both herder and 'young maiden').[58] Finally, women might even be involved in such activities as cutting timber: travelling from La Coruña to Oporto in December 1808, for example, one traveller professed himself 'surprised to see little girls of about ten years old cutting wood at the height of sixty to eighty feet from the ground'.[59]

If plenty of women worked in the fields in the peasant-dominated agriculture of northern Spain, in the central and southern provinces the situation was rather different. With the countryside largely parcelled out into great estates founded on monoculture farmed by day-labourers, opportunities for women were extremely limited, not least because much of the workforce had to live away from home herded together in remote farmsteads known as *cortijos*. Left behind in the miserable 'agro-towns' into which the bulk of the populace was concentrated, the wives of the day-labourers might derive some small income from gleaning: for example, travelling from Zaragoza to Madrid in 1778 the British naturalist, John Dillon, observed large numbers of women gathering the parasite that produces cochineal, whilst across Andalucía it was common for women to cut wild esparto grass that could be woven into such items as baskets.[60] Otherwise, other than exploiting their own bodies by means of prostitution or wet-nursing, with little space available in the cramped townships which they inhabited to keep pigs or chickens, their only chance was to take in laundry—something for which there was not much call in a society where the vast majority of the population was desperately poor—or obtain domestic work in the homes of the local élite, this last being something that was often exploited to obtain clothing, cooking utensils and crockery (until comparatively recently, it was common for female domestics to wheedle such items out of their employers).[61] The limited nature of such opportunities did not mean that women were wholly unimportant—if a man needed a favour from his employer, it was generally his wife who was deputed to obtain it, whilst in some districts it was customary for the bonus paid out at the end of the harvest to be ceremonially solicited by a posse of pretty girls—but the fact is that women were much less economically active than was the case elsewhere.[62]

With regards to agriculture, then, we have a very mixed picture. This, however, is not the case with regard to artisanry. In so far as this was concerned, women were heavily involved. If they could not always become master-artisans themselves, marriage to an artisan almost always brought with it involvement in his work, and all the more so as artisans generally worked either in the home itself or very close to it, whilst the pattern of work was often such that women could easily combine a stint in the workshop with the domestic routine.[63] At all events it is clear that a whole range of auxiliary tasks fell to their lot. Indeed, although guild regulations often prevented them from doing so on a permanent basis, there seems no reason to doubt that, depending on the levels of skill which they had managed to acquire, they on occasion even took on the role of the master-craftsman himself. And this, meanwhile, was just the wives of the artisans: particularly in the clothing trades young women were frequently able to obtain paid employment, the famous Manuela Malasaña being, as we have seen, an embroideress.[64]

To go out to work in the style of Manuela Malasaña was as yet the experience of only a tiny handful of women: apart from the handful of embroiderers and seamstresses from whose ranks she stemmed, practically the only women who did so in any numbers were those who by 1800 had begun to find employment in the new mills that were just beginning to spring up to serve Catalonia's nascent cotton industry (in the course of the reign of Charles III some opportunities had also been available in the various industrial establishments that had been founded by the crown at such places as Guadalajara, Brihuega and Talavera de la Reina as part of its drive to promote scientific and industrial development, but by the close of the eighteenth century these had all collapsed). This development should not be exaggerated—the eighty textile factories that existed in Catalonia in 1784 employed only 1,740 women as opposed to 4,607 men—but it was not necessary to have a place of employment in order to earn money in the textile industry. Thus, in many parts of Spain women spun and wove in their own homes as part of the 'putting-out' system, whilst they could also be engaged in such activities as making lace. As Patterson wrote of Bejar, then: 'The chief employment here is carding and cleaning wool for the cloth manufacturies. The females are constantly occupied in this business, assembled in groups at their doors and windows, picking the wool and getting it ready for the loom'.[65]

Even in areas of unskilled labour that were dominated by men, it seems that, aided perhaps by the fact that their wages were much lower than those of their male competitors or other issues specific to the particular locality, women were on occasion seemingly in much evidence. Here, for example, is Dillon on Bilbao (the capital of a province from which many thousands of young men habitually took ship for the American colonies): 'In other countries women are oppressed with the slightest fatigue. Here they work as much as the strongest men, unload the ships, carry burdens and do all the business of porters. The very felons, confined to hard labour in the mines of Almadén, do nothing in comparison with these females: they go bare-footed and are remarkably active, carrying burdens on their heads which require two men to lift up'.[66] If the lot of the women noted by Dillon was doubtless very hard, at least they appear to have been benefiting from a gap in the labour market. Elsewhere, however, the situation appears to have been very different: in nearby Burgos women who were unable to contribute to the domestic economy by any other means appear to have been forced into working as porters and treated little better than beasts of burden.[67] That said, it is possible that there is some confusion here with another issue in that in northern Spain many women had become involved in long-distance trade. Thus, Galicia, Asturias, Santander and the Basque provinces were all possessed of resources that were unavailable in much of the rest of Spain in the form of dairy products and plentiful supplies of fish, these traditionally being exported by means of female labour. 'These women', wrote Buckham, 'carry two baskets behind them like a soldier's knapsack. The lower basket is in the shape of a funnel, the point of which reaches nearly to their heels; on top of this is placed an oblong basket, the ends of which protrude beyond their shoulders. These baskets, when filled, weigh four *arrobas,* equal to 128 pounds, and beneath this load the women walk, nearly bent double, at the rate of three miles an hour, and often make a day's journey of six or seven leagues. . . . They travel in troops of thirty or forty and you meet with them on all the high roads'.[68]

Whilst it would be advisable to assume that the situation witnessed by Dillon was by no means the norm, there were nonetheless many areas of the urban economy where women were prominent or, indeed, had made it their own. Let us begin here with small-scale commerce. As with artisanry, the chief entrée here was the need to provide husbands or sons with direct assistance in the management of petty businesses: a woman who was married to a market trader might very well help him to man his stall, just as the wife of a fisherman might take charge of selling his fish or the wife of a peasant travel into town to sell his produce. Yet here too women succeeded in—literally—penetrating the market in their own right. In Barcelona, for example, they were by tradition allowed to acquire licences as street traders from the relevant guilds, these rights often later being transmitted from mother to daughter, whilst in many places women sought to set themselves up illegally, very often as itinerant street sellers, setting up a proper stall making them too vulnerable to denunciation and arrest. At all events, women had a very marked presence in the streets and markets (not that this was necessarily an advantage, the women concerned having, for obvious reasons to be tough, combative and highly vocal, the result was to add fuel to the flames of Spanish misogynism).[69]

Having observed the street sellers and small holders at work in places like the Puerta del Sol and the Plaza Mayor, the visitor to Madrid had but a short walk to see even greater numbers employed in another sector of the economy. Thus, the sandy banks of the river Manzanares (and, it may be assumed, those of the rivers of other cities) were perpetually lined by large numbers of washer women. Here, for example, is Christian Fischer:

> The *lavanderas* are to be found from the Segovia gate almost as far as that of Toledo. They have a vast number of small stalls covered in summer in linen, and near which are also places to dry. The hooting, singing and quarrelling of these ladies of the tub . . . forms a chorus which is truly infernal.[70]

If women at work were a common enough sight in the streets, so they were in the houses of the propertied classes. Thus, titled households employed hundreds of servants of whom many—indeed, the majority—were women. At the top of the scale in this respect came *camaristas*—women with at least some pretensions of gentility who lived out their lives as ladies' companions—whilst below them came a vast array of cooks, maids and housekeepers. Generally speaking, the resultant mass of women consisted of girls aged from fifteen to twenty-five, but their ranks also included older women who had been forced to look for employment when their husbands died or who had forgone the chance of marriage to remain in the pay of their employers. Included amongst them, meanwhile, were many young women who had migrated from the countryside rather than having grown up in the major cities—Madrid, Seville, Barcelona. As for conditions, these were often grim in the extreme: in addition to frequently being the victims of long hours and every form of abuse—court records suggest that many young women in service were raped by members of the families for whom they were working or, for that matter, butlers, chamberlains or footmen—servants often received nothing more than board and lodging, although in fairness there were households in which they were treated more graciously, maids in such families sometimes even being provided with dowries when they decided to get married.[71]

For the vast majority of Iberia's women, the world was one of work, not to mention one in which their subordination to husband or father was as complete as it was brutal and humiliating: 'The Valencians', noted Henry Swinburne, 'still retain much of the features and manners of their old Saracen masters. To this day the farmers won't allow their wives to sit at table, but make them stand at their elbow and wait upon them'.[72] At the same time, however, it was also one of great vulnerability. The vast majority of the populace were desperately poor even in times of relative plenty: if we take Madrid as an example, of the c.150,000 people who lived in the capital in 1750, approximately seventy per cent were drawn from the artisanate or below, and of these it has been estimated that only fifteen per cent received wages of more than ten *reales* a day, and, further, that two thirds got only six *reales* a day. However, for women the situation was even worse: whereas a skilled male weaver might get as much as eight *reales* per day, an equally skilled female lace-maker could not expect more than two.[73] The lot of most women, then, was hardship and privation, but a number of factors put them at particular risk of absolute destitution. As we have already implied, few women could hope to survive without a male protector, but therein lay a major problem in that on the whole women lived longer than men. In short, sooner or later large numbers of women faced the problem of widowhood, whilst a further problem was that the female population was in any case starting to outstrip its male counterpart.[74] Nor, meanwhile, was demography the end of the problem, the disparity between men and women being worsened still further in certain parts of the country by the fact that large numbers of young men regularly emigrated to America or were swept up by conscription.[75]

The consequences of all this can be imagined all too well: in brief, many women either never managed to obtain a husband at all, or were unable to contract a second marriage in the wake of the demise of their first partner, thereby being left to bring up their families more-or-less on their own: in the second half of the eighteenth century, there were parts of the country where households headed by women reached twenty-five per cent of the total and very few where the figure was less than ten per cent.[76] With rates of pay insufficient to support even one individual, let alone a family, and extended kinship groups unable in most instances to take in extra mouths, the net result in many instances was great difficulty. Faced by the threat of starvation, the legions of single women made head as best they could. Thus, widows might often let out rooms in their homes (very often, it seems, to other single women) or care for children while their mothers went out to work, while women who were lucky enough to be in milk would seek to rent themselves out as wet nurses, this being a device that was also open, of course, to women who were still living *en famille*.[77] Meanwhile, still others became washerwomen or street traders, offered their services as midwives, disguised themselves as men so as to work as labourers—there were certainly cases of this amongst the migrant workers of Galicia[78]—or fled to distant cities in search of work.[79] And, of course, a regular means of making life a little easier was the abandonment of infant offspring to the various foundling hospitals. Taking that of Barcelona as an example, according to Townsend, at the time of his visit to the city this was taking in an average of at least 500 babies a year.[80]

Sadly for the women concerned, the desperate battles to survive in an unkind world in a more-or-less honourable fashion that are encapsulated in this brief paragraph frequently ended in failure. Indeed, with the economic situation steadily worsening—apart from the serious effect of the war with Britain that broke out in 1796, from the 1780s onwards Spain was in the grip of mounting price inflation—such failures seem to have become more and more frequent. If we look at the figures for admissions to the hospital of San Juan de Díos in Murcia, for example, there seems no doubt that the picture was dark indeed: in the period 1740–49, then, the number of admissions had amounted to 3,941 men and 2,389 women, but in 1790–99 the same numbers were 5,944 men and 5,791 women. Meanwhile, as if it was not bad enough that the proportion of women who were becoming so indigent that they had no option but to turn to charity was increasing, the statistics also show, first, that women were turning to the system at a much younger age and, second, that far more were unmarried, and therefore either very young women or spinsters who had been unable to find a husband.[81]

Faced by the final disaster of disappearance into a welfare system whose charity was at best very cold, many women who reached the end of every other resource turned to other ways of maintaining themselves and their families (if, that is, they had not done so already). Petty theft, then, was common, whilst thousands upon thousands of women slid into prostitution. The best that can said here is that this was in some cases disguised, this being particularly so of the many relationships that appear to have been forged with members of the clergy. In raising this subject, the author is once again painfully aware of the problem of popular anti-clericalism: in brief, just because all parish priests had housekeepers, it does not mean that all parish priests had mistresses. Many of the positions of this type that were offered to poverty-stricken widows were therefore beyond doubt offered out of Christian charity, whilst it is equally beyond doubt that there were priests who sheltered needy members of their own families in their presbyteries, some of whom, inevitably enough, were female.[82] That said, there are simply too many ecclesiastical complaints of clerical incontinence to believe that offers of shelter did not in at least some instances come with certain very clear expectations, or, for that matter, that the women concerned did not offer their prospective hosts sexual favours in return for the promise of shelter. Such remarks as the following may therefore be nothing more than the fruit of prejudice, but they therefore cannot be wished away:

> I have observed that in Spain the prettiest girl in every gentleman's house is the niece. The *padres* particularly are the luckiest fellows in the world in having the handsomest brothers and sisters of any man living—not that I have seen the brother or sister of any one of them, but then I have seen 999 *padres,* and each had his niece at the head of his establishment, and I know not how it happened, but she was always the prettiest girl in the parish.[83]

For the sort of women referred to here, life was probably by no means unbearable: indeed, Fischer even suggests that some of them were eventually enabled to get married thanks to dowries given them by their grateful protectors.[84] Meanwhile, a few women emerged as high-class courtesans, setting themselves up 'in very fine houses and pretending to be young widows'.[85] But for most prostitutes, life was inevitably very grim, the same author describing how in Madrid they lived clustered together in the most miserable districts of the periphery 'plying for custom at the corner of every little street or lane', earning no more than a single *real* for each transaction and often living under the thumb of 'mercenary lovers or bullies'.[86] Nor was it just a question of the daily misery of life in the streets. Also a factor was the constant hostility of the authorities. Thus, if Dalrymple saw 'fifteen prostitutes drummed out of the town for their malpractices . . . placed upon the steps of ladders carried horizontally upon men's shoulders with the hair of their heads and [their] eyebrows shaved off' in El Ferrol, in Lisbon Beckford witnessed one of the numerous 'wretched sibylls' who survived by 'telling fortunes and selling charms against the ague' being dragged off in a most distressed condition for interrogation.[87] Note, then, that arrest was not limited to women who were beyond doubt prostitutes. On the contrary, many women were arrested for no other crime than that of vagrancy, selling goods in the streets, frequenting taverns, living in sin, being on the streets late at night, or even simply laughing and joking with men who were not their husbands. Prostitution, it would therefore seem, was in many ways but a pretext for a much wider round-up of women who had transgressed against the prevalent social norms.[88]

Whoever was taken, however, the results were much the same. Thus, in towns which lacked the necessary facilities, the women were probably simply whipped and driven out of town, but elsewhere they were incarcerated along with the unruly wives and daughters we have already met in one of the various houses of correction scattered around the country. Once sentenced to confinement, the women concerned could be kept without trial for months, whilst they were invariably subjected to a régime of brutality and forced labour, whilst those institutions run by nuns also insisted on forcing inmates to dress as postulants and take part in the daily round of religious ceremonies.[89]

For the vast majority of women, then life was very far removed from that enjoyed by the privileged few. That said, however, they may be said to have had one thing in common. Thus, within their separate spheres, both groups can clearly be seen to have been pushing against the boundaries that kept them in check. Amongst the élite this revolved around such matters as advancing the frontiers of sociability, securing access to the fruits of the new consumer society, enjoying the games centred on the person of the *cortejo* and, last but not least, in a very few instances, penetrating the world of intellectual debate. Amongst the lower classes, however, we see a much greater degree of vigour that is, perhaps, encapsulated in the figure of the *maja*. Impossible to translate with any ease, this is a word that is best left 'as is'. That said, however, the *maja* is easy enough to depict. In brief, prostitute, seamstress, washerwoman or maid-servant, she was a young woman of the lower classes who at all times affected a haughty and challenging mien, and in the evenings and on Sundays and other feast days joined together with other young men and women of her age to wander the streets having fun, and jeering at any passersby who they spotted wearing French-style costume (a particular feature of the *maja* and her male counter-part, the *majo,* was the affectation of an exaggerated form of traditional dress).[90] On one level, then, the *maja* was a defender of Spanish tradition in the face of the spread of foreign influence, but, brassy, bold and defiant as she was, she was also a *de facto* champion of the right of the Spanish woman to occupy the public space and, to the extent that she was a single woman, live beyond the bounds of male control. To quote Fischer, 'It is impossible to imagine creatures more loose, more wanton and more shameless'.[91]

If the aggressive style of the *majas* was one way of standing up for the cause of women, there were others that achieved results that were more concrete. Let us take, for example, the issue of the *leva*. Husbands, as we have seen, could denounce their wives to the authorities if they failed in what they perceived to be their duty and have them placed in a house of correction, but the same applied to wives. Thus, every time a *leva* was called, *vagos* were not just swept from the streets, but also picked up in response to denunciations presented by their kith and kin, wives who had been deserted, beaten or neglected by their husbands were provided with a chance of getting their revenge. Thanks to Pérez Estévez, who suggests that around ten per cent of *vagos* owed their arrest to complaints by angry wives, we can even cite a number of such cases. In July 1774, for example, a carter was declared a *vago* in El Pardo after his wife had denounced him for having failed to provide for either her or her children, sold much of the family's clothes and furniture to buy wine, and regularly beaten her up, for good measure also turning on his neighbours when they had tried to intervene, while in 1759 the same fate befell a notary from Valseca who was condemned for having neglected his family on account of his fondness for wine.[92]

Whilst the *leva* could be a useful way of getting rid of a wife-beater or drunk, it was something that at best happened once every few years. More useful, then, in many respects were the ordinary courts and magistrates. By 1808, then, the figure of the female plaintiff was one that had become very common. Particularly in cities with a high incidence of emigration to America, large numbers of women whose husbands had made such a choice whilst yet leaving them behind petitioned the courts to order the return of their husbands, while still others tried to take them to court for reneging on promises to marry them (this was a much more important issue than these bare words reveal: for the women of the lower classes, the only dowry they had to offer was their virginity, and, so desperate were many of them to acquire a husband, that they were prepared to part with this for a mere promise of marriage; if they were then betrayed, the chances were that they would then lose all hope of reaching the altar). And, finally, the ecclesiastical courts found themselves dealing with many requests from women who wanted to separate from their husbands on the grounds of mistreatment. Talk of a significant revolt would be premature, but, even so, it is clear that at least some women were fighting back.[93]

Meanwhile, even when they were not actually fighting back, women had long since evolved patterns of interaction that allowed them to make contact with one another, share their troubles and exchange strategies and ideas. For hundreds of years isolated in the confines of their parlours, the women of the upper classes started with an obvious disadvantage here, but in the course of the eighteenth century they had been provided with a way out through the emergence of the *tertulia*. Yet attending church, as they did, every day, even before that they had had an important outlet, in which respect we might quote a letter written by one Mariquita de las Virtudes that appeared in the *Correo de Sevilla* on 27 June 1804. In brief, this painted an affecting picture of the courage shown by many women in struggling to keep their households going by a policy of make-do and mend in the face of wastrel husbands who spent all their time putting the world to rights, gaming, or gadding about town with their cronies, and denied them the few pennies they needed for basic necessities, thereby leaving them with no option but to turn to the charity of their neighbours, and at the same time make use of their church-going as a means of seeking the support of other women and lamenting their many ills.[94] For the women of the lower classes, the church porch or patio must doubtless have provided just the same sort of solidarity—it is beyond doubt for this reason that, throughout the 200 years of decline that has followed, church attendance throughout Spain has remained a lot higher among women than among men—but they also often had their work environment: thus, the communal cooking areas in which they had to prepare food for their families, the market places in which they obtained that food, the scrubland in which they engaged in gleaning, the corners in which they squatted to spin, sew or make lace, and the riverbanks on which they did their washing all afforded them environments in which they could talk to one another, and, what is more, do so safe from the prying ears of men.[95]

There was, of course, one other way of fighting back and that was to run away. As we have seen, as the eighteenth century wore on, many desperate single women, whether spinsters or widows, abandoned economic situations that had become ever more intolerable and made for cities such as Madrid in the hope of securing a better life. However, such behaviour was not just open to women who were on their own: married women could also take to the road—hence the various cases we have observed of women who were sent into 'houses of correction' after deserting their husbands. Such flights, however, did not just have to end in Madrid or other large cities. On the contrary, exactly as in Britain and France (see below), large numbers of women threw in their lot with the Spanish army and became campfollowers. How this option worked is unclear—a brief reference in Buckham's memoirs to the women being on half rations suggests that wives may have been taken 'on the strength' in the same fashion as the British army (see below)[96]—but work it did, for when a Spanish division was sent to Denmark under the Marqués de la Romana in 1807 women featured very strongly in the works of several German illustrators who were evidently fascinated by its presence.[97] Finally, as in other armies of the period, a tiny handful of women may have disguised themselves as men so as to become soldiers. Certainly, cases of such 'cross dressers' did exist—in the seventeenth century, for example, a runaway nun named Catalina de Erauso had successfully hidden her identity and become a soldier of fortune in America[98]—while the theme was one that was regularly exploited in the theatre. At the same time, too, the women of Spain and Portugal perhaps had more reason than most to try it. Yet it was at best a difficult option to embark upon and one may doubt whether the feat was ever pulled off on more than a handful of occasions.[99]

To conclude, then, what sort of picture have we elaborated of the position occupied by the women of Iberia in 1808? In the first instance, it has to be said that this was extremely dark. At the top of society, certainly, there had been some progress. Thanks to Feijóo, a serious intellectual debate had been unleashed with regard to the role of women in society, and this had in turn given a few élite women the chance to participate in the Enlightenment. Meanwhile, on a somewhat less exalted plane, wider changes in patterns of fashion and sociability had given élite women in general the chance to escape the confines of the home, enjoy a variety of luxury products, participate in a varied social life and even experience a degree of sexual adventure. Yet too much should not be made of these developments. Even among the élites these advances had not been universal: if the *tertulia* was the rule in Madrid and Lisbon, it is by no means clear that this could be said of the provinces. As for society as a whole, the situation was very different: the vast majority of women lived lives of utter misery. However, whilst it should be stressed that many thousands of women, perhaps even many hundreds of thousands of women, were content to accept their lot, and that some of them might even have been perfectly happy, the female population was by no means a passive force. Beneath the surface, indeed, there is plenty of evidence of a willingness to challenge the reigning structures. Thus, women shared their sorrows in social spaces that they had made their own, used the *cortejo* system to live out fantasies of role reversal, adopted a persona—that of the *maja*—that was the very personification of pride and defiance, exploited a variety of mechanisms to rid themselves of violent husbands, developed a range of professional skills, and frequently left the parental or marital home to seek survival elsewhere. Meanwhile, in Spain they also began to emerge as veritable symbols of national identity. Thus, on the one hand we have the *petimetra*—the genteel noblewoman dressed in her French fashions, adorned with her French *coiffure* and reclining on her French *chaise-longue*—and, on the other, the *maja*—the tough, foul-mouthed woman of the streets who, unable to clad herself in anything other than traditional clothing, turned her poverty into a statement of not just female pride but national identity. It is an arresting combination and one which suggests a number of possible responses to war and invasion. Would the women of Iberia choose the path of patriotism, or would they rather turn traitor? Or would they rather ignore such issues, or, at least, subordinate them to more pressing matters related to the survival of themselves and their families?

3

Baggages

Like all their counterparts for the past 200 years, armies of the Napoleonic period did not march alone. Thus, for the simple reason that their paymasters could not afford the various auxiliary corps that were to become a feature of later forces, the troops of the belligerent states were dependent on the services of a swarm of non-combatants. Some of these figures (above all, teamsters, waggoners, muleteers and drovers) were men, but, generally speaking, the so-called 'other army' was made up of a mass of more-or-less unruly female campfollowers who, setting aside a variety of less legitimate activities, assisted with a myriad menial tasks in barracks and campsite alike, catered for the sexual needs of the troops, acted as nursing auxiliaries and supplied the soldiers with a variety of creature comforts.[1] Alongside the common 'drabs' who marched with the rank and file, meanwhile, were often to be found many other females, namely officers' wives and mistresses and perhaps even a few 'cross-dressers.' In the Peninsular War, then, the armies of all the belligerents were accompanied by thousands of women. As the conflict went on, the ranks of this 'monstruous regiment' were augmented by new recruits from Spain and Portugal, but right up until the end of the war a large proportion remained foreign. British, French, Belgian, Dutch, German, Italian and even Polish, these were the women who came to the war, and they are as much a part of our story as the women to whom the war came.[2]

Let us begin with the figure of the campfollower, and, in particular, the issue of why women became campfollowers or, more particularly, soldiers' wives. In discussing this, let us first set aside any reference to some supposed 'spirit of the age'. Rather, whilst the increased size of armies meant that there were more such women, the most that can be said is that, thanks to the greater prominence enjoyed by the military estate, soldiers may have become more attractive as partners. For the rest, one is clearly dealing with a phenomenon that is eminently traditional. Throughout the eighteenth century, then, barracks and encampments had swarmed with women. Of course, many of the females concerned were prostitutes attracted by the chance of easy money, but at any given time many thousands of soldiers were living with wives and, very often, children as well. Given that the soldiers of the period were much despised by society, why was it that they were seemingly able to conquer women with so little difficulty?

The first area that we must look in this context concerns the experiences of civilian women in their own homes, and, more particularly, their contacts with recruiting parties, the soldiers stationed in their towns and villages and, on occasion, actually billeted upon them, or, finally, regiments marching from one place to another. Here we may begin with a song which certainly dates back to at least the eighteenth century. Entitled 'A Soldier Boy for Me', this takes as a theme an issue that will serve us very well as a point of departure. To judge by its cadence and structure, sung as an accompaniment to such tasks as spinning, hoeing the soil or washing clothes, this expresses something of the longing for excitement and glamour that must have filled the minds of many young girls growing up amidst the monotony and toil of life in a village or small country town, lives, moreover, that were all too often accompanied by domestic violence and sexual abuse. Such a longing was natural enough, but what is particularly interesting here is the figure which encapsulates this longing. Thus, the text centres on a discussion of possible husbands, and specifically rejects a variety of more-or-less respectable possibilities in favour of taking up with that most risky of prospects, the soldier.[3] That young girls should have fantasised about such an ideal is hardly surprising. Dressed in uniform, soldiers offered a splash of colour in a world otherwise dominated by drab homespun. At the same time, too, soldiers travelled, saw the world and had adventures, whilst, by virtue of their very profession, they might easily be invested one-and-all with notions of honour, courage and vitality, not to mention the hope of social advancement: did not 'Over the Hills and Far Away'—probably the most well-known of all the many English ballads that dealt with the military world—speak of soldiers returning from the wars 'all gentlemen'?[4] In a most literal sense, then, soldiers seemed to offer young girls a way out, and, with soldiers themselves often all too happy to 'buckle their swash', there must have been many who thrilled at the arrival of a recruiting party or detachment of troops. As the rifle officer, John Kincaid, remembered, 'Of all the evils with which a sober community can be cursed, there is none so great as a guardhouse, for, while the notable housewife is superintending the scouring of her kitchen coppers and the worthy citizen is selling his sweets, the daughters are as surely to be found lavishing their's upon their gaudy neighbour'.[5]

The teenage dreams and sexual excitement aroused by the figure of the soldier are all too obvious.[6] In the eighteenth century, however, marriage was rarely the stuff of either. What was wanted was rather reliability and solid economic advantage, and in these soldiers were notoriously deficient. In consequence, girls who took up with such men faced an uncertain future. Yet marry soldiers all too many women did, and that despite the fact that girls who so much as associated with them ran the risk of immediately losing their reputations, whether they wed with them or not.[7] In brief, the barracks had the capacity to offer thousands of women perhaps the only hope they would ever have of altering the terms of their existence for the better. Indeed, so desperate were some women to take advantage of the opportunity that they literally put themselves up for sale: in March 1805 a drummer of the Fourth Foot bought such a girl in the market at Hythe for six pence.[8] Who this girl was or what her circumstances were, we have no idea, but it is probable that she was a foundling, an orphan or one of the thousands of children whom desperate or uncaring parents simply turned loose on the streets. For such unfortunates, life was particularly precarious, and it may be that, as Cardoza has pointed out in respect of a French girl named Marie Pierrette who was abandoned by her parents at the time of her birth in 1757 and eventually married a soldier, the army 'offered a sense of security and family that her earlier life lacked'.[9] Also on the edge, of course, were the eighteenth century's legions of prostitutes, and some of them, too, might well have seen marriage with a soldier as a way out.[10] Poverty, then, was an important factor; as witnessed by the well-documented case of eighteenth-century France, the majority of such women came from lowly peasant or artisan backgrounds.[11]

Yet it was not all calculation or sexual excitement. Thus, plenty of soldiers' wives fell in love with their men or even married them prior to them joining the army and then followed them into the ranks. One such woman was the Dublin maidservant who found herself beating a path to the barracks after her sweetheart was forced to enlist following a fight in which he badly injured a man who had tried to steal her away from him, and still another, Mary Young, the daughter of a Scottish excise officer. In brief, an attractive girl of eighteen, Mary fell in love with a highlander named Duncan Stewart. Very soon discovering that they were expecting a baby, the couple got married secretly (being old enemies, their respective fathers were opposed to them even seeing one another). Eventually, the time came when all would necessarily have to be revealed, but at this point the young man panicked and ran away to join the army rather than having to face the storm. To his credit, however, having obtained permission from the commanding officer of his regiment, Stewart sent word for Young to join him, and, despite now being in advanced state of pregnancy, she made the long journey to Duncan's current station at Hythe and was finally reunited with him on the very eve of his battalion's departure for the Peninsula.[12] Mary Young, it will be noted, had originally fallen not for a soldier, but for a civilian, but there were also women who clearly succumbed to redcoats in spite of their uniforms rather than because of them, one such probably being the wife of William Surtees of the Ninety-Fifth, the lady in question being 'a young woman whom I had known from my boyhood, she having been one of my earliest school fellows', and another Nancy McDermott, a lady's maid in a good household who to the fury of her family married a sergeant of the Eighty-Fifth Foot.[13]

Thus far, we have spoken solely in terms of the soldier's wives who emerged from the ranks of civilian society. Yet, important though this group was, many campfollowers came rather from another source. We now come to the so-called *children of the regiment.* In brief, army couples were no less likely to produce offspring than their civilian counterparts, and for all of them the question sooner or later emerged as to what was to become of the products of their union. For boys the answer was easy enough—there was always the regiment—but girls were more of a problem: posts in service, for example, were hard to come by for young women whose mothers were seen as little more than glorified prostitutes (while it is possible that army families may have possessed far fewer prejudices in this respect, the pool of employers that they constituted was distinctly finite).[14] For the daughters of army families, then, marrying a soldier was as good a way out as any, in which respect even a girl who was only moderately favoured had a reasonable chance of finding a husband, not least because, having been habituated to the life of a campfollower since birth, it could be assumed that she would cope with the demands of army life. Something else that needs to be considered here, meanwhile, is the issue of institutionalization: for army children, the regiment was the only home that they had ever known and civilian life a rather frightening concept that, at best, promised no more than bare subsistence. Both the British and French campfollowers therefore beyond doubt included many women of the stamp of the wonderfully named Catherine Campagne, a French girl who spent the first sixteen years of her life in a classic barracks family, before marrying a soldier and following the drum right up till 1814.[15]

It should not, of course, be thought that armies were prepared to throw open the barrack gates to all and sundry, not the least of the problems here being the fact that women were by no means regarded as an unmixed blessing. A soldier with a wife, true, was likely to be better cared for, and therefore less vulnerable to disease and exhaustion, than one without one, while he was also far less likely to desert, a further issue here being that marriage would encourage monogamy and thereby reduce the incidence of venereal disease. Equally, there was some hope that marriage might induce men to fight harder by giving them a family to protect. Alongside these advantages, however, went many disadvantages.

In the first place, the soldiers' wives and children necessarily represented a considerable economic burden. In the second place, while soldiers were subject to military discipline, women and children were not. In the third place, the presence of large numbers of non-combatants was an encumbrance. In the fourth place, campfollowers were notoriously quarrelsome, whilst they often provoked fights among the men. And, finally, in the fifth place, women and children were less likely to cope with the hardships of life on campaign, whilst there was also room to question how, ill-paid as they were, soldiers could provide for a family. There were, then, a number of conflicting pressures, and these were resolved by a compromise which saw soldiers only being allowed to marry with the permission of their commanding officers. By no means granted with any facility and sometimes limited by some sort of quota system, such agreements also came with strings attached: the women concerned had to be able to demonstrate a good character, and to promise to perform a variety of useful services for the units which they were joining, including maintaining items of uniform and equipment, taking in laundry, helping with the sick and wounded and preparing food; indeed, in the French army the standard official term for a soldier's wife was a *blanchisseuse*—a washerwoman.[16]

If wedding a soldier was difficult, this was probably just as well, for the reality of a military marriage was far from romantic. There being no special provision for married couples, they lived in the same crowded, sordid and uncomfortable accommodation as everyone else, whilst the rations were at best insufficient and frequently downright inedible. All this, of course, was no worse than what could be expected in civilian life, but, even so, dreams of a fresh start must have been shattered in a matter of hours. And it was not just the question of the conditions. Thus, drudgery was the norm—given their insufficient rations, women depended on taking in laundry and providing other small services in order to survive—while they were at constant risk from sexual harassment and the danger of prostitution: an unscrupulous husband who wanted a few extra coins for food or drink might very well pressure a wife into making herself available to other soldiers. Alternatively, women might simply be discarded, a soldier of the King's

German Legion named Johan Mämpel claiming, for example, that he saw a man of the Tenth Foot sell his wife to a drummer for two pounds, the latter then passing the woman on to the battalion armourer for two Spanish dollars.[17] Finally, with exploitation came brutality: even had the law not been biased against women to begin with, soldiers were in any case left pretty much to their own devices when it came to the imposition of marital discipline, a grenadier of the Eighty-Eighth Foot who stabbed his wife to death after she absconded with another man being recorded as having escaped with nothing more than a reprimand.[18]

How many women entered the military world as wives, it is difficult to say. In the French army relatively few such unions were sanctioned prior to 1789—a guess might be no more than two for every hundred men—but other forces were more generous: in Prussia at least one third of soldiers were married in the mid-eighteenth century, while in Britain the figure seems to have fallen somewhere in between the two.[19] Yet, in the British army at least, simply being 'put on the strength'—the process whereby the newly married campfollower was placed on the regimental rolls and thereby entitled to a half-ration each day[20]—was not sufficient to guarantee a married couple security. On the contrary, whilst it was accepted that at least some women would have to accompany their men in the field, there was a determination to cut the number of non-combatants to an absolute minimum. When a battalion was ordered abroad, then, a ballot was held to determine which wives should go to war (generally speaking, this was done at the last moment so as both to allow all those concerned to keep a modicum of hope and to safeguard the preparations for departure from disruption).[21] Generally speaking, the number was six for every company, but sometimes it was as few as four.[22] However, particularly if a battalion had been at home for any length of time, the number of wives in any given company could be as many as twenty or thirty. The result was scenes that were harrowing in the extreme. Assembled in the office of the pay-sergeant, the women drew tickets marked 'to go' or 'not to go' out of a hat.[23] For those chosen to go all was well, but for those left behind the result was disaster. Thus, in an instant, they had been stripped of not just their husbands but the only home they possessed, while, often encumbered with several small children, they were given no other assistance than a certificate that entitled them to food and shelter in the course of what could well be a long journey back to their places of origin. Given that they could rarely expect much of a welcome, what faced the women concerned was very often a slide into prostitution.[24]

Even if this is an overly negative assessment of the situation, for many couples it was still a time of untold grief. Here, for example, is Gleig's account of the moment when the unfortunate Mary Stewart discovered that she was to be left behind:

> When Mary unrolled the slip of paper and read upon it the fatal words . . . she gazed upon it for some minutes without speaking a word, though the rapid succession of colour . . . upon her cheeks told how severe the struggle was that was going on within, till, at length, completely overpowered . . . she crushed it between her palms, and fell senseless.[25]

At the actual moment of parting, there followed further scenes of despair. However, help there was none, not least because so many other couples faced precisely the same misfortune. All too frequent, then, are passages such as the following:

> What an affecting scene took place between the married men and their families! It was truly distressing to see the anguish of the poor women . . . some of whom were nearly frantic [and] others fainting away [with] their children crying by their sides or in their arms . . . The hardest heart must have been moved at the sight: many of these pitiable creatures never saw their husbands more.[26]

How many women were abandoned in this fashion is impossible to say, but over the years it is clear that the number must have run into many thousands: to take just one instance, when the Eighteenth Light Dragoons embarked for Spain in July 1808, the regiment left behind no fewer than ninety-one wives, this last being a figure that suggests that, in the course of the first six months of the Peninsular War alone, the overall total was around 4,500.[27]

So much for the arrangements of the British army. In the French army, by contrast, the situation was rather different. As we have seen, before 1789 women entered the military world in much the same way as they did in Britain, albeit probably in rather smaller numbers. Unlike their British counterparts, however, they had been accorded a semi-professional status in that they were referred to not in terms of who they were—*femmes*—but rather what they did—*blanchisseuses*. On top of this, meanwhile, there was yet another difference in that the military world also included women who were there by reason of their economic function or who had at least obtained an economic function within it. We come here to the so-called *vivandières* or sutleresses. In the eighteenth century all European armies were, as we have seen, accompanied by an enormous train of non-combatants who made their living from the soldiery. Aside from common prostitutes, the largest component of this 'tail' consisted of a variety of traders from whom the troops could obtain such items as alcohol, tobacco, cheese, ham and sausage, and these traders in turn included many women, initially, perhaps, just in the capacity of wives or helpmeets, but increasingly as independent operatives, generally widows or daughters carrying on the family business in the wake of its original proprietor's demise. So far, so good, but in the French army in particular these women were afforded a semi-official status. Thus, all traders were supposed to be attached to a particular regiment, and each regiment limited to a total of eight such positions, the result being that all *vivandières* in effect carried an official licence (the fact that, having once taken on the role, many of the women concerned later took soldiers as second husbands is by-the-by). To put it another way, unlike in Britain, women could occupy a position in the military estate without being the wife of one of its members. Furthermore, in a small number of cases at least, the services that they rendered were even recognised by the state, various erstwhile *vivandières* who had fallen on hard times being provided with substantial cash payments.[28]

It is sometimes suggested that this situation was transformed by the French Revolution, but, in reality, the effect of this was rather to confirm it. Thus, driven by the chaotic scenes that ensued from the complete breakdown of all control on the number of women who were allowed to follow the army that resulted from the events of 1789–92, from 1793 onwards successive regimes took firm action to restore order. In brief, then, as symbolised by the gradual adoption of the single catch-all term, *cantinière,* the position of the *blanchisseuse* and the *vivandière* was amalgamated, while the number of women attached to the army strictly limited (eventually to just four per infantry battalion and two per cavalry squadron), and all those concerned forced to apply for licenses of the sort seen prior to 1789, there also being a very strong expectation, albeit one that was never quite laid down in law, that *cantinières* would be the wives of soldiers. By the time that the Peninsular War broke out, then, the situation in the French army could not have been more different from that in its British counterpart. In the first place, the soldier's right to be accompanied by wife and family had been severely circumscribed; in the second, such soldiers' wives as were permitted in the ranks were there not because they had chosen to marry a man in uniform, but rather because they had applied for a particular position; and, in the third, irrespective of their marital status, all the women attached to the army were in effect independent businesswomen who made their living by selling food and drink, taking in laundry and offering a variety of other services such as mending uniforms.[29] Tending to put paid, as it does, to romantic assumptions that the women of the French army were a new breed of revolutionary heroine whose presence was the product of some political awakening, this last point is most important. That said, something of the spirit of Napoleon's army certainly rubbed off on the women who marched in its wake. When the forces of General Junot were marched through Lisbon prior to being embarked for repatriation after Vimeiro, then, their camp-followers were undaunted in the face of the abuse they faced from the angry crowd. To quote Charles Leslie: 'The French soldiers' wives . . . made a good fight of it . . . I heard some of them tell the mob, "You shall pay for these outrages: our victorious armies will return again, and we will wash our hands in Portuguese blood."'[30]

As to the question of who the *cantinières* were, the answer is that they were almost exactly the same sort of women as the *blanchisseuses* and *vivandières* had been prior to 1789. Thus, some of the older ones were actually veterans of the Bourbon army; others were girls who had married soldiers in the less regulated days of the early 1790s; and still others were 'children of the regiment'. Of these three categories, perhaps the most interesting is the second. As implied above, it has sometimes been suggested that the women concerned were *femmes révolutionnaires*—in other words women who had become *femmes militaires* as the next best thing to actually fighting for the Republic. This idea, however, is at best impossible to substantiate. With military service now far more evenly spread than it had been before, the women concerned had a wider range of home towns, while they also tended to embark on the role for the first time at a somewhat earlier age—the result, perhaps, of the intense privations to which France was subjected in the 1790s—but otherwise their social profile was all but unchanged. In short, if they had become *femmes militaires,* it was not because they were *femmes patriotiques,* but because they were *femmes pauvres,* even *femmes désesperées.*[31]

So much for the origins of the campfollowers, and so much too for the ways and means that brought them to Spain and Portugal (it will be noted here that, thanks to the reforms of which we have just spoken, in the French army there was no equivalent to the 'to go or not to go' ballot).[32] As to the numbers involved, these were very considerable. In all, some 40,000 British troops were sent to the Peninsula in 1808, and so, if we assume the conservative rate of four women for every 100 soldiers, it may be assumed that they were accompanied by some 1,600 women. As for the French army, the first Armée d'Espagne totalled 160 battalions of infantry and sixty-seven squadrons of cavalry, this suggesting a minimum of 774 *cantinières.* Enough, though, of types and statistics. What of the roles and experiences of the *cantinières* and campfollowers once they had either landed at Lisbon or crossed the Pyrenees? Beginning with the *cantinières,* they obviously had a strong military function and, what is more, one that they fulfilled with considerable aplomb. Thus, on the one hand, they had a vital role to play in the upkeep of morale, whilst on the other there is no doubt that in at least some instances they were fiercely loyal to the men they served, the regiments to which they were attached, and, last but not least, the cause of France. However, all that said, if *cantinières* can seen as forerunners of the uniformed women's auxiliary services of the two World Wars, they were also *entrepreneurs,* and this in turn produced the extraordinary spectacle of women emerging as small-scale business tycoons. Let us here trace the story of how this might have worked. In the beginning the *cantinière* was just a girl—literally in many instances—whose stock in trade was limited to what little she could carry, her own body, and, if she was lucky, quick wits, a pretty face, and a winning smile. Thus equipped, the girl would launch out on a personal odyssey in which success depended above all on establishing a strong *rapport* with the men of her unit.[33] On the one hand, they were potential clients, of course, but, on the other, they were also both protectors and willing hands—men who would come to the rescue in moments of crisis or help put up a tent at the end of a day (for this reason, it made sense that most of the women selling food and drink were also soldiers' wives, although this, of course, meant that, in addition to earning their living, they also had to provide for the needs of husbands and, very often, children too). When we hear, then, of *cantinières* dispensing brandy for free on days of battle or taking pity on some hungry conscript by giving him a bit of sausage, we should not think so much of angels of mercy as canny businesswomen investing in their own futures. And, by the same token, when we hear of girls rushing into the front line to rescue wounded soldiers, encourage the troops or even snatch up a musket, we should think not so much of patriotic viragos, but rather shopkeepers eager to show solidarity with their customers.[34] One can, of course, take all this too far—amongst all the women who served in the French army, there were beyond doubt hundreds of cheerful, generous and even heroic souls who really did conform to the stereotype[35]—but this is neither here nor there. Particularly if she was willing to provide sexual services—something that certainly did not always happen[36]—lend a few coins to needy soldiers, or engage in a spot of sharp practice, it would not be long before the girl would be able to acquire a mule or a donkey and a tent and thereby start to increase her stock-in-trade and turnover. Next would come, perhaps, another woman—some local girl displaced by the horrors of war, perhaps—and a wagon, and in time one wagon would become two or three or even four. Just to keep such a convoy on the move—a task that obviously required constant negotiation with the military authorities—would have been difficult enough at the best of times, but in Spain and Portugal it was obviously all the harder, even if those countries, by virtue of their very poverty and want of comfort, also offered special advantages. The risks were high, then, and the challenges even greater, but with them came the chance of achievements that were simply inaccessible by any other means.[37] What cannot be denied, meanwhile, is that the *cantinières* were, of necessity, a most resourceful band. Well worth recounting here is the story of Madame Leczakowska, a much-respected *cantinière* in the Legion of the Vistula: thus, unable to get her team to pull her wagon up a steep track, she secured the assistance of a party of Spanish prisoners in exchange for 'just a few cups of hot chocolate and some glasses of schnapps'.[38]

Turning away from the subject of *cantinières,* we come to the subject of the campfollowers.[39] Like the *cantinières,* they, too, carried out their traditional avocations. On the march veritable beasts of burden laden with tents, blankets, spare clothing, cooking utensils, pots and pans, it would fall to them to set up camp in the evening and cook their husbands' rations whilst at the same time scavenging for firewood and doing what they could to organise a little extra for the pot. What is more, all this had to be done in the face of military protocols that insisted that women should march at the rear of their regiments, this being something that guaranteed that they would arrive last at any encampment when in reality they needed to get there first. Add in the demands of caring for any children they might have, not to mention taking in mending and laundry so as to bring in a little money and helping to look after the sick and wounded, and a picture is conjured up of a life that was potentially every bit as miserable and exhausting as anything on offer in civilian life, in which respect it is probably no coincidence that the reality of the 'baggage' was hardly celebrated at all in the otherwise copious musicography of the period.[40]

Certainly campfollowers presented a dismal appearance after a few weeks of campaigning. As an anonymous officer of the King's German Legion wrote of the women of Wellington's army as they looked in the wake of the battle of Talavera: 'The wives . . . were now completely barefooted, and with scarce a whole garment, and, seated on meagre crazy-footed donkeys, cut a figure altogether forlorn'.[41] Still worse, in principle they were every bit as vulnerable as they might have been at home. In this respect mention has already been made of the minimal protection they received at the hands of military law, but, utterly dependent on their married status to safeguard their positions in their regiments, they were also exposed to much humiliation and abuse. Sometimes this was simple bullying, as witness, for example, the case of a woman who one rainy night was rudely ejected from a pigsty she had secured for herself and her husband by an officer who had no intention of going wet for the sake of a mere campfollower.[42] But sometimes it was something more sinister: for instance, assuming that the details can be trusted, the case of a woman of the Tenth Foot being sold from hand to hand for an ever-depreciating price that we have already encountered in the memoirs of Johan Mampel of the King's German Legion looks like nothing so much as a case of downright chattel slavery.[43] With their lowly position, meanwhile, probably went a variety of jobs that were both difficult and dangerous, as witness a report that appeared in *The Times* in respect of the siege of Burgos: 'The besieged are in great want of water. They have got some poor women whom they let down over the wall, giving them four *reales* for every bucketful they bring them'.[44]

In so far as individuals are concerned, we have few means of bringing the thousands of soldiers' wives who served in the Peninsular War to life. However, two in particular have come down to us through detailed accounts in the memoirs. Of these the first is Mary Anton. A girl from Edinburgh who wed a sergeant in the Forty-Second Foot named James Anton when he was sent to the city with a recruitment party in 1812, this young woman was fortunate enough to draw a 'to go' ticket when the resultant party of reinforcements travelled out to Spain in 1813, and spent the last eight months of the war caring for her husband from San Sebastián to Bayonne.[45] Given that Mary Anton emerges as a rather stylised figure who throughout is the very model of patience and resignation, the second case—namely, the redoubtable Bridget Skiddy—is rather more interesting. Thus, the wife of an Irish soldier who had been taken on as a servant by Ensign George Bell of the Thirty-Fourth Foot, Mrs Skiddy positively explodes from the page. Physically, she was not very prepossessing: Bell calls her 'a squat little Irish woman, and broad as a big turtle'.[46] Yet what she lacked in looks, she more than made up for in competence, courage and character. To quote Bell again, then, 'She was a devoted soldier's wife, and a right good one, an excellent forager, and never failed to have something for Dan when we were all starving'.[47] To illustrate this point, meanwhile, we are told a number of moving anecdotes. First of all, there is the picture of 'Mother Skiddy' defying the orders that the campfollowers should always march in the rear, insisting on being 'foremost on the line of march' the day after a group of provosts had shot the donkeys belonging to some of her fellows as a punishment for the women having tried to push ahead so as to get things ready for their husbands when they fell out at the end of the day's march.[48] Then there is Mrs Skiddy, complete with her donkey, 'The Queen of Spain', once again defying orders to remain in the rear at the crossing of the Rive Nive on 8 December 1813 on the grounds that if her husband was killed there would be no one to bury him.[49] And, finally, there is the Mrs Skiddy who carried her husband on her back for many miles when he collapsed from exhaustion during the terrible retreat to Ciudad Rodrigo in November 1812.[50]

The life of the campfollower, then, was very hard. Yet the situation was not entirely negative. Women might have been at the very bottom of the military hierarchy, but their ability to offer the common soldier a higher standard of living brought them a certain status, and all the more so when armies were operating in environments as bleak as that of Spain and Portugal. Nowhere is this clearer than in respect to the constant re-marriage that was part and parcel of the experiences of a soldier's wife. To remain 'on the strength', in the British army women had to be married to soldiers, and this in turn meant that should their husbands die in battle or fall prey to disease, there was but one course open to them, this being to get married again as soon as possible. Yet, unless she was truly the worst of harridans, few women had any trouble finding a replacement. Thus:

> The daring . . . of these creatures . . . is not to be described. They had no hesitation in engaging themselves three or four deep to future husbands, and according to the activity in mis-

> chief of each was the number of candidates for her hand in case of disaster to her lawful lord, and one of them has been heard to reply to a soldier who offered himself as successor to her then commanding officer [i.e. husband], 'Nay, but thou'rt late as I'm promised to John Edwards first and to Edward Atkinson next, but when they two be killed off, I'll think of thee'.[51]

This being an aspect of the life of army women that shocked many observers, it is certainly something that is worthy of further comment. Thus, the knowledge that rapid re-marriage was the norm may well lie at the heart of the assumption that all soldiers' wives doubled as prostitutes, while it also fuelled notions that they were utterly lacking in normal feeling.[52] Quite clearly, however, such ideas are unfair. A few women may have run prostitution rings, been habitually unfaithful to their husbands, or allowed other men access to their bodies to raise a little extra money or in some way ease the way for their husbands.[53] We hear, then, of the wife of a soldier of the Eighteenth Light Dragoons who was struck over the head by her husband with a bottle when he caught her in the arms of a black ship's cook, and of Mrs Coleman of the Ninety-Fifth who became known as 'the wife of the regiment' and is alleged to have spent some months 'fishing in all the loose dollars which were floating about in gentlemen's pockets by those winning ways which ladies know so well'.[54] More generally, meanwhile, Joseph Donaldson of the Ninety-Fourth Foot offers a comment that is as plausible as it is sensible:

> During our campaigns in the Peninsula . . . the poor women who followed us . . . were assailed by every temptation which could be thrown in their way, and every scheme laid by those who had rank and money, to rob them of that virtue which was all they had left to congratulate themselves upon. Was it to be wondered at, then, if many of them were led astray, particularly when it is considered that their starving condition was often taken advantage of by those who had it in their power to supply them, but who were villains enough to make their chastity the price?[55]

Finally, such caveats aside, there were some campfollowers who were simply adventuresses or even downright promiscuous, one such probably being an Irish girl from Clonmel married to a sergeant of the Seventh Foot who abandoned him for a British colonel.[56] Yet there is plenty of evidence that at least some soldiers' wives genuinely loved their men. If this was not obvious enough already in the case of the redoubtable 'Mother Skiddy', in her case we can also point to the intense distress she is recounted as having displayed when news reached her at the end of the battle of the Rive Nive that her husband had been shot in the leg.[57] Also worth citing here is the grief shown by the wife of a corporal of the Forty-Second Foot named Cunningham who was killed at Toulouse, and the desperate efforts that she made to ensure that he received a decent burial, not to mention the anguished state of a woman whom Donaldson witnessed discover the body of her husband beneath the walls of Badajoz: 'She raised the dead soldier . . . and, looking on his pallid features . . . gave a wild scream . . . Sinking on her knees, she cast her eyes to heaven . . . The blood had fled her face . . . and all her faculties were absorbed in grief'.[58] Finally, there is the case of the Nancy McDermott mentioned above: this young woman was by all accounts genuinely extremely happy with her soldier husband, and, when the latter was decapitated by a roundshot during the siege of Bayonne in 1814, she therefore sank into a deep depression from which nothing could rouse her.[59] One may assume, then, that it was not lust that drove women to seek new partners, but rather necessity.[60] Here, for example, is James Anton: 'Although slightingly spoken of by some of little feeling . . . this [practice] is, perhaps, the only alternative to save a lone, innocent woman's reputation . . . The peculiar situation in which she is placed renders it necessary . . . to feel grateful for a protector'.[61]

To the extent that army wives had hard hearts, then, it may be assumed that it was because they knew that they were likely to be assailed by frequent sorrow, and were inclined to insulate themselves against it: to take just two examples, one campfollower in the Fifty-First Foot lost no fewer than three husbands between June and November 1813, while by the end of the war a woman of the Sixty-Eighth Foot was on her sixth partner.[62] Also attendant on the life of all army women was considerable privation and danger: the fate of the sergeant's wife mortally wounded by a cannon ball during the retreat from Burgos (just, poignantly enough, as she was putting a pot of chocolate on the fire for her husband's breakfast), or the Mrs Riley of the Forty-Second Foot who was drowned in the harbour of La Coruña while trying to board a transport, or the woman swept away with her child during the passage of the Adour could have occurred during any campaign of the Napoleonic Wars.[63] That said, some of the experiences that had to be endured in the Peninsula were hard even by the standards of those struggles. First of all, there were the extraordinary distances that the armies were regularly forced to march—the Iberian Peninsula, after all, is approximately 500 miles across in every direction. To long marches were added the most severe climactic conditions. We might think here of the baking heat of summer, but far worse was the misery that was endured during such events as the retreat to La Coruña in January 1809:

> It was a pitiable sight to behold the forlorn condition of the women and children. Those who could not get upon baggage wagons, trudged along with painful steps, scarcely able to bear up the weight by which they were encumbered. Many sank during the bitter night famished, way-worn and in the snow, with infants at their breasts or in their arms, and in this situation were found lifeless and frozen on the following morning. Others took refuge from the storm in the dismantled ammunition carts that lay about the road, and, trying to get shelter there, perished with their children . . . as they crouched in groups together. The whole exhibition was one of appalling wretchedness that would harrow up the feelings even of those who had long been familiar with lamentable scenes.[64]

Amidst all this women continued to be affected by the natural rhythms of life: Private Stephen Morley of the Fifth Foot actually saw one give birth by the roadside.[65] The road to La Coruña, then, was littered with female bodies.[66]

The appalling scenes witnessed during the retreat of January 1809 probably constitute the extreme end of the scale in so far as the horrors of war as experienced in the Iberian Peninsula were concerned.[67] A more chronic problem, however, was want of food. In times of crisis the supply system broke down altogether—during the retreat to Ciudad Rodrigo no bread or biscuit was issued for five days—but even at the best of time armies were quite literally on starvation rations: for example, assuming that it was issued in full and was entirely edible, the basic daily ration in the British army only amounted to 2,400 calories as opposed to the minimum of 3,600 needed by a grown man (it will be recalled that women received only one half of this amount).[68] This in turn meant that food frequently somehow had to be acquired from other sources, but, with the countryside generally stripped of such few resources as it possessed, this was often very difficult. Thus, even if food was available for purchase, it could command prices that were far beyond the capacity of most campfollowers. 'I paid six shillings for a loaf of bread', wrote George Bell, 'my daily pay being five shillings and three pence, less income tax'.[69] Famine conditions, then, were common, and gallantry scarce. As John Green of the Sixty-Eighth Foot wrote of an incident that occurred in the course of the retreat to Ciudad Rodrigo in 1812: 'One of our party got a loaf of bread and shared it amongst us. At this time a poor woman belonging to the army came by, and in a most affecting manner begged for a morsel of bread, saying [that] she had not eaten any for three days, but such was the scarcity of that valuable article that we could not spare her one morsel, not knowing when we should get another supply'.[70]

To all this was added a level of savagery rarely seen elsewhere. In general, the campfollowers of the British and French armies could expect reasonable treatment at the hands of enemy regulars, but from time to time even these norms were transgressed by troops whose blood was up, the worst such incident probably being the massacre of a crowd of British stragglers at Bembibre on 2 January 1809. This was certainly a brutal affair. As Robert Blakeney recalled, for example, 'Frantic women held forth their babies, suing for mercy by the cries of defenceless innocence, but all to no purpose. . . . Drunkards, women and children were indiscriminately hewn down'.[71] At Bembibre, too, a campfollower of the Forty-Third Foot who had been left behind 'stupid with intoxication' on the third floor of a convent was apparently 'most horribly mangled' when some French soldiers threw her out of a window.[72] According to Louis Fantin des Odoards, a sub-lieutenant in the Thirty-First Line, some of the women who were spared were even sold by their captors as *de facto* slaves.[73] Yet Bembibre was beyond doubt an exception. At Vitoria for example, the large numbers of French campfollowers who fell into the hands of Wellington's soldiers were treated very well, while a considerable party of British women taken prisoner during the retreat from Salamanca to Ciudad Rodrigo in November 1812 were returned unharmed the next day.[74]

If French women were safe enough as prisoners of the British, those taken by the Spaniards could face a much grimmer fate. We come here to the atrocities allegedly committed by Spanish irregulars whenever they captured French prisoners (women who fell into the hands of the regular army, by contrast, generally had little to fear). The extent of these is open to question, but there is no reason to doubt that women whose captors were no more than gangs of bandits on many occasions experienced a terrible end. Marching on Madrid in November 1808, for example, an *aide-de-camp* named Aymar de Gonneville saw a sight that was probably typical enough. Thus: 'A few leagues beyond Burgos we found on the road a civilian cantineer [sic] and a child of twelve with their throats cut: they were artistically posed to display the barbarity that accompanied the act'.[75] Equally, Jean-Baptiste Barrès, a sub-lieutenant in the Sixteenth Light Infantry remembered that in March 1810, having dropped behind, 'a few grenadiers and a woman canteen-keeper' were captured and had their throats cut 'with refinements of cruelty'.[76] Meanwhile, even women taken by combatants of a more regular nature may not have been entirely safe: when Vigo was taken by the recently organised Division of the River Miño in April 1809, five French campfollowers were reputedly thrown into the sea.[77]

Such horrors were bad enough, but by far the worst fate experienced by the French campfollowers who served in Spain and Portugal was probably that reserved for the hundreds of women taken prisoner at Bailén. The wives of the officers were all soon repatriated to France, but those of the rank and file were left to endure the fate of their menfolk. This, alas, was miserable indeed. After several months' confinement in various towns on the mainland, the prisoners were transferred to a number of hulks moored in the bay of Cádiz. Conditions on these vessels were terrible, but the women supposedly showed great courage, in particular doing everything they could to care for the growing numbers of sick.[78] Yet there was even worse to come. Following the invasion of Andalucía by the French early in 1810, all the surviving prisoners were deported to the uninhabited Mediterranean island of Cabrera. The arrangements made for supplying them proving to be completely inadequate, several thousands starved to death. Shipped to Cabrera with all the rest, the women died by the hundred too, but one at least of them now discovered that virtue had its rewards. Thus:

> Amongst the *vivandières* was to be found the widow of a sergeant. On board the pontoons she had dedicated herself day and night to the care of the sick, but in the course of the voyage she had been brought to bed, and the result was that she was now nursing two charming little twins. However, this did not prevent her from rushing with the utmost speed to make herself useful to the prisoners whenever their poor state of health required her care. It is very much to the credit of that generous women that, despite the fact that she was still beautiful, we desisted from any pretentions in her respect: it was decided unanimously that we 'Robinsons' would be the godfather of the two children.[79]

Whether this woman survived is unknown, but it is to be hoped that she had better fortune than a group of fifteen or so women noted by an infantryman named Louis Gille who were seemingly sold by their husbands or lovers into the hands of a self-appointed pimp and then auctioned off to the highest bidder, only for the same women then to be sold on again and again at an ever lower price, one of them—a once pretty Polish girl who was supposed actually to have fought in the ranks of her parent regiment—even ending up being drawn for in a lottery at a price of four *sous*.[80]

In the face of the horrors of life on campaign, it is scarcely surprising to find that, while most campfollowers were fiercely loyal to their units, some women drifted away from the armies' encampments. Such women had necessarily to fend for themselves, and it is probable that many ended up by becoming prostitutes. Yet, by one means or another, at least some managed to find a rather better fate. For example, travelling from Lisbon to join Wellington's army in June 1813, Captain John Blakiston of the Portuguese Third Caçadores recounts staying in 'a miserable inn kept by a Scotswoman' at Villafranca, while in another place the same author complains of 'jackals who, in the capacity of sutlers, generally contrive to go between the natives and the army, and to pick up a livelihood at the expense of both parties', many of whom were 'soldiers' wives, or widows, who, on the demise of their lords had set up for themselves, and, having possessed themselves of a mule, carried on a lucrative, if not very honourable, traffic'.[81] Failing anything better, meanwhile, there was always the chance of becoming a 'kept woman', one such being a French woman named Madame Durand whom Patterson found co-habiting with a man named Pedro González in Madrid in October 1812, and another a redoubtable female encountered by a commissary named Graham in the house of a fellow commissary named Macleod:

> Macleod gave me a bed in his own house: he kept a lady named Margaret, a very termagent for temper. For some time she behaved well, but broke out one day at dinner, when Macleod happened to say something that displeased her. She then took hold of the table cloth, and . . . sent everything on the floor. . . . This, to her, was genteel and in style, and that night she got drunk with brandy, saying [that] it was the finest comfort in nature.[82]

In the fiery Margaret, we see the very epitome of a 'baggage'.[83] Rather more sophisticated, perhaps, was a campfollower mentioned by the German commissary, Augustus Schaumann. The woman—originally one Anne Luke—clearly being a consummate adventuress, her story is worth recounting in full. Thus:

> In Coimbra, whither I repaired occasionally, a variety of pleasures awaited me. As a rule I stayed in the house of Commissary

> Gordon, who, however, as a travelling depot-commissary, was almost always absent. I had fallen in love with his alleged wife, a beautiful woman who ruled the household . . . She had come to Portugal as the wife of a man in the Third Dragoons, but, endowed by nature with the most extraordinary beauty and talent, she soon felt she was not in her proper place. Mr Gordon, who came across her while acting as a commissary to the regiment, took her with her husband's consent, and in return paid the man a *solatium*. When this man was killed in a small engagement and Mr Gordon entered the Spanish service, she married Commissary-General Boyes . . . She was fair . . . had the most beautiful blue eyes I ever saw in my life . . . and was quickly able to acquire the most refined manners: nobody would have suspected her of being the wife of an ordinary dragoon.[84]

Few, then, of the campfollowers of the Peninsular War were saints.[85] Yet their behaviour was at least in part a reflection of the terrible conditions which they experienced. To feed their families—indeed, to survive at all—they had at the very least to be sharp in their dealings, whilst there were some, perhaps many even, who became absolutely bereft of all the normal constraints of morality: Browne, for example, speaks of 'a fearful and melancholy change' gradually coming over the women of the army, whilst, as he continues, by 1812 'all ideas of conduct and decency had disappeared: plunder and profligacy seemed their sole object and the very soldiers their husbands evidently estimated them in proportion to their proficiency in these vices'.[86] For an example of a fairly minor transgression we may cite the example of a story told by John Kincaid. In course of Wellington's march on Madrid Kincaid bought a brace of chickens from a pair of King's-German-Legion campfollowers (chickens, incidentally, which the women had almost certainly stolen). However, hardly had he got back in his saddle than his horse bolted and the chickens escaped, only for them immediately to be seized by their vendors, the unfortunate Kincaid being left with no option but to buy them anew. As he remarked, 'They were each six feet high and as strong as a horse, and I felt convinced that they had often thrashed a better man than myself in the course of their military career'.[87]

The sort of pilfering engaged in by the two campfollowers who bested Kincaid was widespread. Here, for example, is Charles Leslie:

> After proceeding about two leagues we were encamped at Zarza Mayor, a small Spanish town. Here several of the soldiers' wives, having preceded the column, had taken the liberty of helping themselves to various articles in the shape of vegetables and other eatables. On complaint being made by the injured inhabitants, Lord Hill consigned the delinquents to the provost who exercised schoolboy discipline on a few as an example to the rest.[88]

However, there was, alas, much worse. To habitual pilfering, then, was added active participation in such affairs as the sack of Badajoz.[89] Nor do things appear to have been much better in the French army, and all the more so as most *cantinières* had no means of replenishing the stocks on which they depended other than plunder. To quote Blayney, for example, 'In the act of spoliation, the female campaigners are worse than the men, for, being lost to every feminine virtue, they plunder and murder with the greatest coolness and composure'.[90] In saying this, however, it has to be admitted that 'plunder and murder' were also to be found amongst British campfollowers. According to Browne, for example, in the aftermath of Salamanca, large numbers 'were seen stripping and plundering friend and foe alike', whilst he adds that it was 'not doubted that they gave the finishing blow to many an officer who was struggling with a mortal wound'.[91] Yet one may fairly ask, with rations so inadequate, food prices so high and pay so short, how else were campfollowers of either army to provide for themselves and their families? To take just one example, a donkey was at the very least a key part of their equipage, and yet throughout the war animals of any sort could command sums that most of the women concerned could only dream of: in early 1813, for example, George Woodberry of the Eighteenth Light Dragoons paid 150 dollars for a mule.[92]

If the women plundered, they also drank, this being something else that is frequently held up to illustrate their brutalization. As

Richard Henegan wrote of a group of stragglers he encountered in northern Portugal early in 1809, for example, 'The women seemed to have lost every attribute of their sex but their name . . . The well-filled canteen of *aguadiente* [i.e. brandy] was an ever constant companion, strapped across the shoulder to ensure its safety and showing good cause for the livid lips to which it was unceasingly applied'.[93] At the same time the constant drinking at times gave rise to scenes that were genuinely shocking as when a group of women who had come up from the rear looking for their husbands during the battle of the River Nivelle plundered a captured French store depot and 'freely [partook] of the damnable potion until they had transformed themselves into something more like fiends than angels of mercy'.[94] Yet drunkenness was no more purely the fruit of vice pure and simple than larceny was. Thus, there was a fixed belief in British society that alcohol was both a preservative against illness and a stimulant that rendered the body more robust, whilst its use also serves to fend off sorrow, cold and hunger alike.[95] At the same time the increasing availability of cheap spirits in eighteenth-century England had led to the emergence of heavy drinking as a response to despair and alienation, the 'gin craze' having put down its deepest roots among the wives and daughters of poorer artisans and the labouring poor—in other words, women who were precisely the sort of women who became campfollowers.[96] It was not necessarily, then, pure beastliness that produced the sad sight witnessed by Blakeney during the retreat to La Coruña of a woman lying dead in the snow with her head in a pool of rum, or, for that matter, the rather more comic incident in which Grattan found the wife of his soldier-servant lying dead-drunk on his cot when he returned to his tent in the wake of the storm of Badajoz.[97]

Over and over again, then, it appears that campfollowers cannot just be stigmatised as the scum of the earth. On the contrary, they earned the esteem of officers and men alike. We hear, indeed, of many cases in which they were in one way or another recognised or rewarded for their services, or simply afforded assistance. We have already seen the cases of the *cantinières* who were rescued from drowning in the river Douro in Portugal and cared for by a group of sergeants on Cabrera, but there were many others. For example, the wife of a sergeant-major of the Eighteenth Light Dragoons having fallen ill in the course of the unit's voyage to Portugal in 1813, a cornet of the regiment who had had the foresight to bring a coop full of hens along with him presented her with one of them.[98] Equally, when Lieutenant William Cooke of the First Dragoons died at Albergaría on 26 September 1811, he left a guinea to each of the wives of the sergeants, corporals and common soldiers of his troop.[99] And, finally, when they were lost, they were often lamented. Writing of the action of El Bodón in September 1811, then, Grattan remarks: 'Mrs Howley, the black cymbals-man's wife of the Eighty-Eighth, was captured by a lancer. The . . . loss of Mrs Howley was a source of grief to the entire division. . . . Perhaps in the entire army such another woman could not be found'.[100] Indeed, the veterans of the conflict are often fulsome in their praise. 'Without the labours of the fair sex', wrote John Patterson, 'we should not have been able to get on, and I shall ever respect the heroine who has . . . served with honour a campaign or two'.[101]

Thus far we have spoken of women of the lower classes only, but these were not the only females who travelled to the Peninsular War. In both the British and—especially—the French armies, the wives and mistresses of officers and generals appeared in Spain and Portugal in considerable numbers. In general, such women gravitated to the relative safety of cities such as Madrid, Barcelona, Seville and Lisbon—a good example here is the redoubtable Laure Junot, who in 1810 travelled to the Peninsula to join her husband, then a corps commander in the forces of Marshal Masséna, and ended up spending a miserable autumn and winter in Ciudad Rodrigo.[102] Yet even a relatively civilian lifestyle was not without its dangers and privations: Madame Junot was almost captured by guerrillas whilst out riding with the wife of General Thomières near Salamanca, for example, while others found themselves in the direct line of fire when the convoys they were with came under attack, or were even held to ransom by bandits.[103] Finally, at the battle of Vitoria the collapse of the French army led to a number finding themselves in the very midst of the fighting as the French baggage train was over-run. One such was the wife of the commander of the so-called 'Army of the South', Honoré Gazan. Herewith the recollections of Thomas Browne:

> I well remember . . . seeing amongst other ladies who were descending from their carriages in great alarm, the Countess Gazan, the wife of the Quartermaster-General [*sic*] of the French army. As I passed her, she declared to me in a scream who she was. I recommended her to re-enter her carriage, shut the door and remain quiet. . . . It appears that, after I had ridden on, she . . . was taken to Lord Wellington's headquarters, and remained there some days.[104]

Other women also habitually travelled with the armies. Thus, the wife of the French cavalry commander, Lasalle, was present at Medina de Río Seco, while the French prisoners at Bailén included the wives of General Schramm and General Chabert.[105] Equally, the young and beautiful wife of Marshal Suchet was often to be observed riding with her husband's headquarters during the fighting in eastern Spain, while at Busaco Masséna was accompanied by a mistress arrayed in hussar costume, and Edouard Simon, a brigade commander in Loison's division, by 'a young Spanish lady arrayed in male attire', the girl in question being sent across the lines to join Simon in captivity when he was taken prisoner, yet another senior officer who sought to assuage the discomfort of life on campaign being the notoriously unruly cavalry commander, François Fournier, who appeared at Burgos in 1808 accompanied by 'a pretty Calabrian girl whom he had stolen away from her parents in the Kingdom of Naples and was dressed as a man'.[106] From Fantin des Odoards we learn of a German woman who had married a French commissary in the wake of the Prussian defeat at Jena and travelled with him to Spain where she appears to have spent her time poking fun at the successive members of the clergy on whom her husband was billeted.[107] Finally, at Salamanca 'a beautiful young woman' was observed 'running wildly with her hair loose about the spot from which the Third Division had first attacked . . . searching for the body of her husband, a young lieutenant who had lately joined the Eighty-Eighth Regiment and had been killed in the action'; equally tragic, at first sight, was a woman whom Ross-Lewin encountered being escorted into the city in a state of shock after having learned that the captain to whom she was married had also fallen in the battle, though the effect was rather spoiled by the fact that a few days later Ross-Lewin spotted her 'leaning on a young commissary with two gold epaulettes and evidently enjoying excellent spirits'.[108] In short, even if it might also bring tragedy—the surgeon, Adam Neale, for example, recalls the wife of a British officer dying of fever in Lisbon in the autumn of 1808[109]—for some women of the upper classes, at least, the Peninsular War brought opportunities for travel and excitement that many appear to have relished, and with them, if they so chose, the chance to show their mettle on the battlefield: at Roliça, for example, the senior Royal-Engineer officer attached to Wellesley's forces came across a well-dressed woman walking calmly across the battlefield a few yards behind the main British line and urged her to take shelter, only to be told in tones of some asperity, 'Mind your own affairs, Sir: I have a husband before me', while at Salamanca the 'delicate and beautiful wife of Colonel Dalbiac . . . forgetful of herself, impelled by strong affection for her gallant knight . . . rode amidst the enemy's fire, exposing herself to imminent peril'.[110]

For a woman, however, 'imminent peril' was not just a matter of enemy bullets. Travelling from Lisbon to the frontier to join her husband, one officer's wife was accused by Portuguese militia of being a spy and marched back to the capital under close arrest.[111] Less romantically, meanwhile, even reasonably genteel campfollowers could easily find themselves suffering both want of privacy and casual sexual harassment: returning to Portugal from leave in England in October 1811, for example, George Bowles found himself sharing a cabin with nine officers, a commissary, a surgeon and, last but not least, the wife and daughter of an officer already serving in Portugal. Until the last night of the voyage, the two women just endured overcrowding and discomfort, but at this point two of the men got extremely drunk, and 'offered very improper solicitations to the ladies'.[112]

In the British army, despite exceptions such as Mrs Dalbiac, comparatively few of these women travelled to the front. Larpent, for example, says that the only woman at Wellington's headquarters at the isolated Portuguese border village of Fresnada in January 1813 was the wife of the leading intelligence officer, George Scovell, whilst a chance encounter with the wives of two artillery officers at Malhada Sorda in May the same year was clearly something that came as a considerable surprise to Augustus Frazer.[113] In practice, most of the officers' wives who came out to Spain remained clustered in and around Lisbon. On the whole, however, this did not make for a happy situation. Bored and frustrated, the women concerned in at least some cases took to drink, while in others they became embroiled with the many officers hanging around Lisbon playing truant from the army, the result being a series of discreditable affairs that in one instance ended in a sensational murder trial.[114]

In this survey of the women who came to the war, we have thus far looked solely at those who did so in the conventional feminine roles of campfollower, consort or courtesan. What, though, of that other category, the cross-dresser? Mercifully, however, this subject can be dealt with very briefly. In the course of the French Revolution a certain number of women had openly enlisted in the French army, but from 1794 onwards they were very quickly weeded out, the principle of female enlistment eventually being abolished altogether. The idea being just as abhorrent to the British army, we may safely say that no women fought as women in the forces of either Napoleon or Wellington.[115] Whether any enlisted secretly and fought in male garb is another matter, however. Precisely because the aim was to avoid discovery, we cannot be certain that it did not happen, but, at least in so far as the Peninsular War is concerned, the fact is that there is almost no record in either song or story of it having done so.[116] Women do appear here and there dressed in male attire, but the aim was clearly either to enhance their allure or increase their own comfort—a good example here would be the hussar outfit adopted by Masséna's mistress[117]—or to ensure their own safety. Such, at least, is probably the explanation for, first, the Spanish girl who was taken prisoner dressed as a drummer with a French officer by a group of Spanish irregulars outside Salamanca in July 1812, and, second, the 'smart young French officer' taken at Vitoria who 'proved to be a beautiful Catalonian girl who had been mistress of a French colonel for two years'.[118]

To conclude, then, if it is clear that many thousands of foreign women experienced the Peninsular War in some form or other, it is just as clear that they for the most part did so in forms that had been familiar for the past century or more, the fact being that the patterns of military life had in this respect been but lightly affected by the French Revolution. Sadly, the women concerned have left us with almost no record of their existence of their own, but their presence was yet one that was as constant as it was prominent. At the same time, too, they made a considerable contribution to the success of the armies of which they formed a part, above all, by sustaining the morale and physical well-being of the soldiery. Saints the women of the rank and file most definitely were not, but their sins were the fruit not of the inherent bestiality sometimes imputed to them, but rather the circumstances in which they were placed, circumstances in which they were denied the wherewithal to support themselves and their families whilst enduring conditions that were as bad as anything ever experienced in the Napoleonic Wars. Their story, then, is worth the telling, and their sacrifice worthy of commemoration.

4

Heroines

As has already been noted, the most famous combatant of the Peninsular War is a woman. We refer here, of course, to Agustina Zaragoza Domenech, a young Catalan girl who in 1808 was, at the age of twenty-two, the wife of a sergeant in the First Regiment of Artillery named Juan Roca. Stationed at Barcelona at the outbreak of the Spanish uprising against Napoleon, like many other soldiers of the garrison, Roca fled the French-occupied city, and eventually made his way to Zaragoza where he offered his services to the insurgent garrison commanded by the famous José Palafox. Very soon, however, Roca was sent out of the city to join a Spanish force that was being organised in the vicinity of Teruel, and the result was that Domenech, who had travelled to Zaragoza with her four-year-old son to join her husband, was on her own in the city when the French closed in on the defenders. Thus was the scene set for an incident that to this day remains absolutely central to the traditional Spanish view of the Peninsular War. On 2 July 1808 the French launched a massive attack on the defences, and, like many of the women of Zaragoza, Domenech busied herself carrying food and water to the walls and succouring the wounded. As she was approaching a battery that had been established at the Portillo gate, however, a shell touched off an expense magazine, the resulting explosion being so great that most of the gunners were killed or incapacitated. With the French in the very act of entering the battery, Domenech touched off a cannon in their very faces, whereupon the remaining defenders returned to their positions and fought off the enemy.[1]

The participation of Domenech in the defence of Zaragoza has been seized upon by a variety of historians as an emblem on which to centre two main arguments: first, the claim that Spain was engaged in a 'people's war', and, second, the idea that Spanish women were conscious of themselves as citizens possessed of the same interests and duties as their male counterparts. However the matter is viewed, then, Domenech is a deeply political figure, a Spanish precursor, perhaps, of Delacroix's famous heroine of 1830, and even a harbinger of female emancipation. This is all very well, but let us consider a story from Canada that predates the Peninsular War by more than 100 years. We come here to Marie-Madeleine Jarret de Verchères. Famous as 'the girl who saved the fort', Jarret was born in 1678 in a small fortified settlement near Montreal. The daughter of the governor, on 22 October 1692 she found herself all but alone in the place when it was suddenly attacked by an Iroquois war party. Nothing daunted, however, the girl managed to slam the gates in the raiders' faces, and then mounted the walls and let fly with a small cannon, the Iroquois eventually retiring to search for easier pickings elsewhere.[2]

Like Domenech, Jarret became a national heroine, while her story, which was already well-known in educated circles in1808, has obvious parallels with that of the 'maid of Saragossa'.[3] Why include it in a study of women in the Peninsular War, however? In brief, the answer is obvious. Exactly as was to be the case with Domenech, Jerret found herself in a situation in which her life was in direct danger and in which she could only rely on herself for protection. In short, history had not entered a new age at all: in certain exceptional circumstances, it had clearly always been acceptable for women to take up arms, whilst, just as importantly, there had always been women who were prepared to do just that: from the American War of Independence, then, we have the famous story of Mollie Pitcher, whilst Spain provides us with the example of María Pita, a woman who according to legend played a leading role in beating off an assault on La Coruña during the British attack on the city in 1589.[4]

In many respects, then, there is nothing particularly surprising about the case of Domenech: she was not in any sense a 'new' woman, and it is ahistorical to consider her in such a light. At the same time, it has to be accepted that she was in many respects a figure who was artificially created. This is not to say that the exploit that brought her to fame did not happen: on the contrary, given the panic inspired by the French at this stage of the war, something of the sort is entirely plausible. What is less clear, however, is why it was her who was singled out for recognition. By all accounts many women took part in one way or another in the fighting of 2 July, while Domenech's heroism was hardly the turning point in the battle. What made the difference, then, was in all probability rather a single word. Thus the happy coincidence by which her patronym was none other than 'Zaragoza' meant that the moment she fired her cannon she at once became a living symbol of the city's spirit of resistance.[5]

This was not the only manner in which chance took a hand in the story of Domenech, however. In other cities her actions might well have gone unrecognised. However, José Palafox, the Spanish commander at Zaragoza, was one of the most remarkable figures in the entire Spanish War of Independence. In 1808 an officer in the royal bodyguard, he had in the last few years become caught up in an aristocratic *fronde* whose adherents were determined to overthrow the hated royal favourite, Manuel de Godoy, turn back the creeping tide of enlightened absolutism and restore the much eroded power of the magnates. The story is a highly complicated one that has already been told at length elsewhere, but, in brief, it was largely the machinations of this group that had led, first, to the efforts that were made in the autumn of 1807 to obtain a Bonaparte bride for the future Ferdinand VII, and, second, to the court crisis known as the Affair of El Escorial. Meanwhile, it was this group, too, that had organised the military coup of 17–19 March 1808 that had ejected Godoy from power and forced Charles IV to abdicate in favour of Ferdinand. This should have been a moment of triumph—Ferdinand being notoriously cowardly and unintelligent, the conspirators believed that he would prove a mere figurehead who could be manipulated by them almost at will—but to their horror the best efforts of the new regime proved insufficient to win the recognition of Napoleon, the latter having by now resolved to remove the Bourbons from the throne of Spain.

Still worse, very shortly, as Spain was gripped by revolt so the alliance with the French empire which the conspirators had looked upon as the ultimate guarantee of their strategy had evaporated and been replaced by the near certainty of war. Faced by this situation, whilst some of the conspirators elected to throw in their lot with the French, others responded by seeking to seize control of the uprising and pursuing their goals in the new political context which it offered, their general aim being to establish a regency dominated by themselves and their adherents.[6]

In all this José Palafox was a prime mover. The officer charged with escorting Godoy into exile in France when Napoleon had insisted on his release, he had briefly waited upon Ferdinand VII at Bayonne and then returned to Zaragoza, where he had played a leading role in the uprising and engineered his nomination to the post of Captain General. Bound up with this move were undoubtedly hopes that the whole of Spain would rally to his lead and acclaim him as regent, but this did not occur, and Palafox therefore found himself competing with a whole range of other authorities. In this contest, however, Palafox proved himself to be extraordinarily gifted. If he was both a very poor general and a coward, he was also a consummate politician. On the one hand, then, he quickly realised that his only chance of success was to transform Zaragoza into a beacon of resistance, while on the other he was acutely aware of the need to maintain control of the street: the uprising against Napoleon had everywhere been both linked to and fuelled by intense social unrest, and this was as much the case in Zaragoza as it was everywhere else.[7]

From all this there followed two consequences. On the one hand Palafox bombarded Spain with a series of grandiloquent proclamations that portrayed the resistance of Zaragoza in the most exaggerated terms and took great pains to heap praise upon the devotion of the populace.[8] And on the other he gathered around himself a coterie of acolytes and cheerleaders drawn from the ranks of the crowd, one such being the popular peasant farmer, Jorge Imbort. In the circumstances, then, it is not hard to divine what happened with Domenech. Hearing by one means or another of her actions, Palafox immediately realised that she was an ideal tool of his policy, whether it was a matter of trumpeting his power-base's heroism to the rest of Spain or reinforcing his status as a demagogue. In brief, whether or not Domenech had actually been a heroine, she was now to be made a heroine.[9] At all events, this was now exactly what occurred. In this respect the embellishment of her story for public consumption to which we have already referred was only the beginning. Thus, Domenech was immediately given both a pension of six *reales* per day and the rank of gunner, and accorded the right to wear a special badge inscribed with the words *defensora de Zaragoza,* while she was henceforward kept at Palafox's right hand, and, following the abandonment of the siege by the French, introduced to prominent visitors to the city, including Goya, Vaughan and the British liaison officer, Charles William Doyle.[10]

By the autumn of 1808, then, Domenech had become a national heroine, indeed, even an international heroine. Thereafter, however, her story becomes ever more clouded in legend. In the summer of 1809 she was certainly in Seville, for on 12 August of that year she petitioned the provisional government for aid, the story that she told being extremely exciting. In brief, having engaged in further heroics when the French attacked the city for a second time in December 1808, she fell victim to the dreadful typhus epidemic that assailed the defenders, the fall of the city therefore finding her prostrate in a hospital bed. Summarily dragged out by the French along with her son, she was forced to march for the frontier with a long column of prisoners, and would have died had a friendly officer not placed her on the back of a mule. Thus assisted, Domenech survived to reach Puente la Reina, where she somehow managed to make her escape. Sadly, her son perished shortly afterwards, but she herself made her way to the headquarters of the nearest Spanish army, from whence she was dispatched to Seville. Greeted as a heroine as she was, she was promptly given a commission as an ensign (thereby becoming the first female officer in the history of the Spanish army) and provided with the money she needed to rejoin her husband, who was now stationed at Tarragona.[11]

From Seville, then, Domenech travelled to Cádiz, from where she took ship for Catalonia, though not before she had thoroughly charmed the commander of the British naval squadron stationed off the city, Admiral Purvis.[12] Thus far, thus good, but the story thereafter becomes increasingly implausible. Seemingly, Agustina never managed to reach her husband: caught at Tortosa when that fortress was besieged by the French in January 1810, she evaded captivity when it was overcome, and then made her way to La Mancha where she supposedly joined the guerrilla band commanded by Francisco Abad before finally attaching herself to the division of General Pablo Morillo and taking part in the battle of Vitoria. That she was in the vicinity of Vitoria in June 1813 seems certain enough, but the only British eyewitness who recorded seeing her unfortunately makes it clear that he encountered her hastening towards Vitoria from the east some days after the battle so it seems very unlikely that she was actually there.[13]

There is, then, much in the story of Agustina Zaragoza that is open to doubt. Yet even if her exploits were entirely fabricated, she was not the only woman who distinguished herself at Zaragoza. Two of these heroines, indeed, we have already met in the persons of Casta Álvarez and Manuela Sancho, of whom the former acquired much fame for her handling of musket and bayonet, and the latter was wounded helping to defend the convent of San José, while others who have been identified include Benita Portales, Juliana Larena and María Lostal.[14] Yet the extent of direct female involvement in the fighting even in the very special circumstances constituted by the sieges of Zaragoza—in each case wholly urban struggles in which the defenders were hopelessly inter-mingled with the civilian population (in the first siege, indeed, the defenders to all intents and purposes *were* the civilian population)—may well have been exaggerated. Passages describing women rushing to the walls are extremely numerous in British, French and Spanish accounts alike.[15] Yet it would be wrong to lay too much stress on such accounts. In the first place, they do not provide us with much in the way of evidence for women actually fighting the French, rather laying far more stress on their role of auxiliaries engaged in the traditional feminine roles of succouring the wounded and keeping the men supplied with food and drink. Still worse, when we do hear of women warriors, it is clearly in the context of moments of extreme emergency when it was literally a case of kill or be killed. Indeed, it was in precisely such a fight that Casta Álvarez appears to have made her name, the traditional account stating that, suddenly finding herself surrounded by French horsemen whilst bearing refreshments to the walls, she snatched up a discarded musket and laid about her.[16]

Something else that needs to be assessed is the issue of Palafox's own intentions. Prepared though he was to turn Domenech's's act of heroism to good account, initially at least it is probable that he had no intention of mobilising the women of the city *per se.* Note, for example, the following proclamation. Issued on 15 June 1808, it clearly implies an adherence to the doctrine of separate spheres. Thus: 'Brave men of Aragón! Continue in the spirit of ardour and nobility that is animating you. Look, too, upon the heroic conduct of the women of Zaragoza: inflamed with love for their Fatherland, their king and their religion, they have rushed to bring you assistance of every kind!'[17] This document can admittedly be countered by a second proclamation of 30 January 1809 which is far more militaristic in tone: 'In you, the women of Zaragoza, is to be found more energy than is to be found in any other women. Rally, then, dear ladies: do not leave the laurels of victory to the men alone. . . . The French soldiers fear you. . . . Your presence alone will be enough to intimidate even the bravest of them'.[18] However, striking though this proclamation is, its date tells its own story: the French were within the walls and the defenders falling prone to typhus by the hundred, the real archtype of the *defensoras* of Zaragoza therefore being not Agustina Zaragoza but rather María Agustín, a woman of humble birth who was severely wounded carrying food and water to the defenders of the Carmen gate on 15 June 1808.[19]

A further point to note in discussing all this is the issue of class. In so far as the general refrain is concerned, the model is very clear: in brief, women rush to take part in the defence without reference to their station in society—all are *españolas* and all have an equal interest in the defence of their country. Yet, as even historians who are anxious to discern feminist stirrings among Spain's women recognise, despite the manner in which the Brambila prints dressed Palafox's kinswoman, the Condesa de Bureta, up as a common woman of the streets and placed a musket in her hands, such an image was wildly misleading. Those women of the *zaragozano* élites who were in a position to make an independent choice certainly in many instances supported the independence struggle—as beneficiaries of feudalism or representatives of the Church, they had a strong interest in opposing Napoleonic reform, while in several cases they were closely connected with the Palafox family—but they did not dirty their hands in the same style as peasant girls. Indeed, so far as is known, they did not come under fire at all. Typified by the Condesa de Bureta, the Marquesa de Ayerbe and the prioress, María Rafols, they lavished money on the war effort, promoted recruitment and sought to look after the sick and wounded and displaced, but stand in the front line they most certainly did not.[20]

What, however, did happen at Zaragoza? Let us begin first of all with the context. In a manner that occurred almost nowhere else in Spain, a combination of a demagogic local leadership closely associated with the almost millennial hopes inspired by the advent of Ferdinand VII, a direct threat to life and limb, the recent example of the Dos de Mayo, and a military situation that was entirely comprehensible, drew forth a response from the populace that was as vigorous and determined as it was confused and inchoate. In the face of the French attack on the city, then, the people put up a desperate fight, and in this situation the female population could not but be drawn into the struggle, and all the more so once the enemy troops had managed to break through the walls and enter the streets. However, the women had not just been drawn into the fighting in some small way, but had also shown real heroism. If this was so, in contemporary eyes it was because particular circumstances were operating in the Peninsula that did not pertain elsewhere. Let us here turn to the French *aide-de-*camp, François Lejeune: 'It was the friars, above all, who exercised the most hostile influence against us. Their ascendancy being at their greatest amongst women, their despotism could reign all the more freely. . . . They excited in them the most ardent passion to defend . . . their Church, their fatherland and their liberty'.[21] Yet, just as Domenech's heroism on the walls was prefigured by that of Jarret, Pita and Pitcher, so the involvement of women in such tasks as helping the wounded and provisioning the defenders had also been seen in other conflicts. This was particularly so in sieges when women, first, were trapped and therefore possessed of a strong interest in putting up a stout defence as the only protection against sack and pillage; second, provided an abundant source of cheap or even free labour; and, third, were frequently deprived of their normal sources of income and therefore only too eager to earn the few coins that might be on offer from work of a military nature. Here and there, there had even been cases where, as might be argued in the case of Zaragoza, involvement in the fighting was fuelled by political or religious factors. One thinks here of Dutch towns besieged by the Spaniards in the Dutch revolt, Puritan towns besieged by the Royalists in the English Civil War—a conflict that was also notable for the manner in which aristocratic women often found themselves taking charge of the defence of one stronghold or another—and finally Irish towns besieged by the New Model Army, while in terms of Spanish history the obvious example is the Duke of Berwick's attack on Barcelona in 1714; to quote Henry Swinburne, 'The burgesses, animated by despair, rejected all offers of accommodation, and seemed determined to bury themselves under the ruins of their city. . . . The women, the children, breathed the same spirit and shared the labours of the defence with their husbands and fathers'.[22] The phenomenon, however, was simply too general to allow of explanation by reference to special pleading: in brief, throughout the early-modern period, whenever towns were besieged, women took part in their defence.[23]

All this serves to put the more overblown claims of some of the historiography in their proper perspective. In Zaragoza there were certainly women who were both in a position to adopt a leadership role and willing to do so, just as there were circumstances that provided women with greater opportunities actually to take part in the fighting, but the reality is that what occurred was not really so very out of the ordinary. If it seems so, indeed, it is solely because it was seized upon by a self-propagandist of great genius as a means of consolidating his power and influence, and later exploited by a highly self-conscious attempt to turn the War of Independence into a national epic. Also worth noting, meanwhile, is the distinctly uncritical manner in which the affair was reported by those outsiders who were first on the scene—primarily

Vaughan and Doyle, but also in their different ways Brambila and even Goya—and, last but not least, the lack of historical context that is evident in the work of almost all those who have discussed it thereafter. At the same time, even if something out of the ordinary happened in Zaragoza in the summer of 1808, it cannot really be used as an exemplar for the whole of the Peninsular War. Even in Zaragoza, indeed, conditions changed between the first siege and the second in that, by the time the French appeared again, the female population had been formally organised into a species of auxiliary force whose remit did not challenge social conventions in the same fashion as Domenech.[24]

This development did not quite mean that women were now officially to be excluded from the fighting, but there was clearly henceforth to be far less spontaneity. And it was not just that the women of the city had been placed under greater control. Whereas the defence of the city in the summer of 1808 had been a highly improvised affair conducted by crowds of armed civilians, Palafox had spent the autumn forming large numbers of new regiments, while two divisions of Valencian troops had also been incorporated into the garrison following the battle of Tudela. In consequence, the defences were now lined by thousands of regular soldiers (very raw regular soldiers, perhaps, but regular soldiers nonetheless). In short, there was now far less opportunity for women to take to the walls. At all events, whatever the reason, we hear far less mention of women in the second siege, and that despite the fact that the French once again got into the city and were forced to fight for it street by street and house by house. As witness the accounts of Lejeune and the Polish officer, Josef Mrozinski, woman warriors do appear from time to time, but plenty of women can be assumed never to have adopted such a role, instead huddling with their families in some place of safety. For example: 'Wishing to forget their misfortunes and seek comfort, the women gathered together in the houses of friends or relatives, and in this fashion as many as twenty persons might come to eat and sleep in some cramped cellar. Fearing the bombs, they did not dare go out into the streets'.[25]

Even in Zaragoza, then, the woman armed was almost certainly by no means a common figure, whilst it is also probably true that formal involvement in the war effort even in a non-combatant capacity was less frequent than is commonly supposed.[26] And, as in Zaragoza, so in the rest of Iberia. Setting aside the usual more-or-less invisible minority of cross-dressers who had by one means or another insinuated themselves into the ranks of the armed forces—a group that *may* have been larger than it was elsewhere due to the utter misery that beset the civilian populace—those women who became involved in actual combat generally did so in circumstances where their only hope lay in catching up the nearest weapon and trying to fight off their assailants, this being a pattern that was established as early as the Dos de Mayo. As hardly needs to be said, this affair was in many respects the keystone of the entire Peninsular War. In brief, on the morning of 2 May 1808 a riot broke out in Madrid that had very soon escalated into a city-wide revolt, only for Napoleon's lieutenant in Spain, Marshal Murat, to send in troops from all sides and crush the insurgents. The significance and nature of what happened will doubtless remain the subjects of debate for many years to come, but one of the few points that is generally agreed upon is that the populace feared that they were in imminent danger of massacre. If there were many women amongst the crowds who flooded into the streets, then, there is no need to explain their presence by reference to theories of politicisation: heroic though some few women undoubtedly were, what mattered was rather the far more elemental issues of self, home and family.[27]

From the Dos de Mayo the story of the Spanish insurrection moves more-or-less seamlessly into the series of provincial uprisings that soon saw every part of the country that was not actually occupied by the French rise in revolt. This development was extremely complex, but, in brief, events followed two main patterns. Thus, in some cities small groups of conspirators drawn from various disaffected elements and interest groups made use of paid agitators to whip up the crowds and at a convenient moment propel them into action, while in others disturbances broke out more-or-less spontaneously among the lower classes in response to the arrival of news of insurrection elsewhere. In each case, however, the result was the same: terrified of wholesale social disorder, the local administrative, military, ecclesiastical and judicial establishment abandoned their initial instinct to obey the orders they had received to collaborate with the French and formed new organs of authority—generally, provincial juntas—that stood a chance of channelling the energy of the crowd away from the political and social *status quo*. At the heart of the uprising, then, was certainly an angry and vociferous street, but what did that street want? The traditional answer here, of course, is that, suspicious of all foreigners on principle, the Spanish people were outraged at the threat to their Church and their king, not to mention the over-weening behaviour of the occupying forces, and further that they were convinced that the Dos de Mayo had amounted to an attempt at wholesale massacre that was set to be repeated in every city of Spain. To a degree this analysis cannot be entirely set aside—there seems little doubt, for example, that Ferdinand VII inspired genuine excitement among the masses and that fear of the French abounded (and not just in respect of possible massacres: also important was the widespread suspicion that Spaniards would soon find themselves being conscripted into Napoleon's armies). However, again, all this can only be understood in the context of a much wider background. Here one must begin with the social and economic situation. In brief, the ten years previous to the event of 1808 had been a period of the utmost trauma. Harvest failures, epidemics and natural disasters had stalked the land and large parts of such trade and industry as existed had been thrown into chaos by the war against Britain, while, to make matters still worse, the disamortisation of one-sixth of the lands of the Church had wrought havoc with the latter's ability to dispense charity. In consequence, misery was widespread, while it was all too easy for the many enemies of the hated *eminence gris* of the régime, Manuel de Godoy, to spread rumours that it was all his fault—even that God was in effect punishing Spain for his sins (Godoy was, after all, as lascivious as he was venal). As for what followed, it was all too simple. In the words of Ronald Fraser, 'Godoy paid the political price. Hatred of the royal favourite grew in all sectors of the population which suffered, to a greater or a lesser degree, the cost of an unpopular war'.[28]

All this puts the situation in a very different light. Thus, what we have is neither a political movement, nor an ideological movement, but a social movement. The ground having been carefully prepared by the conspirators by means of the widespread distribution of a series of scurrilous handbills denouncing Godoy, the accession to the throne of Ferdinand VII on 19 March 1808 had unleashed a torrent of hope among the populace in that, however naively, it was believed that somehow all Spain's ills would be swept away at a stroke.[29] When Napoleon removed Ferdinand from the scene, then, there was much outrage, certainly, but this was linked not so much to the fact of foreign intervention as to the fact that said foreign intervention had at a stroke dispelled the populace's hopes of salvation. On top of this, there was a further twist in the situation. With the legally constituted authorities, almost all of whom were still clients of Godoy, all preaching the need for submission to the French (at the express instructions, be it said, of Ferdinand VII), it appeared that Napoleon's actions were the fruit of a scheme to save the favourite and his adherents: after all, had not the French had Godoy freed from the imprisonment into which he had been flung in the wake of Aranjuez, and given him asylum? For the crowd, then, the enemy was not so much the French, who were actually present only in a very few parts of Spain, as *godoyismo.* To quote Raymond Carr, 'The rising against Napoleon was thus, in part, a revolution of disappointed hopes'.[30]

Yet if *godoyismo* was the enemy, unlettered artisans, peasants and day-labourers (or, for that matter, washerwomen, fishwives and prostitutes) were not much inclined to draw distinctions between one member of the propertied classes and another. What was building in Spain, at least, was not an anti-French revolt at all, but rather a gigantic *jacquerie.*[31] Indeed, even in Madrid the popular unrest that sparked off the Dos de Mayo was at least in part the product of fears that the presence of so many foreign troops would lead to a catastrophic spike in bread prices.[32] All this means that the role played by women in the uprising must needs be reassessed. Feminist writers, of course, have been keen to stress the participation of women in the disturbances as doing so allows them to highlight both their general political awareness and their patriotism, though in fact only in Cádiz, La Coruña, Badajoz and Zaragoza do we have clear evidence of women being in the forefront of the crowds.[33]

Let us assume, however, that women played a major role in the situation everywhere, a situation that is logical enough and certainly cannot be disproved. However, we come here to a theme to which we shall have to return over and over again. Women might have taken part in the disturbances that led to the Spanish revolt in large numbers, but they had always played a prominent role in such disturbances, and all the more so when the cause was related to such issues as high bread prices. For this there were a variety of reasons. In many Catholic countries, for example, traditions of 'carnival' were closely bound up with notions of the world being turned upside down, and this in turn may have instilled women with the notion that in certain circumstances it was legitimate for them to challenge authority. More widely, meanwhile, women were in a safer position than men in that female rioters were traditionally treated much more leniently than male ones, the net result being that the expression of dissent had come to be seen as part of the duty owed by women to the community. And, finally, if the object was to whip up revolt, employing women as paid agitators was always a useful ploy on account of their capacity to shame or seduce men into taking action.[34]

If women took to the streets in Spain in 1808, then, it was not because they were somehow newly energised, but rather because they were acting out traditional roles in what in many respects appeared to be a traditional crisis. Yet in June 1808 riot and insurrection finally became open war. Hardly had this development occurred, meanwhile, than we come across a woman fighting the French, the scene for this event being Valdepeñas. In brief, in 6 June 1808 a column of 1,000 enemy troops suddenly appeared before the town, whose streets had been hastily barricaded by the junta that had taken control in the wake of the uprising. In the fierce fight that followed many women appear to have tried to play their part by manning windows armed with cooking utensils and pans of boiling water, and one at least—a Juana Galán—was later recognised by the town as a heroine. The thirty-one-year-old daughter of a prosperous tavern keeper, Galán armed herself with a club and sallied out into the street where she supposedly took on various French soldiers single-handed, pulling them from their horses and dispatching them one after another with massive blows to the head.[35]

Over the years that followed many other instances may be found of women being caught up in combat in the same fashion as Juana Galán. As in Zaragoza, however, the setting is almost invariably one of either sack and massacre or small-scale riots. Here, for example, is Jean Naylies' description of the aftermath of an attack on the Galician town of Rivadavia in 1809:

> Under the walls of the town, I saw a horrible tableau that summed up the effects of this odious war. Lying nude and disfigured in the midst of a pile of corpses, I saw the bodies of two women. One of them was middle-aged: beside her lay a musket, whilst she was wearing a cartridge box and a sabre . . . and had been killed by a bullet in the chest. . . . The other, who was entirely naked and could not have been more than seventeen years old, had evidently joined a group of peasants in trying to pull a mounted officer from his horse: she had been cut down by a blow from a sabre that had split her skull in two.[36]

Having taken part in various fights in Galicia, Naylies went on to take part in Marshal Soult's invasion of northern Portugal in 1809. Eventually dispatched with his regiment to raid the town of Penafiel on 31 March, he here encountered another female combatant in the person of an unknown woman who supposedly rallied the terrified inhabitants and, sword in hand, led them in battle against the raiders (albeit to no avail: the town was thoroughly sacked and, according to local records, no fewer than 111 of the inhabitants killed, including seven women).[37] Meanwhile, someone else who encountered women amongst the militias who tried to fight off Soult was Fantin des Odoards, the latter reporting, first, seeing large numbers of women amongst the crowds of armed peasants who sought to block the passage of the River Miño on 16 February 1809, and, second, that during the defence of Oporto women 'crewed guns, served wine and carried munitions'.[38] To return to Spain, in Málaga, too, women were involved in the fighting when the city was stormed on 5 February 1810. Its only defenders being an improvised 'crowd army' consisting of nothing more than poorly armed civilians, the French broke into the city almost without firing a shot, but there followed several hours of confusion in which it was thoroughly sacked, a number of women seeking to defend their homes with anything that came to hand.[39] And, finally, also from Andalucía comes the story of Marimarcos (more properly María Marcos), a tavern keeper of La Palma del Condado who played a key role in driving out a small force of French troops that was attacked in the town by Spanish troops on 9 March 1811.[40]

In certain very special circumstances, then, the women of Spain and Portugal certainly fought in the Peninsular War. Indeed, on occasion they were actively encouraged to do so. For example, a blueprint for the liberation of Catalonia that was published in 1811 called for the inhabitants of every village, women included, to murder as many French soldiers as they possibly could.[41] Yet, again as in Zaragoza, the response was by no means a universal one. On the contrary, on plenty of occasions women are specifically mentioned as having put up no resistance. Sent to reconnoitre a village on the north bank of the River Guadalaviar a few miles west of Valencia in December 1811, for example, Aymar de Gonneville, recounts how his fears that his small command—a squadron of cavalry and two companies of Polish infantry—could be heading for trouble were quickly dissipated:

> It was a delicate operation I had in hand: we had to follow a road along the Guadalaviar for four leagues. . . . During the whole of this passage we were in sight of the enemy occupying the further bank . . . but on reaching the end I found that there were no enemies, and I only saw three or four thousand inhabitants of the village I had been directed to examine flying across the river for safety, bearing their children on their shoulders. The women were crying piteously, no doubt imagining that all their dear household stores would be plundered, and that they would find all plundered on their return.[42]

For many women, then, the natural reaction to the presence of French troops was not fight but fright. Indeed, on occasion, women seem even to have attempted to prevent violence. We come here to a curious incident that took place at Tarifa late in 1811. Thus, a Spanish outpost on the extreme southern tip of Andalucía, Tarifa was held by little more than a civic guard. Evidently suspecting that this force was not to be trusted, the governor one day decided to put it to the test by calling a snap mobilisation, only for his fears to be vindicated in dramatic fashion. An eyewitness was Robert Blakeney of the Twenty-Eighth Foot:

> The streets were instantly crowded with women, one seizing a husband, another a son, a third a brother . . . all endeavouring to snatch them by force from out their warlike ranks, [and] loudly . . . exclaiming against the British, who, they cried or rather screamed, being fond of bloodshed themselves, would force others into fighting whether willingly or otherwise. At length, urged by some British officers and breaking away from their wives, mothers, sisters and lovers, in whose hands remained many cloaks, coats, hats and even torn locks of hair, the poor nuts arrived half-shelled upon the ramparts.[43]

Even if we say that this episode was an exception, it is clear that women who got behind the war effort drew water far more often than they drew blood. At all events the most common task which we see them undertaking on the battlefield is that of keeping the troops supplied with food and drink. At Bailén, then, a peasant woman named María Bellido won a place in history for the courage she showed while engaged in this activity, while many women flocked to the walls of Valencia for the same purpose when Marshal Moncey attempted to storm the city on June 1808.[44] At Bailén and Valencia the involvement of women was, if not spontaneous, then certainly *ad hoc*. Much the same, too, is also probably true of women Richard Henegan observed labouring to strengthen the ramparts of Ciudad Rodrigo in December 1808.[45] As time passed, however, so efforts were made to harness women to the war effort in a more formal manner. First seen at Zaragoza in the siege of December 1808–February 1809, these found their most dramatic expression during the defence of Gerona. A key position that completely blocked the main road from the French frontier to Barcelona, Gerona had declared for the Patriot cause at the beginning of the war, and had since then beaten off repeated assaults under the leadership of its redoubtable governor, Mariano Álvarez de Castro. However, isolated deep in the French rear, the city remained extremely vulnerable, and Álvarez de Castro therefore strained every nerve to reinforce its defences. Pressed by necessity, he could not but explore every avenue that was open to him, and thus it was that in the spring of 1809 he gratefully seized upon an offer that was made him by the wives of some of his senior officers to organise a company of female volunteers. Thus was born the so-called 'Companía de Santa Bárbara' (Saint Bárbara is the patron saint of the Spanish artillery). Already (or so the traditional history of the sieges insists) the women of Gerona had sustained the defence of the city in much the same way as had their fellows at Zaragoza, and the result was that when Álvarez de Castro issued a call for 200 volunteers on 28 June 1809, there was an enthusiastic response (though in fact in the first instance only 131 women, most of them seemingly either the wives or daughters of soldiers of the garrison, came forward). Organised into four platoons, each of them led by a commandant and four non-commissioned officers, all of them women, and accorded the right to wear a red sash, this force was given the task of aiding the wounded and carrying food, drink and ammunition to the defenders, and in this capacity served with considerable distinction, a number of its members being killed or wounded, and several being rewarded for their courage by Ferdinand VII after 1814; indeed, Hyacinthe Clémenso, an officer of the Valais Battalion, later recalled them singing patriotic songs and hurling insults at the French troops.[46]

Such auxiliary service, meanwhile, was not just confined to the inhabitants of cities threatened by the French. As the forces of Sir John Moore and the Duke of Wellington marched and counter-marched across Spain and Portugal, then, they on occasion found their efforts seconded by local women of a more or less enthusiastic disposition. A participant in the unsuccessful siege of the castle of Burgos in the autumn of 1812, for example, Ensign John Aitchison of the Third Foot Guards encountered a pleasing scene when he paid a visit to the town: 'I . . . was very happy to find a woman at almost every door busily employed in tearing rags to pieces to make lint for the hospitals. They seem all in great spirits at the prospect of soon being freed from the enemy'.[47] Also worth noting here, perhaps, is the response of the women of Vitoria when Wellington's great victory of 21 June 1813 cleared the French from their city:

> During the whole of the night, conveyances were bringing in the wounded of both nations, every house being converted into a temporary hospital for their accommodation, and here it must be recorded to the honour of the fair women of Vitoria that never did female excellence shine more conspicuously than in their tender care of the poor sufferers. They made . . . lint, and applied it with the delicacy that women only could display; they watched by the bed of agony, and dropped the tear of sympathy on the pallid cheek of him whose sufferings had closed with his last drawn sigh.[48]

Thus far, with the possible exception of the skirmish at La Palma del Condado, where a regular military operation against the French garrison was seconded in the timeliest of fashions by a street riot, all of this is very much in keeping with the norms of warfare in the horse-and-musket period, even the 'Companía de Santa Bárbara' differing from what had gone before in little more than detail. For something rather different we need to look at what might be imagined to be the most quintessentially Iberian aspect of the Peninsular War, namely the so-called *guerrilla.* In this respect, we have already met the Catalan *somatén,* Susana Claretona, but recent research has suggested that women found acceptance in many of the small irregular bands that gave birth to the struggle. In Andalucía in 1812, for example, we hear of two anonymous women, the one from Estepa and the other from Antequera, who were executed by firing squad after having in both cases killed a number of French soldiers, while there are also eyewitness accounts of women taking part in skirmishes in the Serranía de Ronda in 1810.[49]

If Andalucía was the heartland of small-scale guerrilla warfare, similar examples have been spotted in other parts of Spain—the female *somatenes,* María Escoplé, Magdalena Bofill, and Margarita Tona; María Catalina and Catalina Martín, of whom the first was supposedly the wife and the second the aunt of the Castillian chieftain, Toribio Bustamente; Francisca de la Puerta, who seemingly fought in Extremadura and eventually petitioned the junta of that province for permission to form a *partida* of her own; Josefa Bosch, who was hung by the French in Morella (though it is probable that she acted as an informant rather than fighting as a combatant); and an un-named woman from Miranda de Ebro (possibly Dominica Ruíz de Vallejo, the wife of the *riojano* chieftain, Cuevillas) who was actually appointed to the command of a *partida* by the Junta of Molina de Aragón in 1809.[50] At the same time, impelled by the murder of her father and brother in the French occupation of Bilbao in August 1808, a young Basque woman named Martina de Ibaibarriaga Elorriaga for a time headed a guerrilla band in the Cantabrian mountains and eventually gained a commission in the Spanish army, although it is important to note that she did so disguised as a man.[51] Finally, at least one British officer speaks of coming across women serving with bands of irregulars as fully fledged combatants. Thus: 'One of the Spanish women belonging to Don Julián's corps was very remarkable both for her beauty and her dress, which was a sort of uniform with epaulettes, and a sabre and sash, the latter thrown over one shoulder'.[52]

We should, however, do well to take care in analysing such references. In the summer of 1812, for example, three women were executed in Málaga for their part in serious disorders that broke out in the town after it was temporarily occupied by Spanish troops commanded by General Ballesteros on 14 July.[53] Were these patriotic heroines who had rallied to the Patriot cause or rather simply looters out to steal the food and money they needed to keep themselves and their families going for a few more days? What, too, of the 268 women shown by Ronald Fraser to have been tried by the special tribunals set up by the *josefino* authorities to expedite the punishment of those accused of crimes against public order? On the surface, the fact that their offences included providing the *partidas* with information, storing guns and ammunition in their homes, carrying messages for one chieftain or another and keeping company with bands of insurgents might suggest that what we have is clear evidence of the participation of women in the resistance movement, and yet the fact that many of the bands involved in these cases were beyond doubt little more than gangs of bandits cannot but give us pause: what we see might be evidence of female involvement in the resistance, but it might just as well be evidence of female involvement in traditional forms of rural criminality.[54] Indeed, in one or two instances female participants in *la guerrilla* quite simply were bandits: a woman from Samaniego named Juana Ruiz who ended up being sentenced to ten years' imprisonment by the *afrancesado* authorities had so evil a reputation that even fellow villagers referred to her as 'La Briganta', while the band commanded by the famous Martina de Ibaibarriaga eventually caused such havoc that it had to be suppressed by the more dedicated guerrilla commanders, Francisco Longa and Francisco Espoz y Mina (though her followers were all executed, Ibaibarriaga herself was pardoned and allowed to serve in Longa's forces until the end of the war).[55]

The difficulties involved in assuming that cases in which women were in one way or another involved with the *partidas* constitute evidence of female support for the irregular struggle are numerous. Consider, for example, the following passage from the journal of Seymour Larpent: 'My old witch of a *patrona* came in just now . . . and, moving the heavy bed, disappeared down a trapdoor under it to get up a little clean linen. . . . She also produced a guerrilla soldier's shirt, which he had left to be washed, and called for today'.[56] Given that Larpent was in Navarre at the time that he wrote these words, it may be assumed that the soldier concerned belonged to the command of Espoz y Mina, and it therefore on the surface appears that what we have is a woman doing what she can to support the struggle against the invaders. Perhaps, but, then again, perhaps not. In brief, we simply do not know enough about the situation to make such a judgement. Was the woman given any choice in the matter? Was the transaction simply an economic one in which the woman provided a necessary service for cash and in the process put food on the table? Was the guerrilla her son or even her husband, and therefore someone to whom such services were accorded as of right? To none of these questions do we have the answer, and the fact is that, unless we do, it would be unsafe to invest the incident with overtones that are overly patriotic.[57]

Equally ambiguous, meanwhile, is the figure of the female *guerrillera* cited above, for there is no certainty that the woman concerned actually fought as a man, the figure that immediately comes to mind here being Masséna's hussar-clad mistress. And, last but by no means least, there is the issue of the political slant that was given to many of the memoirs generated by the French troops who served in Spain and Portugal. To repeat a point that has been made before, anyone who wrote a memoir with a view to having it published by definition had a strong interest in writing a book that would sell, and that in turn meant filling its pages with the exciting and the exotic. This, of course, applied to British writers as well as French ones, but in the latter instance a number of other factors were in operation that strongly reinforced this tendency. In brief, the French had been defeated in the Peninsula, and the injured pride of the men who had fought there not unnaturally sought to assuage itself by finding some explanation that did not reflect upon their competence. In so far as this was concerned, few ideas were more useful than that of the nation-in-arms: in Spain and Portugal the forces of Napoleon had been facing the enmity of entire peoples and therefore could not have hoped to prevail. At the same time, not only was victory out of reach, but the opponent a particularly savage one who did not respect the usual conventions of warfare and habitually resorted to torture and murder, an opponent, in short, that required great courage simply to confront. However, stressing the idea that the French were fighting the proverbial 'people numerous and armed' was not just useful as a means of explaining away defeat and emphasising the heroism and devotion of Napoleon's men. Just as important was the role that it could play in legitimising what had occurred. Central to the claims both of imperial propaganda, and, indeed, those of the emperor's legions of later apologists, had been the idea that Napoleonic France had been fighting for the ideas of the French Revolution—in effect, that the Napoleonic armies had been the spearhead of a new age of justice and liberty. Opposing them in Spain were the people, but the people, it was generally accepted, merited nothing but scorn, being a mere mob that was superstitious, ignorant, brutal and incapable of rational thought. If the people opposed the empire, then, that alone was a major mark in the latter's favour. However, the people, or so the argument continued, were incapable of acting alone: whilst there might be a street riot here and a peasant rising there, the populace could not possibly have mounted the sort of resistance the French faced in Spain and Portugal on their own account. What was needed, then, was some sort of catalyst, and this, of course, was found in the Catholic Church. Behind every Spanish peasant, in short, there lurked a priest, a monk or a friar, just as behind every Spanish general there lurked a bishop, an abbot or a prior. What was being waged in Spain and Portugal was therefore a struggle between good and evil, between progress and reaction, between the present and the past, and this struggle was in turn but a part of the wider struggle between the French Revolution and the *ancien régime* that lay at the heart of the French (or, at least, Bonapartist) explanation of the Napoleonic Wars.[58]

When we hear, then, of 'furies let loose' throwing themselves with horrible shrieks upon the wounded (note the suggestion that women are cowards who do not fight fair but single out the weak and the vulnerable), we should read such words with considerable caution. Let us accept, however, that, here and there, women were a presence in the fighting elements of *la guerrilla,* albeit a presence that was relatively restricted: even in the savagery of irregular warfare, there were cooking pots to be stirred, campfires to be tended, firewood to be collected, and age-old assumptions about the role of women to be respected. And, if few women got to handle weapons in *la guerrilla,* in the regular army, meanwhile, overt penetration of the male sphere was even more limited, the only woman who is known openly to have served the cause of Spain as a woman in a formal military capacity being Domenech. Nor is this surprising. Thus, notwithstanding emergency measures such as those seen in Zaragoza and Gerona, the Patriot establishment remained deeply opposed to any blurring of the principle of gender separation. Women were certainly expected to bear their part in the struggle, but that part was not to be found on the battlefield or even in the camp. There were, then, no official appeals for women to come forward to serve their country, nor still less any attempt at some sort of general mobilisation.[59] As pamphlet after pamphlet made clear, by contrast, it was the task of the woman to pray for victory and, with this, do penance for Spain's sins; to watch over and guard traditional morality; to welcome home the warrior; and to provide the army with clothing and other necessities. For example, 'Women of Valencia! Spin and bleach linen, make up breeches, sew shirts, make ready thread and bandages. . . . This is what corresponds to your sex; this is what your fatherland demands; this is what our soldiers need'.[60] Also from Valencia, meanwhile, comes the equally telling *Soldado de España,* a pamphlet published in 1811 that assumes the female voice to call upon women to reassure and encourage the fighting soldier:

> Come, my soldier friend, enter my house; honour it with your presence as a worthy citizen of the Fatherland. I will clean away your dust and honourable sweat. This will be my glory: to lavish attention upon the suffering champion who passes so many nights stretched on the floor of some crowded barrack room. . . . Maidens of Spain! To nature you owe the gift of having been given gentle characteristics: keep them safe for the honourable soldiers who will one day return to you covered in wounds. Keep safe, too, your maidenhead so that it might sweeten the sorrows that will be deposited in it, whilst reserving your beautiful arms to embrace those who, crowned with laurels, will come running in search of . . . the greatest prize of honest passion and battlefield daring.[61]

This is not to say that stirrings of something rather different were completely absent from the scene. On the contrary, on 8 June 1808 the *Diario de Granada* carried a very different piece. Thus:

> The conduct of the government thus far has been an offence to the fair sex, and there are now a great many amongst us who quite rightly can no longer contain their sentiments. Are we not useful for anything in the current circumstances? Is it really intended that we should only be used in those tasks that are deemed appropriate to our gender? Our honour is being compromised and we demand complete satisfaction. . . . The sentiments of patriotism that animate all Spaniards have also

> communicated themselves to the fair sex, and we are going to see reproduced in our own days the great acts which have made the latter so admired throughout the centuries.[62]

Such appeals, however, fell on deaf ears: nothing in the style of the Companía de Santa Bárbara was ever to emerge again.[63] What, though, of cross-dressers—in short, women who enlisted in the army disguised as men? As we have seen, this practice was by no means unknown in Bourbon Spain though there is no reason to suppose that it was especially common. With the coming of the Peninsular War, however, it is just possible that the situation may have changed a little. Though we know of only one case of a woman enlisting as a man and serving in that capacity—that of Martina de Ibaibarriaga—it cannot be denied that there was now greater motive for embarking on such a course. First of all, there is the issue of context in that Spain and Portugal both became societies that were subjected to a constant barrage of propaganda designed to foster a sense of duty and patriotism and whip up hatred of the enemy. As for that enemy, he in many instances almost went out of his way to earn that hatred, the French forces leaving a trail of devastation across the countryside. In short, if men heard the call of the Fatherland, women did so too, while, for every man who mourned the loss of father, mother, brother or sister, there was a woman with exactly the same cause to hate the invaders. Those who see the Iberian struggle against the Napoleonic empire in traditional terms will therefore have no difficulty in imagining that the pressures and emotions unleashed in this fashion persuaded at least some women to seek a place in the ranks. At the same time, even those who take a critical view of the war against Napoleon can accept that some degree of cross-dressing took place. The sufferings that the war inflicted on an already much afflicted populace will be detailed in another place and need not be expounded here: suffice it to say that there could well have been many young women who saw no option but to disguise themselves as men and enlist as soldiers, while there may even have been soldiers who colluded in the practice rather than leave *novias* or sisters behind in their home villages to face slaughter or starvation. Yet in the end all this is mere speculation: exactly as is the case with other *ancien-régime* societies, we simply cannot tell how many women became soldiers, and certainly cannot assume that the practice was widespread. Aside from anything else, there were plenty of prejudices against the idea amongst women themselves. To quote Heinrich von Brandt, for example:

> Although women, especially the mature ones, bitterly rebuked the French for their lack of religion and for their insatiable appetites, generally they were of the opinion that it was the duty of the men to fight for the legitimate king, [and] that women should restrict their attention to the housekeeping. This intelligent opinion held sway in the countryside and in the little villages, and it was only in important cities that the women meddled in war and politics.[64]

What, though, of other forms of involvement in the struggle, forms that did not involve actually bearing arms against the French or serving in or near the front line in an auxiliary capacity? Very close to simply picking up a musket and yet at the same time a very long way removed from it was the concept of murdering French soldiers at a moment when they could one way or another be taken unawares, this very often being achieved by means of women exploiting traditional roles that allowed them to take men by surprise. How often such events took place is a moot point, but they do occasionally appear. Travelling to Madrid after the battle of Bailén, for example, the British liaison officer, Samuel Whittingham, was introduced to a peasant woman who was supposed to have killed eight French soldiers by knocking them on the head as they were drinking from her well and then throwing them down its shaft.[65] This case can be dismissed as mere patriotic nonsense, but it is nonetheless interesting that a woman could have persuaded the local community to accept such a claim (and still more interesting that she should have been moved to make it), whilst from time to time rumours also surfaced amongst the French that women were taking unwary soldiers to their beds so as later to do away with them.[66] Highly suggestive, too, is the case of a woman named María Senepe Apri who was jailed for a year when two French soldiers were murdered by insurgents in the house she owned in Alcalá de Gudaira.[67]

If some women contributed to the French cause by murdering French soldiers, others turned to espionage, one such case that has been uncovered being that of María García, a housewife from Ronda who took it upon herself to pass information of all kinds to the local partisans, and two others those of María Isidora de Gastañaga and Manuela Rubín López, both of whom were sentenced to terms of imprisonment for espionage in the Basque provinces.[68] Other cases, meanwhile, have surfaced in Madrid, Barcelona, Córdoba and León.[69] Such women were even rumoured on occasion to have seduced their way into the beds of French generals. Thus, passing through Navarre in the summer of 1811, for example, Aymar de Gonneville heard a most alarming story. As he wrote: 'General Reille was in command at Tudela, and report said that his chief of staff had a Spanish mistress who extracted confidential information from him on the movement of troops [and] the force and composition of detachments, and then sent it on to [Espoz y] Mina. . . . I saw the woman one night at an evening party at the commandant's. She was playing high . . . [and] might be capable of any wickedness judging by her face and manner'.[70]

And, finally, for those not possessed of the courage to play the spy, there was also always the possibility of engaging in acts of symbolic resistance – the French hussar, Albert de Rocca, saw Andalusian women wearing 'English stuffs on which the pictures of Ferdinand VII and the Spanish generals most distinguished in the war against the French were painted'[71]—or, alternatively, solidarity with the Allied cause: when the governor of Seville invited 200 of the leading ladies of the city to a ball celebrating Joseph's saint's day on 19 March 1810, for example, the only guests who turned up were forty who were 'so dishonest that they were the scandal of the crowd that . . . had gathered to inspect the decorations that had been put up to mark the occasion'.[72] At the same time, one may also cite a number of incidents in which local girls succoured British officers who had been taken prisoner by the French or otherwise fallen upon hard times.[73] A variant on the theme, meanwhile, was to shelter fugitives or obstruct the agents of the occupying forces. A member of a British family that had been settled for many years in Oporto, for example, Harriet Slessor kept two police agents participating in the round-up of all British males that followed the initial French occupation of Portugal talking in her front hall while their quarry—her son-in-law, James Walsh—'most nimbly stepped out at a window, jumped onto the tiles and got safe into our neighbour's yard'.[74]

It was not, of course, just British fugitives and prisoners of war who found help. With their commanders defeated in battle after battle by the French, thousands of Spanish prisoners found themselves condemned to participating in what sometimes became veritable 'death marches' on their way to captivity in France. Typical enough, perhaps, was the fate of the garrison of Valencia. Dispatched to the frontier immediately following the fall of the city in January 1812, they were denied food and had no sooner left the coastal plain than they were assailed by the most bitter winter weather. Afforded no shelter whatsoever, hundreds of the prisoners died every night, whilst many others collapsed along the way and were shot where they fell.[75] The sight of such columns could hardly fail to elicit the compassion of the inhabitants of the towns through which they passed, and historians such as Elena Fernández García have therefore been able to cite numerous cases of women bringing prisoners food or helping them to escape (sometimes, ironically enough, by means of dressing them in women's clothing), one such being María Angela Tellería, who spirited a number of officers from French captivity in Santander in 1809, and another Raimunda Bosch y Espino, the wife of a Barcelona architect who assisted a number of prisoners who had escaped their guards in Catalonia.[76] Finally, from the Navarrese town of Tudela, meanwhile, comes the case of Antonia Caparrosa, a woman of the town who after the war was rewarded by a pension of three *reales* per day for her services in this respect.[77]

Finally, if nothing else, there was always the course of simply freezing out the invaders. Here, for example, are the memories of the future conqueror of Algeria, Marshal Bugeaud, of being stationed in Madrid in May 1808: 'I assure you that it is not a good time for playing the flute at night under a beauty's windows. . . . Everyone complains of a dearth of intrigues'.[78] The Madrid of the immediate aftermath of the Dos de Mayo is by no means a fair sample of the relations of French soldiers with Spanish women, but Bugeaud was not the only French soldier to experience the problem. For a good case of a frustrated suitor we can cite the case of Elzéar Blaze:

> When the Spanish women mention the devil, they make the sign of the cross on the mouth with the thumb of the right hand, and the name of Napoleon was treated like that of the devil. I lodged at Pamplona in the house of a young and charming woman. I attempted to flutter around her, but was always repulsed. Whenever I met my pretty hostess and would have enacted the gallant with her, she drew back as far as possible, [and] shrank into a corner, trembling with fear, and there made thousands of signs of the cross to prevent the devil, who, no doubt, was in me, from sallying forth with my words and taking possession of her. Though persevering as he is mischievous, I declare that this time he was completely foiled. Too vigilant a guard was kept: a sign of the cross always made him turn tail, and, devil though one be, one cannot cope with such means of defence.[79]

Denied the pleasures of the flesh, French officers might also be snubbed in other ways, as witness an incident in Covilhão in the autumn of 1807 when the ladies of the town had responded to an invitation to a ball by dressing up their maidservants in their best clothes and sending them in their place.[80] Alternatively, they might simply be subjected to repeated tongue lashings. Stationed at Chiclana during the siege of Cádiz, for example, a military pharmacist attached to the corps of Marshal Victor named Antoine Fée who was billeted in the home of a prominent local citizen named Múñoz found himself constantly assailed by one of the household's three daughters, a fiery young woman named María who 'took hatred of the French to a state of exultation'.[81] Rather quieter, perhaps, but just as brave was a British woman who George Simmons got to know in Lisbon. Unwilling to abandon their substantial property, she and her husband (a British merchant) had resolved to brave the French occupation of Portugal in 1807. Forced to accept several French officers into her home, she countered their denigration of the British army with discreet hints that they would do well to curb their boasting, hints that were, of course, soon vindicated by the battles of Roliça and Vimeiro.[82] Bravest of all, though, was possibly an old woman who had evidently been too frail to flee with the rest of the inhabitants when her home village—a small place near Coria called Montehermoso—was raided by French troops looking for grain in October 1809. Thus, having evidently crawled from her bed to the door of her dwelling, she greeted the enemy soldiers with a volley of abuse and kept up a constant diatribe of curses for the whole time that they remained in the village.[83]

Thus far, the subject of the direct involvement of women in the conflict has been discussed entirely in terms of what occurred in the presence of the enemy. What, however, went on in districts that could be considered to be behind the lines? In so far as this is concerned, it is clear that amongst those groups that had an interest in supporting the war effort, women certainly played their part in keeping up an air of patriotic effervescence. Here, for example, are Charles Leslie's recollections of Ayamonte:

> Being the first English who had landed in Spain . . . we were received with the most enthusiastic demonstrations of joy by the inhabitants. The governor invited all the officers to an entertainment in the evening, and had provided for us billets in all the best houses. The Spanish officers, both of the army and navy, almost crushed us in their fraternal embraces and insisted on . . . introducing us to all the pretty ladies in the place. These dark beauties gave us the most cordial reception, and sang patriotic songs and warlike hymns, accompanied on the guitar or piano. . . . The Patriots having assumed a red cockade, with the cypher 'FVII' worked upon [it], woe to any man who ventured to appear without one. The ladies took a pride in presenting us with this national emblem, embroidered with their own fair hands, as we had been ordered to put them above our black ones.[84]

The warm welcome afforded Leslie was repeated many times. Hardly had British troops landed in Mondego Bay in August 1808, for example, than the local women were expressing their appreciation. Thus: 'Our visitors were not confined to the male sex, for some olive beauties with sparkling eyes and jet-black hair were induced to take a peep at us, and before we parted some of the more favoured of us were presented with flowers and fruit from the hands of these damsels'.[85] Landing in Portugal two years later, meanwhile, John Kincaid encountered a welcome that was still more vigorous, being greeted 'by about a hundred hideous looking Portuguese women, whose joy was so excessive that they waded up to their arm-pits through a heavy surf and insisted on carrying us on shore on their backs!'[86] However, the most dramatic scenes of feminine support for the common cause were witnessed when the Anglo-Portuguese army liberated Madrid on 12 August 1812. As the troops marched in, then, they were mobbed by hundreds of excited women. 'We moved slowly on', wrote William Wheeler, 'amidst the sweet voices of thousands of the most bewitching and interesting little devils I had ever seen. . . . The whole of the windows and the tops of the houses were crowded with Spanish beauty waving white handkerchiefs'.[87] Meanwhile, where blood had been shed to secure their liberation, women sometimes offered something more practical than kisses. If the women of Vitoria rushed to help the wounded, then so did the women of Salamanca:

> Having thus noticed the battle of Salamanca, I must not pass over the behaviour of its inhabitants. . . . During the three days that we were on the heights of Villanes . . . men and women, young and old, visited us, bringing with them loads of fresh water and dry wood. . . . After [our] driving off their enemy . . . even ladies of birth went to the field of battle and lent all their delicate assistance at removing the wounded into their houses and administering every comfort in their power.[88]

The reverse side of the coin to all this, of course, was displays of violent aversion in respect of such representatives of the enemy as offered themselves. Thus the angry crowds that frequently menaced the columns of French prisoners wending their way into captivity in the wake of the battle of Bailén included large numbers of women, women who, what is more, showed no hesitation in hurling themselves into the fray when menace turned to violence.

Here, for example, is Maurice du Tascher on the scenes which took place at Puerto de Santa María when he and a group of other officers were brought down to the quay to be taken out to one of the prison hulks anchored in the bay of Cádiz:

> The women in general showed themselves to be more relentless than the men: they screamed for our heads and demanded that the soldiers should kill us before their eyes. . . . Robbed and bruised by many blows [Huguet] took refuge in a rowing boat, where he underwent a new search. A pretty, well-dressed young woman carried insult . . . a step further. . . . No modesty restrained her greedy hands: she explored his most secret places, and, enraged at failing to find any . . . hidden treasures, she gripped the voluptuous parts that she was outraging, and, with a violent jolt, brought the wretched officer to lie at her feet as white as death. . . . An attractive female tapped on the shoulder of an officer, one who was usually quite conceited. He, thinking that good fortune had come his way as a result of his good looks and long blond moustaches, turned to her with a smile. The amiable female at once covered his eyes and face with spit.[89]

To return to more pleasant matters, friendly cross-cultural gender relations were not just limited to such moments of heightened emotion as the liberation of Madrid. On the contrary, the women of Spain and Portugal generally seem to have been happy enough to fraternise with the British. Here, for example, is George Bell: 'We passed . . . the month of September [1812] in the town of Yepes. . . . There were many pretty girls in the town, all fond of dancing, in which we often indulged of an evening until we became almost of one family; in fact, every young fellow had his sweetheart'.[90] In September 1809, meanwhile, Badajoz saw one of the leading ladies of the city organise a reception for as many British officers as cared to attend.[91] Objectively at least, associating with the British army in this fashion was a political act as well as a social one in that it helped keep up morale. Still more symbolic was the performance of such dances as the *bolero,* the *fandango* and the *jota,* for all of them could be seen as being an overt statement of national identity. Consider, for example, this account by Grattan of a dance he attended at Ciudad Rodrigo in the winter of 1812–13:

> The ball was opened by Avandano de Alcantaro, a young captain belonging to the garrison of Almeida, and Señora Dolores de Inza, a Spanish lady. . . . The dance was the *bolero,* of which I had heard so much but had never seen danced before. All eyes were turned towards the spot which the youthful couple occupied. Avandano danced well . . . but he danced mechanically, like one who had been taught, and his rule more by lesson than by heart. . . . His partner, on the contrary, had all the fire of the true Andalucían breed. Her movements, though perhaps not quite as correct as his, were spirited and drew down thunders of applause from the spectators, and each plaudit, as was natural, caused her to increase her exertions.[92]

One can, however, go too far here. For a simpler explanation of the presence of so many Spanish women at the functions organised by British officers, we need only return to George Bell. Thus: 'The girls were very fond of dancing'.[93] More generally, the presence of a British garrison brought spice to lives that were otherwise all too often deeply circumscribed. As Leslie wrote of his arrival at Valencia de Alcántara, for example, 'This town being at that period out of range of our warlike operations . . . the appearance of a few English officers caused some little sensation among the ladies'.[94]

Let us not, though, be too cynical: the mere fact that female hearts were fluttered by gallant officers does not necessarily mean that those same hearts were not given over to the Patriot cause. At the same time, support for the war effort was also expressed in forms that were more tangible. With thread much needed to make up uniforms and sew wounds, for example, at least some women found a simple means of helping the cause, the newspapers frequently carrying lists of individuals who had contributed balls of their own spinning of one size or another.[95] For those women with money to spare, meanwhile, it was possible to contribute to the Patriot cause in a manner that was less gender-specific. Thus, the lists of donors in money or in kind include many women. To take just a few examples from the richer end of the scale, in June 1808 the Marquesa del Saltillo presented the Junta of Granada with 10,000 *reales;* in August 1808 various female inhabitants of Vélez-Málaga handed over a silver tray, two silver candlesticks, six silver forks and a gold watch; in September 1808 one Ana Requena paid over 100 *pesos fuertes* to a fund established by the Captain General of Guatemala; in November 1808 two residents of Havana named Bárbara Estrada and Josefa Peñalver gave a total of sixty-six chests of sugar.[96] However, gifts did not just come from the propertied classes. Particularly moving in this respect is a list of 190 residents of the notoriously poverty-stricken district of Triana who in the course of 1809 contributed the impressive total of 5,132 *reales* to a special appeal for clothing for the army, those concerned including several women who gave just ten apiece (particularly interesting here is the fact that women actually outdid men in their generosity: whilst the average for the list as a whole was just over twenty-seven *reales* per donor, for the twenty women it reached thirty-two).[97]

Finally, even acts of ordinary human decency could become services to the cause. At Badajoz, then, after George Bell had all his personal possessions stolen by thieves who entered his room through an open window, he was treated to breakfast and given two shirts and a small amount of money by an old acquaintance called Leonor whom he happened to meet in the street, while the terrible retreat to Ciudad Rodrigo saw him sheltered and fed by an old woman living in a cottage at the side of the road.[98] Equally, wounded in the arm at San Sebastián, Captain John Blakiston was billeted on a Spanish woman at Pasajes prior to being sent on by sea to a hospital that had been established at Bilbao. The first night he was much distressed, being tormented both by bugs of various sorts and the pain of his wound, not to mention the great heat, but the woman did her best to care for him, providing him with water and adjusting his dressings, this being an action that Blakiston remembered with much gratitude in view of the lack of warmth which he claims that he and his fellow officers usually met from the families on which they were billeted.[99] And, finally, having fallen very ill near Salamanca in the summer of 1812, George Wood of the Eighty-Fifth Foot was taken in and cared for by 'an old widow-woman'.[100]

Of course, the presence of British soldiers in their homes opened up still another possibility of involvement in the war effort to the women of Spain and Portugal. Thus, just as in areas garrisoned by the French women could make use of the licence afforded them on account of their sex to berate the invaders for having crossed the Pyrenees, so in areas garrisoned by the British women could use the same licence to advocate greater support for the Patriot cause. One British officer who experienced this treatment was George Simmons of the Ninety-Fifth. By the summer of 1810 Spanish patience with the Fabian strategy affected by Wellington was wearing thin, and irritation turned to fury when Wellington's army remained passive on the frontier of Portugal while the French set about the reduction of the Spanish fortress of Ciudad Rodrigo. Simmons being stationed in a little village a few miles from the city, he found himself—in every sense!—in the front line: 'The Spaniards are astonished at us remaining idle, as they term it, and allowing the French to invest their town; consequently, they have no high opinion of our valour. The young women with whom we joke and talk, make no scruple in calling us cowards, and say if we fought as we eat and drink . . . we should be fine fellows indeed'.[101]

Here we see Spanish women acting almost as agents of foreign policy.[102] It was not just British soldiers who could be goaded in this fashion, however. Amongst the family on whom Joseph Sherer was billeted at Mérida in the autumn of 1809, for example, was 'a girl of about seventeen . . . without any exception, the . . . most beautiful woman I saw while in Spain'. Seemingly a would-be amazon, this young woman was quite clear that her sexuality was one more weapon in the service of her country. Thus: 'In the course of our conversation, she . . . expressed herself warmly about the profession of arms, saying repeatedly that she would accept the hand of no man who had not fought for his country, and who was not a true Spaniard'.[103] As usual with such examples, it is impossible to know whether the girl's remarks were anything more than bravado, or how representative she was, or even whether the incident happened at all, but the invaders, at least, believed that the issue was worthy of note. Indeed, in February 1810 an article in the French-controlled *Gazeta de Madrid* even argued that the Patriot propaganda machine had made a special effort to whip up support for the war amongst women as the best means of getting their menfolk to take part in the struggle.[104]

Also worth considering here is the riot. Throughout the period 1808–1810 such events were very frequent in Patriot Spain. In reality these were complex phenomena that had their roots either in intrigues within the Patriot élite or in popular hostility to conscription or taxation, but the rioters almost invariably dressed their actions up in claims that they were out to eradicate traitors in the Patriot leadership or put an end to threats to the security of the populace. As a good example here we might cite the serious riots that gripped Cádiz in February 1809. These are a subject to which we shall return at a later point, but, in brief, they were sparked off by fears among the city's civic guard that it was about to be sent to the front. The Voluntarios Distinguidos, as they were called, were determined to put a stop to this, but they could hardly come out and do so openly. Instead, then, they seized upon, first, the presence in the town of many French prisoners, and, second, the prospect that a battalion of foreign deserters was to be brought into the town as part of the garrison. Given these factors, it could be claimed that the city authorities were putting the populace in danger, and thus it was that the agitators made use of by the Voluntarios Distinguidos had no difficulty mobilising a crowd already radicalised by rising prices and some rather heavy-handed attempts to clamp down on such activities as gaming and prostitution. Nor was the crowd just male. As one French officer remembered, the rioters who made for the building in which he and his comrades were detained included various women who kept up an 'atrocious clamour' and tried to incite their fellow rioters to disarm the guard.[105] On one level, of course, the women concerned were but dupes of the Voluntarios Distinguidos, but it may safely be assumed their presence cannot just be explained by the latter's machinations. On the contrary, they also had their own concerns, not the least of which was personal safety (also important were the particular grievances of prostitutes and other street women who had been hit particularly hard by new police regulations, but even prostitutes have a legitimate interest in the presence of 'enemies within').

On occasion, then, women played their part by spurring on Spanish, British and Portuguese soldiers alike to fresh efforts, and putting pressure on the authorities to behave in a suitably patriotic manner. Played out in the context of daily life, such activity did not require much in the way of social status, but for anything else what was required was property and education. For women possessed of these advantages, however, it was possible to become involved in the war in an overtly political capacity. As we have seen, a tiny handful of Spanish women had penetrated social and political discussion in the years prior to 1808, and this development was to at least some extent stimulated by events thereafter. Let us begin here with the figure of Frasquita Larrea Aherán. Born in Cádiz in 1775, Larrea was the daughter of a merchant from Alava. Given a relatively good education, in 1796 she married a merchant of German extraction named Juan Böhl, and thereafter paid at least two visits to Hamburg to see his family. Comparatively speaking, then, this was a woman who was both widely read and widely travelled, as well as one of considerable independence of mind: though much impressed by the ideas of Mary Wollstonecroft, she conceived a fierce hatred of the French Revolution and Napoleon. Increasingly horrified by the disasters that were afflicting Spain under Charles IV and Godoy, she was therefore delighted by the news of the Motín de Aranjuez, from which it was an easy step to supporting the uprising and going on to join the legion of pamphleteers who were very soon waging war against the French with the pen rather than the sword.[106] By 1810, then, Larrea was the author of at least two patriotic harangues in which she on the one hand heaped obloquy on Napoleon and on the other lauded the Spanish armies to the skies. Living as she was in Chiclana, she was trapped by the French occupation of Andalucía in January 1810, but a safe-conduct issued by the invaders a year later allowed her to make her way to Cádiz, where, having successfully established herself as a political hostess—her home, indeed, became the centre of the most lively and influential *tertulia* in the camp of those opposed to the liberals who dominated politics in the city[107]—she eventually became involved in the so-called Junta de Damas de Cádiz (see below) and celebrated the end of the war by a further volley of pamphlets in which she hailed the newly returned Ferdinand VII as a messiah.[108]

Frasquita Larrea, then, was no liberal, while, initially at least, her sympathy for feminist ideals received little or nothing in the way of expression. Yet her devotion to the cause of *dios, rey y patria* cannot be denied, and in this respect she stands out very clearly as the very epitome of a female Spanish patriot. Nor was she the only example of the Iberian woman politicised. In some ways very different and yet in others very similar was María do Carmen Silva. Of Portuguese origin—she was born in Lisbon at some point in the 1780s—she became the lover of a Spanish army doctor named Fernández Sardina during the occupation of Portugal, and eventually escaped with him to Badajoz where he became one of the editors of the gazette published by the Junta of Extremadura. Following the fall of Badajoz in 1811 the couple somehow made their way to Cádiz, where Fernández Sardina launched the notorious *Robespierre Español.* An outspoken supporter of the revolution that had been unleashed by the convocation of the *cortes* of Cádiz, this eventually went too far, and, after a more-or-less rigged trial, Fernández Sardina was imprisoned for sedition. Left without any other means of support, and seemingly anxious to fight for the same cause as her husband, Silva immediately took over the job of editing the paper, in which capacity she emerged as a champion of the war effort and the cause of reform alike.[109]

Frasquita Larrea and María do Carmen Silva initially both involved themselves in the Patriot cause as individuals. However, they were not alone. In the hothouse atmosphere of the Cádiz of the *cortes,* it was, perhaps, inevitable that the many women of the élites who had either always lived there or taken refuge within its walls should have sought to elaborate structures that could stimulate female enthusiasm and integrate it into the war effort.[110] The idea was around from quite early in the war: in January 1809, for example, an anonymous proposal had reached the Junta Central for the establishment of a Real Hermandad Patriótica de Señoras whose task it would be to collect money for the war effort via a network of local committees.[111] However, notwithstanding the fact that this proposal received a warm welcome, there is no record of it being implemented, and it was not until the shattering blow constituted by the fall of Andalucía in January 1810 that the idea bore fruit. Amongst the many refugees who had reached Cádiz was the Marquesa de Villafranca. The daughter of the Condesa de Montijo, who had, as we have seen, for many years served as the secretary of the old Junta de Damas de Honor y Mérito, the marchioness was resolved to rebuild the old association in a new setting, and on 19 November 1811 duly held the first meeting of a new body entitled the Sociedad de Señoras de Fernando VII. Better known simply as the Junta de Damas, for the rest of the war this dedicated itself to, first, collecting funds for the war effort, and, second, clothing Spain's ragged army.[112]

Dissolved in 1814, this body had by the end of the war raised a total of 888,155 *reales* for the Patriot cause. Yet questions remain. In the first place it might well be asked why so much money proved so lacking in concrete results, the number of complete uniforms provided by the Junta in the end amounting to fewer than 2,000. And, in the second little attempt seems to have been made to mobilise even the women of Cádiz, the latter to the end of the war evidently regarding this last, according to their station, either as a burden or as a pleasant diversion; thus, we hear nothing of mass rallies or patriotic demonstrations.[113] This was not, then, the Unión de Mujeres Anti-Fascistas of the Spanish Civil War, but rather the tool of a tiny handful of élite women intent on reviving the debate on the position of women in society, in which respect it is significant that the manifesto which launched its proceedings did not so much call on women to show heroism as call on men to recognise that women were capable of showing heroism—indeed, more than that, had shown heroism.[114]

At every turn, then, the idea of a female population engaged wholeheartedly in the war effort is being open to question. Some women, albeit a tiny handful only, certainly took up arms, while others aided the Patriot war effort in an auxiliary capacity by raising money, contributing to the cause, encouraging their menfolk to show greater courage and devotion, helping to build fortifications, keeping the fighting men supplied with food and water, assisting the sick and the wounded, attending to the needs of prisoners of war, acting as 'scarlet pimpernels' or serving as propagandists, spies and couriers. All this is very true, and yet it is also very true of most other conflicts in the period from 1500 to 1800: in siege warfare, in particular, there were numerous precedents for what happened in Zaragoza and Gerona. Still worse, everywhere we find great confusion and ambiguity. What did the 'maid of Saragossa' really do in the war? Were the women involved in *la guerrilla* really heroic freedom fighters or were they rather bandits? Were women who passed information to the Allied forces doing so out of patriotism or rather earning a few pennies to keep starvation at bay? Was the Marquesa de Villafranca primarily an ardent opponent of the French or rather a champion of feminism (not, of course, that the one rules out the other)? And, finally, there is not just confusion but contradiction: hard though it might be to accept, many women remained aloof from the war effort and on occasion were actively opposed to it. Women, then, were certainly engaged in a struggle for survival, but, as we shall now see, it was a struggle that encompassed far more than simply fighting the French, and, indeed, a struggle in which fighting the French frequently figured not at all.

5

Survivors

That the Peninsular War was a major disaster for the peoples of Iberia is something that no objective observer could possibly deny. Commerce, industry and agriculture were paralysed; the country-side was stripped of all its resources by the contending armies; thousands of men, women and children were driven from their homes; large numbers of villages and farmsteads were burned to the ground; and many cities were left in ruins after terrible sieges. To the ravages of war, meanwhile, were added the forces of nature, whether these came in the form of repeated harvest failures or the onset of epidemics of such diseases as typhus and yellow fever. For the civilian population the result was suffering of a sort whose scale can be judged by the death rate to which it gave rise: Portugal lost as many as 150,000 dead, and Spain anything from 300,000 to 500,000. Amidst all these trials and tribulations, it hardly needs to be said that, along with children and the elderly, women were particularly vulnerable. Here, for example, is a scene that was witnessed by Schaumann at the Galician township of Manzanal:

> I looked into one of the huts. The fireplace was in the middle, and the smoke went whither it listed, up to the roof or out at the door. The fuel consisted of moist heath . . . the smoke of which makes the eyes smart horribly. The family in this particular hut consisted of a tall, old . . . witch and three ugly children, of whom two were suffering from a hectic fever. Everything was extremely dirty: their hair was matted together and they never seemed to have washed since the day of their birth. Round the

woman's neck hung a rosary. . . . She did nothing except sit over the fire, and shake with cold and . . . the whole place presented a picture of the most appalling misery.[1]

Such scenes, alas, were doubtless all too typical, and in consequence it may be assumed that for many women confronting the invader paled into insignificance beside the struggle for survival. However, the female population's response to the war was not just about putting bread on the table for themselves and their families. On the contrary, also discernible is a willingness on the part of at least some women to make use of the war to effect a change in their circumstances, this in some cases leading them to place even less weight on the duty to fight the invaders. In short, imagining the women of Spain and Portugal as patriotic heroines is distinctly misleading: heroines there may well have been, and that in very great numbers, but only in very few cases did they come in the guise of Agustina of Aragón.

Before considering how women reacted to the stresses and strains of war, we need first to consider the circumstances with which they had to contend in the wake of the French invasion. As we have seen, the vast majority of women had already been living in very precarious conditions prior to 1808, but these now deteriorated still further. Of these, the first, and possibly most important, was the very great impact that the war had on many forms of economic activity. With both the French and Allied armies eager for transport of any sort, for example, mules, oxen and carts were all swept up in the war effort, and this in turn meant that it became increasingly difficult to transport goods from one place to another, the problem being further increased by the ever increasing swarms of bandits. And, if goods could not be transported, migrant labour could not pass: with the roads unsafe for travel, the many communities in Galicia, Andalucía and Portugal who relied on the export of labour were progressively pauperised.[2] Setting aside such logistical difficulties, there was also the issue of the fighting itself. One should not, of course, think of Spain and Portugal being divided by the continuous trench lines of the First World War, but even so many centres of trade and industry found themselves completely cut off from their natural hinterlands.

Finally, with Iberia ever more impoverished, consumer demand (such as it was) could not but fall off very sharply (nor was it just a matter of industrial products here: just as badly hit were such cash crops as the hemp that was extensively cultivated in Granada). Added to these purely internal factors, meanwhile, were a number of external ones such as the break-out of revolution in Latin America in 1810, the activities of French privateers in the Bay of Biscay and the Mediterranean alike, and the blockade which the British imposed on all those ports controlled by the French. When William Jacob visited Seville in late 1809, then, he observed that the great tobacco factory was running at a mere fraction of its normal capacity, and the city's silk industry in a state of what appeared to be terminal decline.[3] Equally, passing through Málaga following his capture in the autumn of 1810, the British general, Lord Blayney, found its once busy port all but derelict.[4]

For thousands of women, then, sooner or later the war brought economic disaster as husbands or sons were thrown out of work, died of disease, or ran away to avoid conscription, or the workshops and domestic industry on which they themselves relied were brought to a standstill.[5] Catastrophic as it was, however, this development coincided with greatly increased pressure on the part of the state, whether Patriot or *josefino,* not to mention the imposition of ever heavier demands in money and kind on the part of the contending armies, demands, indeed, which were frequently passed on to the populace in the most inequitable of fashions. Thus, in areas occupied by the French, the new authorities' first move in almost every case was to demand large sums of money, such *ad hoc* measures later being replaced by a more regular system of taxation that even given the obvious difficulties faced by the officials tasked with its implementation, brought in up to four times the amount that had been raised by the pre-war administration; as for requisitions in kind, meanwhile, despite provisions that the populace was to be left with enough for its own needs, the demands involved were to all intents and purposes limitless.[6] Less well known, perhaps, are the sacrifices demanded of the inhabitants by the Patriot authorities, but these were no less great, culminating in 1813 in the imposition by the *cortes* of Cádiz of a new system of taxation known as the *contribución única.*[7]

Inflicted on a country that was for the most part desperately poor, these pressures were simply unsustainable. However, what made the situation infinitely worse was that the supply of food was falling steadily. Spain had since time immemorial been a net importer of grain, but it was now frequently very difficult to transport it much beyond the ports of its arrival. However, the shortfall could not be made up by an agricultural sector whose productivity had been extremely low at the best of times, and was now reduced still further: faced by a situation in which they stood to lose much of their harvest, the natural response of many large landowners was to let land go out of production (thereby greatly intensifying the squeeze on the hapless labourers who depended on them for employment), whilst in Extremadura in particular there are accounts of *guerrillas* putting such fields as had still been cultivated to the torch rather than see the food they represented augment the magazines of the enemy.[8] With consumption up and supply down, of course, there could be but one result in that prices soared. 'In the month of June [1812]', wrote one resident of Valladolid, 'things reached such a pass in this city that wagon loads of wheat and barley were being sold . . . at 1700–1800 *reales* and 900–1000 *reales* respectively. Since the very beginning of the world such prices have almost certainly never been known either in Castile or the rest of the Kingdom'.[9]

'Price spikes' of the sort described here were nothing new in the recent history of Spain: on the contrary, indeed, they recurred with depressing frequency. What made matters worse in this respect was that the soldiers of all nations showed no compunction in stripping the population of those few financial resources that they had managed to keep out of the hands of the tax collectors of both sides, resources that might otherwise have tided them over until the coming of better times. Such events as the sack of cities like Burgos and Badajoz represented utter destitution for their inhabitants—if an Irish private of the Twenty-Eighth Foot named Charles O'Neill struck it rich by uncovering a substantial cache of gold coins hidden in some old barrels, the family he took it from were left with little chance of surviving the war[10]—while petty theft was a constant problem: for example, William Lawrence describes how he and his comrades stole a cache of 7,000 dollars that had been buried in the cellar of a house in which they were billeted outside Lisbon. An extension of theft, meanwhile, was cheating: Bunbury, for example, recalls how an old woman with whom he lodged during his stay in Lisbon in 1813 was eventually ruined by the refusal of the authorities to pay the bills she had amassed in respect of the numerous troops who had been billeted in her house, while at Cea Buckham came across a case where an officer had bought a horse from a girl only to return it ten days later with a demand for the money he had paid for it to be returned in full on the grounds that it was not suitable.[11] Nor was it just money and valuables. Furniture, for example, was regularly broken up for use as firewood, and not just furniture but such items as doors, shutters, carts, looms and farm implements.[12] Whilst some soldiers shared such food they had with civilians, others had no compunction in stripping them of that as well: in the course of Masséna's retreat from Portugal, for example, Costello seized a loaf from an emaciated half-starved hag, and, despite the fact that she was 'almost cadaverous with want', while, on the eve of Vitoria, having first 'haversacked' some of his sheep, a group of soldiers stripped an old shepherd of 'a four-pound loaf, some cheese and about a quart of wine', the unfortunate man being reduced to tears.[13] So ingrained was the practice, it seems that even officers did not consider it beneath them: travelling from Lisbon to the Spanish frontier in the autumn of 1812 as a lieutenant in the Twelth Light Dragoons, for example, Hay describes how, stumbling on a flock of sheep near Nisa, he galloped into its midst, cut down a ram and then rode off with its bloody carcase slung across a saddlebow.[14]

Bad as all this was, it was not the end to the story. Thus, the poor also found many of the palliatives normally open to them either seriously reduced or swept away altogether. First of all, there was the issue of the commons. In many regions of Spain, part of the municipal lands had generally been set aside to provide the town councils with a regular rental income. Generally, let out in small lots at a reasonable rent, the plots concerned had provided large numbers of families with at least a degree of subsistence, but many town councils were in the course of the war forced to sell off considerable quantities of land as the only means of meeting the spiralling demands of the contending armies, the families who had hitherto lived off the commons in consequence being left to make shift as best they could, there being little hope that they could scrape together the money needed to buy their plots. Thus proletarianised, along with the rest of the agricultural populace, the people concerned could normally have turned to charity, but, with the vast majority of its religious houses either shut down altogether or struggling to obtain any income, the Church was in no position to meet the vastly increased demand for its assistance, while much the same was true of the propertied classes, many communities also being deprived of the source of employment which they represented by the fact that in many instances they fled provincial towns in favour of more comfortable havens such as Cádiz.[15] And, last but not least, in Patriot and *josefino* Spain alike, authorities concerned about internal security and the threat to public order introduced swingeing police regulations that made it much harder for the poor to make ends meet by engaging in such activities as taking in lodgers, becoming involved in prostitution or setting up as pedlars or market traders.[16]

All this, meanwhile, was inflicted amidst a landscape of the utmost devastation. Situated on the main road from the French frontier to Madrid, for example, Burgos was a spot seen by many French soldiers and the women who marched with them. Happened upon by many of them before they had had much experience of the Peninsular War, it appears to have made an indelible impression. 'Burgos' wrote Fée, 'had suffered a great deal from the war: many of the houses were abandoned, and the population appeared to be in a miserable state'.[17] Still more graphic, meanwhile, was the wife of General Junot:

> A desert in which there was nothing to be found but famine, ruin, despair and death . . . extended for four or five leagues in every direction from the town and surrounded it like a belt of misfortune. . . . As for the few inhabitants who remained, they no longer cared whether they lived or died . . . and wandered through the badly paved streets of the city like ghosts. . . . So mephitic was the stench that the plague could have been caught by breathing it alone.[18]

Also very bad were the much fought over regions in the vicinity of the Portuguese frontier. Writing of the area around Salamanca, then, Boutflower remarked, 'The country we pass through is highly fertile, but the corn is everywhere lamentably destroyed. The villages have been systematically plundered by the enemy, the churches destroyed and vast numbers of houses burned to the ground'.[19] Meanwhile, a pamphlet published as a guide to a panorama of the siege of Badajoz exhibited in London in 1813 makes much the same point. Thus: 'The surrounding country presents a scene of universal devastation. Not a tree or shrub relieves the melancholy waste, which appears still more deplorable from the remains of villages and extensive farm-houses, now in ruins, scattered in every direction. The constant warfare carried on in this part of Spain has destroyed the once beautiful face of the country, which was formerly well cultivated, and covered, in many parts, with large plantations of olive trees'.[20] And, finally, from much the same region comes this account of the village of Santa Marta: 'This wretched place was in a sad condition, for it had been occupied alternately by the French and English several times . . . and its resources were completely exhausted. Provisions were dear and scarce, and on every side poverty and want assailed you with imploring prayers'.[21]

The result of the collapse of society which all this amounted to was terrible indeed. In brief, entire communities were plunged into famine. Here, for example, is a scene encountered by an anonymous sergeant of the Light Division in an isolated farmhouse during Masséna's evacuation of Portugal in 1811:

> A large house . . . was discovered near the line of our route. Prompted by curiosity, several men turned aside to inspect the interior, where they found a number of famished wretches crowded together. . . . Thirty women and children had perished for want of food, and lay dead upon the floor, while about half that number of survivors sat watching the remains of those who had fallen. The soldiers offered some refreshment to these unfortunate persons, but one man only had sufficient strength to eat.[22]

If conditions for the civilian population probably reached their nadir in the course of this episode, from 1809 onwards scenes of horror could be encountered almost anywhere, whilst, with the situation worsened still further by the failure of the harvest of 1811, suffering again reached epic proportions in 1812, 20,000 people being reputed to have died of starvation in Madrid alone.[23]

Faced by disaster of the sort that we have detailed, women had a number of courses of action open to them.[24] In the most immediate term, they could take direct action to defend themselves and their families. One means of doing this in the past had been to take to the streets, and there were, in fact, a number of examples of such disturbances. In 1813, then, Bunbury was attacked at Celorico by villagers angered by a quarrel over billeting, and, more generally, the persistent misbehaviour both of the small parties of troops who were constantly passing to and fro and the inmates of a nearby British military hospital. This was quite a serious affair, Bunbury and his small group of fellow travellers only being able to beat off their assailants with some difficulty, but what is most notable about it is that women were well to the fore, one of them even biting off one of the fingers of Bunbury's servant.[25] Much more significant, meanwhile, were the events which took place in Cádiz in February 1809. What took place has been covered in considerable detail elsewhere, but, to reiterate, here too what one contemporary account termed 'the lowest representatives of the other sex' figured very strongly.[26]

If women took the lead in such riots, it was in part because, as we have seen, by long tradition women were afforded a greater degree of indulgence than men. To the expression of grievances, meanwhile, was added the defence of the community against the forces of the state, the assumption clearly being that they had a greater chance of securing a positive result. William Tomkinson, for example, was a cavalry officer who frequently found himself requisitioning forage on the frontiers of Portugal in the autumn of 1811:

> The procuring of forage through this winter . . . was attended with the greatest difficulty. . . . The peasants hid their straw with the greatest care, being the only chance of keeping what few oxen remained to them for the purpose of agriculture alive until the spring. They hid their straw behind stores of wood laid by for fuel, which two or three dragoons would remove with several hours' work, and possibly not find above three or four

> days' supply for three or four horses. The carrying it away was always attended with the complaints and lamentations of the women, who followed us out of the place saying . . . their oxen must now die.[27]

Of course, when such pleas failed, there was nothing to stop resistance from taking a more violent direction: during the retreat of Sir John Moore, for example, Schaumann recorded that, faced by demands that they hand over such food to some Spanish troops, the women of Manzanal 'raised a loud outcry . . . and, tearing their hair . . . endeavoured to defend their property tooth and nail', whilst earlier in the same campaign some soldiers of the Fifty-Second trying to break into a house which they had been assigned as a billet were confronted by an old woman clutching a match-lock musket, 'her hand shaking with age and fright'.[28] Before such tactics, meanwhile, British troops might even give way. Here, for example, is Frazer on the difficulties experienced in respect of the requisition of local guides in the campaign of 1813: 'In one place we had to fight all the ladies of the village. Of course, we lost our guide: there was no disputing the field with the Amazons'.[29]

Similar tactics were, no doubt also employed against French troops who entered Spanish villages looking for food or other assistance. However, given that the invaders were both grimmer in their general outlook, and less inclined to be lenient, it is unlikely that they achieved anything in the way of success. That said, something could still be achieved by means of quickwittedness. Thus, hearing that French troops were bearing down on their village, two young girls who were living in one of the larger houses in the place adopted the stratagem of putting the younger one into bed and making out that she had the plague, the result being that the soldiers who entered the house turned about and fled in panic![30]

It was not just in this fashion that women served family and community. As we have seen, in élite and popular culture alike, prior to 1808 women had played an important role as intermediaries in respect of dealings with authority figures, whether these were political or economic. Given the extreme pressures generated by the Peninsular War, this role now became doubly important. When suspected *afrancesados* were seized by lynch mobs in the Patriot zone, for example, it was often their wives who who took on the task of begging for mercy.[31] As the French army conquered more and more territory, for example, it became vital almost literally to win the hearts of the invaders. Thus, faced by an announcement that Joseph Bonaparte intended to visit their city, the new authorities that had been established in Málaga in the wake of French conquest in 1810 gave orders that the women of the town were to dress in their best, line every balcony along the main street and strew flowers in his path.[32] Meanwhile, just as the young Polish noblewoman, Maria Walewska, had effectively been expected to prostitute herself for her country when Napoleon entered Warsaw in 1806, so something of the sort may explain an incident that is supposed to have taken place at Granada in which 'one of the prettiest women of the town—a member of one of the best families in the province—supposedly wrote to King Joseph to request the favour of being allowed to visit him in his bed-chamber.[33] If this was the case, however, it was only an extreme case of behaviour that was just as visible in the Patriot zone. Indeed, here the practice was taken a stage further still, the *Diario Mercantil de Cádiz*, for example, complaining bitterly that the corridors of power had become overrun with 'a considerable number of well-known women' who had set themselves up as professional intermediaries and spent all their time 'intrigueing and seeking favours . . . whilst at the same time attempting to blacken and undermine all those who come with legitimate business'.[34]

On a more humble level, either individually or collectively, female intercession with the authorities was a frequent weapon in the hands of an increasingly desperate populace. For example, we find women petitioning the French authorities to release arrested family members, and travelling to the headquarters of *guerrilla* bands to secure the release of sequestered sons: as an example of the former, we may cite a petition from one Leonarda de Esparza imploring the French governor of Bilbao, General Thouvenot, to release her husband, Juan María de Iranzu, from imprisonment in Vitoria, while, as one of the latter, we have the mother of the future Spanish statesman, Ramón Santillán, successfully persuading the redoubtable Jerónimo Merino to let him return home after being swept up in a *leva* in his home town of Lerma.[35] Such approaches, moreover, were by no means always personal: in Málaga, for example, the French governor, Jean-Pierre Maransin, was on 15 August 1812 approached by a delegation of twenty women headed by none other than the wife of the head of the *josefino* civil administration who had decided to take advantage of the festivities being held to mark Napoleon's saint's day to appeal for clemency for the forty-four civilians who had been arrested in the wake of the city's temporary occupation by Spanish regular troops a month earlier.[36] And, finally, just to show that what applied on one side of the lines applied just as much on the other, when a small party of British troops pillaged a shop at Puente del Orbigo in December 1808, it was the women of the family who undertook the task of appealing to the first officers they could find for redress and protection.[37]

Interesting as all these incidents are, a wider guide to the situation of the female populace in the occupied regions in particular is provided by the papers of the *de facto* civil governor of Andalucía, the Conde de Montarco. In office from December 1810 till August 1812 Montarco was subjected to a veritable blizzard of petitions from the women living in his area of responsibility. For example, in May 1811 one Francisca de Acosta appealed for the payment of her widow's pension, whilst Manuela Rumbos, the widow of a tax official named Pedro García Miranda, complained that she was receiving only half the pension of three *reales* per day that she was supposed to receive, and asked that it be paid in full on account of the fact that she had become indigent.[38] Similarly in June 1811, Victorina Cuadrada appealed to Montarco to force the administrators of the Hospital de los Ríos to supply her with the dole of food to which she was entitled; María de Araceli Jiménez, the widow of the sub-prefect of Antequera, requested payment of the two months' salary that were customarily paid on death of an incumbent to aid with funeral expenses; and María Dolores Villapol reported that her husband, who was the administrator of national properties at Llerena, had been kidnapped by the insurgents and requested that his salary continued to be paid notwithstanding.[39] And, finally, in November 1811 María Trinidad Ferrer requested that her son be appointed to a vacant post in the tax administration in Seville; María Ruiz requested that she be granted a tobacco kiosk that had become vacant in recognition of the merits of her recently deceased husband, Eugenio Monteleón; and Mariá de la Salud Diéguez wanted Montarco to order that she be paid a sum of 160 *reales* that she had been left in a will.[40]

On all sides, then, women worked to better the conditions in which they found themselves. Yet in the end there was only so much that even the bravest and most determined women could do to defend their communities from the demands of the contending armies, the result being that many towns and villages were plunged into the utmost misery. Consider, for example, the state of a group of civilians seen on 1 January 1809 by Captain Alexander Gordon of the Fifteenth Light Dragoons:

> In the afternoon we passed through a large village which had been completely gutted by fire. The wretched inhabitants were sitting amidst the trifling articles of property they had been able to seize from the flames, contemplating the ruins of their homes in silent despair. The bodies of several Spaniards who had died of hunger and disease, or perished from the inclemency of the weather, were lying scattered around and added to the horrors of the scene. The village had been burned by some of our infantry.[41]

This was, perhaps, the extreme end of the scale, but even places which were spared any fighting did not escape the general poverty. At Portalegre, a Portuguese border town that never heard a shot fired in anger, for example, Patterson found himself in a billet that could scarcely be described even as being Spartan:

> My quarters were at the house of . . . an ancient maiden who had counted at least fifty winters. . . . A dilapidated hovel was the tenement of this . . . sybil, and scanty indeed was the accommodation offered within its . . . walls. Like those in the suburbs of all Portuguese towns, it was fraught with poverty, and, as if to harmonise more with its dingy *patrona,* all the appendages contained therein were of broken, filthy and crumbling materials. I was introduced by the aforesaid hostess into a chamber of

> sadness without the vestige of anything in the shape of furniture to garnish its interior with the exception of two broken chairs and a rickety table, tottering upon three legs gnawed into holes by vermin, hordes of which had long maintained undisturbed possession of the premises.[42]

To misery, meanwhile, was often added extreme danger, whether it was from bandit gangs, marauding troops or punitive expeditions, whilst a few areas—above all central Portugal—were hit by the imposition of scorched-earth tactics that not only deprived the inhabitants of the necessities of life but also forced them from their homes. Here, for example, is Schaumann on the sights that accompanied the retreat of Sir John Moore:

> Starving inhabitants of the country fled . . . past us with faces distorted by fear . . . and the weaker among them—the aged, the children and the women—laden with their belongings and perishing from fear, and from the rain, the storms, the snow and the hunger to which they had been exposed night and day, sank in the mire at our feet, imploring in vain for [the] help which we could not give even our own men.[43]

But, having once fled, what then? Flight might bring temporary relief from danger, but it was unlikely to be attended by economic security. In the course of the French invasion of Portugal in 1810, for example, provided with neither food nor shelter, many thousands of the civilians who at Wellington's behest retired behind the Lines of Torres Vedras died of starvation or exposure.[44] This was, of course, a particularly difficult moment—so many people fled before Masséna's army that a human catastrophe was inevitable—but only the most fortunate refugees could expect anything but the most precarious of existences. Typical enough, perhaps, was a situation encountered by the commissary, Richard Henegan, in December 1808. Thus, retiring into Portugal with Moore's surplus ammunition, at Pinhel he took shelter with a family that turned out to be Spanish. Consisting of a woman, her young daughter and the latter's baby son (the product of an illicit liaison with the girl's childhood sweetheart), this had been forced to flee its home in the province of Zamora after French troops had killed the woman's husband and only son in the wake of the battle of Medina de Río Seco.[45]

What is particularly interesting about this story is the manner in which the women encountered by Henegan were left not just pauperised, but entirely alone. That this was the fate of many women is all too evident, as witness, for example, the many references to such a fate that are encountered in the desperate requests for help that were regularly submitted to the authorities. Thus: 'Doña María de los Dolores Rivero, widow of Captain José de Vargas, begs that she might receive assistance on account of her miserable situation. . . . Doña María Luisa Laglé, widow of Captain José Romero, begs that she be assisted on account of her necessity. . . . Doña María Teresa Eguía, the wife of Captain Francisco de Paula Serrano, who was taken prisoner in the battle at Durango, acknowledges herself to be indigent and begs for assistance'.[46] However, it was not just widowhood that left women alone in an unfriendly world.[47] Given that it did not affect married men, conscription was not the issue that might have been expected here, but thousands of married men undoubtedly took to the hills with bandits or *guerrilla* bands, whilst others were arrested by the French as hostages or suspected Patriot sympathisers.[48] And, finally, there were plenty of wives who were simply abandoned by their husbands, a very good example here being the spouse of the leading *afrancesado* official, Blas de Aranza y Doyle, Carmen Langton Dillon.[49] The daughter of a prominent British merchant whose family had settled in Cádiz early in the eighteenth century, Langton was at least able to seek refuge in England, but many other women evidently had no one to whom they could turn for help at all: in the long list of petitions dealt with by Montarco, then, we find a María del Carmen Nájeras begging for the salary drawn by her husband, Jacinto del Castillo, to be made over to her on the grounds that he had not only abandoned her, but left her without any financial support, and an Ana María Miguéz demanding justice against three men whom she accused of having enticed her husband into a life of dissolution which had eventually led to his leaving her.[50]

Such was the desperate situation that most of the women of Spain and Portugal endured that it often mattered little whether a breadwinner was present or not. In consequence, whatever their precise situation, women were everywhere forced to make such shift as they could. At least some of the involvement in the Patriot war effort that is commonly ascribed to patriotism is therefore open to reassessment, this being particularly true of espionage: information, the population soon learned, was a commodity that could be bought and sold, and it is probable that it was sold at least as often to the French as it was to the British—during the blockade of Pamplona in 1813 the governor supposedly corresponded with the army that was planning to relieve the city by means of letters carried by a woman.[51] Equally we may assume that, if women acted as couriers for the Anglo-Portuguese army when it moved into the Basque provinces in the summer of 1813 after the men of the area had in general refused to act in such a capacity, they were moved not by greater patriotism but by the opportunity to make a little money.[52] However, much of what went on was little different from the efforts that poor women had made to sustain themselves prior to 1808. Prostitution flourished, then, and it seems likely that in areas that were much transited by the rival armies this became the lot of almost the entire female populace. Of one mountain village on the frontiers of Portugal, for example, Schaumann wrote: 'As regards morals, I must confess that in all my travels I have never come across such a Sodom and Gomorrah as that place was. The girls and women of the higher as well as of the lower classes were practically all disreputable. Pure virgins were rare'.[53] Also a common sight were women engaging in petty commerce in the streets. 'The number of poor . . . is very great, many dying in the streets of starvation', wrote John Patterson of a visit he paid to Madrid in the autumn of 1812. 'We met several persons, male and female, who had formerly been possessed of wealth and distinction, endeavouring to obtain a livelihood by selling different items of their dress and household furniture. Others, particularly women, whose looks bespoke their having lived in better days, were reduced to the miserable situation of vending pamphlets or small wares or keeping stalls or even hawking salt fish and vegetables through the city'.[54] Meanwhile, genteel poverty might also find relief in a more dignified fashion: one very much doubts whether the María de Carmen Jaén whom we meet setting up a private school in a room in the Calle del Amargura in Cádiz would have done anything of the sort had it not been for the war.[55]And, finally, there were always begging and prostitution, many observers noting the large number of women who were to be found amongst the mendicants who thronged the streets of the capital, whilst the swarms of girls who clustered round every British officer in sight when the Anglo-Portuguese army liberated Madrid in August 1812 speak, alas, of something far more mundane than patriotic enthusiasm.[56]

Faced by all this, it is extremely easy to understand that some women—many women even—sought salvation in throwing themselves on the mercy of the armies that had established themselves in their midst.[57] Such cases are numerous, indeed. On the eve of the evacuation of La Coruña in January 1809, then, 'a wonderfully pretty girl' from whom Augustus Schaumann bought some chocolate and cigars bewailed her fate should the French arrive and hinted very strongly that he should take her back to Britain with him.[58] Confirmed philanderer as he was, Schaumann did not take the girl away with him, but what is certainly true is that plenty of examples can be found of young women who ended up in either the French camps or their British counterparts, though the fact is that even this was a risky business: Donaldson, for example, has a sad story of a Portuguese girl who became the mistress of a British captain and accompanied him on all his subsequent campaigns, only to be reduced to complete penury when he was killed at the battle of Vitoria and his possessions auctioned off, as was the custom, to provide for the man's wife and family; cut dead by the other officers of the regiment, she was last seen by Donaldson 'struggling through the mud on the line of march with the shoes torn off her feet'.[59]

In this respect let us begin with the invaders. Here we first have several comments of a general nature. 'An immense number of the women of Seville', wrote Alexander Dallas, 'became attached to individuals of the French army. The number which left the town during the period of its stay there to accompany their lovers was computed at upwards of 4,000'.[60] Someone else who comments on the large number of women who took up with the French in Seville and in many cases accompanied them when they evacuated Andalucía in 1812 was the pharmacist, Sébastian Blaze, for whom the 'army of women' that was so great a feature of the retreat 'just proves that great disorder was occasioned by the war, the fact being that many of these women must have been married'.[61] On top of this, meanwhile, there were the scenes that many British soldiers witnessed when the Anglo-Portuguese army over-ran the French baggage train at Vitoria. To quote George Bell, 'Oceans of women—wives, actresses and nuns—were captured, but . . . all of them were treated with respect and allowed to follow their husbands and sweethearts as they found opportunity'.[62]

However, it is not just a question of generalisations. Setting aside the two or three case we have already met of Spanish women who were captured in the company of French officers, on 2 March 1813, for example, we find an officer of the Army of the North named Marenghien pleading with the commander in chief of that force to allow a young Spanish woman who had been living with him to stay with him rather than being forcibly returned to her parents, while Fantin des Odoards describes how in the last days of the campaign in Galicia he rescued a nineteen-year-old girl named María from a group of infantry who had seized her after killing her husband in a skirmish, and thereafter kept her with him in his billet.[63] And, finally, at Andújar Blayney encountered 'a beautiful Spanish girl of about eighteen, whose elegant shape, perfect head and bosom, shaded by . . . hair falling in graceful ringlets over her shoulders, might have entitled her to sit for the picture of Venus' who had supposedly thrown herself on the protection of the governor, General Blondeau, 'to escape the brutality of the brigands' and was now acting as his 'housekeeper'.[64]

In so far as the British army is concerned, whilst there is some suggestion that this force was rather less successful in terms of the number of indigenous women it acquired, the numbers were still considerable. What is true, however, is that, for the simple reason that the British army spent more time in Portugal than it did in Spain, the majority of those concerned were Portuguese rather than Spaniards. As a good example here, we might cite one Jaçinta Cherito, the daughter of the mayor of Campo Mayor who eloped with Drum-Major Thorp of the Eighty-Eighth Foot, the couple securing the girl's escape by blacking her face and disguising her as a coloured cymbals player, whilst, still more notorious, not least because it involved an irritated Wellington in a considerable amount of correspondence, was the case of William Kelly, a lieutenant of the Fortieth Foot who in 1813 ran off with and eventually married a young woman named Ana Ludovina Teixeira de Aguilar.[65] That said, there were also Spanish women involved, the prime example here being Juana de León, a young girl rescued from the sack of Badajoz who married Lieutenant Harry Smith of the Ninety-Fifth Foot, travelled with him for the whole of the rest of the Peninsular War and was eventually, as Lady Smith, commemorated by the town of that name in South Africa, though we might also mention 'a beautiful girl, lightly clothed', whom Captain John Cooke of the Forty-Third Foot saw rush from the crowd to join her lover, a British officer in a Portuguese light-infantry unit, as the last Allied troops were evacuating Madrid on 31 October 1812 (the officer, he said, tied a silk scarf around her neck, and placed her on his saddle-bow before him, later on finding her a soldier's greatcoat to wrap herself in).[66] Meanwhile, in both countries, for every girl who took up with a soldier, there were others who might well have done so had they not been prevented from doing so by one circumstance or another. Thus, in one instance a girl from Reinosa was at the last minute prevented from eloping with an artillery subaltern, whilst, in another, Benjamin Harris of the Ninety-Fifth Rifles might well have acquired a Portuguese wife but for the fact that the girl's parents, who were in this instance entirely happy with the match, insisted that he should both become a Catholic and desert from his regiment.[67] And, even when girls did not join forces with British soldiers, their interest in them was quite evident. If the magistrate's daughter whom Boutflower talked to at Cano was very ignorant, she still had an eye for the main chance: 'She overwhelmed me with questions as to the modes and customs of the English, and was particularly inquisitive as to the ceremony of matrimony: she had been taught to believe that an Englishman was by no means limited in the number of his wives'.[68] Near Toro, meanwhile, one British officer found himself the subject of the Spanish custom known as the *piropo*. Thus: 'A fine woman of about 20 years . . . passed much nearer to us than the rest and, attentively regarding my big friend, Tom, exclaimed, '*Muy guapito!*' ('What a very fine fellow!')'.[69]

The trials and tribulations of war, then, made association with soldiers an attractive option: if a young girl named Eufemia das Neves who had been separated from her family during the retreat to the Lines of Torres Vedras first placed herself under Schaumann's protection and almost immediately allowed herself to be seduced by him, it is scarcely surprising.[70] Yet it was not just a matter of food and shelter. From the very beginning war offered the women of Spain and Portugal both an economic opportunity and a chance to make a break with lives that offered them absolutely nothing.[71] Hardly had the Spanish armies begun to take the field in 1808, then, than they were swarming with campfollowers. Issued by General Castaños at his then headquarters of Utrera on 27 June 1808, the following order is a case in point:

> I have regretfully noted the many excesses given rise to amongst the troops on account of their criminal association with the prostitutes who every day flock to the army. . . . These are a serious affront to the holy religion which we profess . . . and the fatherland which we hope to liberate, not to mention in every way contrary to discipline. Meanwhile, the consequences have already become all too clear. As well as provoking God's anger in the most extreme fashion, these women weaken the soldiers, coarsen their conduct and lessen their readiness . . . whilst at the same time placing them on a level with the French. . . . I therefore command that all women of the sort referred to should be barred from the proximity of the troops, and, further, that all those who are currently living with the army should be immediately conducted to the house that used to belong to Don José Romero in the Calle de Sevilla of this city of Utrera so that they may receive due punishment.[72]

Such denunciations, of course, are far too sweeping, the women of whom Castaños complained undoubtedly also including large numbers of peasant women who looked to do no more than sell their produce to the soldiery.[73] In one sense, however, such distinctions do not matter. Whatever they were selling, the women concerned had gone to the camps for reasons that were essentially economic. Yet the possibility that other factors were present cannot be denied. Consider, for example, the following popular song from the region of Salamanca:

> Ah, ah, ah, ah, ah, ahhh . . .
> I ride with a lancer, a-perching on his lance:
> Is it that he wants to take me to France?
> My lover is a lancer of Don Julián:
> If he loves me a lot, I love him all I can.[74]

Just as interesting, meanwhile, is the fact that there was also interest in plenty in British and French soldiers virtually from the very moment that they appeared in the Peninsula. Here, for example, is Alexander Gordon on his experiences in La Coruña in the autumn of 1808:

> The females in the houses where we were billeted often visited us in the morning before we got up to ask us how we had passed the night and to bring us our chocolate: they then entered into conversation, and sometimes extended their visits to such an extent that we were obliged to request them to retire.[75]

Meanwhile, according to his own account at least, sent to Portugal with Junot's forces in 1807 Oyon found himself the subject of a great deal of attention from successive young women, not, however, that he was disposed to take this very seriously: 'A love letter means no more to a Portuguese girl than a greetings card: not having any recreation other than engaging in dalliances from their window sills, they amused themselves in the same fashion as French girls would when out for a stroll'.[76] Moreover, this interest continued to appear over and over again even in areas where life remained relatively comfortable for the propertied classes—areas, in short, where despair was not paramount: having finally got back to Lisbon in April 1809 in the wake of his departure from Moore's headquarters with the British army's surplus ammunition, Henegan encountered two lieutenants whose acquaintance he had made during the voyage out from England, both of whom were happily engaged in a series of amatory adventures in which it appears that they were as often seduced by local women as they managed to seduce them themselves.[77]

What, however, are we to make of all this? In brief, for once Bonapartist propaganda appears to have had some basis in fact in that, encouraged, perhaps, by French posturing—a good example is a much published decision on the part of General Junot as governor of Lisbon to release a girl who had been imprisoned in a convent in the wake of a foiled elopement[78]—all over Spain and Portugal women were throwing off their chains: not for nothing did a range of conservative ecclesiastics express outrage at the 'immodesty' that the war had in their eyes provoked in many women, in some cases even going so far as to claim that the constant disasters experienced by the Patriot cause were the fruit of divine retribution for such wickedness.[79] Though it is worth noting that here and there we can find cases of women desperate for a return to a lost normality—a good example is a girl from Burgos named Teresa Negreruela who petitioned the town council of that city with the request that it pay her father the salary owing to him as a municipal employee as she would otherwise be denied a dowry[80]—that gender and even generational relations had been thrown into turmoil is certainly suggested by the archives. For example, 'Juan Parra, resident of Rota, petitions in respect of the problems he has been having with his wife, María Aldana, and requests that she be brought to her senses and admonished for her conduct. . . . Being unwilling voluntarily to re-unite herself with her husband, Miguel Rodríguez, María Manuela Brava . . . requests a judicial separation. . . . Doña Rita Cardero and her three sisters lay out the cruelty with which they have been treated by their parents and request permission to remove to the house of Doña Leonor Valderrama y Estrada under the direction of some magistrate or other person of authority'.[81] Rather more open to debate though they are, the French memoirs are also of interest. Here, for example, is Heinrich von Brandt: 'Although women, especially the mature ones, bitterly rebuked the French for their lack of religion and for their insatiable appetites . . . on occasion during our wanderings we had the agreeable experience of meeting ardent francophiles, especially young brides with old husbands'.[82] One such, perhaps, was an attractive young woman from Rota named Margarita who was married to a man much older than she was. Thus, part French in origin, she spent the years of occupation surrounded by veritable crowds of admirers, among them Captain Grivel of the Sailors of the Guard. 'One of the prettiest women in Andalucía', he writes, '[Margarita] lived in a charming villa at the entrance of the town, and entertained many guests. Officers of the highest rank made it their duty to call upon her and pay her homage'.[83]

Not all women who took up with the invaders necessarily went to war. On the contrary, many relationships were evidently rather conducted wholly in the context of garrison life.[84] Though it may be wondered whether what is described is rather prostitution, or, indeed, constitutes nothing other than the fruits of an old man's imagination, of such love affairs the invaders' memoirs are full.[85] Here, for example, is Charles Parquin:

> At Salamanca my duties as adjutant obtained for me excellent quarters in the house of a beautiful Spanish noblewoman, Doña Rosa de la N., whose husband, a colonel in the Spanish army, had died two years previously. Like any widow who still retains a touch of vanity, she had instructed her maid to say she was twenty-five. . . . But this little lie, if indeed it was one, was not at all necessary for . . . Doña Rosa was one of the most enchanting women I have ever seen. . . . She had no children and lived alone with her servants in a house where comfort and even luxury were clearly in evidence. Mine were clearly very good quarters; I could have had none better. Every evening I would spend an hour or two by the fire with my hostess. I had to avoid politics in our conversation as Doña Rosa, who was as proud as any Spaniard could be, would not tolerate contradiction. In the end I persuaded her to banish politics from our conversation. . . . Later on, as one can imagine, I did not stop there. I made further requests and, in short, I was happy, very happy indeed.[86]

It was not, of course, just French officers who enjoyed such liaisons. In the British army, a comparable sexual athlete was probably Augustus von Schaumann, who appears to have made a point of flirting with every girl he ever met, and in many cases carried matters to their logical conclusion, as in the summer of 1810 when he had an affair with a fifteen-year-old girl from the village of Mangualde named María: 'The girl was perfectly built, with beautiful chest development, snow-white teeth, [a] delightfully small mouth, black and fiery eyes, full of voluptuousness, and the daintiest of hips', he recalled. 'Even in our love-making she always retained a certain modesty, and at the first cockcrow she would flee from me'.[87]

In the case of all the many relationships that we have been looking at that involved representatives of the *grande armée,* an obvious question presents itself. In brief, to what extent did a willingness to get into bed with the enemy suggest an acceptance of his principles? This, however, is something that is very difficult to answer. Some of the women concerned were certainly drawn from those elements of society that had been most open to the influence of the Enlightenment, and, as such may have been drawn to the cause of the invaders, but there is, alas, nothing to show that the *grandes dames* of sexual fraternization, including most notably, Joseph's principal mistresses, the Marquesa de Montehermoso and the Condesa de Jaruco, were motivated by anything other than opportunism. Indeed, in the case of the Condesa de Jaruco there is clear evidence that this was so: in 1808 the lady in question was in desperate financial trouble.[88] Still worse, it transpires that at least some of the élite women who actually married senior French officers were acting at the behest of their families, and were therefore not collaborators at all but rather the victims of traditional marriage diplomacy.[89] Given that only two cases—the one a woman named Joaquina de Urdaiba who had a considerable number of the inhabitants of Oñate vaccinated against smallpox at her own cost, and in consequence received the thanks of the French administration, and the other the Condesa de Ega, a leading member of Portuguese society who displayed such enthusiasm for the French cause that she became known as the 'citizen aristocrat'[90]—have been identified of something that resembles ideological collaboration on the part of a member of the female population, it seems likely other issues were far more important.[91]

Whatever the truth of the situation, such *afrancesamiento* as existed in the ranks of France's conquests does not appear to have been especially hardy. Here, for example, is William Surtees on a group of women taken in a skirmish at San Millán on 18 June 1813: 'Along with the captured baggage were a number of Spanish ladies who had been attached to the French officers to whom it belonged, but they did not appear over faithful to their protectors, for most of them, I believe, preferred remaining in the hands of their captors to being forwarded after their beaten and now ill-provided former companions. Such is generally the fidelity to be expected from that sort of people'.[92] Rather less supercilious but just as telling, meanwhile, is a passage from the journal of Thomas Browne:

> I have heard that upwards of 500 Spanish damsels passed into the civil branches of the service. . . . These fair ladies were speedily reconciled to this change in their position. . . . They were found laughing and singing along the whole line of march, perched for the most part on the panniers that were slung over the mules.[93]

For many women, then, the war was something to be exploited, not the least of its joys being the ability that it afforded of wearing comfortable male attire, Cooke remarking, for example, on the fact that many of the women who became the lovers of French soldiers 'travelled about . . . clad in the uniform of Polish lancers or hussars, splendidly embroidered, with crimson trousers made very wide in the Cossack fashion'.[94] Meanwhile, for others it was something that might even be enjoyed, at least in its lighter moments. Thus, the memoirs of the period are full of references to women having fun and relishing a time that was marked both by an increase in personal liberty and a much wider range of stimuli than had been available prior to 1808, this being particularly so of those corners of the Peninsula which escaped the worst of the conflict. Of these, the place of which we know most is Cádiz.[95] Here, for example, are the memories of Thomas Bunbury of the Portuguese Twentieth Line in respect of the family of one of his fellow officers:

> The senior major was married, and his wife and four grown-up daughters, who were rather fine-looking girls, resided with

> him. I was a great favourite with the old couple, who used to regard me in the light of a son, while the girls esteemed me as a brother. They were sad romps and . . . I generally came off . . . with my clothes nearly torn from my back. To the neighbours it must have appeared sometimes that we were going to turn the house out of the window.[96]

Also significant, perhaps, is the same author's account of an incident he witnessed in San Fernando (the chief settlement of the main part of the Isla de León):

> The Spanish ladies are celebrated for their beauty and *salero.* I can only translate this term by our word 'piquancy'. . . . I was one day at the Adjutant-General's office . . . when I heard a great noise outside. On going to see what was the matter, I found a beautiful creature, the niece of the Marchioness of Astorga, endeavouring to mount my charger. . . . In those days side-saddles were unknown in Spain, and the . . . black silk dress then universally worn . . . was not suited to equestrian efforts, and proved very insufficient to conceal the effects of her exertion. . . . The marchioness was sitting on a stone bench, waiting for the carriage which was to convey herself and her niece to Cádiz . . . [and] said to her, 'Dearest Pepita, you are such a mad girl: what will these Englishmen think of you?'. . . . Giving the horse a slight tap with her whip, [the young lady] coolly remarked, 'As I do not intend to marry [any] of them, it is of very little consequence'.[97]

The young women mentioned by Bunbury may possibly have been especially bold spirits, but even so there seems to have been a general determination on the part of the female members of the propertied class, at least, to make the most of their opportunity:

> We had here free access to Spanish society. There were five or six houses open every night where grand *tertulias* were held. . . . At these *soirées* there is a long saloon where dancing is kept up with great spirit, and another where a long gambling table is crowded with fashionable males and females, all eagerly engaged in this demoralising amusement; nay, you might have

> seen . . . young misses as busy as the others, and their mammas engaged in the ball-room. . . . As the evening closes the gentlemen invite the parties of ladies to join them in a glass of some cooling drink in the shops which are fitted up with tables and look like coffee rooms, where ices, iced water, iced punch and confections of all kinds are to be had.[98]

Conditions in Cádiz were particularly conducive to making the war something of a pleasurable experience for at least some women, but even in the provinces there were moments of enjoyment. Consider, for example, the somewhat rumbustious dances organised by Wellington's officers, a good start here being afforded by a passage respecting an evening entertainment put on for the mayor of the Portuguese town of Meda:

> Major White, finding his host and family very obliging, was desirous to give them an entertainment and to please the two daughters, each about 20 years of age, invited all the officers . . . to a ball and had the band in attendance. It was rather a strange sight to see so many men dancing together, but everyone seemed determined . . . to keep up the affair with spirit. . . . The whole went off remarkably well to the great delight and gratification of the *capitan mor,* his wife and daughters. The young ladies joined us and were much charmed with the animation . . . of our country dance and no wonder, for their country dance is the most stupid monotonous concern imaginable.[99]

Such opinions are, of course, only to be expected in the British memoirs, yet it is difficult to believe that, even if their own entertainments were not quite so inferior as this suggests, the women of the many little towns and villages which temporarily became the headquarters of one regiment or another were completely impervious to the fresh faces and escape from routine which such visits offered. To quote Kincaid, 'We invited the villagers every evening to a dance at our quarters. . . . We used to flourish away at the bolero, fandango and waltz and wound up . . . with a supper of roasted chestnuts. Our village belles . . . made themselves perfectly at home'.[100]

Meanwhile, if the various social events that were occasioned by the presence of British troops were exciting for the younger members of society, for older women, and particularly widows, having guests in their homes could make for a pleasant change. Billetted one night at Ituera in the home of a blind woman of about sixty, Kincaid describes her as being 'as merry as a cricket', and as attempting to amuse her guests by 'chanting "Malbrook" and other ditties with a voice that at one time might have had a little music in it, but had then degenerated into the squeak of a penny trumpet'.[101] As witness the following passage from the correspondence of William Keep in respect of a brief stop that he made in a small village near San Sebastián, nor was the experience so terrible for young girls:

> At a hamlet with a few houses . . . my active servant, Robert, got me a good dinner in a billet . . . in a secluded farm house. . . . After this repast, two very pretty girls about sixteen and eighteen favoured me with their company, why or wherefore it was impossible to tell, their pretty tongues . . . being quite unintelligible to me. . . . I was left entirely to guess who . . . they were, but my eyes convinced me they were extremely attractive. . . . These girls in this sequestered part of the coast, it is to be supposed, had never before seen . . . redcoats at all; their fancies were pleased, perhaps at the sight of our first approach, and one under their roof was an object of such curiosity to them that they couldn't resist its gratification. . . . As we could not speak a single word to each other . . . you will wonder how we amused ourselves . . . but they danced and sang to entertain me, having a tambourine for the music. . . . After the dance a large trunk was opened, and its manifold treasures of lady's apparel, etc., displayed to my wondering gaze with marks of trepidation, tender looks, etc., which unluckily I could only meet with responsive nods of satisfaction.[102]

It is to be hoped that the two sisters who dressed up for Keep did not go on to fall out over him in the same manner as two cousins in Llerena who became so furiously jealous in respect of William Swabey that one ended up stabbing the other.[103] Be that as it may, given that all this is a very long way from the formality and downright seclusion that had already been in steady retreat in 1808, the Peninsular War may therefore be said to have played a major role in accelerating the pace of social change in Spain and Portugal.[104] At all events there seems no reason to doubt that for many women the departure of British regiments was a source of sincere regrets. Here, for example, is the account of the anonymous 'soldier of the Seventy-First' of the day that he and his comrades left the village in which they had spent the winter of 1812–13: '[The] morning we marched, the town was deserted by its inhabitants, who accompanied us a good way, girls weeping or running into the ranks to be protected from their parents, and hanging upon their old acquaintances, parents tearing away and scolding their children'.[105] Meanwhile, plenty of women were also experiencing an expansion in their areas of responsibility. Though there is no evidence readily accessible of this tendency, it is clear that as craftsmen and artisans fell victim to want or disease, so their widows must in at least some instances have attempted to secure their income by taking over the family business themselves. Once again, of course, there was nothing new in this development as such, but it cannot but be suspected that one effect of the war was to increase its frequency, just as the war certainly increased the pressure on those few women who had become involved in such issues as poor relief: in Madrid, for example, the female section of the Sociedad de Amigos del País found itself struggling to cope with a situation that had by 1812 collapsed into outright famine with nothing but the support of a *josefino* régime that was all but bankrupt.[106] Meanwhile, one area where we do have plentiful evidence of greater female involvement in matters economic is estate management, the correspondence of such figures as Montarco being full of petitions from female representatives of the landed classes asking permission to sell off one portion or another of their estates so as to raise the money needed to meet their share of the dues exacted by the French.[107] To take just two examples from the autumn of 1811, then, such requests were received from both a Manuela Bonifaz and a Beatriz Manuel de Villena.[108] Meanwhile, on issue after issue pertaining to the demands which French occupation imposed on the estates of the propertied classes, we find women corresponding with the authorities: in June 1811 the Marquesa de Salar asked that a contribution of wheat and barley that had been levied on an estate belonging to her patrimony at Santaella be lifted on the grounds, first, that the estate concerned was in a state of complete abandon, and, second, that she was quite unable to meet any such demand; in December 1811 Josefa Victoria Bernuy petitioned Montarco asking to be paid the money owing to her for a large consignment of timber she had supplied for the construction of the flotilla of small craft that was built for a putative amphibious attack on Cádiz; and in January 1812 the Marquesa de Benameji requested that substantial amounts of foodstuffs which she had sent from an estate at Alcalá la Valle to the French garrison of Ronda should be discounted against future contributions.[109] Nor did these preoccupations come to an end with the departure of the French, women also being prominent in the many attempts that were made to secure compensation from the Anglo-Portuguese authorities in the last months of the war: in November 1813 we find one María Francisca Martín demanding payment from Wellington for 227 *fanegas* of wheat and twenty-one *fanegas* of chickpeas whose harvest she claimed she had lost in the battle of Salamanca.[110]

In embarking on these transactions and other negotiations, women were clearly acting in the capacity of heads of households.[111] On occasion, however, it was not just money that was at stake. Consider, then, the case of Pascuala Alonso. The wife of a petty functionary in Zaragoza, Alonso had lost her husband when he was lynched on 1 February 1809 on trumped-up charges of hoarding, and had then been flung into prison along with her young son and a servant named Teresa Pérez. Sadly, the boy had then died of disease, but Alonso had refused simply to accept her fate. On the contrary, following the fall of Zaragoza, she applied to the French for justice and demanded the rehabilitation of her husband. Feeling unable to deal with the matter himself, the commander of the French forces in Aragón, General Suchet, passed the case to the city's high court, the latter eventually declaring the man to have been innocent of all guilt. How far such an exoneration would have been of use in the wake of the French evacuation is a moot point, but that is by-the-by: if the taint of treason never left the family, the person at fault was certainly not Pascuala Alonso.[112]

To conclude, then, the women of Spain and Portugal's experience of the Peninsular War was in many respects extremely negative: impoverishment, flight, disease, starvation, bereavement and death were all commonplace, whilst, as we shall see in a later chapter, the soldiers of every army engaged in the struggle routinely engaged in sexual harassment and, on occasion, rape. Indeed, fear stalked the land. On outpost duty in Extremadura, for example, the cavalryman William Swabey had a telling experience: 'The house we left at Santa Marta belongs to a most interesting family, a widow and two daughters, who, on seeing the troop retiring, were in the utmost distress, uncertain whether they should go to the mountains or wait the approach of the French'.[113] That said, many very sad individual cases aside, helpless victims the female part of the population most certainly were not: on the contrary, on all sides we see women demonstrating considerable resourcefulness in what had increasingly become a struggle for survival, and even turning the war into something which they could exploit to make a bid for a better future or simply enjoy for its own sake. In recognising this last tendency in particular of course, we are implicitly rejecting the notion that all women flung themselves into the war against the French: to the extent that the female population had any interest in matters political at all, it was frequently ready to cast loyalty to the Patriot cause aside when its own goals could best be served by collaboration.[114] In short, whilst it might be pleasant to believe that every woman of the Peninsula was a potential Agustina of Aragón, it is probably more accurate to see every one of them as a potential Marquesa de Montehermoso.

6

Virgins

Let us begin this chapter with a story. In the first years of the nineteenth century a young nun named Teresa was growing up in a convent at Salamanca. Deprived of her parents at an early age, she had been given shelter by the nuns, and since then had been struggling to adjust to the environment in which she found herself. On one level she was not unhappy. The nuns had been kind to her, and she believed in God; indeed, sometimes she was even certain that He wanted her to give her life to Him. But she also knew that there was a world beyond the walls of the convent, a world that was exciting and mysterious and filled her with a strange sense of curiosity. In her mind, then, there was much tension, and increasingly the young nun and the young girl had come into conflict with one another: hence the scoldings for daydreaming that Teresa was getting on what sometimes seemed a daily basis. And then suddenly Spain was at war, and Salamanca full of soldiers: first Frenchmen, then Spaniards and finally red-coated Britons, including a particularly handsome young officer who one morning came knocking at the convent gates to enquire about making use of the convent as a hospital. Such, more-or-less is the beginning of the 1959 film, *Miracle,* this telling the story of how Teresa falls in love with the British officer and literally throws aside her habit to run out into the night and elope with him. What follows is a complicated tale, but, in brief, Teresa becomes separated from her lover and takes up with a band of gypsies. Discovering by chance that the young man (or so she believes) is dead, in her grief she rejects God entirely, denounces Christianity as a fraud, and leaves Spain and becomes a famous singer. What we have, then, is a story that, so far at least, is strongly anti-clerical. Thus, trapped into an unnatural way of life against which she is soon in a state of rebellion, Teresa is, for all its tragedy, liberated by the Peninsular War and enabled to find her true destiny, whilst, having become a military hospital, her convent is literally thrown open to the world and the nuns compelled to make a more useful contribution to society.[1] Excruciating though *Miracle* is, it nonetheless immediately provides us with an obvious starting point for this chapter. In brief, how did the Barefoot Carmelites, the Poor Clares and the rest respond to the greatest crisis in their history prior to the Spanish Civil War?

Let us begin by setting the scene. In 1808 there were about 18,000 nuns in Spain and perhaps another 7,000 in Portugal (the nearest precise figures that can be obtained are those of the Spanish census of 1797 and its Portuguese counterpart of 1765; these give totals of 24,471 and 11,428 respectively, but in the latter case recruitment had been considerably cut back by the reformist administration of the Marques de Pombal, while in Spain various factors had slashed the number by as much as one third).[2] Exactly how many separate orders made up these numbers, or how many communities they lived in, has proved impossible to establish, but Spain alone possessed twenty-nine of the former and 1,122 of the latter, whilst the nunnery was a prominent feature of almost every town and city: Seville had thirty-two, Burgos twenty, Lisbon and Barcelona eighteen apiece, Badajoz nine and Ecija eight, whilst few places of any size had none at all. As for the size of the different communities, taking the province of Valladolid as an example, we find that there were thirty-six separate convents with a total of 689 fully professed nuns, including 228 Franciscans, 162 Dominicans, eighty-eight Augustinians, seventy-two Bernardines, forty-nine Carmelites, thirty-six Trinitarians, thirty Brigidines and twenty-four Capuchins, this giving an average for each house of just over nineteen (there were, in addition, 820 lay dependants, including 111 servants, but, interestingly, only six novices).[3] What, however, did these communities stand for, and what role, if any, did they play in society? The first thing to say here is that they were in no respect a popular institution. In so far as their composition was concerned, although there were exceptions—in Portugal, for example, a leading spirit in a convent that was founded in Vila

Pouca da Beira in 1780 was Sister Genoveva Maria do Espiritu Santo, a young peasant girl who according to tradition was so horrified by an incident in which the town's parish church was vandalised that she was impelled to embark upon a campaign to establish a new religious community in reparation for what had occurred[4]—they were beyond doubt highly élitist. Women from the poorer classes might find shelter within their walls as servants or lay sisters—drudges in either case—but to enter the cloisters proper in most orders usually required a substantial dowry that by the 1780s generally ranged from 9,000 to 16,000 *reales* (by contrast, marriage dowries averaged around 3,500).[5] The result, of course, was that convents became bastions of the rich, with many nuns being recruited from the aristocracy: in Asturias, for example, the first three Marqueses de San Estebán contributed no fewer than seven daughters to the region's convents, while several aristocratic widows are known to have used them as a form of retirement home).[6] Indeed, according to William Dalrymple, in one convent he visited in Salamanca in 1774, practice was converted into principle. Thus: 'The nuns are women of family, and none but those who can prove their nobility are admitted'.[7]

The association between the nunnery and privilege was reinforced by a number of different factors. In the first place, there was the issue of occupation. Over the centuries repeated attempts had been made to found orders that would in one way or another reach out to the community, whether by turning the convents into centres of teaching, poor relief and health care, or by sending nuns out into the world to live and work amongst the poor. Yet in Spain and Portugal alike these initiatives had proved stillborn with the result that all female religious had been restricted to a life of prayer and contemplation and shut up in their convents: not only was the idea of large numbers of sisters operating in the community independently of any immediate male control profoundly worrying, but, precisely because women were seen as being so inherently sinful, it followed that nuns needed to shun society. Not until 1804, then, do we see anything resembling Saint Louise de Marillac's wildly successful Sisters of Charity and even then we are talking about nothing more than one tiny community based in Barcelona.[8]

For this enclosure of the nun, however, the Spanish Church was to pay a heavy price. In the first place, precisely because they knew that nuns would not have to engage in work which they regarded as menial and degrading, the wealthy were encouraged to continue incarcerating their surplus daughters. And, in the second, unable to show that they made any concrete contribution to society, the female religious orders became the target of ever increasing levels of hostility, and that on many different levels. Among educated groups influenced by the Enlightenment, there was a strong feeling that nuns were mere parasites while among the populace stories were rife of good living and immorality alike: even today there are, as Higgs points out, 'numerous Portuguese desserts and cakes with names like "Nun's Delight"'.[9] How justified these criticisms were is another matter. Genuine scandals do seem to have occurred from time to time in the form of love affairs between nuns and their confessors, but it may be assumed that stories of nunneries that were little more than brothels were wildly exaggerated.[10] However, a far more pervasive issue was a general air of *laissez faire* that saw many orders move further and further away from the ideals that had inspired their foundation. Both convents as a whole and the cells allocated to individual nuns became characterised by their comfortable furnishings and high standards of decor (more than one convent came to house impressive collections of art, for example); inmates were allowed to keep large quantities of personal possessions, to wear richly ornamented habits made of the finest cloth, to live in *de facto* family units with aunts, sisters, cousins and other acquaintances who had entered the convent with them, and to receive frequent visits from friends and relations; and convent kitchens became a byword for their cuisine.[11] Also clear is the fact that, often being very wealthy, the orders enjoyed the services of many servants: in Asturias in 1797 the region's 196 nuns were looked after by no fewer than ninety-two domestics, this being a ratio that also appears to have been on the increase (in 1766 there had been 216 nuns but only seventy domestics).[12] As for the daily round, it was scarcely onerous: whilst the office was generally complied with, many nuns seem to have spent their free time, not praying and studying the scriptures, but engaging in such crafts as embroidery and, yes, making confectionary.[13] Meanwhile, for those who were so inclined, it was possible to follow up interests in science, music, history or literature.[14] All in all, then, it was generally a very comfortable life, and one that left the nunneries wide open to attack: in Portugal, as we have seen, Pombal placed many restrictions on the admission of new postulants, while in Spain Charles III ordered a series of full-scale investigations that on occasion produced serious attempts at renovation.[15]

What, though, does all this say about the nuns themselves? Brought up as many of them were in atmospheres of intense religiosity in which attendance at church was central to their daily life, it should not be wondered at if some of them took the veil in a spirit of genuine devotion, and it may well be that this religiosity lasted into their lives as nuns, though rarely with the flamboyance of the past (in this respect, it has to be said that by 1808 it was a long time since a nun had achieved real prominence as a writer on matters spiritual). For others, however, it may be surmised that enthusiasm was lacking, that they entered upon their vocations, in fact, in much the same spirit as they might have entered upon some arranged marriage.[16] Yet in truth their fate was not so very bad. On the contrary, becoming a nun even offered certain benefits, whether they were freedom from physical abuse and the dangers of childbirth, access to learning, or the chance of rising to positions of greater or lesser status and authority. For at least some women of intelligence, indeed, the cloister was not a prison at all, but rather a space in which they could find real fulfilment. To quote Silvia Evangelisti, 'Removed from society, convents acted as catalysts for female freedom and individual development. No other institution could be compared to them. They were unique'.[17]

For a few nuns entering a convent might even be a career choice. Herewith, for example, Thomas Bunbury on a young Portuguese woman he met at various *tertulias* after the war:

> A canon from the cathedral at Lamego, with his niece (generally supposed to be his daughter) was always at these parties. . . . The young lady was good looking, with light hair, [and] went by the name of *da lorda,* a sobriquet she had acquired from having been a great favourite of Lord Wellington's, who was so

> pleased with her performance on the pianoforte at the convent of Viseu, where his lordship and [his] staff were wont to repair almost every day during their stay there, that he made her the present, I have heard it said, of a piano which he had sent out to her from England. She certainly played well, and was about to take the veil and be engaged as organist at a convent at Oporto where none but ladies of rich and noble families professed. As she was fond of society, I was surprised at her desire to immure herself for life in a convent, and I frequently talked to her on the subject. It did not appear to me that she was affected by any particular religious veneration . . . and I think the salary of the appointment, together with the influence and consequence it would give her in the convent, and [the manner in which it served] as a provision for life, had a great deal to do with her decision. [This,] she told me, was fixed, and [she also said] that she preferred the society she would there meet with, describing it as more enjoyable than any she had ever met outside the walls.[18]

All this cannot but lead us to reassess the *mentalité* of Iberia's nuns on the eve of the Peninsular War. Some less mature heads were capable of being turned by handsome young officers, doubtless, while even wimpled heads of greater maturity may have reached such a pitch of frustration that they were desperate for rescue, but with their life in general so pampered and comfortable it is difficult to believe that the cloisters were on the brink of rebellion.[19] A few individuals aside, then, the most that can be said is that the war may in some instances have afforded a welcome diversion. Here, once again, is Thomas Bunbury:

> A lady, the widow of a major Feijoo, had three daughters, who were very nice girls. With this family . . . I frequently went to visit the nunnery of Santa Clara [at Vilafanca]. On one occasion the nuns gave a breakfast to these and other ladies, and requested them to bring the officers of the battalion. The convent put me very much in mind of a menagerie at feeding time. . . . The imprisoned nuns crowded the gratings to see us eat. When we had finished, they ordered the things to be cleared

away for dancing, as they were anxious to hear the fine band of our battalion and to see us tread the light fantastic toe.[20]

So much for the personal, but what about the political? That the nunneries were opposed to the French may be taken as read, but that does not mean that they emerged as a prominent force in the Patriot zone. A Gillray cartoon that appeared in Britain in on 15 August 1808 entitled 'Spanish Patriots attacking French Banditti' showing a horde of Spaniards throwing themselves upon the invaders in the wake of a solitary British grenadier features two nuns brandishing knives dripping with blood.[21] Yet the reality was very different. Although numerous abbots and priors became members of the large numbers of juntas that sprang up to direct the insurrection, not a single instance has been uncovered of one of their female counterparts being accorded a similar honour, while, even in such episodes as the siege of Zaragoza, there is no record of a latter-day Catalina de Erauso.[22] Indeed, only in moments of the greatest crisis do we hear of nuns acquiring a public role of any sort, as, for example, in January 1810 when a Junta Central reeling from the castastophic defeat of Ocaña seemingly conjured up several 'inspired priestesses' who assured the inhabitants of Seville 'that, if ever the French should see the walls of that town, the fire of heaven would fall upon them and destroy them before they should reach its gates'.[23]

Even on those occasions when opportunity really offered, nuns do not appear to have come to the fore. If we take the obvious case of Zaragoza, Madre Rafols certainly won renown for the courage and commitment which she showed in her care of the sick and wounded, but she seems very much to have been an exception: to judge from the chronicles they left behind, the vast majority of the city's nuns sat out the fighting huddled in such refuges as the Pilar basilica.[24]

If such behaviour is scarcely a picture of heroism, the nuns concerned had at least chosen to endure the same fate as the people amongst whom they lived. In some cases, however, even the most minimal solidarity was lacking. For some two hundred years, for example, Lisbon had housed a small community of English nuns belonging to the Order of Saint Bridget. Recruited entirely from the recusant aristocracy and known in Lisbon as the Order of Sion, these women had weathered the French occupation of 1807–1808 well enough, but the bloody conquest of Oporto by Marshal Soult in March 1809 appears to have instilled the community with such terror that it took ship for England and remained there until 1814.[25] Just as unheroic, meanwhile, is the history of the Dominicans of the *zaragozano* convent of Santa Inés: having fled the city for the safety of Huesca during the first siege, during the second all but twelve nuns who were too old or infirm to travel retreated to Alcáñiz, from where they eventually migrated to Palma de Mallorca.[26] Few communities, of course, had the means of removing themselves from the theatre of war altogether, but even so, particularly at the start of the war when fears of the French were at their worst, flight was a common option, some abbesses choosing to conceal their flocks in convenient refuges in the neighbourhood until such time as they judged it safe to return to their convents (convents which, alas, they then often found to have been thoroughly sacked) and others embarking on epic journeys which sometimes stretched to many hundreds of miles.[27] For example, having decided to abandon their home in the wake of the battle of Gamonal in November 1808, sometimes walking all night and constantly menaced by French cavalry patrols, the Barefoot Carmelites of Burgos travelled on foot through bitter winter weather to sister houses in, first, Lerma, then Segovia and finally Avila, from whence they dispersed to similar institutions in Palencia and Valladolid.[28]

Yet it would be wrong to think of nuns simply as passive spectators whose only concern was their own safety.[29] On the contrary, they may be found supporting the war effort in a wide variety of ways. Here and there nuns are encountered among the swarms of clerical pamphleteers damning Napoleon and all his works and preaching holy war, perhaps the most interesting of these being one Madre María Rosa de Jesus who suddenly appeared in Cádiz in the summer of 1811 claiming that she had succeeded in paying a visit to the captive Pius VII and that the latter had told her that she should get the *cortes* to proclaim Our Lady of Sorrows commander-in-chief of the Spanish armies and have her image added to the standards of every single regiment: ignored by the *cortes,* she then made an impassioned appeal to public opinion in general in which she repeated her claims and for good measure blamed the manner in which she had been ignored on the fact that the *cortes* was full of Jansenists and Freemasons.[30] At Portalegre we find a community that had taken in many female refugees, and at Villanueva del Arzobispo one which hid a number of fleeing Spanish soldiers.[31] At Granada, Zaragoza and Tordesillas we find convents making generous donations to the Patriot cause.[32] And, finally, all over Spain and Portugal British officers were greeted as liberators, entertained by impromptu concerts, given gifts of confectionary and preserved fruits, and plied with requests for news of the campaign, while nuns were regularly seen waving from their windows whenever British troops marched through the streets.[33]

Within the walls of the convents, meanwhile, it is probable that still more fervour was on display, the traditional rituals of the Catholic Church providing nuns with an extremely potent means of engaging in the war effort. Thus:

> For a long time the whole community maintained a watch on the Blessed Sacrament in such a fashion that at all times there were two nuns . . . imploring the Divine Husband to lift the scourge of His justice from we who had so justly merited it. Meanwhile, the processions that were held in the cloister cannot be numbered, and in these each member of the community . . . practised the most rigorous mortifications, whether it was by carrying a heavy cross on their shoulders or wearing tightly fastened cilices of the most punishing sort, or making use of other devices whose nature would take too long to go into here; on each occasion, meanwhile, these devotions concluded with a prolonged act of the most strict discipline. . . . On top of all that, who can number the particular and secret exercises with which each one of these chaste Wives of the Lamb attempted to divest the Divine Husband of the righteous anger that sinners had stirred up in Him?[34]

Whether prayer and penance did anything to save Spain and Portugal from their travails is beyond the competence of this author to judge, but what is clear is that in psychological terms it was vital, binding communities together and giving them the strength to endure the travails of French occupation. These were many and varied. It would perhaps be tempting to see the nun as a figure that was especially vulnerable to the horrors of war, but, to judge from their chronicles, in fact experiences varied enormously from one community to another. Even in parts of Spain that were crossed and recrossed by the rival armies, particular convents could suffer no harm. As an example, one can here cite the Barefoot Carmelites of Alba de Tormes. Situated in the main square, their convent was a prominent landmark in a town that was repeatedly occupied and fought over by the field armies, and yet not once did it come to harm, and that despite the fact that both the other convents in the town were sacked at one time or another. Following the Spanish defeat at Alba de Tormes in November 1809, French troops poured into the town and slaughtered many Spanish fugitives, but not one enemy soldier even tried to force the doors, whilst their victorious commander extended the nuns the courtesy of sending them rations of bread and meat the next day. Much the same happened in July 1812 on the night of the battle of Salamanca except that this time the French were in retreat, the nuns again being kept from harm by orders that placed the convent under guard until the last troops had left the city. And, finally, in November 1812, the arrival of French forces in the town yet again in the course of their pursuit of Wellington's retreating forces was accompanied by no worse an intrusion than that of two respectful officers who wanted to get a view from the convent's roof.[35] Rather similar, meanwhile, was the experience of the Barefoot Carmelites in Seville: not only was the convent left in peace on the arrival of the French forces in January 1810, but friendly French officers even kept the nuns supplied with communion wine.[36]

Given the fears aroused in ecclesiastical circles by the coming of the French, such acts of decency doubtless came as a great surprise. However, whereas the policy of the invaders eventually encompassed the abolition of all the male religious orders without exception, the female ones were a different matter, not least because shutting them down would have had the socially undesirable result of turning loose large groups of masterless women. The result, then, was the adoption of a much more gradualist approach. Thus, rather than being shut down, convents were left alone other than a ban being placed on the acceptance of new novices, existing nuns being given permission to apply for secularization and communities with fewer than ten members being forced to amalgamate with others, the hope being that the figure of the nun would ultimately literally die off. To quote Sébastien Blaze, 'As convents would become the preserve of old women, the number of inmates would steadily diminish, and this in turn would allow for . . . reductions in the number of houses. Indeed, within twenty-five years they would have vanished altogether'.[37]

The fact that the French did not go to extremes does not mean that their rule was benign, however. Here and there individual enemy officers might treat the orders with kindness and courtesy, but other men were more committed to the ideological agenda inherited from the French Revolution, the result being that there were communities that suffered constant harassment, while here and there others found themselves driven from their homes for no better reason than that the French wished to use them as fortresses or make use of the ground they occupied to lay out one of the new squares that earned Joseph Bonaparte the alternative nickname of *rey de las plazuelas*.[38] As the years of occupation went by, meanwhile, convents lost more and more of their valuables: to take just one example, in 1814 the abbess of the convent of Las Huelgas in Burgos reported that, amongst many other items, since 1808 her foundation had lost a marble statue of Christ, eight large oil paintings, three tabernacles, eight golden chalices, seventy-two brass or silver candlesticks, three bejewelled crucifixes, forty-eight silver place settings, three silver ewers, nine silver trays, six silver lamps, a silver writing stand and the convent's golden seal.[39] And, last but not least, whatever the attitude of the authorities, many convents, for example, found that badly hit by the disruption in the countryside, their incomes fell away almost to nothing on account of the disruption to agriculture, and that much of what little they had left went in paying the levies imposed by the French. Indeed, vows of poverty now became only too real. As one barefoot Carmelite remembered, 'Our misery . . . reached such a pitch that all we had to eat were some . . . dried peas that were given us out of charity, and even these were full of grit. Nor was there very much to go round: when we got so much as a plateful we were very happy. . . .

We went about the place faint from hunger. Indeed, one day while I was in the porter's lodge I was completely overcome and had a bad fall'.[40]

Nor was it just poverty that threatened the Peninsula's nuns. On the contrary, there was also the issue of the behaviour of France's troops. On occasion, this was merely annoying, as, for example, when a group of young French infantry officers whose battalion had just occupied the Navarrese *pueblo* of Puente la Reina suddenly took it into their heads to invade the private quarters of its only convent to pay the nuns a visit.[41] How the nuns dealt with this intrusion is a matter to which we shall return in due course, but suffice to say that the affair did not end badly for them. On other occasions, however, communities were less lucky. Especially in areas gripped by the 'little war' or at moments when discipline was at a low ebb amongst the occupying forces, they could at any time find themselves at the mercy of troops who had become little more than bands of marauders. For a particularly grim episode, one might cite the fate of a convent in the *pueblo* of Cienpozuelos whose inhabitants were reportedly gang-raped and then put to the sword by retreating French troops in the summer of 1812, the only survivors being two elderly sisters who managed to take refuge in a nearby house.[42]

Such atrocities, perhaps, were not as common as might be expected. Much more common than murder or even harassment was almost certainly inconvenience of the sort that occurred when Fantin des Odoards' regiment requisitioned a nunnery at León for use as a barracks during the campaign of La Coruña: the nuns found themselves confined to a small part of the building and lost both their kitchen and their refectory, but otherwise, or so it is claimed, were left in peace.[43] Heaven, then, could often be thanked for small mercies, but, even so, life was still difficult enough. That being the case, it might well be thought that many nuns who found themselves in the French zone would have leapt at the chance of a new life with which they were suddenly presented. How far this took place is a moot point, however. That some nuns applied for secularization cannot be denied, the Conceptionist convent of San Juan de la Palma in Seville losing at least two sisters in this fashion.[44] However, while no detailed study has ever been conducted of the phenomenon, it seems probable that conventual solidarity was much stronger than the French anticipated. Thus, the Barefoot Carmelites of Seville did not experience a single secularization in two and one half years of French occupation, whilst in his detailed study of the clergy of Valladolid, Álvarez García has only identified one case of a nun—one Manuela Mauricia Bulnes—who decided on such a course of action.[45]

Yet perhaps this is not so very strange. Setting aside the issue of institutionalization, with Spain and Portugal in the grip of the Peninsular War, the outside world was a frightening place, while nuns who returned to their old lives were not only unlikely to receive the warmest of welcomes, but also risked ostracisation. The pensions allocated to secularised nuns being distinctly meagre—at between three and six *reales* per day, they were no more than what might be earned by a common seamstress—this was scarcely an inviting prospect, and all the more so we know from numerous petitions that the perennial shortage of money that dogged the *josefino* administration meant that they were very frequently not forthcoming at all.[46] Yet, once the decision was taken, there was no way back, all attempts by erstwhile nuns to return to their communities being firmly vetoed by the authorities, the result being that the few secularised nuns of whom we have any details appear to have had little option but to live on the coat-tails of the occupying forces as campfollowers or informers.[47]

The number of nuns who opted for secularization, then, was in all probability very small. However, this policy was not the only factor that caused a move outside the cloisters. Thus, in a number of instances abbesses ordered their nuns to return to their own homes until such time as life had returned to normal.[48] From one point of view, such a decision was logical enough: with convents running short of food, nuns might well be better off with living with their families, while their absence obviously reduced the number of mouths that needed feeding. Thus released, it is possible that some nuns found solace in the new forms of vocation that had hitherto made so little progress in the Peninsula: wounded at Talavera, for example, Charles Leslie found himself in the hands of 'a most charming nurse, no other than a daughter of our host . . . a nun of the Order of Saint Clare [who] had returned to take refuge in her father's house'.[49] If at least some nuns discovered as a result that there could be more to taking the veil than a life of contemplation, this was all very well, but for younger women especially exclaustration carried with it obvious dangers. At Santiago de Compostela, then, we hear of a nun who also set herself to care for the sick, but ended up becoming the lover of one of the officers for whom she was caring.[50] Nor is this the only such case, Heinrich von Brandt claiming to have had love affairs with such women at both Daroca and Calatayud.[51]

Naïve and lonely, such young women were easy targets for dashing French officers. Yet even in their own communities their heart-strings were not much safer, Napoleon's men being, like their British counterparts, much given to visiting convents in an attempt to try their luck. We here return to the incident at Puente la Reina that has already been mentioned. This, however, is interesting in another sense for it provides us with a good example of how nuns were quite capable of manipulating the invaders. According to Desboeufs, the French soldier to whom we owe our knowledge of the story, when he and his three friends entered the convent, every nun in the place rushed to the parlour into which they were shown to inspect them, four of the youngest and prettiest then remaining behind to entertain them with songs and music. This pleasant interlude having come to an end, the officers took their departure, but the next day the four of them all received little packages from the convent. Interpreting the confectionary that these contained as conveying one message and one message only, the officers immediately returned to thank their companions of the day before, and soon found themselves in the grip of a most romantic adventure. This time they were not admitted to the enclosure, but were forced to conduct their business via the grilled viewing slits cut in the firmly barred main gates. Nevertheless, everything proceeded in satisfactory fashion, the nuns presenting them with further gifts and tearfully begging them for some token of affection in return, four thoroughly beguiled young officers then returning to their billet to concoct appropriate love poems, these last being duly passed back into the convent.[52]

Evidently convinced that he was an Adonis who had only to walk into a convent for every one of its inmates to fall at his feet, Desboeufs recounts this story without the slightest hint of self-doubt (indeed, he even includes his lamentable attempt at poetry). Reading between the lines, however, what actually took place is all too clear. Not to put too fine a point on it, the convent's visitors had been thoroughly bamboozled. Thus, concerned both to contain the intrusion represented by her uninvited guests and to maintain good relations with the occupying authorities, the abbess clearly instructed the youngest and prettiest of her charges to embark on a flirtation with Desboeufs and his friends with a view to obtaining lasting evidence that her community had behaved in a friendly fashion towards the occupying forces. If tears really did run down the cheeks of the four nuns, then, the chances are that they were tears of mirth.[53]

If such is the truth of the matter, then clearly an important factor in the situation of any given convent under French rule was the character of its Reverend Mother, the fact being that ingenuity and wit could play great dividends. To cite just two examples, Carrión de los Condes' convent of Santa Clara supposedly bought immunity from French persecution by means of guaranteeing to keep the garrison supplied with the speciality confectionary for which the nuns were renowned, while at Tordesillas the abbess of the Franciscan convent made such an impact on Napoleon when he paused at her convent for refreshment during his shortlived pursuit of Sir John Moore that he gave her 1,000 *francs* for her community to treat itself to a banquet in his honour and had an order posted up threatening any soldier who molested the community with death.[54] Also very useful, meanwhile, was pathos: according to Fantin des Odoards, for example, he was so moved by the pleas of Consuegra's nuns to be allowed to keep their homes that he was dissuaded from requisitioning either of the town's two convents as a military hospital.[55] And, finally, there was always guile: no abbess could hope to resist a direct order to take in nuns from a convent that had been shut down on the grounds of having become too small to be viable, but that did not mean that the lives of the new arrivals could not be made so unbearable that they would soon beg to be given alternative accommodation.[56]

To put it mildly, then, the female religious orders made a spirited attempt to maintain their integrity in the face of French pressure. So much is this the case, indeed, that it would be pleasant to report that their travails ended with their liberation at the hands of the Anglo-Portuguese army. Nothing, alas, could be further from the truth. Except in certain very particular cases, the soldiers of Moore and Wellington did not represent any physical danger to the convents and their inmates: the few incidents in which nuns were seriously molested by British soldiers all took place in the context of the capture of fortified cities such as Badajoz and San Sebastián.[57] At the same time, the British army's baggage train did not contain a reformist agenda akin to that brought to Spain by the French.[58] If sexual violence was limited and institutional reform non-existent, however, sexual harassment was not: Kincaid, indeed, positively boasts of molesting nuns that he happened to encounter in the street.[59] In those parts of Spain and Portugal traversed by Wellington's army, then, there was the endless embarrassment caused by the behaviour of young officers steeped in a Protestant myth that regarded convents with a mixture of fascination and horror, and convinced to a man, first, that the 'fair inmates' had been incarcerated in them by cruel brothers or step-fathers and, second, that, having been denied all contact with men, nuns must be even more avid for sex than their secular sisters.[60] Matters were not helped, meanwhile, by the sinister aspect of many convents.[61] With officers, perhaps, precluded from indulging their sexual needs with the common prostitutes that were the only sources of such solace open to most of them, in every town the Anglo-Portuguese army occupied, every convent was soon besieged by scores of subalterns intent on making contact with the nuns or simply indulging their fantasies; indeed, a party of officers headed by the surgeon of the Thirty-Fourth Foot who had got very drunk at a dinner held to celebrate the first anniversary of the Battle of Albuera even attempted to take a convent at Trujillo by assault.[62] Yet what is interesting is not so much the behaviour of young men blinded by lust and prejudice, but the response of the nuns. Over and over again, then we find officers insisting that individual sisters welcomed their advances and even begged them for rescue: at Olite that George Woodberry had 'the vanity to think the youngest nun would leave the convent and share the fate of the Eighteenth Light Dragoons in defiance of her vows', and that despite the fact that another nun from the same convent had reportedly run away with a French officer two years before, and been brought back and placed in solitary confinement, eventually dying of a broken heart.[63]

How far it is possible to give credence to such stories, it is difficult to say, but it is not impossible that the attentions which were lavished on them by such men as Woodberry unsettled at least some of the younger nuns. As much as had been the case under the French, then, Mother Superiors were confronted with a range of difficult issues that allowed for more than one solution. One way forward is visible at a convent visited by Sherer at Portalegre: in brief, to allow a limited degree of contact so as to inject both sides with a dose of reality.[64] For an alternative, however, we may cite the story of a visit by a group of equally bumptious British officers to a convent in the Portuguese town of Vila Pouca da Beira:

> We were admitted into the chapel during the afternoon service. The nuns were in the organ gallery, screened by a thick trellis . . . so that we could only perceive their sparkling eyes peering down upon us. Their singing was very delightful: some of them had the most melodious voices. . . . After the service we were informed that one of the sisters was an Irish lady and would be happy to speak with any one Irish officer. Lieutenant Clarke accepted the invitation, but was greatly chagrined that he was not able to see the fair incognita, who was ensconced in a dark closet with a small latticed window. She, however, told him of her name and family, and that she was placed there by her parents twenty years ago. From this and the sound of her voice, Clarke inferred that the bloom of the peach had long since faded.[65]

By contrast with the tactics adopted at Portalegre, here there was no room for ambiguity: soldiers and nuns alike were kept firmly in their respective places and dialogue with the outside world conducted by one of the older members of the community in conditions that were strictly controlled in accordance with the norms of the previous century.[66] Elsewhere, meanwhile, British officers had even less luck: in the course of the Light Division's long march to join Wellington at Talavera in the summer of 1809, Leach and his friends tried to, as he put it, 'get a peep' at communities at both Castelo Branco and Coria, only to find that their inmates remained firmly *incommunicado*.[67] Finally, still another tactic was to let the intruders in but to allow them to see no one other than the abbess.[68] In short, exactly as had been the case under the French, convents were not just passive victims, but can be observed as making choices and even fighting back, in which respect it is particularly pleasant to be able to record the sharp 'come-uppance' that Bunbury received at the hands of the aspiring organist that we have already mentioned:

> I said to her on one occasion, 'You have been . . . at liberty in the wicked world we live in to do as you please: pray tell me honestly, have you, when in company with any young gentlemen, never found yourself possessed of some innate . . . feeling that you are placed on this earth for some other purpose than to struggle against nature, and to finish by shutting yourself up for life a prisoner in a convent?' She replied, 'I know this world is all vanity and folly, but, if you are going to talk nonsense, I shall get up and leave you'. And thus our conversation ended.[69]

Curiously, despite all the temptations, in at least some religious houses the war may have strengthened the norms of conventual life rather than weakening them. There were exceptions: in one Bernardine convent in Valladolid, for example, a violent dispute broke out amongst the nuns between one group that was said to favour the new regime and another that was fiercely opposed to it.[70] But let us here return to the convent of the Barefoot Carmelites in Seville. By contrast, with many other nunneries, this community survived the experience of French occupation relatively unscathed. If it did so, this was undoubtedly because it was far removed from areas of counter-*guerrilla* warfare in which Spanish settlements were regularly plundered by brigands-cum-insurgents on the one hand and devastated by French punitive columns on the other: to cite just one example of a community of nuns which found itself subjected to this sort of misfortune, situated in the Navarrese village of Tulebras, the Cistercian convent of Santa María de la Caridad was first raided by French troops from the garrison of nearby Tudela and then pillaged by Spanish marauders belonging to the command of the famous *guerrilla* leader, Francisco Espoz y Mina.[71] But to return to the Barefoot Carmelites of Seville, they were also fortunate in another respect. With the capital of Andalucía in effect an open city that could not be defended, it was therefore, by extension, immune from the horrors of a Badajoz-style storm. In consequence, the nuns were never likely to be in physical danger, while the need of the French commander, Marshal Soult, to keep the capital of Andalucía as a showpiece of Napoleonic rule and, more particularly, cultivate the selfsame élites who for generations had been keeping the Carmelites and their sister orders supplied with fresh postulants, ensured that they were likely to be treated with at least a modicum of respect. However, this was not how the matter was interpreted within the cloister. Terrified by the arrival of the French in January 1810, the sisters had made a desperate attempt to shield themselves from harm by placing a statue of the infant Jesus at the main entrance to the convent in the belief that the same statue had saved it from harm during an outbreak of rioting in 1580 by miraculously coming to life and sending the convent's assailants fleeing in all directions. The one miracle was not repeated, alas, but the nuns nonetheless attributed their salvation to the statue's influence, and all the more so as the incident in which a French soldier caused the nuns serious problems took place on a day on which it had been moved back into the convent for cleaning.[72] The consequence, of course, was that pride in the community and religious faith were renewed, whilst the very fact that the convent survived the French occupation so well left the nuns full of self-righteous zeal. Thus:

> Other than the mercy of the good Lord in respect of his wives, the charity which was experienced in a time of such great calamity, not only from our benefactors and other persons who remained unknown, but also from the very French and those who followed their standards, is attributable to the rigor and observance with which the common life was maintained in the

> community. Everything that was received—alms, gifts from the families of one sister or another, in fact anything whatsoever—immediately became as much the property of one and all as it did of the person who received it. In this fashion the entire community shared in abundance and want alike.[73]

For all the pressure that the French exerted on Spain's nunneries, then, it is arguable that the experience of the Peninsular War actually left the conventual ideal both strengthened and revived. This is, perhaps, a view that is overly roseate, but it is nevertheless difficult not to be impressed by the evident determination of many communities to rise from the ashes come what may. Typical of these, perhaps, was that of the Barefoot-Carmelite convent of San José in Zaragoza. Having not only lost their home but seen no fewer than six of the sixteen members of the community die in the course of the second siege, the survivors had eventually set out on foot for Huesca. With the road full of French troops, it was a difficult journey—whilst some soldiers jeered at them, others demanded money—but they eventually reached their destination unscathed. Here, however, fresh trials awaited them, the town's own Barefoot-Carmelite community proving singularly unwelcoming, and many of the remaining nuns succumbing to typhus. Eventually, a reasonable *modus vivendi* was arrived at, but even so it was a difficult time, the nuns having to earn sufficient money to pay their keep, the fact being that the income from their estates quickly evaporated in the face of the disruption caused by the war. At length, though, the French evacuated Zaragoza, and the surviving nuns set out to return home in the hope of re-building their pre-war lives only to find that, a staunch liberal hostile to the religious orders, the new provincial governor who had been appointed in the wake of liberation would not let them take possession of the shattered ruins that were all that was left of their convent, the result being they were forced to take refuge in the house of their erstwhile gardener. Here they lived for many months in poverty and discomfort, and it was not in fact till Ferdinand VII returned to Spain and overthrew the constitution of 1812 that the nuns finally returned home. It was an emotional moment that must have been shared by many other communities:

> How sad it was for us to see our church full of rubbish and stripped of its roof, its altars, its statuary, its furniture and its floor tiles. Yet we all gave praise to God and set about cleaning His house, whilst at the same time rejoicing to find ourselves back in our enclosure (for, the outer wall having been the one thing to survive intact, enclosure there still was, however much damage it may have suffered). Yet comfort and amenities there were none: we slept in an upper room whose walls were punctured by thousands of holes through which the wind . . . blew incessantly. . . . In the eyes of human prudence, setting ourselves up in this fashion amongst a mere heap of ruins with neither money nor adequate clothing . . . must seem quite mad, but, as nothing is impossible to God, a God, moreover, who never fails to reward sacrifice suffered out of love of Him, the church now has everything that it needs, whilst we nuns each have a cell of our own, there even being four novices. Let us, then, give thanks to God and offer up everything for His glory.[74]

It is fitting that we should end this chapter with images of reconstruction, for in the end the nunnery was not vanquished by the eagle. Some nuns chose the path of secularization certainly, but the vast majority did not, while great efforts were made to restore many of those convents that had been reduced to ruin. Meanwhile, thanks in part to the heroism of María Rafols and her fellow Sisters of Charity of Saint Anne, the new model of conventual life that had grown with such speed in France in the eighteenth century and gathered fresh pace under the rule of Napoleon finally made a start on supplanting the pattern of aristocratic seclusion that had been so characteristic of the *antiguo régimen* in Spain and Portugal: after 1814 Spanish and Portuguese nuns began to work much more actively with the poor and the sick (the community headed by Madre Rafols, in particular, took over the running of Zaragoza's foundling hospital), while they also began to gather recruits from the humbler elements of society and, perhaps, to refresh their leadership cadres. At the same time, even amongst those orders that changed their outlook but little, the travails of the Peninsular War brought a revival of their spiritual life and a return, if only *faut de mieux,* to the ideals of their founders, whilst many communities had shown extraordinary courage and resourcefulness in the face of danger and privations of all sorts: for all its many faults, the cloister had risen to the massive challenge posed by the Peninsular War more creditably than might ever have been imagined.

In stating this, curiously enough, we find ourselves returning to *Miracle*. Thus, notwithstanding the summary of the plot retailed at the start of the chapter, this does not proclaim the collapse of the religious life at all. On the contrary, thanks to the fleeing Teresa's substitution by an image of the Virgin to which she had been much devoted that comes to life, arrays itself in her discarded habit and literally takes her place among the sisters, her departure causes not a ripple in the community: there is bewilderment as to why the statue has suddenly disappeared, certainly, but otherwise the only puzzle is why Teresa has suddenly turned into a model nun. Moreover, still more symbolically, at the end of the film a Teresa who, absurdly enough, has been wrongly convinced a second time of the demise of her lover, this time at the battle of Waterloo, returns to the convent and slips in without being noticed whereupon the apparition who had taken her place duly reverts to her status as a statue. And, as Teresa is back in her convent, so God is back in the heavens: according to local tradition, it is the loving intercession of the convent's Virgin that causes the rain to fall, and the fact that the statue's absence coincides exactly with a long drought leads unerringly to the conclusion that Teresa's actions had provoked the anger of the Lord, an anger that could only be assuaged when she turned her back on her sins.

In the end, then, faith is reaffirmed. Yet in the real world, all was far from well. For an analogy of the impact of the Peninsular War on Spain's nuns, we can do no better than look to an event which took place in Salamanca at about half past six in the morning of 6 July 1812. In brief, the garrison that the French had left behind in the improvised citadel they had constructed to overawe the city when the Anglo-Portuguese army of the Duke of Wellington arrived at the gates the previous month having finally been forced to surrender, a start was quickly made on dismantling the fortifications and removing the supplies of munitions that still remained in their magazines. The captured powder was placed in a building near the Augustinian convent of the Purísima Concepción, but, as the convent's chronicler remembered, the results were all but apocalyptic:

> Thanks to a most dreadful want of care, on 6 July the magazine blew up. The noise was terrible, while the damage was such that many houses were flattened and their occupants buried in the ruins, the many people who died in this fashion including our good priest and sacristan, Don Francisco Caraciolo, and, with him, his mother and sister. The wall of our prioress's cell was blown in, but, through an act of divine providence, she was not inside at the time, while a sister who was caught in the patio amidst a hail of shells and cannon balls escaped with no other injury than a blow from a stick that also came flying through the air. However, the truth is that we were all in the gravest danger, for the entire convent was so shaken that afterwards nothing was to be seen but ruins: every interior wall was down, every window blown out. A body smashed a hole in the roof and landed in the loft, while bits and pieces of several others were found scattered in the gardens. As for the chunks of masonry that crashed down upon us, one was found to weigh ten *arrobas*. . . . Through His particular mercy, the Lord saved us all, but, setting aside the great fright we had all had, the damage incurred in those few moments could not be repaired for under 200,000 *reales*.[75]

No image could be more expressive: along with the rest of the Catholic Church, the female religious orders had suffered a grievous blow. As if it was not bad enough that many of their establishments were in a greater or lesser state of dilapidation—going back to the convents at Santarem where he had joined many other officers in flirting with the nuns in 1809 following the French occupation of central Portugal in 1810–11, Leach found them 'nothing but piles of filth, disgusting beyond description'[76]—their income had been slashed, either because their tenants had ceased to pay any rent or because their estates had been expropriated and sold off in the course of the French occupation (given the pre-war policies of the Bourbon administration, it is no surprise whatsoever to find that much of the land was never returned and that that portion which was recovered was only returned after bitter legal battles). Particularly badly hit were those communities that had been forcibly amalgamated with others on account either of a desire for rationalization or because the invaders wanted to requisition their buildings: when the Augustinians of the convent of Santa Isabel were driven out in October 1810, for example, they were only allowed to take their personal possessions with them, everything else having to be left for the benefit of the French and their supporters.[77] To gain a sense of the scale of the losses, we can do no better than turn to the words of an unknown nun who was a member of a convent at Lerma:

> The riches possessed by the community had been immense. Its founder, the Duke, had made every effort to ensure that the convent would be all but a royal palace. To achieve his object, he had outdone himself in the sumptuous nature of its furnishings: the slightest thing that serves to please the eye and encourage devotion in the soul had been adorned in the most magnificent fashion. As for the sacred vessels and other utensils, they were graded according to the calendar: on days of great solemnity, everything was of the purest gold. . . . In addition to being equipped in so generous a fashion, the convent had been supplied with abundant rents . . . while its treasury also contained the many valuable jewels that the various titled aristocrats who had entered the community over the years had brought with them as gifts. Taken all in all, it constituted an accumulation of wealth and beauty of incalculable value, but, sadly, along came the black hand of the French Revolution, and everything disappeared as if by magic.[78]

At the same time, everywhere numbers were under pressure: if relatively few nuns had taken the opportunity to turn their backs on their convents, many had died or been killed, while several years' worth of recruitment had been almost entirely lost.[79] Precise statistics are not available, but something of the scale of the damage is suggested by the fact that in Portugal the 7,000 nuns of 1808 had been reduced to 3,093 in 1822 (in Spain the fact that no fresh census of the population was carried out until 1857 makes it impossible to give figures which are even this meaningful, but it is generally reckoned that the ecclesiastical population was reduced by about one third).[80] For just one example of the gaps that had appeared in the ranks, of the thirty Recollected Augustinians living in that order's convent in Salamanca in 1808, twelve had died of illness or old age and one more killed by a shell during the siege of the French citadel in June 1812.[81] Gone for good, too, were many individual communities—to take the case of the Augustinians alone, houses were lost at Valladolid, Medellín and Arenas de San Pedro—whilst those that survived were often burdened by terrible debts.[82] Nor had very much been obtained in the way of credit: a pro-active policy that had taken the nuns out of their cloisters and put them to work among the ever more desperate masses might have gained them considerable popularity, but we instead see a picture of community after community huddling together in one refuge or another in the hope that the storm would pass them by. If Iberia's nuns were on their knees, then, it was not just because they were praying.

7

Liberators

The story of the female experience of the Peninsular War is, of course, one that is just as much about men as it is about women. Thus, at every moment the treatment of women was conditioned by the attitudes of the men who waged it, and it is therefore to these attitudes that we must now turn. In brief, there would seem to be three questions that we must answer in this respect. In the first place, what impressions did the soldiers of Britain and France have of the women of Iberia prior to being sent to Spain and Portugal? In the second place, what impact did the soldiers' experience of Spain and Portugal have upon those views? And, in the third place, how did the soldiers treat the women whom they encountered? Linking all this together, however, there is but one theme. Sexual violence, it is sometimes argued, is inherent to all wars, and, still, more so, wars which are waged against or in the presence of a racial, ethnic or cultural 'other'. The soldiers of Britain and France alike seeing the Spaniards and Portuguese as just such an other, to what extent is this generalization borne out in respect of the Peninsular War?

Beginning with the question of the general impression that was entertained of the women of Spain and Portugal in Britain and France at the start of the Peninsular War, as usual, we can do no better than turn to the travelography, this being the only source that British and French officers had to prepare them for conditions in the Iberian Peninsula. As for the messages which the various works concerned portrayed, these were very simple and straightforward: in brief, the women the contending armies would meet were in the first place beautiful, and in the second ripe for liberation, not to say avid for sex. Let us begin with the question of physical appearance. In so far as this was concerned, many visitors to the Peninsula were unsparing in their praise. Here, for example, is the French diplomat, Bourgoing:

> The sensation which you experience at the approach of a handsome Spanish lady has something so bewitching that it baffles description. Her coquetry is more open and less restrained than that of other women. . . . If she neglects nothing which is likely to carry her point, at least she disdains affectation, and owes very little to the assistance of her toilet. The complexion of a Spanish woman never borrows any assistance from art. . . . But with how many charms is she not endowed as a compensation for her paleness? Where can you find such fine shapes as theirs, such graceful movements, such delicacy of features and such lightness of carriage?[1]

However, it was not just that the women of Spain and Portugal were generally extremely attractive. Just as important was the fact that, thanks to the state of repression which they were commonly supposed to endure, they were perceived as being in every sense ripe for the picking. In so far as this view is concerned, pride of place may once again be assigned to Bourgoing. According to him, then, Spanish women were sexually insatiable, and had to satisfy this urge by taking lovers: 'In this respect depravity knows no bounds. It infects all classes of society and even those whom one would expect at least to have the appearance of shame . . . and it is not rare to receive advances from that sex destined by nature not to provoke but to await them'.[2] Nor do the sweeping generalizations and blatant prejudice end here, Bourgoing concluding his remarks with the ludicrous claim that there were comparatively few prostitutes in Spain, a situation that he ascribed to the fact that women were so freely available that the oldest profession was hardly necessary.[3] It was not just in the French literature that such remarks were to be found, however. For a good example, let us quote some remarks on the part of Phillip Thicknesse:

> They are very much addicted to pleasure, nor is there scarce one among them that cannot, nay will not, dance the fandango

in private, either in the decent or the indecent manner. I have seen it danced both ways by a pretty woman than which nothing can be more immodestly agreeable, and I was shown a young lady at Barcelona who in the midst of this dance, ran out of the room, telling her partner, she could stand it no longer. He ran after her, to be sure, and must be answerable for the consequences.[4]

We shall return there to the issue of the fandango later. Meanwhile, let us stay with more general issues. Herewith, then, William Dalrymple:

> The conjugal bed is not held very sacred by men of fashion, and, since the Bourbon family has been seated on this throne, jealousy has lost its sting. The ladies are not behindhand with their husbands: every dame has one *cortejo* at least and often more. . . . Amongst the people of rank, gratification is their object, and they stop at nothing to accomplish it. . . . Intrigue is one of the great pursuits of both sexes. At church, in the streets and at all public meetings, the fair carry the appearance of saints, but, no sooner has the sun rolled down the beamy light, than all restraint is thrown aside, and every bird seeks its mate: no single woman can appear abroad without her *dueña,* who is an old woman that generally assists her in carrying on her amours.[5]

To complete the picture, meanwhile, it was avowed that the men of Spain were no longer the proud heroes of the past, but rather degenerate cowards for whom almost anything went. Thus: 'There is no country in Europe that can boast of so few jealous husbands. The women, who were formerly deprived of all intercourse, who could hardly be seen through the grates of their windows . . . now enjoy perfect liberty. Their veils, the only remains of their ancient slavery . . . now serve no other purpose than . . . to render them more attractive. . . . Coquetry has made [them] one of its most seductive items of dress, and, in favouring half-concealment, has indirectly encouraged . . . stolen glances of love'.[6]

If any proof was needed of the lasciviousness of Iberia's women, it was found in a series of wild new dances that came in in the course of the eighteenth century in the form of the fandango and the bolero. As we have already seen, these were believed to have the power completely to sweep aside such natural inhibitions as still managed to exist in the female breast, but, even if the story retailed by Thicknesse is apocryphal, there is no doubt that they had a powerful effect, and confirmed the impression of the Iberian as an extremely sexual being. One witness was Henry Swinburne: 'Our evening ended with a ball where we had for the first time the pleasure of seeing the fandango danced. It is odd and entertaining enough when they execute with precision and ability all the various footings, wheelings of the arms and crackings of the fingers, but it exceeds in wantonness all the dances I ever beheld. Such motions, such writhings of the body and . . . the limbs as no modest eye can look upon without a blush! A good fandango lady will stand five minutes in one spot, wriggling like a worm that has just been cut in two'.[7]

Another phenomenon that attracted the interest of visitors to Spain was the bullfight. This attracted a number of responses, most of them negative, but what matters here is the further evidence they seemingly offered of the flames that burned within the female breast:

> If women acted consistently, it were to be wondered at how those who would either faint, or feign to faint, at the sight of a frog, a spider, etc, can delight in spectacles so barbarous as these are, where they are certain of seeing . . . bulls expire in agony, horses with their bellies ripped open, men tossed on the beasts' horns or trampled to death, and every other species of cruelty exhibited, but, as they do not act consistently, the wonder ceases: the greater the barbarity, and the more the bloodshed, the greater enjoyment they testify, clapping their hands, waving their handkerchiefs and hallooing, the more to enrage the bull.[8]

To conclude, then, despite the occasional voice of caution—Richard Croker, for example, specifically noted that he had met none of the sexual abandon that he had expected during his captivity in Arcos de la Frontera[9]—the women of Spain and Portugal were almost universally perceived as, in the first place, beautiful beyond measure, and, in the second eager for sexual adventure. Communicated to the forces of Britain and France (or, at least, their more educated elements) not just through the works of the many travellers who had visited the Peninsula, but such plays and novels as Sheridan's *The Duenna,* Fletcher's *The Chances* and, above all, Lesage's *L'Histoire de Gil Blas de Santillane,* such notions ensured that the many of those who found themselves intervening in the conflict did so to the accompaniment of considerable excitement. Here, for example, is William Keep: 'I must endeavour now to forget the charms of my own countrywomen and prepare to pay my devotions to the Spanish *señoras.* Some of our officers who have been there paint them in very attractive colours. . . . I anticipate great pleasure from serving with our fine army in that interesting country'.[10] But it was not just this. Thus, Iberia represented a cultural 'other', a geographical space that did not seem to belong to Europe at all. As Thirion wrote, indeed, 'Spain's inclusion in Europe is an error of geography. In her blood, in her customs, in her language, in her life-style and in her manner of fighting, she is African'.[11] From this, however, followed an unfortunate consequence, for, if Spaniards were 'African', it followed that their women were not protected even by such vestigial consideration as survived the horrors of war in Europe. And, as if all this was not enough, there was also the military culture of the French army. In brief, Napoleon's men were driven by an ethos that placed great weight on an aggressive masculinity that, first, saw the French soldier as a sexual athlete; second, specifically identified sex as one of the rewards that the French soldiers could expect; and, third, saw French soldiers as being irresistible to the women whom they encountered.[12]

The sexual baggage that underpinned the Peninsular War was therefore considerable. Meanwhile, all the impressions which we have had cause to note in this respect struck a strong echo with the hundreds of thousands of foreign men who were brought to Spain by the Peninsular War. A good place to start in this respect is with Lord Byron, who travelled from Lisbon to Gibraltar in the course of his journey to the eastern Mediterranean in the summer of 1809. Having on the way enjoyed liaisons with Spanish women both at Seville and Cádiz, he waxed lyrical with what he had discovered. Thus: 'Cádiz! Sweet Cádiz! It is the first spot in creation. The beauty of its streets . . . is only excelled by the loveliness of its inhabitants, for, with all national prejudice, I must confess the women of Cádiz are as far superior to the English women in beauty as the Spaniards are inferior to the English in every quality that dignifies the name of man'.[13] And again: 'Long black hair; dark languishing eyes; clear, olive complexions; and forms more graceful . . . than can be conceived by an Englishman used to the drowsy, listless air of his countrywomen . . . render a Spanish beauty irresistible'.[14] Needless to say, few of the soldiers whose impressions are of most concern to us could possibly hope to equal Byron's prose, but even so it is clear that they were anything but disappointed by what they saw around them—that the reality, indeed, very much lived up to what they had been promised.[15] The women encountered by friends and foes alike, however, were not just beautiful: they were also exotic—the fact that many of them smoked is an obvious starting point here[16]—and, above all, or so it was generally assumed, lascivious. As Byron continued in the second of the letters we cited earlier, 'I beg leave to observe that intrigue here is the business of life: when a woman marries she throws off all restraint, but I believe their conduct is chaste enough before. If you make a proposal which in England would bring a box on the ear from the meekest of virgins to a Spanish girl, she thanks you for the honour you intend her and replies, "Wait till I am married, and I shall be too happy." This is literally and strictly true'.[17] Very interesting, too, is the following passage from Sir John Carr:

> When a stranger contemplates the massy bars by which the windows of all the houses here, not lately erected, are barricaded, he cannot help entering into reflections not very favourable to the morals of the Spanish ladies. Time, without strengthening the virtue of the women, has conveniently reduced the jealousy of the men so low that anyone acquainted with the present manner of Spain might suppose, though ridiculously enough, that those very bars have been constructed for the sole purpose of preventing over-heated and romantic lovers from the hazard of injury by attempting to enter the window of their mis-

tresses when they can have access to them with perfect safety through the door whenever they please. . . . The insensibility of that man must be great indeed who cannot find a *querida* . . . and destitute of every attraction must that woman be who does not meet with a *cortejo* . . . among the men. In carrying on intrigue, the Spanish ladies are singularly dextrous. Wrapped up in the masquerade of fable and parable, they carry on an amorous conversation with their admirers in public without the fear of detection. In the language of the fingers they are also very expert: with one hand they are enabled to form an alphabet.[18]

The French view, meanwhile, was very similar. Here, for example, are Oyon's recollections of the women of Lisbon:

> Having some pretension as to the beauty of her legs and feet, [the Portuguese woman] is always well shod, while she walks in a fashion that is grave, but at the same time very graceful. She never looks at you other than with downcast eyes, but the glance which she directs at you is nonetheless full of fire, full of spirit, full of lustre. Large and dark, her eyes brim with voluptuousness. . . . In vain does she affect an air of reserve: she is not proof against the slightest look of admiration. . . . On the contrary, you have only to glance at her in a tender fashion.[19]

To this account may be added the views of the *aide-de*-camp, Alfred de Saint Chamans:

> The women of the Kingdom of Seville . . . are avid for pleasures, and, above all, those of love. Their eyes tell of this more than their lips do on account of the fact that they are always closely watched, but often they are set to watch each other, and when this happens they are assured of mutual indulgence. . . . Summing everything up . . . I believe that they are the most seductive women in the whole world.[20]

And, last but not least, there is Fantin des Odoards. Thus: 'Without hesitation, one can affirm that their habits of life were more than easy. How could it be otherwise under such a sky and amongst so many monks?'[21]

Physically, then, the troops who occupied Spain and Portugal considered themselves to be in the midst of something of a dream come true. Meanwhile, they were in many instances convinced that, victims of both a backward culture and a torrid climate as they were, Spanish and Portuguese women were morally inferior to those of their own nation. Of this idea there are many examples. Newly arrived in Lisbon, for example, George Simmons attended a performance at the opera. As he afterwards wrote to his parents, 'The dancing was too indelicate to give pleasure; at least, I felt it so, and blessed my stars I was an Englishman. The Portuguese ladies seemed to enjoy the performance with great rapture, which must make a Briton turn from them with disgust'.[22] Though much less of a prude than Simmons, his fellow officer in the Ninety-Fifth Rifles, Jonathan Leach, was just as horrified when he attended a bullfight in Madrid following the Anglo-Portuguese liberation of the city in August 1812. Thus:

> The countless numbers of Spanish females of all ages belonging to the higher class of society, dressed as if for a grand ball and taking intense interest in this cruel amusement, did certainly puzzle us Englishmen not a little and was a convincing proof of what an early habit will effect. If an opinion of the general character of Spanish females is to be formed from seeing them once only, and that at a bullfight, one would naturally conclude them to be utterly devoid of feeling, and a most inhuman set of devils in the garb of angels. But when it is remembered that from their earliest infancy they are taught to look forward [to a bullfight] as the first, the greatest and most delightful of all amusements . . . our wonder will cease to a great measure. I should, nevertheless, be much better satisfied . . . if they abhorred the diabolical process of torturing the noble animal to death, and turned from it with the same disgust as the females of other parts of Europe naturally would do.[23]

Finally, summing it all up, we have Charles Boutflower. As he remarked of Badajoz, for example, 'From habit and bad example the women here even of the first rank have contracted an immodesty in their ideas and conversation which would shock the most abandoned in England'.[24]

If even better-born women attracted the scorn of their liberators, what chance did their lower-class sisters have? In this respect it is quite clear that, prepared to consort with them though they were, British officers regarded them with little respect. Here, for example, is George Simmons:

> We usually give a ball once a week to the ladies of the village.... If you saw them, they would astonish you. They dress in short brown jackets and petticoats of the same, very coarse [and] figured with ridiculous patches of red cloth. These delicate ladies feed so grossly and eat so much garlic that it is enough to suffocate a person being in the room with twenty or thirty of them.[25]

As for scruples, these were few and far between. Betrothed to a young woman in Brighton named Amelia Perkins, Woodberry did not let that circumstance trouble him one whit. Thus, having reported himself to be 'getting quite desperate in love with Señora Zacarias' and, further, that 'I actively think nothing of telling a dozen females here the same tale', he stilled his conscience with the thought that emotions felt in Spain were not equivalent to their British counterparts: 'It is not the kind of love that attacks a mortal in England: here it only lasts in the sight of the object, while the English version pierces the heart so deeply that only death erases it'.[26] Himself another swaggering young blade, Kincaid says much the same, but is, perhaps, more honest: 'When month after month . . . continued to roll along without producing any change, we found that . . . rustic beauty furnished but a very poor apology for the illuminated portion of nature's fairest works, and ardently longed for an opportunity of once more feasting our eyes on a lady'.[27] In short, much as Pérez Galdós' tragic heroine, Asunción, women who became involved with foreign soldiers risked heartbreak and betrayal. Let us here quote Charles Leslie's memories of Tarifa:

> There was one lady, as elegant and accomplished as she was beautiful, who . . . so captivated a noble lord, then on an

> amateur military expedition in southern climes, but who, of course, had more opportunities of displaying his gallantry in devotion to the fair than in active operations in the field, that he proposed to put his heart and fortune at her disposal, and, on his proceeding to England on urgent affairs, he, with the consent of her parents, placed her in a convent on a handsome allowance in order to finish her education or perhaps to place her out of the way of other rivals. His lordship, however, proved no true knight. This Dulcinea, had Don Quijote been in existence, might fairly have called upon him to right her wrongs. She, however, most sensibly took the matter very quietly, came forth from the convent and consoled herself by marrying a man of her choice who, being her own countryman, was a more suitable match.[28]

To quote John Kincaid once again, 'A woman was a woman in those days, and . . . we were only birds of passage'.[29] From all this what can be expected was at the very least high levels of sexual harassment. As has already been discussed, convents were a particular target of this abuse, but it was a phenomenon that was encountered on a very widespread basis. Let us begin here with the British army.[30] Thus, at Tarifa, a district where the women still kept their heads completely swathed, Moorish fashion, we find Lieutenant-Colonel Browne of the Twenty-Eighth Foot, 'a most wild and eccentric character', amusing himself by stopping each woman that he met so dressed and forcing them to 'open the *mantilla* that he might have a fair peep at them'.[31] Not much better was Augustus Schaumann. Herewith, for example, his recollections of an incident that took place shortly after the battle of Vimeiro. 'At one house on the road we bought a turkey from an old peasant woman. She had a charmingly pretty . . . daughter, a real beauty in face and build, with whom we had great fun, for, among other things, we made her kiss us each in turn before taking our leave, and, as the last to be kissed always ran round to the tail of the line in order to be kissed again, the poor girl never came to an end with her kissing'.[32] Finally, in Lisbon one officer made himself such a nuisance in respect of one unfortunate young woman that he eventually had to de driven off by a humiliating practical joke that, somewhat improbably, saw the object of his desire substituted for a barbary ape![33] And where the officers led, the men followed. Herewith part of Richard Henegan's account of his escape from Spain in the wake of the retreat of Sir John Moore:

> There was a corporal in my party by the name of Dalglish, by birth an Irishman, and a sad, wicked dog, though a great favourite with everyone. He had a turn for gallantry, guitaring, singing and all the lighter accomplishments . . . and, withal . . . was constantly getting into some scrape in the pursuance, not of his duties, but of his pleasures.[34]

Life in the company of this individual was inclined to be problematic. According to Henegan, for example, having gone with Dalglish to a small village in Beira to try to negotiate the hire of some boats with which to transport a consignment of ammunition that he had been ordered to get back to Oporto down the river Douro, he and the corporal were entertained to a meal and invited to spend the night, only to be forced to flee after Dalglish was set upon by an angry crowd, the latter's explanation being, 'Och, please, Your Honour . . . 'twas nothing at all, at all, but a woman fell in love with me, and you see her husband didn't like it'.[35] Nor was the incorrigible Dalglish at all repentant. On the contrary, chided by Henegan that he thought of nothing but women, he responded 'Your Honour doesn't seem to understand the thing at, all. It's the women that can think of nothing but me, please Your Honour'.[36] As for being the only such rogue to be found in Wellington's army, this is highly unlikely. Indeed, Grattan laughingly recalled that, told that they must pack up to leave, his soldier servant, Daniel Carsons, had remarked 'that he did not know how the devil he could get away at all at all without taking three women, besides his wife, Nelly, with him'.[37]

If even the British forces behaved in this fashion, little more was to be expected from the French. Here, for example, are Andrew Blayney's recollections of an incident that he witnessed while a prisoner of war of General Sébastiani in Andalucía: 'At Archidona we halted to breakfast. . . . We were attended by four extremely pretty girls, whom the French officers, to show their gallantry, pinched and pulled about until the poor girls were afraid to approach the table, and, although I did not join in tormenting them, I suffered as if I had, and was obliged to assist myself'.[38] Not all French officers were such brutes. Indeed, at least some British officers maintained that they were at least more subtle in their approach to the opposite sex than their opponents. As William Grattan of the Eighty-Eighth Foot remarked, 'It is a singular fact, and I look upon it as degrading one, that the French officers while at Madrid made in the ration of five to one more conquests than we did! How is this to be accounted for? The British officer has the advantage of appearance: his exterior is far before that of a Frenchman; his fortune, generally speaking, ten times as great, but what of all this if the one accommodates himself to the manners, the whims, of those he is thrown amongst, while the other, disregarding all forms, sticks to his national habits, struts about and not only despises, but lets it be seen that he despises, all he meets save those of his own nation. What a fatal error!'[39] To judge from their memoirs, meanwhile, the sort of behaviour remarked on by Grattan was by no means unknown: for example, Marcel inveigled his way into the bed of the widow he had an affair with at Ledesma by the simple expedient of insisting on accompanying her to Mass every day, and the following summer succeeded in seducing a fourteen-year-old girl named Manuelita at Vitigudino by cultivating the couple with whom she lived and in general pretending that he was 'a good boy and really honest with it'.[40] Given the cultural norms prevalent in the French army, however, it is difficult not to believe that 'rough wooing' was endemic: set loose in Seville after nearly two years of confinement at the hands of the Spaniards, for example, Sébastien Blaze appears to have set out to throw himself upon literally every woman that he came across.[41] Meanwhile, whilst Blaze was at least a man of some sophistication who probably made some pretence of courting his targets, it is probable that there were instances in which women were treated in a manner lacking even the faintest veneer of romance. That such was the case is suggested by a story that Dallas claims to have got from a Belgian officer whom he met in the course of the Waterloo campaign. In brief, stationed in a small village with two other officers, the Belgian ordered the local mayor to provide him with three pretty girls, including, not least, his own daughter, the young women concerned then seemingly being kept as sex-slaves.[42]

It is greatly to be hoped that this story is apocryphal—that the thousands of women who had liaisons or relationships with British or French soldiers whose experiences we have examined in the previous chapter were able to exercise at least a degree of freedom of choice in initiating such a course of action. What cannot be wished away, alas, are the numerous reports of outright rape. Here about the best that can be done is to suggest that, in the British army at least, this crime tended only to occur in certain situations of a quite specific nature, not least because soldiers who made unwelcome advances to women in, say, ordinary garrison or bivouac situations ran a very serious risk of severe punishment, or could well find, like Dalglish, that they had bitten off more than they could chew. Shortly after his arrival in Portugal in 1808, for example, Bunbury was caught up in a serious disturbance at Lamego which he claims to have been the result of the conduct of 'an amorous Hibernian youth', whilst angry relatives threatened Woodberry's life after he attempted to seduce a Portuguese girl at Cartajo.[43] Still worse, in October 1811 two men of the Twenty-Eighth named McCann and Ludley were stabbed to death in Alburquerque after they were accused of making free with the women of the house in which they were billeted, while in July 1813 a captain of the Ninety-Fourth Foot named Gore was shot dead in Pamplona by a party of Spaniards who had come to snatch a girl he had persuaded to run away with him.[44] That said, if casual acts of rape were uncommon in the British army, they did occur, one such seeming very likely to have taken place at the Pyrenean village of Legasa on 30 August 1813. Thus:

> Ensign Pollen of the Forty-Eighth . . . had been long in the Peninsula and given many proofs of his bravery. He forded the river with his party . . . and took possession of one of the houses, the mistress of which was the only inhabitant who remained to take care of the household wealth. Pollen detected his men when about to debase the poor woman, drove them out and then committed the vile act himself.[45]

In the French army, perhaps, the situation was rather different in that the soldiers were less constrained by military discipline and driven by an ethic that was much more strongly sexual, as well as operating in a context in which the civilian population were much more restricted in terms of their response: any attempt at riot, for example, was clearly liable to provoke the most brutal repression. Yet, particularly in the dark and winding streets of such cities as Seville and Córdoba, murder was by no means an impossibility, French soldiers therefore being well aware that to go too far was to risk a knife in the ribs. To quote Levavasseur, 'Any sort of gallant enterprise—for that matter, even the payment of the most innocent courtesies—was, we felt, ruled out by the tragic events that were happening every day: all too often French officers were found lying murdered in the street'.[46]

To return to the central theme of this chapter, it should by now be quite clear that, for all that they often found them very beautiful, the soldiers of Britain and France had little respect for the women of Iberia and treated them accordingly.[47] However, that said, it seems probable that overt sexual violence was not the norm. Rape was certainly a common occurrence, but, in so far as we can judge, it was only a common occurrence in certain specific situations, most of them, as we shall discover, moments in which officers had lost control of their men. Before we deal with these, however, we should first look at the one instance in which violence against women, and, with it, rape, was clearly integrated into the conduct of the war. We come here to the punitive expedition, and, more particularly, the operations which the French conducted against the more irregular elements of the Patriot forces. In the face of the popular uprisings which they faced from 1793 onwards, the armies of the French Revolution and Napoleon had evolved a doctrine of counter-insurgency based on the most savage violence. No sooner did bands of irregulars emerge, then, than columns of troops were sent into the areas affected with orders not just to root out the offenders, but to punish the civilian population with fire and sword. Given that by involving themselves in the war effort, the populace were deemed to have contravened the so-called 'laws of war' and thereby forfeited the protection which these were supposed to give them—in theory, the rights to life, property and the ability to go about their lawful business as normal—the results were extremely grim, it being the norm for every village in the path of the troops concerned to be burned to the ground and the male inhabitants subjected to mass executions (women, by contrast, were generally spared). Should they resist their assailants, meanwhile, the populace risked a fate that was still worse in that they were deemed to have opened themselves not just to execution, but to wholesale massacre.

From the very beginning, this was the policy that was applied in Spain and Portugal: indeed, prior to the Dos de Mayo Napoleon even expressed the hope that there would be a revolt in Madrid for the precise reason that this would afford an opportunity for the populace to be taught a salutary lesson. With extreme violence further justified by the fact that, in theory, opposition to the French amounted to rebellion against the legitimate government of the state—a crime that throughout the eighteenth century had been dealt with in the most brutal of fashions—the result was that the punitive columns that the French dispatched in all directions in response to the uprising behaved with great savagery, and, what is more had no hesitation in cutting down as many women as they did men: when the village of Boada was sacked on 30 March 1809, for example, the five dead that it suffered included a women named María Antonia Rodríguez.[48] As the war went on and the French troops began to be contested by bands of armed civilians, so such acts of repression inevitably grew ever more terrible. First of all, in this respect comes the account of Sergeant Marcel of the Sixty-Ninth Line. Ordered to Galicia in pursuit of the forces of Sir John Moore, Marcel soon found himself hunting down not fugitive British soldiers but rather detachments of the local home guard known as the *alarma*. Possibly influenced by the fact the conditions they encountered in Galicia were particularly primitive—'In these Galician villages', wrote Marcel, 'one finds neither tables nor beds nor cooking utensils; as for their inhabitants, the serfs of the most wretched parts of Poland are better off than they are'[49]—Marcel and his fellow soldiers set about eliminating the threat with the greatest ruthlessness. Typical enough was the fate suffered by the coastal village of Camariñas. Thus, ordered to march on the village to investigate reports that a French patrol had been massacred in the vicinity, the column found the way barred by a mass of civilians armed with pitchforks, flails and a few muskets. Quickly dispersed though this array was, the fact that it had stood to arms was deemed to be proof of Camariñas's guilt, and so, having already killed many of the peasants who had tried to oppose them including many women and children, the French fell on the village without the least compunction. Most of the inhabitants had already sought safety by taking ship in the many fishing boats moored in the port, but there were plenty left behind either hiding in the houses or crowding the quay in a last-ditch attempt to reach safety, and, 'despite their tears, their pleas for mercy and their protestations of innocence', these were all put to the sword, though not before the women had been subjected to 'the last outrages'. As for the town, it was pillaged of all it contained and in large part burned to the ground.[50]

Perhaps the most savage counter-insurgent operations of the war were those that took place after 1810 in Andalucía. With the latter very much the home of the irregular *guerrilla* band rather than the semi-militarised commands that dominated the scene elsewhere, bands, moreover, that frequently committed the most appalling atrocities in respect of such prisoners as fell into their hands. For example, an officer of the Sailors of the Guard named Pierre Baste who had the misfortune to serve in the army of General Dupont describes the fate of a French detachment that was massacred near Montoro in June 1808: 'We had the great sorrow to see several of our unfortunate soldiers on the road: one had had his arms cut off, another his legs; several had had their ears, eyes, nails and genitals removed. I myself saw one whom these tigers had crucified on a tree'.[51]

Dominated by counter-insurgency operations as it was, the fighting that raged in Andalucía during the French occupation of 1810–12 was therefore frequently a savage affair whose character is best caught by the memoirs of another sergeant, François Lavaux. Lavaux's regiment, the 103rd Line, forming a part of the division of General Gazan in Mortier's V Corps, following the fall of Seville he initially found himself marching north in an abortive attempt to seize the fortress of Badajoz, but within a few weeks he was back on the Guadalquivir. The troops were exhausted—by the time they reached Seville they had been four days without bread—but there was no rest. With the countryside up in arms, on 10 April Lavaux's regiment marched northwards together with a few cavalry with orders to burn down every village which offered resistance and put the entire population, children and babies included, to the sword. After first sacking the town of Branes on the grounds that a few shots had been fired at them, Lavaux and his comrades headed for Constantina from whence news had reached the French that the insurgents had established a base in the town. The 103rd having come in sight of the town, the defenders were offered fair terms, but the latter answered that they would never surrender to the French, and, so after a speech from the regiment's commanding officer in which he specifically promised the troops that they would be allowed to sack the place, Lavaux and his comrades fell on with a will whereupon the defenders fled in panic, many of them being cut down by the French cavalry as they attempted to reach the hills that surrounded the town. There followed scenes of absolute horror:

> We eventually entered the town, the latter immediately being pillaged and reduced to ashes. A number of soldiers entered a convent, and . . . raped and murdered the nuns they found inside. In the evening, after the brigands had dispersed, we were billeted in the town. Hardly anybody was left in any of the buildings, but the few people we did find were immediately bayonetted.[52]

Following the affair at Constantina, the French column returned to Seville, only for Lavaux and his comrades to be sent out for a second time, this time against a nearby village in which a number of insurgents had reportedly taken refuge. Sensing that discretion was the better part of valour, most of the *partida* concerned melted away, but a picket of thirty-two men were taken prisoner and executed there and then without further ado. Having done what was required of then, the French returned to Seville for a third time, only almost immediately to march off to war again. This time the target was the Serranía de Ronda, and on 2 May 1810 the 103rd arrived at Algodonales. What followed was, as the *afrance-*

sado press claimed, a bloody affair. In the first charge, Lavaux says that twenty-four men of his own *voltigeur* company fell, but the fire of the insurgents was not sufficient to deter veteran French soldiers forever and very soon the attackers were advancing through the streets towards the centre of the town. Even now, however, the Spaniards did not give up, and their assailants were further enraged to see women carrying ammunition to their husbands and even taking an active part in the defence. The result was wholesale slaughter:

> Whilst we were waiting in the gardens outside the town, the general had ordered us not to spare anyone: even the women and children were to be killed. The horrible carnage that we therefore engaged in had to be seen to be believed. Most of the inhabitants were hiding, and, as I advanced, I came across several women and young girls. Out of pity, I spared their lives, but the *voltigeurs* who were following me ran all of them through with their bayonets. Further on I found a number of others who were trying to hide their husbands by lying on the ground and covering them with their own bodies. . . . I levelled my musket at them, but they begged me for mercy so piteously that I could not refuse them. A number of my comrades then came on the scene. . . . Dragging the women aside, they thus revealed their menfolk, some of whom were found still to have guns in their hands. None of those concerned were long for this life: the whole lot were bayonetted. . . . At last we reached the centre of the village. All the houses were being set alight, while the soldiers seized everything that they could lay their hands on. The worst thing I saw was in the courtyard of a windmill. This was strewn with eighteen bodies, and amongst them I saw a little child of no more than three or four years of age lying cradled in the arms of its dead mother, the latter having been bayonetted several times.[53]

Led by a local insurgent leader named José Romero Álvarez, the so-called Alcalde de Montellano, the insurgents made their last stand in a large house on the *plaza mayor*. Barricading themselves in, they kept up a heavy fire and for some time managed to keep the French at bay. With casualties mounting, the invaders decided to burn Romero and his men out, and had soon managed to stack large quantities of wood and hemp against the walls. Still more inflammable material having been thrown onto the balconies and through the windows, the building was duly fired. Very soon, meanwhile, it had become an inferno, the flames having spread to a large quantity of olive oil that had been in storage in an adjacent outhouse. Trapped inside, some of the defenders, including Romero, chose to die in the flames, but others rushed out onto the balcony, only to be shot down by the vengeful troops waiting outside. With French tempers inflamed by an incident in which a women had shot a soldier who thought that she was trying to surrender, hardly anyone was allowed to escape, practically the only survivors being Romero's wife and three young children.[54]

As both Marcel and Lavaux admit, then, the rape and murder of women was a regular part of counter-insurgency operations, and one that may well have been officially encouraged. Indeed, Gonneville goes so far as to elevate the reality to the status of a definition. Thus: 'The word pillage in the sense it carries in such a case implies not only spoliation, but also violation and murder: in a word, all the excesses that men released from discipline can commit in rivalry with each other'.[55] On most other occasions, however, such behaviour only tended to occur when troops had got out of formation or left their units altogether. Let us begin here with the phenomenon of the sack, which is here defined as the wholesale plundering of a village, town or city that had been left undefended in the face of the likelihood of enemy occupation. This fate befell a number of places that had the misfortune to have field battles take place in their vicinity that were lost by the Spaniards, the most obvious examples being Córdoba, Medina de Río Seco, Burgos and Uclés. In each case, the pattern was the same: bursting into the towns concerned hot on the heels of Spanish fugitives, the victors, who were often for obvious reasons out of formation and beyond the control of their officers, quickly turned from pursuit to pillage. Still worse, with sporadic fighting going on in the streets as desperate Spanish fugitives here and there turned their muskets on their pursuers, the impression was created that the towns were being defended, even that they had been taken by assault. This, alas, provided the French soldiers, many of whom were only too eager to take out their fear, fatigue and frustration on a populace whom they, after all, despised, with just the excuse they needed. The most detailed account of the scenes that followed comes from the pen of Pierre Baste. Thus:

> It was close to 2.30 PM when the bulk of the division came close to Córdoba. At our approach, the Spanish abandoned their position . . . and our troops launched themselves into the town at the charge. We found it deserted by the Spanish troops, who were fleeing in the greatest disorder. . . . But it became impossible to restrain the greed of the soldiers who, running through the streets with bayonets fixed, forced passage for themselves everywhere and spread throughout the houses in order to pillage. An early column, still marching in closed ranks, arrived in one part of town to be met by musketry from the windows of several houses; this fact led us inevitably to the persuasion that the inhabitants had taken up arms and were defending themselves. So a form of street-to-street combat broke out and served as a pretext for our soldiers to sack Córdoba and deliver it up to all the horrors of a town taken by assault. The soldiers scattered by platoons or singly, fully armed and unmoved by any representation made to them. Murder and pillage were soon joined by the rape of women, virgins and nuns, the theft of sacred vessels from the churches—sacrilege accompanied by the most atrocious circumstances. Some officers—even some generals—demeaned themselves by indulging in such dishonour, even when grief-stricken parents sought to solicit the protection of the first officers they encountered. Happily for the name of French honour there were some sensible and generous souls who, in saving more than one family, protected them from the outrageous behaviour of a soldiery even more difficult to rein in once they had broken all the leashes of discipline. I had the good fortune to be able to save several women and some Spanish men who would otherwise have become victim of the soldiers' blind fury. Called to the aid of a woman in the greatest distress, I was almost forced to kill three frenzied members of a light battalion who, despite my efforts and the entreaties of the

unfortunate woman, persisted in forcing their brutal attentions on her daughter, a charming young woman.[56]

In cases such as that of Córdoba, disorder was the product of victory, but it could just as easily be the product of defeat. Thus, French armies that were experiencing logistical difficulties, or, still worse, forced to retreat, were apt to get ever more out of hand, there being a strong tendency for the men to disperse in small groups to shift for themselves and take what they wanted from the populace. Meanwhile, not least because the troops in one way or another held the inhabitants responsible for the privations that they were generally suffering, the latter often came in for the roughest possible treatment. Although there are other examples, by far the worst example came in respect of the French invasion of central Portugal in 1810. In brief, ordered by Napoleon to march on Lisbon, some 65,000 French troops duly invaded central Portugal under Marshal Masséna and headed for the capital. In following this course of action, however, they were marching straight into a trap in that Wellington had ordered the countryside in the path of the invaders to be evacuated and stripped of all its resources, whilst at the same time blocking off all access to the Portuguese capital by means of a series of specially constructed defences known as the Lines of Torres Vedras. By the time that Masséna reached the Lines, the autumn rains had set in, but the central problem that he faced was that there was almost nothing for his men to eat, his troops having long since consumed the limited supplies that they had been able to bring with them. A most determined soldier, the marshal resolved to maintain his position for as long as he could in the hope that help would arrive from, say, the French commander in southern Spain, Marshal Soult, and the result was months of misery for his troops, the latter soon being reduced to a state of semi-starvation. 'We had wine in abundance', wrote Marcel, 'but bread was so rare that, like many others I once did not see it for seventeen days. In place of it, we made a substitute out of corn, but the quality was very poor, while we soon ran out even of that'.[57]

The result of this situation is only too easy to imagine. Either in organised foraging parties or in groups of mere marauders, large numbers of the invaders dispersed into the countryside that had been occupied by Masséna's forces in a desperate search for food. In the process, meanwhile, all discipline broke down. As Louis Fririon wrote in his account of the campaign:

> In the face of destitution, the officer became impotent: he simply did not have the will to subject the soldier who brought him the food he needed for his survival and was willing to share a prize that had cost him incalculable danger and trouble. Very soon, indeed, hunger became the principal motive force amongst the multitude, and marauding their chief activity. . . . First of all it was a handful of isolated individuals quitting the ranks; then, it was a steady trickle; and, finally, it was men running off in entire companies. Having run away, the most daring of the soldiers concerned grouped together in bands, spread out through the valleys, and deprived the unfortunate inhabitants who had taken refuge in their most hidden corners of the slender resources that remained to them. The travails that our soldiers were experiencing, the obstacles which confronted them, the hunger which devoured them, all these excited the worst passions among them.[58]

Understandably enough, French accounts are fairly reticent as to the details of the treatment that was meted out to those members of the civilian population who had elected to stay in their homes rather than retire within the Lines of Torres Vedras.[59] It is, then, only through the accounts written by British soldiers of what they found in the zone occupied by Masséna's forces after the latter finally retreated in March 1811 that it becomes clear that the crimes of the French troops included not just pillage and murder, but also wholesale rape.[60] Meanwhile, as Wellington's army retraced its steps towards the Spanish frontier, many British officers found women who had been violated by the fleeing invaders, some of them having then been put to death in the most horrible circumstances. As George Simmons wrote, for example, 'Two young ladies had been brutally violated in a house that I entered [in Pernes] and were unable to rise from a mattress of straw. . . . In a village . . . named [Cerdeira] I saw a woman laid in the street near her own door murdered. The ruffians had placed upon her bosom a huge piece of granite taken from the market cross, so heavy that it took me and six men to remove it. The blood was running from her ears and mouth. Her dress upwards was most respectable, but her lower habiliments had been dragged off her'.[61] Other women, meanwhile, were subjected to various forms of bullying and extortion. For example:

> At daybreak we followed the French and passed through several towns on fire. . . . A little cottage by the roadside struck my fancy. I took up my abode in order . . . to be sheltered, [it] being rainy. The woman of the house welcomed me in and offered me her chair. She had four children lying near her literally starving. The French had robbed her of everything worth taking. Some of the soldiers cut her with their swords for endeavouring to stop them taking away her daughter, and one villain had the meanness to return to the house and tell her, 'Your children are starving; if you will give two dollars for this loaf, you shall have it'. She went where the last of her money was secreted; he watched her . . . took the money, abused her and walked off.[62]

Clearly, then, women were the targets of much violence. However, as the same author makes clear, this violence was not just directed against women, but was rather indiscriminate. Thus:

> Kincaid and I went into a house where an old man was seated: he had been lame in the legs for many years. A French soldier . . . had given him two deep sabre wounds on the head and another on the arm. . . . It is beyond everything horrid the way these European savages have treated the unfortunate Portuguese. Almost every man they get hold of they murder. The women they use too brutally for me to describe. They even cut the throats of infants. The towns are mostly on fire—I have seen such sights as have made me shudder with horror, and which I really could not have believed unless an eye-witness of them.[63]

Thus far we have mostly had cause to speak of atrocities that were committed by the French army. It should not be thought, however, that British troops were incapable of such actions. Thus, when wholesale straggling broke out during the retreat of Sir John Moore, scenes were witnessed that rivalled those seen in central Portugal in March 1811, and all the more so as Moore's army laid all the blame for their current predicament upon the Spaniards and were furious at what they perceived to be the hostile attitude of the Galician populace. Here, for example, is Anthony Hamilton:

> The soldiers whose strength still allowed them to proceed, maddened by the continual suffering of cold and hunger, were no longer under any subordination. In such circumstances, pillage could not be prevented. . . . Enormities of all kinds were committed, houses and even villages were burning in all directions. The ravages of the most ferocious enemy could not have exceeded in atrocity those perpetrated by a British army on their allies.[64]

Also notorious, meanwhile, was the behaviour of the small parties of British troops who from 1809 onwards were forever making their way to and fro between Lisbon and the quarters of their respective regiments. To quote Richard Henegan, 'Relieved from the responsibility and discipline attached to each individual in an organised force, their route is marked, with few exceptions, by violence and rapine. The arms they bear for the service of their country are turned against the peaceful inhabitants of the districts they pass through, and bloodshed but too often follows the commission of plunder'.[65] On the whole, though, it may be presumed that, in so far as the various opportunities for serious violence against women that we have looked at so far are concerned, the lion's share of the guilt lay with the French, not least because a keen sense of the need to maintain good relations with the local populace led Wellington to take a much harsher line with discipline than was ever the case in the French army.[66] This, however, is not the case with the last area that we should look at, namely the storm. In the course of his campaigns, Wellington had to besiege three French-held cities—Ciudad Rodrigo, Badajoz and San Sebastián—all of which had eventually to be taken by assault.

In all three actions the British troops who took part showed great courage and suffered heavy casualties, but in all three they also fell prey to serious disorder, in the course of which numerous women appear to have been raped or otherwise molested.[67]

That these atrocities occurred is uncontested. On the contrary, they are widely testified to even by British observers, this being particularly so of Badajoz. Let us begin with George Bowles: 'A British officer was shot by one of his own men whom he had endeavoured to prevent ill-using an old woman, [and] nearly a dozen females were actually murdered or died of ill usage'.[68] Then there is Robert Blakeney who had entered the city with his regiment, and, according to his own account at least, managed to save a number of women from assault, sometimes fighting off drunken marauders in the process, and ended the night standing guard over a woman in labour with a fellow officer, though he admits the only way they secured her from further disturbance was by smashing up some furniture and strewing books, papers, crockery and personal possessions of all sorts all over the floor so as to make it appear that the house had been thoroughly pillaged and was therefore of no interest to anyone else:

> There was no safety for women even in the churches, and any who interfered or offered resistance were sure to get shot. Every house presented a scene of plunder, debauchery and bloodshed committed with wanton cruelty . . . by our soldiery, and in many instances I saw the savages tear the rings from the ears of beautiful women. . . . Men, women and children were shot . . . for no other . . . reason than pastime; every species of outrage was publically committed . . . and in a manner so brutal that a faithful recital would be . . . shocking to humanity. Not the slightest shadow of discipline was maintained. . . . The infuriated soldiery resembled rather a pack of hell-hounds vomited up from the infernal regions for the extirpation of mankind than . . . a well-organised, brave, disciplined and obedient British army.[69]

And finally there is Edward Costello, a rifleman who actually participated in the sack, who describes in graphic detail how a woman and two girls who were discovered hiding in a house in which he and a group of other soldiers had settled down to get drunk were dragged out and raped. [70]

The issue, then, is not whether women were raped. Much more to the point is the question of why this happened. In so far as this is concerned, there were certainly factors in the situation that were systemic rather than situational. Thus, whilst such evidence as we have suggests that rank-and-file British soldiers did not engage in rape on a general basis, this was in part because for the bulk of the time they were held in check by the bounds of discipline.[71] Talk of them being merely 'the scum of the earth' may be unfair—as Coss has shown, in most instances they were not habitual criminals on the run from the gallows, but rather labourers and artisans who had fallen on hard times[72]—and, given a fair chance, in civilian life it is probable that many of them would have proved law-abiding, hard-working family men. However, it cannot be denied that long withdrawal from civilian society, constant privation and the horrors of war all had a brutalising effect on even the most decent of individuals. Writing of the aftermath of the retreat of the British army from Burgos in November 1812, for example, Thomas Browne recalled, 'I think it was about this time that I began to remark the . . . effects of a continued warfare like that of the Peninsula on the character of the . . . common soldiers. The latter appeared to me to become daily more ferocious and less fit for return to the duties of citizens, and I sometimes apprehended that, when they should be disbanded in England after the restoration of peace, the country would be over-run with pilferers and marauders of every description'.[73] To this, meanwhile, we must add a certain assumption that soldiers had a right to the spoils of war, and that these spoils included free access to women. And, if this was true in a general sense, it was even more true in the case of cities taken by storm. Throughout the military world of the 'horse-and-musket' period, it was generally understood that governors who continued to defend their city after a practicable breach had been opened in the walls and attempted to withstand an assault not only laid their garrisons open to being executed en masse, but exposed the civilian population to rape and pillage. Of the detail of all this the rank and file of Wellington's army would have been but dimly aware, but many references in the memoirs suggest that they felt that, having stormed the walls, they had the right to throw aside the bonds of discipline, whilst there even seems to have been a belief that they had specifically been given license to do so. 'When the town surrendered and the prisoners were secured', wrote Joseph Donaldson, 'the gate leading into the town from the castle was opened, and we were allowed to enter the town for the purposes of plundering it'.[74] Still more interesting as coming from the perspective of an officer is the testimony of Ensign George Hennell of the Forty-Third Foot: 'Soon after daylight, the bugle sounded for two hours' plunder. . . . By the laws of war we are allowed to kill all found in a town that stands a storm'.[75]

Yet the terrible scenes witnessed in Ciudad Rodrigo, Badajoz and San Sebastián were not unleashed in and of themselves.[76] Instead, they were the product of particular circumstances. In the first place, in all three cases the attackers suffered heavy casualties amid scenes of the most dreadful horror, the result being that, having obtained their objective, they had a desperate need to find some sort of emotional relief.[77] In the second place, there was little to check the men: the civilian population had no arms, the towns concerned were a maze of narrow streets into which they could disperse with the greatest ease, and the few officers who were still on their feet had no means of bringing the men to order: indeed, to attempt to do so was to risk their own lives.[78] In the third place, there was in two of the three cases a serious degree of anger and frustration: Badajoz had withstood an earlier siege in 1811, while San Sebastián had beaten off a massive assault before it fell, there also being stories that both towns were pro-French or, at least, that the populace had shown little in the way of patriotic determination. And in the fourth place, and finally, all three incidents came at the end of what for many of the men concerned were several years of campaigning in some of the roughest and least hospitable terrain in Europe with the support of allies who were often deemed to have left the British to do all the fighting and amidst a civilian population that seemed at best indifferent to the soldiers' suffering. What happened, then, was that, several times over, a deep well of resentment in the heart of many soldiers overflowed and spent itself in a few hours of savagery.[79]

To conclude, then, it is quite clear that, on the whole, the women of Spain and Portugal were not well treated by the foreign soldiers who found themselves in their midst. To start with, the men concerned were the product of military cultures that encouraged soldiers to assume that plunder was very much their right and that women were a legitimate part of that plunder, and, in the case of the French, of an empire that both physically and psychologically nourished its armies from the resources of its subject territories. However, as if this was not enough, those of their number who had any conception of the Iberian peninsula at all could not but be filled with visions of a society in which women were both deeply repressed and by nature possessed of the most powerful sexual cravings. Having once come to Spain or Portugal, meanwhile, the soldiers of Britain and France found that in many instances the women of Iberia really were extraordinarily beautiful, whilst they all around them observed, or, at least, believed that they observed, examples of the behaviour that had given them the reputation they had acquired prior to 1808 (to take just one obvious example, the willingness of many women to seek out a protector in one army or another could all too easily be mistaken for a sexual strategy rather than a survival one). Although it is impossible to say for certain, the result was very probably that, whilst there were exceptions to the general rule, the treatment of the female populace was far worse in Spain and Portugal than was the case in most of the rest of Europe. A part of that exploitation, of course, was outright sexual violence, and there can be no doubt whatsoever that many unfortunate women experienced not just harassment and exploitation, but also rape. That said, however, it is by no means clear that rape was systematic. Thus, whilst it was in all probability ever present as an individual phenomenon, it seems likely only to have reared its head on a general basis in certain very specific situations. This is, though, but cold comfort, while, for all the claims of the French, in particular, that, by freeing many individual women from the grip of elderly husbands, repressive fathers and other such evils, they liberated them and gave them access to a new life, it is quite clear that in most cases they had no basis in reality: thus, a drudge who ran away with some soldier and became a campfollower was likely simply to have exchanged a hearth for a campfire.

Epilogue

In April 1814 peace finally returned to Spain and Portugal, both of which thereafter embarked on a long (and much troubled) process of recovery. As the news of the end of the war and the return of the exiled King Ferdinand VII spread, so women throughout the Peninsula must have heaved a sigh of relief and, indeed, joined in the general celebrations, their participation doubtless being all the more fervent as, in the mind of the crowd at least, Ferdinand VII was seen as a redemptive figure whose coming would usher in a new golden age.[1] Meanwhile, with the initial excitement out of the way, they began to piece together the fragments of their shattered lives. Indeed, with the French cleared from almost the whole of the Peninsula by the end of 1813, they had already started to do so, as witness, for example, the many advertisements placed in the Cádiz press by women who had (or so one can assume) been displaced by the war, and wanted to set out on the long and difficult journey home by attaching themselves as servants or wet nurses to families heading back to Madrid or other cities.[2]

What hopes and dreams were tied up in these pathetic little notes, we cannot say. What is evident, however, is that all the trauma, anguish and suffering of the years that had passed since 1808 had produced almost no change in the situation of the women of Spain and Portugal, the rows of women whom Buckham observed frying dogfish on the quayside in Oporto when he arrived in the Peninsula in May 1812 being highly symbolic in this respect: with the fighting now hundreds of miles away, the female populace were settling back into the same roles as they had played prior to 1808.[3] A tiny handful, true, had seen their lives transformed beyond all recognition: once a peasant girl from the Castillian village of Fuentecén, Catalina de la Fuente, now found herself the wife of one of the most famous and successful generals of the Spanish army, the erstwhile private soldier she had married in 1795 having been transformed into the famous *guerrilla* commander, Juan Martín Díez, el Empecinado. However, in general, as far as the female population was concerned, the Spain and Portugal of 1814 were very much the Spain and Portugal of 1808: the railing of conservative clerics determined to restore the gender relations of the Golden Age notwithstanding, the changes in the lifestyle of the women of the propertied classes that had been set in motion in the course of the eighteenth century were extended and solidified, certainly, but for the vast majority there was nothing. Take, for example, the case of María Josefa Siero. The daughter of a prosperous inhabitant of Fuentes de Oñoro, she was typical enough of the thousands of attractive young women whose dreary lives had suddenly been brightened up by the presence of hundreds of dashing young officers, and, like many others, had allowed herself to be seduced by one of them. Yet, all too soon, the war had moved on and with it her lover, leaving her both devastated and exposed to endless petty vindictiveness at the hands of her outraged family.[4]

Surprisingly, perhaps, the picture is not rendered very much brighter by looking at the many thousands of women who had turned their backs on their pre-war lives by turning to foreign husbands or protectors. What happened to all these women is a story that deserves more attention than it can be given here, and certainly one that requires greater research. Sufficient is known, however, to offer some suggestions. In the short term the women concerned in many cases doubtless saved themselves from starvation and secured themselves at least a degree of protection, though those who ended up as ordinary campfollowers still endured much misery and sometimes lost their lives in any case. Beyond that, however, there is a clear difference between those who took British husbands or partners and those who took French ones. Thus, for the latter group, it may probably be assumed that, in many cases, if not most, when the regiments they had attached themselves to were called back to France or driven across the Pyrenees, they simply went along with them and either met their fates in some other campaign—above all, that of Russia[5]—or eventually found some sort of niche in society.[6] Assuming that they were married to them, where the men concerned were officers who went on to make a distinguished career after 1815, their fate was very comfortable.[7] Yet plenty of other officers did not do so well and ended their days on half-pay, while the many thousands of sergeants, corporals and privates who were simply turned loose to fend for themselves found even less in the way of reward, the fact being that large numbers cannot but have experienced great financial difficulty. Given the general horror which the war in the Peninsula occasioned in France, it is also probable that they did not get much of a welcome: according to the Swiss cadet, Sylvain de Larreguy, his mother refused even to meet the young Extremaduran girl whom his elder brother, François, had secretly married while serving in Spain.[8]

If there were difficulties in France and her erstwhile satellites, in the case of Britain the situation was in general much worse. In contrast to the French army, the return home meant a voyage by sea, this being something that for many of the women concerned constituted an insuperable obstacle. Thus, the authorities for the most part would only meet the cost of the journey in the case of women who were legally married, which most of the Spanish and Portuguese women were not.[9] When the British army took ship at Bourdeaux in the wake of the fall of Napoleon, then, several hundred women found that they were to be left behind. Shocked by the news, a number of regiments appear to have raised subscriptions to help the women, the vast majority of whom were absolutely destitute, whilst a few men deserted rather than forsake their partners, but in general there was nothing to be done, the embarkation going ahead amidst scenes of the utmost despair, the campfollowers concerned eventually being sent back across the Pyrenees in the company of a brigade of Portuguese infantry.[10]

What the future held for the 950 women concerned does not bear thinking about. Many had probably never been forgiven by their families for running off with British soldiers, while others had no homes to return to. A handful, perhaps, managed to find husbands in their wanderings, but the fact that few could have provided even the humblest of dowries could not but have told against them. Sadly, then, we may assume that, *faut de mieux,* many ended up as common prostitutes, and all the more so as the fact that they had run off with foreign soldiers without contracting the bonds of marriage almost certainly precluded them from obtaining any of the limited compensation that was available from the state (in so far as this was concerned, in Spain, at least, it was decreed, first, that pensions should be paid to the widows of men killed in the war, and, second, that girls who had been orphaned in the conflict should be provided with dowries; in practice, however, little money was actually paid out, in the first place because the Spanish state was all but bankrupt, and, in the second, because the countless women of whose husbands there was no trace had no means of proving that they were actually dead).[11]

As for the women, whether British or Iberian, who did make it across the Bay of Biscay, the story is at best mixed. Some of the more fortunate seem to have done well enough, indeed, even to have thrived. Thus, sent home from south-west France in the spring of 1814, for example, being much liked and respected, Nancy McDermott was provided with a considerable sum of money raised by means of a subscription amongst the officers and men of her husband's unit and thereby enabled to live out her days in relative comfort in her native Ireland.[12] Still luckier, perhaps, was Maria da Silva. A village girl from the vicinity of Elvas, at the age of sixteen or seventeen, Da Silva had married a soldier of the Forty-Eighth Foot named Stephen Palmer round about the time of the battle of Albuera in 1811, and remained with the regiment until her husband, now a colour sergeant, was discharged from the army in August 1814 on the account of serious injuries he had received during the storm of Badajoz and the battle of the River Nivelle. Fortunately for her, however, Palmer seems to have been a reliable and hard-working individual of some intelligence, and in the years that followed he succeeded in making a reasonable living as a carter in his home village of Burwell, the couple also proceeding to add nine more children to the son that was born to them in Portugal.[13] Finally, another girl who fell on her feet was one María de la Encarnación Delgado Olivero, a girl from the village of Gallegos de Argañán in the present-day province of Salamanca who at the age of about twenty-six ran away with a redcoat remembered only as Isaac, and after the war lived with him in England for many years. At some point in the 1850s, however, her old soldier died, whereupon she threw herself upon the mercy of the family she had left behind in her home village. Yet she was certainly not a pauper. On the contrary, welcomed home as a prodigal by her surviving relatives, according to family tradition she astounded them by the wealth of personal possessions that she brought back with her.[14]

Other women, meanwhile, experienced lives of great hardship and would probably have ended their days in the workhouse had their cases not come to the attention of the public and even, on occasion, figures as prominent as the Duke of Wellington and Queen Victoria, two such being Agnes Reston, the wife of a sergeant of the Ninety-Fourth Foot who had shown great heroism in the course of her regiment's participation in the defence of Cádiz in 1810, and Mary Anne Hewitt, another campfollower of the Forty-Eighth Foot who had joined its ranks at about the same time as Maria da Silva.[15] However, the story of the rank-and-file of the Peninsular army was not a happy one—discharged by the thousand, Wellington's veterans discovered not only that their return to civilian society coincided with the onset of a great depression, but also that the pensions to which they were entitled were scarcely sufficient for their own needs, let alone those of a family as well—and it may therefore be surmised that the vast majority of the army's wives ended their days as paupers. Consider, for example, the following story from the letters of Augustus Frazer:

> I met a most interesting case in Coimbra a few days since in a blind soldier of the Eighty-Eighth Regiment, only twenty-five years old, with a decent-looking wife carrying an infant of five months in her arms and another little girl, two years and a half old, running by her side. I was struck with the children and stopped the poor fellow to hear his story. He was going to Lisbon to be invalided, was quite cheerful, and seemed only to feel for the little girl, whom he was obliged to carry on the march, and who was both frightened and hurt when he fell down for want of sight. They had been possessed of a donkey, he said, but

it had been stolen from them. I never saw more cheerfulness or resignation.[16]

This, perhaps, represents a particularly extreme case, but such were the economic conditions of the moment that even families in which the husbands were discharged in a fit enough condition to work were scarcely in a better state. A typical story, then, is probably that of Katherine Exley, a campfollower of the Thirty-Fourth Foot who lost three children in the course of the Peninsular War: left a widow when her husband died in 1829, she thereafter eked out a living, first, as the mistress of a 'dame school' in her home town of Batley and then as a textile worker before finally dying in poverty at the age of seventy-eight in 1857.[17] For officers' wives and (sometimes) mistresses, of course, the situation was on the whole somewhat more optimistic: Juana Leon de Smith, for example, went on to enjoy a privileged position in British and colonial society alike.[18] Yet, even so, the keynote was as often uncertainty as it was security. Peace meant the disbanding of many unwanted regiments and battalions, and this in turn meant that many officers found themselves placed on half-pay. Unless the men concerned had private means (which many wartime officers did not), the result was generally years of hardship. One such story is recounted by Richard Henegan. In brief, this concerns no less a person than a countess who fell in love with a lieutenant, and eventually agreed to leave her husband and run away to England with her soldier-lover under cover of a convenient leave of absence which the latter had applied for for that very purpose. When the husband died, the couple got married, but their life together was by no means easy: no position being available in the army for the man concerned, he spent the last fourteen years of his life on half-pay and died in 1828, leaving his Spanish bride to endure the miseries of genteel poverty.[19] Still worse, perhaps is a story that comes to us from the Portuguese army. Thus, posted to Oporto with his regiment in 1814, Bunbury came across a British captain of the Third Caçadores who was absolutely penniless and living with his wife in a state of complete misery in 'a small cottage . . . redolent with the state of rum and in great disorder'. Such men had often been long-serving sergeants in the British army who had switched their allegiance on the promise of preferment, and they therefore had little to their name beyond their pay, this being something that in the Portuguese service was both inadequate and likely to be long in arrears. As for their wives, to the extent that they were British, one imagines that their lot had at best been extremely difficult, not least because they would have had few companions of their own nationality, and in this instance the strain appears to have become all too much, the woman concerned having sought solace in the bottle and become an alcoholic.[20]

In many instances, then, escape did not lead to a better life. On the other hand, it has also to be said that it did not necessarily make life worse either, the fact being that many of the wives and mistresses who ended their days as paupers would probably have ended their lives as paupers anyway. Worth pointing out, too, is the fact that, whatever persecution they may have faced at the hands of family or neighbours, the thousands of women who at some time or another engaged in some form of fraternization with the enemy do not appear to have faced much in the way of official revenge. Here and there cases may be found of women being prosecuted for such crimes as having French soldiers in their homes—one such was a María Margarida Maxima, who was imprisoned for two months following the liberation of Oporto in May 1809[21]—while there are also reports of collaborators being subjected to more-or-less severe measures of arbitrary justice in the course of the war.[22] Also worth noting are various pamphlets and newspaper articles that sought to demonise fraternization.[23] However, in the end, whilst certain *afrancesada* exiles who had managed to escape to France at the end of the war deemed it prudent never to return to Spain—the most notable example is the Marquesa de Montehermoso—the consequences do not appear to have been very great, not the least of the reasons for this being that women accused of collaboration could generally claim that their actions had been the result of compulsion.[24]

What is interesting here is that there seems to have been almost no suggestion that women collaborated with the invaders out of a sense of ideological affinity: rather, fraternization was explained in terms of frivolity—weak-willed, irrational and ignorant, women were, by extension, as incapable of controlling their impulses as they were of understanding that indulging in an affair with a French officer constituted a betrayal of the Fatherland. However, if the prevalence of such views is far from surprising, they do run clean contrary to the one gain that the women of Spain and Portugal made from the war. Thus, already visible in the streets and polite society, women for the first time became visible in political discourse. In the case of plays and pageants this was the literal truth—in a number of such instances, we hear of Spain being represented by the figure of a beautiful young girl[25]—whilst women and girls also became an integral part of patriotic ceremony. Consider, for example, the events that took place when Wellington returned to Ciudad Rodrigo following the fall of Badajoz in April 1812. Thus, we learn that, having first been greeted by a guard of honour of little girls armed with toy weapons, the British commander was serenaded across the bridge over the River Agueda by twelve young women dressed in traditional costume equipped with tambourines and the Spanish woodwind instrument known as the *dulzaina,* showered with flowers by yet more women as he processed through the streets to his headquarters, and, finally, presented with a elaborate bouquet by the wife of some unnamed local dignitary.[26] Women, then, were used to give life to patriotic platitudes, but the need to argue that the struggle against Napoleon was backed by the people ensured that, whatever the truth of the matter, the Patriot propaganda machine went one step further, and on many occasions accorded women a prominent role in the reportage of events.[27] Not just that, meanwhile, but they were also accorded a voice of their own in that newspapers sometimes published accounts of this or that incident that were ostensibly written by women, a very good example being two letters describing the siege of Gerona that appeared in the *Gazeta del Gobierno* (Patriot Spain's *de facto* official gazette) in July 1809.[28] In the latter instance, we hear of women actively taking part in the struggle via the manufacture of sandbags and cartridges, and from 1808 onwards the idea of figures such as Agustina of Aragón actually fighting the French became a standard part of Patriot propaganda. Nor was it just a case of engaging in heroics on the walls of embattled cities. Thus, particularly on the stage, women were portrayed as defending the Fatherland in the context of their day-to-day lives. Thus, in one play set in occupied Logroño, to the huge amusement of their fellow stall holders, two market women named Marica and Frasquita are witnessed treating a pair of unfortunate French soldiers who visit their stalls to a dazzling display of insolence and low wit from which the latter emerge looking utterly ridiculous, and all the more so as they are evidently completely unconscious of the insults that have just been heaped upon them.[29] With a few educated women themselves actively contributing to that propaganda, the result was that it henceforward became much harder to deny the idea that women were political beings who were capable of making reasoned judgements on the issues of the day, and all the more so as a curtain was quickly drawn on the extent of female fraternization with the enemy.

Did any of this make a difference to the fortunes of Spanish and Portuguese women? In the short term, this question must be answered in the negative: the constitution of 1812, for example, made not a single concession to the cause of female emancipation. However, this does not mean that nothing had been gained. Thus, unlike their eighteenth-century counterparts, nineteenth-century Spanish feminists were able to draw upon the services of both a powerful myth that has in many ways survived intact down to the present day. At the same time, just possibly, feminist ideas had begun to penetrate a wider circle of Spanish women than the tiny handful of intellectuals who had come upon them in the eighteenth century. When Cádiz was gripped by rioting in February 1809, the female voices in the crowd seemingly did not just belong to prostitutes. To quote a letter written by the British diplomat, Sir George Jackson, 'One peculiarity of the mob . . . was that very well-dressed women, much above the common class, were observed . . . actively inciting and encouraging the people in their riotous proceedings'.[30] As to why this was so, he had no doubts: '[Villel] has been playing the Bishop of Durham with regard to women's dresses, and has actually sent a lady to a convent who refused to conform to his orders on that head and . . . told him to his face that it was very hot, and that she would wear no more clothing than she pleased, it being also no object with her to dress to please him. This has excited all the women against him'.[31] Evidently, then, there were individual Spanish women who were resentful of the trammels that society had imposed upon them, and were subsequently radicalised by their experiences in the Peninsular War. Equally, would the two women observed by Frazer making vigorous attempts to drag a recalcitrant male home from a tavern in Espinal one day in early January 1813 have dared be half as bold and vociferous as they actually were but for the events of 1808–14? We do not know, but it is interesting to note that they not only prevailed but obtained the support of an angry crowd.[32] And, finally, what, too, are we to make of the incident in which the attempt of the liberal parish priest, Juan Antonio Posse, to reprove a group of Galician women whom he encountered crossing a stream for hitching up their skirts too far was met by a barrage of jeers and catcalls that soon had him fleeing the scene in a state of great embarrassment?[33] If Iberian feminism for the most part remained a cause that was waiting to happen, by 1814 it appears to have acquired greater momentum in six years of armed conflict than it had in almost a century of enlightened debate. This was not much, perhaps, but it was at least a beginning.

Notes

Preface

1. Some obvious points of reference include the following: L. Grant de Pauw, *Battle Cries and Lullabies: Women in War from Prehistory to Present* (Norman, Oklahoma, 1998); A. Venning, *Following the Drum: the Lives of Army Wives and Daughters* (London, 2005); B. C. Hacker, 'Women and military institutions in early-modern Europe: a reconnaissance', *Signs*, VI, No. 4 (Summer, 1981), pp. 643–71; and J. Lynn, *Women, Armies and Warfare in Early-Modern Europe* (Cambridge, 2008).

2. *Cf.* T. Cardoza, *Intrepid Women: Cantinières and Vivandières of the French Army* (Bloomington, Indiana, 2010); T. Cardoza, '"Habits appropriate to her sex": the female military experience in France during the age of revolution', in K. Hagemann *et al.* (eds.), *Gender, War and Politics, 1775–1830* (Houndmills, 2010), pp. 188–205; S. Conner, 'Les femmes militaires: women in the French army, 1792–1815', *Consortium on Revolutionary Europe Proceedings*, XII (1982), pp. 290–302; D. Hopkin, 'The world turned upside-down: female soldiers in the French armies of the Revolutionary and Napoleonic Wars,' in A. Forrest *et al.* (eds.), *Soldiers, Citizens and Civilians: Experiences and Perceptions of the Revolutionary and Napoleonic Wars, 1790–1820* (Houndmills, 2009), pp. 77–95; R. Dekker and L. van de Pol, 'Republican heroines: cross-dressing women in the French-Revolutionary armies', *History of European Ideas*, X, No. 3 (May, 1989), pp. 353–64; K. Hagemann, 'Female patriots: women, war and the nation in the period of the Prussian-German anti-Napoleonic Wars', *Gender and History*, XVI, No. 2 (August, 2004), pp. 397–424; K. Hagemann, '"Heroic virgins" and "bellicose amazons": armed women, the gender order and the German public during and after the Napoleonic Wars', *European History Quarterly*, XXXVII, No. 4 (October, 2007), pp. 507–27; K. Aeslestad, 'Patriotism in practice: war and gender roles in Republican Hamburg, 1750–1815', in Hagemann *et al.*, *Gender, War and Politics*, pp. 227–46; F. C. G. Page, *Following the Drum: Women in Wellington's Wars* (London, 1986); C. Kennedy, 'From the ballroom to the battlefield: British women and Waterloo' in Forrest *et al.*, *Soldiers, Citizens and Civilians*, pp. 137–56.

3. *Cf.* J. L. Tone, 'Spanish women and the resistance to Napoleon', in V. L. Enders and P. Radcliff (eds.), *Constructing Spanish Womanhood: Female Identity in Modern Spain* (New York, 1999), pp. 259–82; J. L. Tone, 'A dangerous Amazon: Agustina Zaragoza and the Spanish revolutionary war, 1808–1814', *European History Quarterly*, XXXVII, No. 4 (October, 2007), pp. 548–61.

4. Minor conference papers aside, the chief contributions here are I. Castells *et al.* (eds.), *Heroínas y patriotas: mujeres de 1808* (Madrid, 2009), and E. Fernández García, *Mujeres en la Guerra de la Independencia* (Madrid, 2009). For an interesting general essay that covers the subject in a much better manner than the equivalent sections of either of these two works, *cf.* M. Cantos, 'Las mujeres en la prensa entre la ilustración y el romanticismo' in M. Cantos *et al.* (eds.), *La guerra de pluma: estudios sobre la prensa de Cádiz en el tiempo de las cortes (1810–1814), III: sociedad, consumo y vida cotidiana* (Cádiz, 2008), pp. 161–336. In fairness to the individuals concerned, it should be said that some of the essays in the collection edited by Castells *et al.* adopt a much more critical line, but the general tone of any such festschrift, alas, is that set by its editors.

5. As discussed below, the one exception here is J. J. Sánchez Arreisegor, 'Mujeres en la guerra', in F. Miranda (ed.), *Guerra, sociedad y política, 1808–1814* (Pamplona, 2008), I, pp. 691–722.

6. For two discussions of the memoir material, *cf.* N. Ramsey, *The Military Memoir and Romantic Military Culture, 1780–1835* (Farnham, 2011); L. Montroussiet-Favre, 'Remembering the other: the Peninsular War in the autobiographical accounts of British and French soldiers', in A. Forrest, E. François and K. Hagemann (eds.), *War Memories: the Revolutionary and Napoleonic Wars in Modern European Culture* (Basingstoke, 2012), pp. 59–76. In addition, D. Yépez, 'Víctimas y participantes: la mujer española en la Peninsular War desde la óptica británica', *Revista Historia Moderna y Contemporania,* VIII (2010), pp. 156–78, is notable as the only effort that has ever been made to analyse the accounts of the women of Spain found in the British memoirs.

7. By contrast, the term 'Anglo-Portuguese army' will be used to refer to the troops directly under the command of Duke of Wellington in the period April 1809–April 1814.

Chapter 1

1. The most convenient place to access the collection is the relevant pages of the Biblióteca Virtual del Patrimonio Bibligráfico, an on-line library of facsimiles organised by the Spanish Ministry of Culture; *cf.* http://bvpb.mcu.es/independencia/es/catalogo_imagenes/grupo.cmd?posicion=13&path=249 (accessed 20 March 2011).

2. Of these images, perhaps the best known example is Sir David Wilkie's 'The Defence of Zaragoza'. Dating from 1828, this painting is particularly notable for the manner in which it implies that Domenech (see below) is, quite literally, directed by religious feeling: whilst one ecclesiastic gives the order to fire with a wave of his crucifix, in the background another is seen writing a message or order; *cf.* http://www.royalcollection.org.uk/eGallery/object.asp?object=405091&row=0&detail=about (accessed 20 March 2011). For a much more secular version of the genre, *cf.* Marcos Hiraldez de Acosta's 'Agustina of Aragón': dating from 1879, this is devoid of any clerical figure. *Cf.* http://www.asociacionlossitios.com/boletin15.htm#diputacion (accessed 20 March 2011). Finally, for an extended discussion of the popularization of the image of Domenech in the course of the nineteenth century, *cf.* E. Ucelay, 'Agustina, la dama del cañón: el topos de la mujer fálica y el invento de patriotismo', in Castells *et al.*, *Heroínas y*

patríotas: mujeres de 1808, pp. 193–265. Finally, on a point of usage, Agustina de Aragón's surname would ordinarily be shortened to 'Zaragoza', but, given the need to avoid confusing the woman with the city, in this instance 'Domenech' will be used instead.

3. For reproductions of these images, *cf.* http://goya.unizar.es/InfoGoya/Aragon/Azlor.html (accessed 20 March 2011), and http://www.asociacionlossitios.com/boletin15.htm#diputacion (accessed 20 March 2011).

4. For reproductions of these images, *cf.* http://artillerosdearagon.blogspot.com/2009/04/grabados-sitios-de-zaragoza.html (accessed 20 March 2011), and http://fr.wikipedia.org/wiki/Fichier:Maurice_Orange,_Les_d%C3%A9fenseurs_de_Saragosse.jpg (accessed 20 March 1811).

5. For good examples, *cf.* Joaquín Sorolla's 'Defensa del Parque de Artillería de Monteleón' accessed at http://gie1808a1814.tripod.com/meses/mayo.htm, 20 March 2011, and Manuel Castellano's 'Muerte de Daoiz y Velarde', accessed at http://www.google.co.uk/imgres?imgurl=http://www.madrid.es/UnidadWeb/Contenidos/ContenidoGenerico/Ayuntamiento/HistoriaDeMadrid/HistoriaModerna/FOTOS/MUERTEDAOIZ.jpg&imgrefurl=http://www.getdomainpics.com/keyword/daoiz/&usg=__mVQcD1Q_waUIzpnlXWznIWWEJ-g=&h=4260&w=5300&sz=1631&hl=en&start=45&zoom=1&tbnid=WJJb6Sp9qAqADM:&tbnh=127&tbnw=148&ei=pending&prev=/images%3Fq%3DDaoiz%2Band%2BVelarde%26hl%3Den%26sa%3DG%26biw%3D947%26bih%3D567%26gbv%3D2%26tbs%3Disch:10%2C1316&itbs=1&iact=hc&vpx=654&vpy=140&dur=47&hovh=201&hovw=250&tx=216&ty=126&oei=3SKGTZ7KCMa1hAe884nABA&page=4&ndsp=15&ved=1t:429,r:4,s:45&biw=947&bih=567, 20 March 1811.

6. 'El tres de mayo', accessed at http://upload.wikimedia.org/wikipedia/commons/thumb/a/af/El_tres_de_mayo_de_1808.jpg/200px-El_tres_de_mayo_de_1808.jpg, 22 November 2011.

7. Image accessed at http://biclaranja.blogs.sapo.pt/363877.html, 20 March 2011. For a discussion of the iconography of the disaster at Oporto, *cf.* F. Vlachou, 'Painting the Battle of Porto, 29 March 1809: the *desastre da ponte das barcas* in its Portuguese and French context', *Revista de estudos anglo-portugueses,* XVIII (2009), pp. 49–68.

8. F. de Goya, 'Ataque a un campamento militar', accessed at http://picasaweb.google.com/lh/photo/FX3IxXHnry8JRDd0cJJWyg, 1 November 2011.

9. For an interesting discussion, *cf.* H. Thomas, *Goya: The Third of May 1808* (London, 1972), pp. 69–71. Thomas would not go as far as the current author, but he does admit that the prints are 'perhaps less anti-French than they seem at first sight', and, further, that, in general, they 'simply bemoan the evil of war without making any specially patriotic comment'.

10. For a convenient means of accessing 'Los desastres de la guerra', *cf.* www.gasl.org/refbib/Goya__Guerra.pdf (accessed 6 February 2010). Meanwhile, note the discussion in M. D. Antiguedad, 'Goya y la genesis de un nuevo modelo femenino en la Guerra de la Independencia', *Revista Historia Moderna y Contemporánea,* VIII (2010), pp. 8–24.

11. J. A. Tomlinson, 'Mothers, *majas* and *marcialidad:* faces of enlightenment in Spain', in Jaafe, C. M., and Lewis, E. F. (eds.), *Eve's Enlightenment: Women's Experience in Spain and Spanish America, 1726–1839* (Baton Rouge, 2009), p. 234.

12. F. Monzón and E. Mendoza, *Agustina* (Zaragoza, 2009), n.p.

13. Image accessed at http://www.cqout.com/item.asp?id=4923219 (accessed 19 March 2011).

14. Image accessed at http://www.google.co.uk/imgres?imgurl=http://www.mediastorehouse.com/image/wellington-at-madrid-1812-c1850s_1226664.jpg&imgrefurl=http://www.mediastorehouse.com/pictures_1226664/wellington-at-madrid-1812-c1850s.html&usg=__X8LydyScVVIVnlcWmmRPdghWadQ=&h=450&w=403&sz=112&hl=en&start=0&zoom=1&tbnid=qLj_UHqKrjWCVM:&tbnh=141&tbnw=126&ei=712GTdD306eJ4gaVv7HUCA&prev=/images%3Fq%3Dwellington%2Bat%2BMadrid%2B1812%26um%3D1%26hl%3Den%26sa%3DG%26biw%3D1659%26bih%3D865%26tbs%3Disch:1&um=1&itbs=1&iact=hc&vpx=123&vpy=57&dur=765&hovh=237&hovw=212&tx=115&ty=137&oei=k12GTdubDc6zhAeikqWxBg&page=1&ndsp=49&ved=1t:429,r:0,s:0, 20 March 2011; for a discussion of 'Malasaña y su hija' and many of the other paintings discussed here, see L. Triviño, 'Percepción e iconografía de la "heroicidad de género" en la Guerra de la Independencia' in A. Ramos and A. Romero (eds.), *1808–1812: los emblemas de la libertad* (Cádiz, 2009), pp. 541–58. In reality, Manuela Malasaña was executed by firing squad after the fighting was over, but that is by-the-by.

15. For a good example of the popularization of these images, *cf.* 'Los sitios de Zaragoza en la tarjeta postal', accessed at http://www.dpz.es/turismo/cadiz-zaragoza/doc/ilustradores.pdf, 20 March 2011. *Cf.* also L. Martín Pozuelo, 'Quereís recordar el Dos de Mayo? Estampas populares de la Guerra de la Independencia' in C. Demange *et al.* (eds.), *Sombras de mayo: mitos y memorias de la Guerra de la Independencia en España, 1808–1908* (Madrid, 2007), pp. 321–44.

16. *Cf.* Tone, 'A dangerous Amazon', p. 553. Interestingly, it was not just representatives of Spanish monarchism that attempted to shelter behind the skirts of *la artillera.* Thus, a conservative Republican who was desperate to ingratiate himself with the élite, in 1872 Emilio Castelar eulogised Agustina Zaragoza in a long speech in which he effectively explained her bravery in terms of the facts, first, that she was Aragonese and, second, that the Aragonese were the very epitome of *hispanidad; cf.* R. García Carcel, *El sueño de la nación indomable: los mitos de la Guerra de la Independencia* (Madrid,2007), pp. 175–76.

17. For an introduction to Pérez Galdós as a historical novelist, *cf.* H. C. Berkowitz, *Pérez Galdós: Spanish Liberal Crusader* (Madison, Wisconsin, 1948); also helpful here is F. C. Saínz, *Pérez Galdós: vida, obra, época* (Madrid, 1970). Meanwhile, a discussion that is specifically relevant to the Peninsular War may be found in G. H. Lovett, 'Some observations on Galdós' *Juan Martín, el Empecinado*', *Modern Language Notes,* LXXXIV, No. 2 (March, 1969), pp. 196–207.

18. *Cf.* B. Pérez Galdós, *El 19 de marzo y el 2 de mayo* (Madrid, 1873), in F. C. Saínz de Robles (ed.), *Bénito Pérez Galdós: obras completas* (Madrid, 1963), p. 460.

19. *Cf. ibid.*, p. 468.

20. M. E. da Câmara, 'A imagem da mulher na ficção literária antinapoleónica', *Revista Historia Moderna y Contemporánea,* VIII (2010), pp. 25–32; *cf.* also M. F. Marinho, 'A memoria e a ficçao da segunda invasão francesa', in L. Valente de Oliveira(ed.), *O Porto e as invasões francesas, 1809–2009* (Oporto, 2009), IV, pp. 205–32. For Arnaldo da Gama in particular, *cf.* A. Gomes Fernandes, 'Da baioneta à pena: as invasões francesas na obra de Arnaldo Gama' in M. L. Machado (ed.), *A Guerra Peninsular: perspectivas multidisciplinares* (Lisbon, 2007), I, pp. 587–609.

21. M. Gomes da Torre, 'A segunda invasão francesa em *The Sisters of the Douro*', in Machado, *A Guerra Peninsular: perspectivas multidisciplinares,* I, pp. 541–49.

22. For all this, *cf.* M. Salgues, 'La Guerra de la Independencia y el teatro: tentativa de creación y de recuperación de una epopeya popular, 1840–1868', in Demange *et al.*, *Sombras de mayo,* pp. 267–87.

23. *Cf.* M. García Guatas, 'La imagen costumbrista de Aragón' in T. Buesa and J. C. Mainer (eds.), *Localismo, costumbrismo y literatura popular en Aragón: V curso sobre lengua y literatura en Aragón* (Zaragoza, 1999), pp. 115–151.

24. Lyrics accessed at http://www.forosdedebate.com/letras-de-jotas-aragonesas-vt2443.html, 22 November 2011.

25. For Toreno's account of the uprising of 1808, *cf.* Conde de Toreno (ed.), *Historia del levantamiento, guerra y revolución de España,* ed. R. Hocquellet (Pamplona, 2008), pp. 80–149 *passim.* The role played by women in such atrocities is also commemorated in *Los desastres de la guerra:* in 'Populacho' ('Mob'), the inanimate body of a man is belaboured by a woman armed with a club while being dragged through the streets of some town or village.

26. *Cf.* A. Alcaide, *Historia de los dos sitios que pusieron a Zaragoza en los años de 1808 y 1809 las tropas de* Napoleón (Burgos, 1830), I, pp. 58–59.

27. E. Rodríguez Solis, *Los guerrilleros de 1808: historia popular de la Guerra de la Independencia* (Barcelona, 1895), I, p. 539. Be it noted that the story of Susana Claretona is not just some folk memory: on the contrary, the account given by Enrique Solis is taken almost word for word from that given in *Diario de Tarragona,* 4 October 1809, pp. 2145–46. Though coming to the subject from a position diametrically opposed to that of the political establishment, republicans were by no means slow to celebrate the idea of female heroism, not least because it reinforced the idea of the dynamism and patriotic ardour of the Spanish people. *Cf.* García Carcel, *Sueño de la nación indomable,* pp. 174–75.

28. C. R. Vaughan, *Narrative of the Siege of Zaragoza* (London, 1809), pp. 14–16.

29. R. W. Southey, *A History of the Peninsular War* (London, 1823–32) I, p. 362; C. Oman, *A History of the Peninsular War* (Oxford, 1902–30), III, p. 23.

30. W. Napier, *History of the War in the Peninsula and the South of France* (London, 1828–40), I, pp. 59–60.

31. For all this, *cf.* J. Gómez de Arteche, *La mujer en la Guerra de la Independencia* (Madrid, 1906). *Cf.* also A. Coy, *Agustina Saragossa* [sic] *Domenech: heroína de los sitios de Zaragoza* (Ceuta, 1914).

32. *Ibid.*, p. 25; for the historical context, *cf.* C. J. Esdaile, *Spain in the Liberal Age: from Constitution to Civil War, 1808–1939* (Oxford, 2000), pp. 200–205.

33. As late as 2002, when the organizers of a conference on the War of Independence that is held every year at Bailén resolved to adopt 'women and war' as the theme for that year's meeting, they found themselves having to fill up the sessions with papers that were either wholly generic or directed towards conflicts far distant from that of 1808–14; *cf.* F. Acosta (ed.), *Conflicto y sociedad civil—la mujer en la guerra: actas de las cuartas jornadas sobre la batalla de Bailén y la España contemporánea* (Jaén, 2003).

34. For all this, *cf.* J. Maroto, *Guerra de la Independencia: imágenes en cine y televisión* (Madrid, 2007), and E. Fernández García, 'Heroínas del cine', *Revista Historia Moderna y Contemporánea,* VIII (2010), pp. 64–78. It has to be said, meanwhile, that outside Spain the image of the role played by women in the conflict

was no different. Thus, in Robert Leonard's 1937 production, *The Firefly*, the chief protagonist is a singer who becomes a spy for the Patriot cause, while, produced twenty years later, Stanley Kramer's *The Pride and the Passion* features Sophia Loren as Juana, a young girl who has joined a guerrilla band.

35. For some remarks on the interest of Franco, in particular, in making use of film to help attain his political objectives, *cf.* J. Maroto, 'La Guerra de la Independencia en el cine' in F. Acosta (ed.), *Bailén a las puertas del bicentenario: revisión y nuevas aportaciones—actas de las septimas jornadas sobre la batalla de Bailén y la España contemporánea* (Jaén, 2008), pp. 153–54. In this respect, it might be noted that, though an American film, *The Pride and the Passion* was produced in Spain and deeply influenced by the cultural norms of the Franco era (indeed, Franco took considerable personal interest in its progress).

36. For all this, *cf.* J. Maroto, 'La Guerra de la Independencia en los tebeos', in J. Armillas (ed.), *La Guerra de la Independencia: estudios* (Zaragoza, 2001), I, pp. 387–416.

37. J. D. Casamayor, *Te Deum: victoria o muerte* (Zaragoza, 2006), p. 188.

38. For a general discussion of the post-Galdosian Spanish novel of the War of Independence, *cf.* J. Maroto, 'La Guerra de la Independencia en la novela del siglo XX', in F. Miranda (ed.), *Guerra, sociedad y política, 1808–1814* (Pamplona, 2008), pp. 386–403.

39. L. Doumergue, 'Goya, las mujeres y la guerra contra Bonaparte', in M. Reder and E. Mendoza (eds.), *La Guerra de la Independencia en Málaga y su provincia, 1808–1814* (Málaga, 2005), p. 243.

40. Aside from the Triviño paper already cited, *cf.* E. Fernández García, 'El liberalismo, las mujeres y la Guerra de la Independencia', in A. Moliner (ed.), *Occapació i resistència a la Guerra del Francès, 1808–1814* (Barcelona, 2007), pp. 203–10; A. M. Jiménez Bartolomé, 'Las mujeres en la Guerra de la Independencia: propaganda y resistencia', in *ibid.*, pp. 247–56; Sánchez Arreiseigor, 'Mujeres en la guerra'. To be fair, the contribution of Sánchez Arreiseigor demands a little more notice than it is here given: the only Spanish contribution to the subject that displays a convincing empirical knowledge of the wider experiences and role of women in the age of 'horse and musket' warfare, it is also more critical in its approach than most of its fellows.

41. *Cf.* A. Moliner (ed.), *La Guerra de la Independencia en España, 1808–1814* (Barcelona, 2007).

42. *Cf.* Castells *et al.*, *Heroínas y patriotas;* Fernández García, *Mujeres.*

43. M. J. de la Pascua, 'Las mujeres en Andalucía en la Guerra de la Independencia', in J. M. Delgado and M. A. López Arandia (eds.), *Andalucía en guerra, 1808–1814* (Jaén, 2010), p. 218.

44. For an English-language version of this tendency, *cf.* Tone, 'Spanish women and the resistance to Napoleon'.

45. For an extended discussion of this evidence, *cf.* C. J. Esdaile, *Fighting Napoleon: guerrillas, bandits and adventurers in Spain, 1808–1814* (London, 2004).

46. Most extraordinary of all here is the fact that Pascua has remained a voice crying in the wilderness, Gloria Espigado even going so far as to deny the very idea that a specifically feminist agenda survived the coming of war. Thus: 'The reinvindicative tone of such earlier voices as those of Inés Joyes and Josefa Amar was now lacking. It was as if the war in Europe had changed the agenda and the priorities of women's discourse—as if women had renounced the explicit defence

of their capacities and the outright demanding of their rights.' *Cf.* G. Espigado, 'Europeas y españolas contra Napoleón: un estudio comparado', *Revista Historia Moderna y Contemporánea,* VIII (2010), p. 61.

47. A. R. C. Dallas, *Felix Alvarez* (London, 1818), II, p. 13.

48. W. H. Maxwell, *The Bivouac, or Stories of the Peninsular War* (Nonesuch Classic reprint, 2008), pp. 161, 217–18. Such references do not prevent Maxwell from retailing a more conventional view of women's experiences in the Peninsular War, as witness, for example, his graphic description of the scenes of mass rape that accompanied the sack of Badajoz in 1812. *Ibid.*, p. 257.

49. Maxwell does provide us with one other possible female role model in the person of La Martina, a young woman who formed a guerrilla band in the Basque provinces. At first sight this might seem a genuflection in the direction of the myth of Agustina of Aragón, but in fact La Martina, as the woman was known, is represented as little more than a brigand who was so indiscriminate in her rampages that she terrorised the civilian population as much as the French and eventually had to be suppressed by the much more famous guerrilla leader, Francisco Espoz y Mina; *cf. ibid.*, p. 219.

50. G. A. Henty, *The Young Buglers: A Tale of the Peninsular War* (London, 1880), pp. 149–63.

51. G. A. Henty, *With Moore at Corunna* (London, 1897), p. 225.

52. *Ibid.*, p. 151.

53. *Ibid.*, pp. 305–10. In fairness, in the sequel to *With Moore at Corunna*—Henty did do something to remedy this very negative portrayal of the women of Spain and Portugal. Thus, in its pages we meet Nita, a young Spanish girl who helps O'Connor escape when he is taken prisoner at the battle of Fuentes de Oñoro in May 1811, and, what is more, refuses his offer of financial recompense on the grounds that he had come 'to take the French away'. *Cf.* G.A. Henty, *Under Wellington's Command* (London, 1899), pp. 131–34. For another portrayal of Spanish female gallantry, one can turn to *The Young Rifleman,* in which a young British officer shipwrecked on the coast of Galicia is helped to make his way to his regiment in Portugal by the wife of a Spanish guerrilla leader. Needless to say, the couple fall in love, but what makes the text particularly worth noting is the fact that the woman clearly sees the journey as a liberating break from routine which is to be seized with both hands. Thus: 'Doña María . . . gave ample scope to her enjoyment. She seemed like a bird, just escaped from its cage, and laughed, and sang, and chatted with a degree of hilarity and abandon . . . that absolutely startled me.' *Cf.* Captain Rafter, *Percy Blake or the Young Rifleman* (London, 1855), II, pp. 94–95.

54. For two interesting discussions of Henty, *cf.* G. Davies, 'G. A. Henty and history', *Huntingdon Library Quarterly,* XVIII, No. 2 (February, 1955), pp. 159–67 and R. A. Huttenback, 'G. A. Henty and the imperial stereotype', *ibid.,* XXIX, No. 1 (November, 1965), pp. 63–75.

55. *Cf.* C. S. Forester, *Death to the French* (London, 1933); G. Heyer, *The Spanish Bride* (London, 1940).

56. Pérez Galdós, *Cádiz,* in Saínz , *Bénito Pérez Galdós,* pp. 942–43.

57. *Cf.* E. M. Flores, 'El gran teatro del mundo: el Cádiz de las cortes de Galdós', *Cuadernos de ilustración y romanticismo,* No. 10 (2002), pp. 45–58. For some further suggestions that women were less caught up in the issues of the struggle than has sometimes been imagined, *cf.* J. M. Pedrosa, 'Canciones y

leyendas en torno a la Guerra de la Independencia: historia y folclore', in Ramos and Romero, *1808–1812,* pp. 133–62.

58. *Cf.* C. Oman, *Wellington's Army* (London, 1913), pp. 274–78. At least Oman does mention the campfollowers: from some other accounts of Wellington's army, they are entirely absent.

59. For a good example, *cf.* B. Cornwell, *Sharpe's Company: Richard Sharpe and the Siege of Badajoz, January to April 1812* (London, 1983), p. 111. Cornwell also provides graphic accounts of the horrors experienced by Spanish and Portuguese women at the hands of British and French troops alike, but the few indigenous female characters that he develops—a Portuguese courtesan who has fetched up with Wellington's army, a beautiful countess turned spy, a peasant girl who becomes the common-law wife of the redoubtable Sergeant Harper and a ruthless *guerrilla* commander named La Aguja—are little more than stock figures. To return to camp followers, a detailed picture of two women in particular—this time French *cantinières*—emerges from the pages of R. F. Delderfield's *Seven Men of Gascony* (London, 1949).

60. A. Eaglestone, *Forward the Baggage!* (London, 2004), p. 6.

61. *Cf.* R. F. Delderfield, *Too Few for Drums* (London, 1964).

62. *Cf.* E. V. Thompson, *Cassie* (London, 1991).

63. *Cf.* S. Tillyard, *Tides of War* (London, 2011). There is no absolute proof that Wellington had a mistress in the Peninsular War, but there is no denying that he enjoyed the company of women, and all the more so if they were young and attractive.

64. For the text of *Our Soldier Boy, cf.* http://www.gutenberg.org/files/21371/21371-h/21371-h.htm (accessed 27 November 2011).

65. This is not the place to engage in literary criticism, but it is difficult to imagine a finer novel ever being written on the Peninsular War than *Joseph.* Its command of the social and geographical background is outstanding, whilst the author's decision to concentrate on the civilian aspects of the conflict gives it a very different aspect to most of its competitors.

Chapter 2

1. M. V. López-Cordón, 'La situación de la mujer a finales del Antiguo Régimen', in R. M. Capel (ed.), *Mujer y sociedad en España, 1700–1975* (Madrid, 1982), pp. 51–52.

2. For the Church's demonization of women, *cf.* J. M. Higgins, 'The myth of Eve: the temptress', *Journal of the American Academy of Religion,* XLIV, No. 4 (December, 1976), pp. 639–40, and M. A. Denike, 'The Devil's insatiable sex: a genealogy of evil incarnate', *Hypatia,* XVIII, No. 1 (Winter, 2003), pp. 10–43.

3. For the concept of honour in Spanish society in the *antiguo régimen, cf.* J. L. Sánchez Lora, *Mujeres, conventos y formas de la religiosidad barroca* (Madrid, 1988), pp. 41–44.

4. For all this, *cf. ibid.,* pp. 52–58. *Cf.* also M. Fernández Álvarez, *Casadas, monjas, rameras y brujas: la olvidada historia de la mujer española en el Renacimiento* (Madrid, 2002), pp. 96–107.

5. J. Townsend, *A Journey through Spain in the Years 1786 and 1787* (London, 1791), II, pp. 318–19.

6. Sánchez Lora, *Mujeres, conventos y formas de la religiosidad barroca,* pp. 60–68; Fernández Álvarez, *Casadas, monjas, brujas y rameras,* pp. 119–25.

7. *Cf.* C. Martín Gaite, *Love Customs in Eighteenth-Century Spain* (Berkeley, California, 1991), pp. 15–17.

8. It was not just women who were subject to these controls. For example, when the future Spanish general, Pedro Girón, made the mistake of pursuing an unsuitable match too ardently, he was shut up by his own father until he promised to desist from his intent; *cf.* Earl of Ilchester (ed.), *The Spanish Journal of Elizabeth Lady Holland* (London, 1910), p. 120.

9. López-Cordón, 'Situación de la mujer, pp. 81–89 *passim;* I. Pérez Molina *et al.*, *Las mujeres en el antiguo régimen: imagen y realidad, S. XVI–XVIII* (Barcelona, 1994), pp. 31–35.

10. Pérez Molina, *Las mujeres en el antiguo régimen*, pp. 40–48.

11. Sánchez Lora, *Mujeres, conventos y formas de la religiosidad barroca*, pp. 45–51.

12. A. de Laborde, *A View of Spain* (London, 1809), V, p. 270.

13. *Cf.* Sánchez Lora, *Mujeres, conventos y formas de la religiosidad barroca*, p. 49.

14. There were, of course exceptions. In the house of the mayor of Golegão, for example, Ormsby found that the eldest daughter was 'a fine and glorious talker' whose 'education had been most carefully attended to insomuch as there was not a celebrated theologian whose works she had not read'. Interestingly, enough, meanwhile, she had not kept within the bounds assigned her. On the contrary: 'From a motive of curiosity or rebellion, she had by stratagem obtained *La nouvelle Héloise*, and could very nearly repeat it by heart. I seriously asked whether she preferred that captivating book or *La vie des onze milles vierges*, and she seriously replied that she thought Rousseau, on the whole, a more interesting writer.' *Cf.* J. W. Ormsby, *An Account of the Operations of the British Army and of the State and Sentiments of the People of Portugal and Spain* (London, 1809), I, pp. 191–92.

15. S. A. Kitts, *The Debate on the Nature, Role and Influence of Women in Eighteenth-Century Spain* (Lewiston, New York, 1995), p. 3.

16. E.g., C. Boutflower, *The Journal of an Army Surgeon during the Peninsular War* (London, 1912), p. 28; C. Leslie, *Military Journal of Colonel Leslie, K. H., of Balquhain, whilst serving with the Twenty-Ninth Regiment in the Peninsula and the Sixtieth Rifles in Canada, etc., 1807–1832* (Aberdeen, 1887), p. 132; G. Bell, *Rough Notes by an Old Soldier* (London, 1867), pp. 59–60; R. K. Porter, *Letters from Portugal and Spain written during the March of the British Troops under Sir John Moore* (London, 1809), p. 45.

17. Such, at least, is the general impression found in the British accounts. *Cf.* R. Croker, *Travels through Several Provinces of Spain and Portugal* (London, 1799), pp. 279–80; J. Patterson, *The Adventures of Captain John Patterson* (London, 1837), pp. 148–49.

18. V. López Barahona, *El cepo y el torneo: la reclusión feminina en el Madrid del siglo XVIII* (Madrid, 2009), pp. 122–26. As will become clear below, it is particularly interesting that Olmos was caught with a group of soldiers.

19. For an excellent description of a female prison, *cf.* Townsend, *Journey*, pp. 126–28.

20. G. Larpent (ed.), *The Private Journal of Judge-Advocate Larpent attached to the Headquarters of Lord Wellington during the Peninsular War from 1812 to its Close* (London, 1854), p. 31.

21. H. Blayney, *Narrative of a Forced Journey through Spain and France as a Prisoner of War in the Years 1810 to 1814* (London, 1814), I, pp. 100–101; note, too,

Blayney's comment on p. 99 re the pleasure which women derived from such childish games as blind-man's bluff. For a rather similar view, *cf.* A. de Saint-Chamans, *Mémoires du Général Comte de Saint-Chamans, ancien aide de camp du Maréchal Soult, 1802–1832* (Paris, 1896), p. 206. Meanwhile, for a feminine perspective, *cf.* M. de Santa Cruz, *Memorias y recuerdos de la Señora Condesa de Merlin* (Havana, 1853), I, pp. 9–36, the author being a wealthy *criolla* who moved to Spain with her mother, brother and sister at an early age, and was brought up in a highly traditional atmosphere that she later remembered as being one of endless boredom and frustration.

22. Kitts, *Debate on the Nature, Role and Influence of Women,* pp. 13–96 *passim;* M. Bolufer, 'Neither male nor female: rational equality in the early Spanish Enlightenment', in S. Knott and B. Taylor (eds.), *Women, Gender and Enlightenment* (Basingstoke, 2005), pp. 389–409.

23. W. Dalrymple, *Travels through Spain and Portugal in 1774* (London, 1777), p. 72.

24. López-Cordón, 'Situación de la mujer', pp. 92–93. A further influence here was beyond doubt that of Spain's queens. Thus, throughout the eighteenth century the Bourbon monarchs took care to portray their wives as competent and responsible women who managed the affairs of court and palace with great competence and provided them with wise and effective counsel. *Cf.* M. V. López-Cordón, 'Women in society in eighteenth-century Spain: models of sociability', in C. M. Jaafe and E. F. Lewis (eds.), *Eve's Enlightenment: Women's Experience in Spain and Spanish America, 1726–1839* (Baton Rouge, Louisiana, 2009), pp. 106–107. The most prestigious of the women's colleges was the Colegio de Doncellas Nobles in Toledo: in 1812, the British artillery officer, William Swabey danced with an Irish officer's orphaned daughter who was being educated there, and found that she was proficient in English, French, Italian and German alike. *Cf.* F. Whinyates (ed.), *Diary of Campaigns in the Peninsula for the Years 1811, 12 and 13 written by Lieutenant William Swabey, an Officer of E Troop (present E Battery), Royal Horse Artillery* (Woolwich, 1895), pp. 129–30.

25. One such was María Luisa de Valleré, the half-French, half-Portuguese daughter of the French soldier of fortune who had been placed in charge of modernising the defences of Elvas after the Seven Year's War; *cf.* L. A. Limpo Piríz, *Badajoz y Elvas en 1811: crónicas de guerra* (Badajoz, 2011), pp. 62–64. In 1763, meanwhile, the shadowy Beatriz de Cienfuegos had founded *La Pensadora Gaditana,* this being a newspaper that ran to fifty-two issues and was the first publication in Spain to cater specifically for a female readership; *cf.* J. Pérez and M. Ihrie, *The Feminist Encyclopaedia of Spanish Literature* (Westport, Connecticut, 2002), pp. 135–36.

26. It should be noted that women did not just write about the issue of their role in the world. On the contrary, the eighteenth century saw women also writing as novelists, playwrights, poets and translators. *Cf.* E. Palacios, 'Noticia sobre el parnaso dramático femenino en el siglo XVIII', in L. García Lorenzo (ed.), *Autoras y actrices en la historia del teatro español* (Murcia, 2000), pp. 81–131.

27. For a discussion of wider female participation in intellectual debate, *cf.* D. Whitaker, 'A new voice: the rise of the enlightened woman in eighteenth-century Spain', in G. Adamson and E. Myers (eds.), *Continental, Latin-American and Francophone Women Writers: Selected Papers from the Wichita State University Conference on Foreign Literature, 1986–1987* (Lanham, Maryland, 1990), II, pp. 31–40;

M. Bolufer, 'Women of letters in eighteenth-century Spain: between tradition and modernity', in Jaafe and Lewis, *Eve's Enlightenment*, pp. 17–32; M. P. Zorrozúa, *Escritoras de la ilustración española* (Deusto, 1999).

28. For a recent biography, *cf.* M. V. López-Cordón, *Condición femenina y razón ilustrada: Josefa Amar y Borbón* (Zaragoza, 2005). A comparable figure, meanwhile, was Inés Joyes y Blake, an army officer's wife who in 1798 published a powerful feminist pamphlet entitled *Apología de las mujeres; cf.* M. Bolufer, *Mujeres e ilustración: la construcción de la feminidad en la España del siglo XVIII* (Valencia, 1998), pp. 290–94.

29. *Cf.* J. B. Grinstein, *La rosa trágica de Málaga: vida y obra de María Rosa de Gálvez* (Charlottesville, Virginia, 2003); D. S. Whitaker, 'An enlightened premiere: the theater of María Rosa Gálvez', *Letras femeninas,* XIX (1993), pp. 21–32.

30. For the Condesa de Montijo, *cf.* R. Herr, *The Eighteenth-Century Revolution in Spain* (Princeton, New Jersey, 1958), pp. 406–407. Lady Holland describes her as having 'an uncommon share of wit and talent and a satirical bent which she is apt to indulge at the expense of the court'; *cf.* Ilchester, *Spanish Journal of Elizabeth, Lady Holland,* p. 193. Meanwhile, a useful general discussion is afforded by Palacios, 'Noticia sobre el parnaso dramático', pp. 93–99. It should be noted that parallel developments took place in the ranks of the Portuguese élite. Here the leading figure was the Marquesa de Alorna, who established a name for herself as an accomplished poetess, and gathered around her a number of like-minded women including the Condesa de Viimeiro and the wife of Luis Pinto de Sousa, who was chief minister from 1788 to 1801 and then again in 1803; *cf.* H. Cidade, *A Marquesa de Viana: sua vida e obras* (Oporto, 1929); R. Bello, *Mulher, nobre ilustrada, dramaturga:* Osmia *de Teresa de Mello Breyner no sistema literário português, 1788–1795* (Lisbon, 2005).

31. Kitts, *Debate on the Nature, Role and Influence of Women,* pp. 136–72.

32. To the *tertulia,* of course, should be added the ball, another new development that really requires no comment.

33. J. T. Dillon, *Letters from an English Traveller in Spain in 1778* (London, 1781), p. 158.

34. For a hilarious description of a provincial *tertulia* in which 'the polite society' had made little progress, *cf.* Patterson, *Adventures,* pp. 291–94. More stately but just as segregated was one attended by Lady Holland in January 1803, this being 'a dull assembly where the ladies sit round the room and the gentlemen stand at the end, each as much separated as if they were in different provinces'; *cf.* Ilchester, *Spanish Journal of Elizabeth, Lady Holland,* p. 23.

35. *Cf.* Townsend, *Journey,* II, pp. 139–42.

36. Dalrymple, *Travels,* p. 15; for an excellent contemporary discussion of the phenomenon of the *tertulia* in general, *cf.* Laborde, *View of Spain,* V, pp. 298–99. If its form differed from household to household, this may have been because these last stood at different points along a curve of change in which they passed from a situation in which men and women alike clung to a semblance of segregation to one in which they finally mingled freely with one another; *cf.* Martín Gaite, *Love Customs,* p. 23. The vast majority of the material available relating to Spain, the bulk of the section that follows refers to that country. However, such evidence as we have suggests that much of what is said refers just as much to Portugal; *cf.* B. Alexander (ed.), *The Journal of William Beckford in Portugal and*

Spain, 1787–1788 (London, 1954), pp. 54–56, 65–66; Ormsby, *Operations of the British Army,* I, pp. 139–42.

37. J. M. Blanco, *Letters from Spain* (London, 1808), p. 324; *cf.* also A. Berazáluce (ed.), *Recuerdos de la vida de Don Pedro Agustín Girón* (Pamplona, 1978), I, pp. 98–99; J. García de León y Pizarro, *Memorias de la vida del Excmo. Señor D. José García de León y Pizarro escritas por el mismo,* ed. A. Alonso (Madrid, 1894), I, pp. 105–106.

38. Dalrymple, *Travels,* p. 17; H. Swinburne, *Travels through Spain in the Years 1775 and 1776* (Dublin, 1779), p. 210.

39. E.g., C. Fischer, *A Picture of Madrid taken on the Spot* (London, 1808), pp. 52–53. For the *paseo, cf.* also Laborde, *View of Spain,* V, pp. 292–93; Townsend, *Journey,* II, p. 138.

40. Fischer, *Picture of Madrid,* p. 103. Communal bathing was not just restricted to Madrid. Returning to Puerto de Santa María one evening by boat following an excursion to Cádiz, for example, George Landmann claims to have come across a group of as many as 100 women of the propertied classes 'bathing in a cluster and only waist-deep in the water, all screaming and making as much noise as they were able'. Emboldened by their sheer number, perhaps, the women concerned also displayed little willingness even to pay lip service to maintaining a submissive demeanour. Thus, 'As we passed within ten yards of them, they abused us in the most perfect Billingsgate style, and endeavoured to splash us with water.' *Cf.* G. Landmann, *Recollections of my Military Life* (London, 1854), II, pp. 61–62.

41. F. de Guzmán, *La España de Goya* (Madrid, 1981), pp. 38–42. For some descriptions by contemporary visitors, *cf.* R. Twiss, *Travels through Portugal and Spain in 1772 and 1773* (London, 1775), pp. 254–55, and Alexander, *Journal of William Beckford,* pp. 287–88.

42. Laborde, *View of Spain,* V, p. 304.

43. Of the *mantilla,* a British officer later noted, 'The Spanish women are much handsomer than the men . . . You may tell their rank in a great measure by the handkerchief over their heads as they are universal, from the finest lace veil to the dish cloth.' *Cf.* M. Glover (ed.), *A Gentleman Volunteer; the Letters of George Hennell from the Peninsular War, 1812–13* (London, 1979), p. 42.

44. Bolufer, *Mujeres e ilustración,* López Barahona, *Cepo y el torneo,* pp. 159–62; Fischer, *Picture of Madrid.,* pp. 240–41.

45. *Ibid.,* p. 181.

46. Croker, *Travels,* p. 132.

47. Laborde, *View of Spain,* V, p. 283. It cannot be stressed too strongly that it would be very wrong to go too far here. In Madrid, certainly, upper-class women had more freedom than before, but this advance was only achieved at the cost of giving considerable ammunition to the cause of Spanish misogynism—by following the dictates of fashion in all its various forms, women could not but lay themselves open to charges of frivolity, extravagance and sexual licence—and may well have produced a reaction in other areas of Spain. As Ruiz Carnal has shown, for example, published from 1803 to 1805, *El Correo de Sevilla,* was replete with complaints in respect of the behaviour of the new Spanish woman; *cf.* J. Ruiz Carnal, *Dependientes y esclavizadas: historia de la mujer sevillana, 1803–1805* (Seville, 1993), pp. 18–27. And at Arcos de la Frontera Croker and his fellow prisoners-of-war found themselves at the centre of a considerable storm when some of

the younger officers 'put into the hands of the young women of the houses in which they lodged French books of a very improper tendency'; *cf.* Croker, *Travels,* p. 168.

48. For all this, *cf.* Martín Gaite, *Love Customs,* pp. 1–13; Townsend, *Journey,* II, pp. 142–47.

49. An exceptionally well-informed female eye-witness implies very strongly that sexual adventure was widespread. Thus: 'The dissolute manners of the women are disgusting . . . Several of the highest rank, possessing youth, beauty and consequence, have from their libertinage destroyed their health.' *Cf.* Ilchester (ed.), *Spanish Journal of Elizabeth, Lady Holland,* I, p. 28. Yet, though at the time and since reputed to be the lover of Charles IV's queen, María Luisa, the greatest *cortejo* of them all, namely, the royal favourite, Manuel de Godoy, was almost certainly guiltless in this respect. What is true, however, is that the queen's encouragement of Godoy's transparent attempts to advance his career by—in a most literal sense!—courting her favour gave a further stimulus to the generalization of the *cortejo* as a figure in polite society. *Cf.* Martín Gaite, *Love Customs,* pp. 90–92. At the same time, if sex was by no means a necessary part of the arrangement, the whole phenomenon was clearly underpinned by a strong *frisson* of sexual excitement. Here, for example, is William Beckford: 'I must take care or I shall kindle a flame not easily extinguished. I am surrounded with fires: it is delightful to be warmed, but unless I summon up every atom of prudence in my composition I shall be reduced to ashes.' *Cf.* Alexander, *Journal of William Beckford,* p. 308.

50. There were obviously many exceptions here, but the remarks of Henry Swinburne in this respect are, alas, all too believable: 'Most of the ladies about court . . . do not seem to have any ambition of passing for clever or accomplished: not one talent do they possess, nor do they ever work, read, write, or touch any musical instrument; their *cortejo* seems their only play-thing.' *Cf.* Swinburne, *Travels,* II, p. 218. Meanwhile, of the 341 subscriptors to *El Correo de Sevilla,* just three were female; *cf.* Ruíz Carnal, *Dependientes y esclavizadas,* p. 18.

51. E. Buckham, *Personal Narrative of Adventures in the Peninsula during the War in 1812–13* (London, 1827), p. 236. *Cf.* also Swinburne, *Travels,* II, p. 217; Fischer, *Picture of Madrid,* pp. 288–89, 296–97.

52. An important point to note here is the role of the theatre. Thus, far from becoming more progessive in line with the spirit of the age, Spanish playwrights of the eighteenth century rather competed with one another to damn every attempt on the part of women to better themselves. *Cf.* B. Miller, 'A school for wives? Women in eighteenth-century Spanish theatre', in B. Miller (ed.), *Women in Hispanic Literature: Icons and Fallen Idols* (Berkeley, California, 1983), pp. 184–200.

53. J. A. Oyon, *Campagnes et souvenirs militaires, 1805–1814* (Paris, 1997), p. 146. Just as interesting are Patterson's recollections of the remote provincial town of Coria in the early months of 1813 in that he noted that the women never left the confines of their own homes 'unless at those times when they tottered . . . to chapel'; *cf.* Patterson, *Adventures,* p. 269. Finally, for some interesting comments on La Coruña, *cf.* H. C. Wylie (ed.), *A Cavalry Officer in the Corunna Campaign: the Journal of Captain Gordon of the Fifteenth Hussars* (London, 1913), pp. 25–34 *passim.* For example, 'The French mode of dress is pretty generally adopted by the

ladies, but many still adhere to the ancient Spanish costume.' *Ibid.*, p. 33. Meanwhile, if progress in Spain was patchy, in Portugal it seems to have been still more limited. According to William Stothert of the Third Foot Guards, for example, 'The Portuguese . . . keep their wives in the greatest restraint.' *Cf.* W. Stothert, *A Narrative of the Principal Events of the Campaigns of 1809, 1810 and 1811 in Spain and Portugal* (London, 1812), p. 53; *cf.* also Ormsby, *Operations of the British Army,* I, pp. 112–13. Equally, travelling through northern Portugal in 1813, Edward Buckham came across a house where the women were kept perpetually locked away from any contact with the outside world whatsoever, whilst the only household in which he was allowed to mingle freely with its female members was the establishment of a grandee with strong links to the court; *cf.* Buckham, *Personal Narrative,* pp. 101–103, 122.

54. E. Warre (ed.), *Letters from the Peninsula, 1808–1812, by William Warre* (London, 1909), p. 131. Also interesting here is Porter's description of the products of the new sociability that he encountered in Salamanca in the autumn of 1808: 'The females [dress] without taste . . . being equipped in bad imitation of what the French wore twenty years ago.' *Cf.* Porter, *Letters from Portugal and Spain,* p. 151.

55. The very patchy penetration of Spanish society by more liberal mores is clearly suggested by the fact that Leandro Fernández de Moratín's powerful *El Sí de la Niñas* was first staged as late as 1806. Meanwhile, the forces of conservatism were by this stage mounting a fierce counter-attack: a court intrigue secured the banishment of the Condesa de Montijo to the provinces, for example, while the scorn that was heaped upon Queen María Luisa by the opponents of Godoy may in part have had their roots in the manner in which she was perceived as exemplifying the 'new woman'.

56. The very beginnings of female public education are visible at this time in that in 1783 Charles III ordered the establishment of thirty-two primary schools for poor girls in Madrid and called for this example to be taken up elsewhere, but in the event very few such institutions ever saw the light of day, whilst the few that did often became the subject of furious local opposition. *Cf.* G. Desdevises, *La España del antiguo régimen,* ed. A. Gónzalez Enciso (Madrid, 1989), p. 753.

57. For some details of public midwives and female teachers, *cf.* López-Cordón, 'Situación de la mujer', pp. 73–77. One other group of professional women that is worth mentioning is constituted by the actresses encountered in Madrid, Lisbon and some other cities, important names here including Rita Luna García, María del Rosario Fernández and María Ladvenant. So far as can be established, however, all such women owed their positions to the fact that they had been born into theatrical dynasties. For some details, *cf.* M. Gómez García, *Diccionario del Teatro* (Madrid, 1987); A. Peléz, 'María Ladvenant y Quirante: primera dama de los teatros de España', in García Lorenzo, *Autoras y actrices,* pp. 133–53.

58. The women of the Basque country seem to have made a strong impression on foreign observers. Here, for example, is William Surtees, who served as a quartermaster in the Ninety-Fifth Rifles: 'They . . . do the same kind of work as the men, that is, they plough and labour at all sorts of husbandry, but what seemed most remarkable to us was their sole management of the ferry boats about Pasajes and San Sebastián: they row as well as any men, being amazingly strong and active.' *Cf.* W. Surtees, *Twenty-Five Years in the Rifle Brigade* (Edinburgh,

1833), p. 268; *cf.* also E. Sabine (ed.), *Letters of Colonel Sir Augustus Simon Frazer, K.C.B., commanding the Royal Horse Artillery in the Army under the Duke of Wellington written during the Peninsular and Waterloo Campaigns* (London, 1859), p. 194. For the general role played by women in the agricultural economy, *cf.* López-Cordón, 'Situación de la mujer a finales del antiguo régimen', pp. 65–66, whilst the *laya* is discussed in L.L. Lande, *Basques et navarrais: souvenirs d'un voyage dans le nord d'Espagne* (Paris, 1878), p. 7. Note, however, that it was not just in areas that made use of the *laya* that women took part in primary labour in the fields: in León, noted Joseph Townsend, 'Women hold the plough.' *Cf.* Townsend, *Journey*, II, p. 67. Finally, for a case-study of Asturias, *cf.* A. Menéndez González, *El barranco de las asturianas: mujer y sociedad en el antiguo régimen* (Oviedo, 2006), pp. 75–86.

59. F. S. Darwin, *Travels in Spain and the East, 1808–1810*, ed. F. D. Darwin (Cambridge, 1927), p. 7.

60. J. T. Dillon, *Travels through Spain* (Dublin, 1781), p. 29. For the esparto industry, *cf.* E. Pardo, *El esparto: noticia sobre su descripción, cría, cúltivo y aprovechamiento* (Madrid, 1888).

61. The combination of the relative scarcity of jobs and the prolonged absence of many men on the great estates produced a result that was all but unavoidable. As Sir John Carr wrote of Algeciras, for example, 'The women in general are . . . well known for carrying on [a] . . . considerable contraband trade in the commerce of love.' *Cf.* J. Carr, *Descriptive Travels in the Southern and Eastern Parts of Spain and the Balearic Islands in the Year 1809* (London, 1811), p. 127.

62. For an excellent discussion of the functioning of society in the agro-towns of Andalucía, and the role of women therein, *cf.* D. Gilmore, *The People of the Plain: Class and Community in Lower Andalucía* (New York, 1980).

63. Exactly what the situation was in respect to female masters is unclear. Taking Asturias as an example, by the middle of the eighteenth century there were certainly a surprising number of such figures: in 1750 women controlled seven of the town of Jovellanos's eleven workshops, whilst women were almost equally dominant in Oviedo, where there were eleven male masters and twelve female ones, but all the women concerned appear to have been widows who had taken over the family business on the demise of their husbands. Only later in the century did changes in guild legislation introduced by Charles III allow women to begin to work their way up to the top in their own right. *Cf.* Menéndez González, *Barranco de las asturianas*, pp. 86–96.

64. Pérez Molina, *Mujeres en el antiguo régimen*, pp. 63–74. In later years the most emblematic figure of the woman in paid employment was to be the tobacco worker. However, in 1808 the *cigarrera* was still in very large part a phenomenon of the future.

65. Patterson, *Adventures*, p. 299; *cf.* also López-Cordón, 'Situación de la mujer', pp. 66–67.

66. Dillon, *Travels through Spain*, p. 184.

67. Desdevises du Dézert, *España del antiguo régimen*, p. 752.

68. Buckham, *Personal Narrative*, pp. 278–79. What is not clear from this account, of course, is the relationship of the women with their burdens.

69. Pérez Molina, *Mujeres en el antiguo régimen*, pp. 77–80. In Lisbon, for example, John Dobbs observed that 'every corner had a woman frying and selling sardines' and that elsewhere the same might be said of roasted chestnuts; *cf.*

J. Dobbs, *Recollections of an Old Fifty-Second Man* (Waterford, 1863), pp. 6, 8. As for the combativeness of the women concerned, one might cite Neale's description of the scene he observed in the Plaza Mayor in Salamanca: 'The women of the lower classes are irascible to a degree. There is generally a pitched battle among them eight or ten times a day. Their tongues are the grand weapons of attack, and . . . the language they use is not much inferior to that of the fair inhabitants of Billingsgate.' *Cf.* A. Neale, *Letters from Portugal and Spain* (London, 1809), p. 226.

70. Fischer, *Picture of Madrid,* pp. 123–24.

71. López-Cordón, 'Situación de la mujer', pp. 72–73; Menéndez González, *Barranco de las asturianas,* pp. 100–12. For the issue of rape in the workplace, *cf.* R. Fraser, *Las dos guerras de Espana* (Madrid, 2012), p. 91.

72. Swinburne, *Travels,* p. 102. It may be assumed, alas, that this subordination was accompanied by a high degree of violence and, in addition, sexual abuse: until very recently it was customary in some remote villages in Extremadura for groups of women literally to mount guard over the daughters of men who had just been widowed. Meanwhile, a deeply disturbing picture of the general feminine experience is afforded by the autobiography that was written by one Madre Isabel de Jesus, an illiterate peasant girl who began life as a goatherd and then endured twenty-four years of an arranged marriage to a man much older than herself before finally entering a convent as a lay sister. *Cf.* E. Arenal, 'The convent as catalyst for autonomy: two hispanic nuns of the seventeenth century', in Miller, *Women in Hispanic Literature,* pp. 147–83.

73. López Barahona, *Cepo y el torneo,* p. 13; F. Valenzuela, *La sociedad de Jaén ante la invasión napoleónica, 1808* (Jaén, 2000), p. 30. For a detailed snapshot of poverty in rural Spain in 1800, and, in addition, one that shows all too clearly that the situation was deteriorating ever more sharply, *cf.* P. Carasa, *Pauperismo y revolución burguesa: Burgos, 1750–1900* (Valladolid, 1987).

74. *Cf. Censo de la población de España de el* [sic] *año de 1797 ejecutado del orden del rey en el de 1801* (Madrid, 1801).

75. López-Cordón, 'La situación de la mujer a finales del antiguo régimen', pp. 52–54; Menéndez González, *Barranco de las asturianas,* pp. 35–51. The issue of conscription is worth a mention here. Strictly speaking, married men were exempt from the *sorteo*—the ballot that was imposed whenever the Spanish army required reinforcements—but they were not exempt from the *leva* or levy, this being a police measure that was made use of on a more-or-less regular basis to scour Spain's streets of beggars and ne'er-do-wells, the bulk of whose male victims being thrust directly into the armed forces. Thus, in 1764 of 8,659 men picked up in this fashion, no fewer than 3,618 left behind wives who, it may be assumed, in most cases immediately faced absolute catastrophe; *cf.* R. M. Pérez Estévez, *El problema de los vagos en la España del siglo XVIII* (Madrid, 1976), pp. 132–33. In Málaga disease may have been a further issue: according to Sir John Carr, in the epidemic of yellow fever of 1800 'the men suffered in proportion to the women as forty-seven to one'; *cf.* Carr, *Descriptive Travels,* p. 45.

76. M. J. de la Pascua, 'Women alone in Enlightenment Spain' in Jaafe and Lewis, *Eve's Enlightenment,* p. 132.

77. Women did not just obtain work as wet nurses in their home towns, but often travelled long distances to seek work elsewhere, very often achieving their goal by means of placing advertisements in such newspapers as existed:

in Madrid, then, young women from the Basque provinces who were working in this capacity were much in evidence (thanks to a tendency to portray their homeland in terms that were strongly idyllic, Basque women were seen as being particularly strong and healthy); *cf.* Fischer, *Picture of Madrid,* pp. 192–93. For the issue of sub-letting, *cf.* C. Bertrand and A. Diéz 'Mujeres solas en la ciudad del siglo XVIII' in M. V. López-Cordón and M. Carbonell (eds.), *Historia de la mujer e historia de la familia* (Murcia, 1997), pp. 165–72.

78. Ruiz Carnal, *Dependientes y esclavizadas,* p. 13.

79. For a case study in female emigration, *cf.* M. C. Ansón , 'El papel de la mujer aragonesa en el proceso emigratorio aragonés a fines del siglo XVIII', in López-Cordón and Carbonell, *Historia de la mujer e historia de la familia,* pp. 241–60. Particularly in times of dearth, such emigration was a most precarious remedy: having reached such cities as Madrid, the women concerned would necessarily have found themselves in competition with thousands of fellow migrants, not to mention the equally desperate populace. For an account of the parlous situation that pertained in Madid during the subsistence crisis of 1800–1804, *cf.* M. V. Vara, 'Crisis de subsistencia en el Madrid de comienzos del siglo, 1800–1805', in L. Otero y A. Bahamonde, *Madrid en la sociedad del siglo XIX* (Madrid, 1986) II, pp. 245–66.

80. Townsend, *Journey,* I, pp. 133–34. The fate of those foundlings who survived infancy (in which respect, it should be noted that two-thirds did not live beyond their first year) was grim: some effort, it seems, was made to find boys apprenticeships, but the girls were surrendered to virtually anyone who would take them, and therefore probably ended up either as prostitutes or the victims of domestic abuse.

81. J. J. García Hourcade, 'Asistidas, recogidas, corregidas: el lugar de la mujer en el sistema asistencial del siglo XVIII' in López-Cordón and Carbonell, *Historia de la mujer e historia de la familia,* pp. 233–40.

82. A good example here is the Leonese parish priest Juan Antonio Posse: one of the latter's sisters having become deaf on account of a childhood fever, in 1794 he took her in as his housekeeper. *Cf.* R. Herr (ed.), *Memorias del cura liberal Don Juan Antonio Posse con su discurso sobre la constitución de 1812* (Madrid, 1984), p. 51.

83. J. Kincaid, *Random Shots from a Rifleman* (London, 1835), pp. 84–85; *cf.* also A. M. Ludovici (ed.), *On the Road with Wellington: the Diary of a War Commissary* (London, 1924), pp. 213–16. In fairness, it should be pointed out that by no means all the women living in presbyteries were as attractive as Kincaid suggests: at the home of the priest in the Portuguese village of Chao do Couce, for example, Charles Crowe came across an 'old hag of a housekeeper . . . whose brown and wrinkled hands and face were equal strangers to the purifying quality of fresh water'; *cf.* G. Glover (ed.), *An Eloquent Soldier: the Peninsular-War Journals of Lieutenant Charles Crowe of the Inniskillings, 1812–1814* (Barnsley, 2011), p. 30. A related issue here is sexual harassment on the part of the clergy. Whilst many of the stories that circulated in this respect are simply ridiculous, there seems little doubt that young women could easily find themselves the prey of amorous clerics. An Ulster Protestant, Crowe can hardly be expected to have a favourable view of the Church, but there is a certain plausibility in his claims to have seen 'many bare and bald headed fat priests, monks or friars with lovely girls of gentlewomanly appearance holding reluctantly on their arms'. *Cf. ibid.,* p. 164.

84. Fischer, *Picture of Madrid,* pp. 122–23.

85. *Ibid.*, p. 254.

86. *Ibid.*

87. Dalrymple, *Travels,* p. 104; Alexander, *Journal of William Beckford,* p. 61.

88. López Barahona, *Cepo y el torneo,* pp. 185–47 *passim.* The vulnerability of women to arbitrary arrest was reinforced in certain areas by the introduction of numerous local by-laws that made it near impossible for them to live out their lives without clashing with the authorities in one way or another. Thus, in Asturias, women were prohibited from either living alone or engaging in most forms of economic activity until they had reached the age of fifty; *cf.* Bertrand and Diéz 'Mujeres solas en la ciudad', pp. 165–66.

89. López Barahona, *Cepo y el torneo,* pp. 25–29; Pérez Molina, *Mujeres en el antiguo regimen,* pp. 139–64. Given what follows, it should be pointed out that the women concerned did not always take their fate lying down: one night in 1803, for example, twenty women confined in the Casa de Recogidas in Murcia engineered a mass escape. *Cf.* García Hourcade, 'Asistidas, recogidas, corregidas', p. 239.

90. The most well-known visual depictions of the *maja* are those found in the numerous 'cartoons' painted by Goya in the period 1775–92. However, the pretty and brightly dressed young women of these images are beyond doubt highly romanticised, not least because the rich had no wish to be reminded of the misery in which much of the populace lived. The words 'traditional dress', then, needs to be stripped of all romance. Here, for example, is Patterson on the women of Toledo: 'Females of the lower class wear thick and substantial garments of black or brown cloth of measurement so ample that no opinion can be formed as to the dimensions of their shape'; of those of Coria, meanwhile, he writes, 'To tell the honest truth, I must say that we never beheld a more ugly and forbidding race of damsels.' *Cf.* Patterson, *Adventures,* pp. 229, 269.

91. Fischer, *Picture of Madrid,* p. 207; for a general discussion, *cf.* E. Rodríguez Solis, *Majas, manolas y chulas* (Madrid, 1886). The acute cultural tensions of the sort generated by the transformation of traditional society in Madrid made the *maja* a figure that was particularly associated with the capital. However, there seems no reason to doubt that the same type was visible in other Spanish cities. Also worthy of note here is the strong sexual innuendo that underpins Fischer's remarks. How far the suggestion of promiscuity is accurate is difficult to judge, but travellers' tales certainly suggest that many of the women of the lower classes showed little hesitation in ignoring the bonds of matrimony.; *cf.* Dalrymple, *Travels,* pp. 33–34.

92. Pérez Estévez, *Problema de los vagos,* pp. 71–72, 78–81.

93. M. J. de la Pascua, 'Las mujeres en un mundo de transición: espacios de sociabilidad y conflictividad en España entre los siglos XVIII y XIX', in Acosta, *Conflicto y sociedad civil—la mujer en la guerra,* pp. 105–32. For the issue of the betrayal of promises of marriage, *cf.* Fraser, *Las dos guerras de Espana,* pp. 85–89.

94. *Cf.* Ruiz Carnal, *Dependientes y esclavizadas,* pp. 31–32.

95. Banned from taverns, in the evenings in particular women would also gather on doorsteps or street corners, this being a custom that survived until very recent times in much of rural Spain and Portugal. Another exclusively feminine gathering, meanwhile, was the communal delousing sessions of the sort described by James Hope of the Ninety-Second Foot; *cf.* S. Monick (ed.), *The*

Iberian and Waterloo Campaigns: the Letters of Lieutenant James Hope, 92nd (Highland) Regiment (London, 2002), pp. 69–70.

96. Buckham, *Personal Narrative*, p. 85.

97. For a complete set of these drawings, see G. Cronin and S. Summerfield, *Spanish Infantry, Cavalry and Artillery of 1808: Uniforms, Organization and Equipment* (Cambridge, 2012).

98. *Cf.* P. Castañeda, *Catalina de Erauso, la monja rebelde* (Madrid, 1984), and E. Mendieta, *En busca de Catalina de Erauso: identidades en conflicto en la vida de la monja-alférez* (Castellón de la Plana, 2010).

99. For a discussion of the image of the woman-soldier as it was projected on the stage, *cf.* R. Fernández Cabezón, 'La mujer guerrera en el teatro español de fines del siglo XVIII', *Anuario de Estudios Filológicos,* XXVI (2003), pp. 117–36.

Chapter 3

1. Campfollowers being notorious for their rough character, it is from them that English derives the perjoratives 'baggage' and 'old bag'.

2. A few foreign women who were the wives of neither officers or other officials nor campfollowers also appeared, one such being the hopelessly alcoholic wife of a cobbler who had for many years earned his living following in the wake of one French army or another mending soldiers' boots. *Cf.* Gleig, *The Light Dragoon* (London, 1855), pp. 89–92.

3. For the lyrics of 'A Soldier Boy for Me', *cf.* http://www.mudcat.org/thread.cfm?threadid=53515 (accessed 1 March 2011).

4. For a French example of the same idea, *cf.* the eighteenth-century Norman folk song 'Trois Jeunes Tambours', this describing how three young drummers come home from the wars so well supplied with booty that the king himself would be unable to deny them his daughter's hand in marriage. Lyrics accessed at http://www.ecole-plus.com/Chansons-MUSIQUES/chansons/troisjeunestamb.htm, 23 February 2012. For the lyrics of 'Over the Hills and Far Away', *cf.* http://napoleonicwars.org/music_hills.htm (accessed, 2 February, 2010).

5. Kincaid, *Random Shots,* pp. 208–209. Also interesting is a letter written by William Keep of the Twenty-Eighth Foot: 'Our band . . . enticed the lasses of Brixham and the neighbourhood to visit the garrison, and the fineness of the weather . . . induced many of them to prolong their stay till after dusk. The scene conspired to exhilarate the spirits of all present and frolics ensued.' *Cit.* I. Fletcher (ed.), *In the Service of the King: the Letters of William Thornton Keep at Home, Walcheren and in the Peninsula* (Staplehurst, 1997), p. 92. For a humorous account of a flirtation in London between a cavalry corporal and the proverbial 'girl next door', *cf.* Anon., *Jottings from my Sabretache* (London, 1847), pp. 117–20.

6. For two good examples in the broadside ballads, *cf.* 'The Hieland Soldier' and 'Darby Kelly'; lyrics accessed at http://www.traditionalmusic.co.uk/folk-song-lyrics/Heiland_Soldier.htm, and http://www.mudcat.org/thread.cfm?threadid=30123, 21 September 2010.

7. *Cf.* Venning, *Following the Drum,* p. 9; Lynn, *Women, Armies and Warfare,* p. 88.

8. Venning, *Following the Drum,* p. 13. It is possible, of course, that the girl was rather put on sale by her family.

9. Cardoza, *Intrepid Women,* p. 17.

10. *Cf.* De Pauw, *Battle Cries and Lullabies,* p. 104.

11. *Cf.* Cardoza, *Intrepid Women,* pp. 16–17.

12. G. Gleig, *The Subaltern,* ed. I. Robertson (Barnsley, 2001), pp. 4–7. There is, alas, a tragic end to this story: when the time came, Young drew a 'not-to-go' ticket (see below), but immediately went into labour and died in child-birth, while her husband, left utterly broken-hearted, was killed at the crossing of the Bidássoa. For the story of the Dublin maidservant, *cf.* Kincaid, *Random Shots,* pp. 110–16.

13. Surtees, *Twenty-Five Years in the Rifle Brigade,* p. 73; Gleig, *The Subaltern,* pp. 166–67.

14. Verification of this point is provided by the fact that in 1717 a survey of Berlin's prostitutes revealed that the largest single group amongst their numbers in terms of background was constituted by soldiers' daughters; *cf.* Lynn, *Women, Armies and Warfare,* p. 87.

15. Cardoza, *Intrepid Women,* p. 18.

16. For a succinct summary of all this, *cf.* Venning, *Following the Drum,* pp. 12–15.

17. J. C. Mämpel, *Adventures of a Young Rifleman in the French and English Armies during the War in Spain and Portugal from 1806 to 1816* (London, 1826), p. 324. In this instance we are assured that the woman concerned was well-pleased with her various transfers, but, very clearly, this need not always have been the case.

18. Surtees, *Twenty-Five Years in the Rifle Brigade,* pp. 157–58; *cf.* also E. Costello, *Adventures of a Soldier* (London, 1852), pp. 126–29.

19. Lynn, *Women, Armies and Warfare,* pp. 83–85.

20. Any children that resulted from such unions were also entitled to receive rations, albeit on a much reduced scale.

21. Holding the ballot at the last minute also had the added advantage of impeding attempts to stow away, let alone cross-dress and hide in the ranks.

22. When the first battalion of the Ninety-Fifth embarked for Walcheren in the summer of 1809, for example, the number taken was 'considerably curtailed' on account of the sufferings endured by the unit's women in the retreat to La Coruña. *Cf.* C. Hibbert (ed.), *The Recollections of Rifleman Harris* (London, 1970), p. 114.

23. For an excellent account of such a draw, *cf.* J. Donaldson, *Recollections of the Eventful Life of a Soldier* (London, 1852), pp. 51–53.

24. That this was the fate of many of the women concerned is made all too apparent by the well-known ballad, 'Johnny has gone for a soldier'. *Cf.* http://www.chivalry.com/cantaria/lyrics/shule.html and http://www.contemplator.com/america/johnny.html (accessed 24 January 2010). Meanwhile, the emotional importance of the regiment is suggested by a moving anecdote of a woman of the Twenty-Eighth Foot left behind at Brixham who was observed 'perching upon a rock . . . the tears rolling over her weather beaten features and her fists clenched in a wild paroxysm of grief and heroism, crying out, 'Fight Twenty-Eighth: fight boys, fight 'em!' *Cf.* Fletcher, *In the Service of the King,* p. 102.

25. Gleig, *The Subaltern,* p. 7; for a longer story that was particularly tragic, the husband later being killed at the Ciudad Rodrigo, *cf.* Donaldson, *Recollections,* pp. 54–56.

26. J. Green, *The Vicissitudes of a Soldier's Life, or a Series of Occurrences from 1806 to 1815* (Louth, 1827), p. 27; *cf.* also J. Hope, *Military Memoirs of an Infantry Officer, 1809–1816* (Edinburgh, 1833), pp. 15–16. If a unit had been in garrison some time, even marching from one quarter to another could produce scenes of chaos. When the Eighty-Second Foot departed from Uxbridge in 1806, for example, a crowd of women tried to follow it as it set out on its way, only to be checked by a picket at the bridge over the River Colne, one girl then going so far as to jump in and attempt to swim across. *Cf.* G. Wood, *The Subaltern Officer: a Narrative* (London, 1825), pp. 7–8.

27. E. Hunt (ed.), *Charging against Napoleon: Diaries and Letters of Three Hussars, 1808–1815* (Barnsley, 2001), p. 7. This figure is calculated by working out the ratio of women left behind by the 624 rank-and-file numbered by the Eighteenth Light Dragoons in August 1808 and applying it to the 30,000 soldiers dispatched to the Peninsula from home stations by December of that same year.

28. Cardoza, *Intrepid Women,* pp. 15–29. There has been much discussion of whether pre-Revolutionary *vivandières* sold sexual services along with sausage. As Cardoza points out, there is no evidence either way, but, like him, the author would incline to the view that they did not, or at least not on a general basis. Thus, prostitutes being frowned upon by the army and regularly driven from the camps and barracks and sometimes even flogged or mutilated, for a *vivandière* to have acted as a madam, let alone sold her own body, would have been risky indeed.

29. *Cf.* Cardoza, *Intrepid Women,* pp. 33–34, 60–61.

30. Leslie, *Military Journal,* p. 69.

31. Cardoza, *Intrepid Women,* pp. 34–38, 61–62.

32. This is not to say that no women were left behind: soldiers continued to be allowed to marry relatively freely. What they could not do, however, was to take their wives on campaign (which is not to say that some few wives may have contrived to follow their men to war anyway, one possibility here being to secure employment as a servant of some officer).

33. Sébastian Blaze provides us with the very epitome of a *cantinière* who had made good in this fashion in the form of a young woman who had marched into Spain in 1808 with nothing more than a cask of brandy on her hip but by 1812 was riding in a grand carriage and dressed in the finest clothes. *Cf.* S. Blaze, *Mémoires d'un apothicaire sur le guerre d'Espagne pendant les années 1808 à 1814* (Paris, 1828), II, p. 251.

34. The value of cultivating the troops is suggested by an incident in which a young *cantinière* was saved by a some dragoons when her horse lost its footing crossing the River Esla in the course of the campaign of La Coruña.; *cf.* A. Thirion, *Souvenirs militaires* (Paris, 1892), pp. 68–69. For the reverse side of the coin, we have only refer to an incident that happened a few days later in the ranks of the army of Sir John Moore: 'Few women were still to be seen . . . In one of the villages through which we went, I saw one of them sink up to her waist in a bog, whereupon, the mud and slime preventing her from rising, she fell, and the whole column marched over her.' *Cf.* Ludovici, *On the Road with Wellington,* p. 130.

35. One such may have been Cathérine Baland of the Ninety-Fifth Line who, Lejeune recalls, 'became quite a celebrated character in the army' and was

awarded the Legion of Honour in 1813; at the battle of Barrosa in March 1811, she is supposed to have gone up and down the ranks of her regiment giving the soldiers brandy and saying, 'Drink, drink . . . You can pay me tomorrow.' *Cf.* N. Bell (ed.), *Memoirs of Baron Lejeune, aide-de-camp to Marshals Berthier, Davout and Oudinot* (London, 1897), II, p. 69.

36. It is Cardoza's opinion that, hardly any firm evidence having come to light of this taking place, very few *cantinières* either worked as prostitutes themselves, or acted as madams. That said, married *cantinières* were as capable as any other woman of infidelity, and it is not beyond the realms of possibility that such behaviour bordered on the realms of prostitution, as witness, for example, Marcel's description of an affair that he had at Ledesma in the winter of 1809 with a *cantinière* of his regiment named Reine; *cf.* L. Var, *Campagnes du Capitaine Marcel du 69e de Ligne en Espagne et Portugal, 1808–1814* (Paris, 1914), p. 97.

37. Again, one should not go too far here. As Cardoza has shown, most of the women involved in the end gained very little from the war and ended their lives in poverty. At the same time, even during the war the thriving madam was an anomaly.

38. *Cf.* J. North (ed.), *In the Legions of Napoleon: the Memoirs of a Polish Officer in Spain and Russia, 1808–1813* (London, 1999), p. 178.

39. It should be noted here that, as the war went on, so the French army acquired plenty of women who were not *cantinières* in any formal sense (see below).

40. It is notable that the only ballad that talks of the British army's campfollowers as they appeared on campaign that has thus far been identified—'The Fate of Faithful Nancy and William of the Wagon-Train'—is a very conventional tale of a virtuous wife who is mortally wounded while watching a battle, stumbles onto the battlefield to seek her husband, and, tragically enough, comes across his dead body: the reality, it appears, was too sordid for the public taste. William's unit, meanwhile, was the Royal Wagon Train, a transport corps organised in 1802.

41. Anon., *Adventures in the Peninsula* (London, n.d.), p. 177.

42. J. Anton, *Retrospect of a Military Life during the Most Eventful Events in the Last War* (Edinburgh, 1841), pp. 90–93.

43. See note 17 for this chapter. The public sale of wives was well established amongst the lower classes, its similarity with the practices of slavery being reinforced by the fact that the women concerned were forced to wear halters around their necks.

44. *The Times,* 27 October 1813. I owe my knowledge of this reference to my friend and colleague, Dr Phillip Freeman. Campfollowers who were bullied over much, of course, might well fraternise with the enemy or even run away: one wonders, for example, what lay behind an incident in which a French campfollower helped the secretary of the renowned guerrilla commander, Jerónimo Merino, escape from captivity after he was captured at Peñafiel late in 1809; *cf.* P. Marco, *El Cura Merino, 1808 a 1813: memorias de un contemporáneo* (Madrid, 1899), p. 25.

45. *Cf.* Anton, *Retrospect of a Military Life,* pp. 44–118 *passim.*

46. Bell, *Rough Notes,* I, p. 75.

47. *Ibid.*

48. *Ibid.*

49. *Ibid.*, I, pp. 133–34. A determination to keep up with the action was very much part of the general ethos of the soldiers' wives. At the combat of Redinha in March 1811, for example, John Cooper noticed 'a German woman belonging to the Brunswick Rifles, trudging boldly close behind her husband with a heavy load on her back in the midst of the fire'. *Cf.* J. S. Cooper, *Rough Notes of Seven Campaigns in Portugal, Spain, France and America during the Years 1809–10–11–12–13–14–15* (London, 1869), p. 52. In another place the same author notes that a woman of his regiment was killed at Salamanca giving drink to a wounded man, and that at Toulouse another campfollower miraculously escaped injury when a shell burst beside her; *ibid.*, pp. 117–18.

50. Bell, *Rough Notes*, I, p. 183. Cut from the same cloth as Mrs Skiddy was one Mrs Clarke of the First Foot. Thus, furious at being left behind when her battalion embarked for the Peninsula in 1810, she attempted to stow away, only to be discovered and frog-marched ashore, yelling 'I wish the bloody ship and all that's in it may go to the bottom!' This, however, was not the end of the story: clearly a resourceful individual, within a year she had managed to smuggle herself out to Portugal and rejoin her husband. *Cf.* S. Monick (ed.), *Douglas' Tale of the Peninsula and Waterloo* (London, 1997), pp. 15, 27.

51. R. N. Buckley (ed.), *The Napoleonic War Journal of Captain Thomas Henry Browne, 1807–1816* (London, 1987), p. 174. A good example of the sort of advantage which married soldiers could derive from their wives is encountered in Lisbon in the wake of its liberation in August 1808. Thus, as Ormsby noted, all the taverns and wine shops in the city were declared out of bounds to British troops, but, by an oversight, nothing was said in the relevant order about campfollowers, and the latter were therefore able to keep the troops in alcohol *ad infinitum*, it being Ormsby's opinion that 'in all the crimes and licentiousness of a soldiery, it generally happens that the ladies are the most active agents and abettors'. *Cf.* Ormsby, *Account of the Operations of the British Army*, I, pp. 116–17.

52. *Cf.* W. Grattan, *Adventures of the Connaught Rangers from 1808 to 1814* (London, 1847), I, pp. 193–94; Gleig, *The Subaltern*, p. 62. What neither recognised, meanwhile, is that fates could befall them that all but beggar belief. Thus, a woman who was widowed might well be assured of a new husband, but what of the woman whose husband was badly wounded or, still worse, maimed to such an extent that he had to be invalided out of the service? In this case re-marriage was not an option while few regiments would have tolerated the notion of a wife abandoning a man in such a case. In consequence, what beckoned was the loss of all community, a long and wearisome trek to some base hospital and a future that was dark indeed. When Buckham came across a convoy consisting of a convoy consisting of 'numbers of carts laden with sick and wounded . . . followed by crowds of half-famishing women and children' near Celorico in December 1812, then, he was witnessing a picture of still greater misery than he imagined; *cf.* Buckham, *Personal Narrative*, p. 95.

53. Desperate situations were also inclined to produce such behaviour. During the period of severe famine that assailed Wellington's army after Talavera, for example, Schaumann saw soldiers' wives who had evidently already sold most of their clothing to buy food offering themselves to anyone who wanted them for half a loaf of bread; *cf.* Ludovici, *On the Road with Wellington*, p. 205. That said, in normal times, there were plenty of other ways of earning money: one woman of

Swabey's artillery battery, for example, was taken on by him as a cook; *cf.* Whinyates, *Diary of Campaigns in the Peninsula*, p. 159.

54. Hunt, *Charging against Napoleon*, p. 58; Kincaid, *Random Shots*, p. 61. The woman concerned in the latter anecdote eventually deserted to the enemy, donkey and all.

55. Donaldson, *Recollections*, p. 219.

56. Cooper, *Rough Notes*, p. 99.

57. Bell, *Rough Notes*, I, p. 143.

58. Anton, *Retrospect of a Military Life*, pp. 141–42; Mrs Cunningham, Anton tells us, was saved from marrying again by a wounded officer who engaged her as his nurse and eventually arranged for her passage back to England. Donaldson, *Recollections of a Soldier*, pp. 160–61.

59. Gleig, *The Subaltern*, p. 167.

60. In fairness, in 1811 orders had been issued that all women widowed in Spain and Portugal should automatically get a free passage home. However, whilst this was fine in theory, the practice was not so easy: having sometimes been away for many years, campfollowers often had almost no links with their families and, still worse, little hope of being able to make an honest living, whilst their regiments were also the only homes they had.

61. Anton, *Retrospect of a Military Life*, pp. 142–43. In fact, it is not true that all women who lost their husbands remarried. Widowed at the battle of Roliça and utterly distraught, for example, a Mrs Cochan of the Ninety-Fifth rejected a proposal from Benjamin Harris—a steady man whose trade as a shoemaker made him a very good catch—and went home to England, saying that she had 'received too great a shock . . . ever to think of another soldier'; *cf.* Hibbert, *Recollections of Rifleman Harris*, p. 22.

62. B. H. Liddell Hart (ed.), *The Letters of Private Wheeler, 1809–1828* (London, 1951), p. 141; A. Hamilton, *Hamilton's Campaign with Moore and Wellington during the Peninsular War* (Troy, New York, 1847), p. 37; Green, *Vicissitudes*, p. 102.

63. *Cf.* Green, *Vicissitudes*, pp. 99–100; Anton, *Retrospect of a Military Life*, pp. 116–17.

64. Patterson, *Adventures*, pp. 92–93. Some attempt was made to avoid these horrors in that, after Moore's army had concentrated in Salamanca, its wives were provided with money and ordered to make their way back to Lisbon. However, in testimony to their feelings for their husbands and their regiments alike, most returned to the ranks after a token absence of a few days only; *cf.* C. Steevens, *Reminiscences of my Military Life from 1795 to 1818* (Winchester, 1878), p. 71.

65. S. Morley, *Memoirs of a Sergeant of the Fifth Regiment of Foot containing an Account of his Service in Hanover, South America and the Peninsula* (London, 1842), p. 61. One woman recorded as having died in childbirth on the road to La Coruña is a Mrs Thomas, who was married to a pay sergeant of the Forty-Third Foot, but others managed not only to survive but to save their babies; *cf.* Hamilton, *Hamilton's Campaign*, p. 47, and Anon., *Memoirs of a Sergeant late in the Forty-Third Light Infantry Regiment previously and during the Peninsular War* (London, 1835), pp. 63–64. Much luckier than either was the wife of a soldier of the Twenty-Seventh Foot who went into labour while her battalion was sheltering for the night in a ruined church at Punhete whilst on the march in Portugal in 1812: there being no pressing danger, she was allowed to remain behind to rest, her

husband eventually being sent back to pick her up with a pony belonging to a sympathetic officer. *Cf.* Glover, *Eloquent Soldier,* p. 26.

66. E.g., Anon., *Journal of a Soldier of the Seventy-First, or Glasgow Regiment, Highland Light Infantry, from 1806 to 1815* (Edinburgh, 1819), p. 82. So terrible were the conditions that at least one observer maintains that virtually none of the women who were with the army survived the retreat; *cf.* Ludovici, *On the Road with Wellington,* pp. 130–31. One wife who did make it back to England, however, and that despite being separated from her husband and raped by French troops, was a Mrs Pullen of the Ninety-Fifth, and another a Mrs Monday of the Twenty-Eighth, the latter distinguishing herself by saving not only herself, but her pet lapdog; *cf.* Hibbert, *Recollections of Rifleman Harris,* pp. 62–64, and C. Cadell, *Narrative of the Campaigns of the Twenty-Eighth Regiment since their Regiment from Egypt in 1802* (London, 1835), p. 73. Meanwhile, women also died during the retreat to Ciudad Rodrigo in November 1812; *cf.* H. Ross-Lewin, *With the Thirty-Second in the Peninsula and other Campaigns,* ed. J. Wardell (Dublin, 1904), p. 207.

67. For the most part , the French forces were spared such scenes. However, during Masséna's retreat from Portugal in 1811, which was also conducted amidst the most miserable weather, the Anglo-Portuguese army came across the bodies of numerous women and children; *cf.* Ludovici, *On the Road with Wellington,* p. 290.

68. E. Coss, *All for the King's Shilling: the British Soldier under Wellington, 1808–1814* (Norman, Oklahoma, 2010), p. 99.

69. Bell, Rough Notes, I, p. 55. *Cf.* also S. A. C. Cassells, *Peninsular Portrait, 1811–1814: the Letters of William Bragge, Third (King's Own) Dragoons* (London, 1963), p. 18; I. Fletcher (ed.), *For King and Country: the Letters and Diaries of John Mills, Coldstream Guards, 1811–14* (Staplehurst, 1995), p. 58.

70. Green, *Vicissitudes,* p. 159.

71. J. Sturgis (ed.), *A Boy in the Peninsular War: the Services, Adventures and Experiences of Robert Blakeney, Subaltern in the Twenty-Eighth Regiment* (London, 1899), p. 51. At least one incident of the same sort occurred in the course of the retreat to Ciudad Rodrigo in November 1812; *cf.* Cadell, *Narrative,* p. 142. Far less easy to condone, however, is an incident that took place on the morning of the battle of Vimeiro when a French cavalry patrol raped (or so it is implied) a group of camp-followers washing clothes in the River Maçeira, though the women concerned were reportedly afterwards more concerned that the men who had assaulted them had also stolen their shoes; *cf.*, Landmann, *Recollections,* II, pp. 199–200.

72. Hamilton, *Hamilton's Campaign,* p. 45.

73. L. Fantin des Odoards, *Journal du Général Fantin des Odoards: étapes d'un officier de la Grande Armée, 1800–1830* (Paris, 2009), p. 143.

74. Liddell Hart, *Letters of Private Wheeler,* p. 103.

75. A. de Gonneville, *Recollections of Colonel de Gonneville* , ed. C. Yonge (London, 1875), I, p. 176.

76. M. Barrès (ed.), *Memoirs of a French Napoleonic Officer: Jean-Baptiste Barrès, Chasseur of the Imperial Guard* (London, 1925), p. 166.

77. Henegan, *Seven Years' Campaigning,* I, pp. 117–18.

78. H. Ducor, *Aventures d'un marin de la Garde Imperiale, prisonnier de guerre sur les pontons espagnols, dans l'ile de Cabrera et en Russie* (Paris, 1833), I, pp. 89–91; Blaze, *Mémoires d'un apothicaire,* I, p. 250. Interestingly, Ducor claims that very

few of the women fell sick themselves, his explanation being that caring for the sick gave them a positive task with which to occupy their time, though, as one of them supposedly remarked, 'If we were to fall sick, what would become of the poor fellows who depend on us?'

79. *Ibid.*, I, pp. 212–13. 'Robinsons'—a reference, of course, to Robinson Crusoe—was the nickname awarded themselves by the prisoners sent to Cabrera. For a full account of their sufferings, *cf.* D. Smith, *The Prisoners of Cabrera: Napoleon's Forgotten Soldiers, 1809–1814* (New York, 2001).

80. P. Gille (ed.), *Mémoires d'un conscrit de 1808* (Paris, 1892), pp. 228–29.

81. J. Blakiston, *Twelve Years' Military Adventure in Three Quarters of the Globe* (London, 1829), II, pp. 144, 227. A second inn run by a British woman was found in Lisbon by George Woodberry of the Eighteenth Light Dragoons; *cf.* Hunt, *Charging against Napoleon*, p. 62.

82. Patterson, *Adventures*, p. 243. W. Graham, *Travels through Portugal and Spain during the Peninsular War* (London, 1820), p. 35. One wonders if it was this same Margaret that figured in a rather sordid affair reported as having taken place in Coimbra in the spring of 1813. In brief, a woman living with a commissary was thrown out by him, only to have her revenge by revealing details of various irregularities in which he had been engaged, the end result being that the man was dismissed and committed suicide; *cf.* Larpent, *Private Journal*, p. 91. By contrast, Madame Durand seems to have been a much nicer character: 'The . . . agreeable disposition of the gay Frenchwoman served to dissipate any melancholy thoughts that might have haunted us. Without being decidedly handsome, she had a very good set of features, and was of such a pleasant temperament that, although she was arrived at a reflecting age, her society was courted by many admiring swains.'

83. Another such was the wife of a commissary named Moore, who, shouted at by her weary and exasperated husband during the retreat to La Coruña, 'retaliated with such a volley of exquisite abuse . . . which, by the bye, she punctuated by flinging . . . all sorts of . . . cups and pots and pans, upon his head, that all those standing by . . . were contorted by laughter.' *Cf.* Ludovici, *On the Road with Wellington*, p. 116.

84. *Ibid.*, pp. 221–22.

85. The worst example that has thus far offered itself is of a woman who was shot dead by a German rifleman on the field of Roliça in the act of murdering a wounded redcoat so that she could rob him of his valuables; *cf.* Landmann, *Recollections*, II, p. 174. It is important, though, to record that the campfollowers included at least some women who were perfectly respectable. Steevens, for example, recalls that, by origin a maid-servant employed in a house in Liverpool, one of the wives lost by the Twentieth Foot in the operations of Sir John Moore, was 'an example of good conduct' whose mistress 'spoke of her in the highest terms and was sorry she married a soldier'. *Cf.* Steevens, *Reminiscences*, p. 71. Moreover, even when misconduct is complained of, it is not always clear what the true story is, as witness, for example, John Cooper's tale of being cheated by one of the wives of his company while lying sick at Badajoz in the autumn of 1809, *cf.* Cooper, *Rough Notes*, p. 33. In this instance, Cooper was certainly short-changed by the campfollower to whom he had turned for help, but we simply do not know why she failed to keep her promises.

86. Buckley, *Napoleonic-War Journal*, p. 174.

87. Kincaid, *Adventures in the Rifle-Brigade in the Peninsula, France and the Netherlands from 1809 to 1815* (London, 1830), pp. 169–71.

88. Leslie, *Military Journal*, p. 123. Another woman who fell foul of such a beating was the Mrs Bishop noted above who ended up as the mistress of a colonel. So desperate were the women for anything that could ease their lot that in the campaign of La Coruña some wives of the Twentieth Foot risked capture by French cavalry rather than abandon their attempts to scoop up a large consignment of bullion that had been abandoned by the roadside; *cf.* Steevens, *Reminiscences*, p. 71.

89. *Cf.* Grattan, *Adventures*, II, pp. 3–5. In fairness, pillage often both had a strong practical bent and was entirely legitimate: for example, many of the horses and donkeys the campfollowers fielded in the later campaigns of the war had been acquired as spoil on the battlefield of Salamanca; *cf.* Anon., *Personal Narrative of a Private Soldier who served in the Forty-Second Highlanders for Twelve Years during the Late War* (London, 1821), p. 136.

90. Blayney, *Narrative*, I, p. 345.

91. Buckley, *Napoleonic-War Journal*, p. 174. One officer who Browne claimed to have died in this fashion was a Major Francis Offley.

92. Hunt, *Charging against Napoleon*, p. 72. The importance of the women's donkeys and other animals is suggested by the rather grim scene that Larpent observed during the battle of the River Nivelle. Thus, while crossing the French frontier, he came across 'ten or fifteen poor women belonging to the baggage . . . lamenting over their dying donkeys and mules, while others were brutally beating some to death because they would not go further'. *Cf.* Larpent, *Private Journal*, p. 298. In this respect Portuguese campfollowers were seen as being 'in respect of economy . . . far superior to the British, as they in general carried all their movables, that is their camp furniture, in a bundle on their heads.' *Cf.* Monick, *Douglas' Tale*, p. 19.

93. R. Henegan, *Seven Years' Campaigning in the Peninsula and the Netherlands from 1808 to 1815* (London, 1846), I, p. 84.

94. Liddell Hart, *Letters of Private Wheeler*, pp. 140–41. In fairness, Wheeler specifically says that some of the women in the group stayed sober and did their best to help care for the wounded.

95. M. Howard, 'Red jackets and red noses: alcohol and the British Napoleonic soldier', *Journal of the Royal Society of Medicine*, XCIII, No. 1 (January, 1993), pp. 38–41.

96. *Cf.* J. White, 'The "slow but sure poyson [*sic*]": the representation of gin and its drinkers, 1736–1751', *Journal of British Studies*, XLII, No. 1 (January, 2003), pp. 5–64.

97. *Cf.* Sturgis, *Boy in the Peninsular War*, p. 67; Grattan, *Adventures*, II, pp. 9–10.

98. Hunt, *Gallopping against Napoleon*, p. 58.

99. Will of Lieutenant William Crosbie, National Archives (hereafter NA.), Prob.11/1580. I owe my knowledge of this document to my good friend and colleague, Phillip Freeman.

100. Grattan, *Adventures*, I, p. 162. It is important to note, however, that there were limits to good will. Thus, campfollowers who transgressed against the rigid

class system of the day could expect short shrift. Herewith, for example, Leslie's memories of an incident that took place at a ball which he attended in the palace of a Portuguese aristocrat in 1809: 'To our surprise, we observed there a great stout fresh-coloured Englishwoman, dressed in a riding habit and sitting between two young and handsome daughters of the hostess. Colonel Oliver immediately said to us, "This is too bad: do not speak to her." We cut our visit as short as decency would permit. It then appeared that this madam was a trooper's wife, and that an English commissary then attached to the Portuguese army . . . had not only taken this soldier's trull under his protection, but [had] had the impudence to introduce her to this and other noble families, and thus bring disgrace on the British character. The colonel went next morning and communicated to the Marquess the whole circumstance and begged to express how much the English officers felt the disgrace that a countryman should have been guilty of such conduct.' *Cf.* Leslie, *Military Journal,* pp. 185–86.

101. Patterson, *Adventures,* pp. 79–80. *Cf.* also the praise lavished on 'a poor Highland woman, the wife of a non-commissioned officer of the Seventy-First Regiment whose leg had been amputated', who waited faithfully on dozens of wounded men for a whole night with the assistance of only a single medical orderly; *cf.* Neale, *Letters,* p. 19.

102. For Madame Junot's adventures, *cf.* L. Junot, *Mémoires de Madame la Duchesse d'Abrantes, ou Souvenirs Historiques sur Napoléon, la Révolution, le Directoire, le Consulat, l'Empire et la Révolution* (4th edition, Brussels 1837), III, pp. 8–104.

103. Junot, *Mémoires,* III, pp. 101–102; for an example of such an attack, *cf.* report of Captain Ilarteguí to General Caffarelli, 10 December 1812, Instituto de Historia y Cultura Militar, Cuartel General del Ejército del Norte (hereafter IHCM. CGEN.) 7343.203. In this attack, the wife of a French officer named Journé was captured along with one of her children, but, far from being put to death, they were treated with every courtesy and handed back to the French some days later. *Cf.* P. Thouvenot to J. M. Caffarelli, 21 December 1812, *ibid.,* 7343.225. Meanwhile another such convoy story may be found in C. Bourachot (ed.), *Souvenirs Militaires du Captaine Jean-Baptiste Lemonnier-Delafosse* (Paris, n.d.), pp. 85–88; in this instance no women were taken prisoner, but the passage is nonetheless notable for the sense which it conveys of the terror that was inseparable from such experiences. Finally, for an example of bandits holding women to ransom, *cf.* B. T. Jones (ed.), *Military Memoirs of Charles Parquin* (London, 1987), pp. 114–16.

104. Buckley, *Napoleonic-War Journal,* pp. 218–19. Caught up in the midst of troops who were completely out of control, Madame Gazan received much rougher treatment than was the norm in such situations, being robbed of a number of valuables by a singularly unpleasant officer of the Eighteenth Light Dragoons named Dolbell. *Cf.* Hunt, *Charging against Napoleon,* p. 114.

105. *Cf.* Comtesse de Beaulaincourt-Marles (ed.), *Journal du Maréchal de Castellane, 1804–1862* (Paris, 1895–97), I, p. 25; T. Rouillard (ed.), *Rélations de la campagne d'Andalousie* (La Vouvre, 1999), p. 121.

106. S. Larreguy de Civrieux, *Souvenirs d'un cadet, 1812–1823,* ed. L. Larreguy de Civrieux (Paris, 1912), pp. 45–46; M. de Marbot, *The Memoirs of Baron de Marbot* (London, 1892), II, pp. 106–107; Stothert, *Narrative,* p. 192; L. S. de Girardin, *Journal et Souvenirs, Discours et Opinions de S. Girardin* (Paris, 1828), IV, pp. 216–17.

According to Larreguy, the sight of Madame Suchet sharing their privations and dangers greatly cheered the troops, while her presence also helped the French commander to forge a variety of useful contacts with the local élite.

107. Fantin des Odoards, *Journal*, p. 152.

108. Buckley, *Napoleonic-War Journal*, pp. 172–73; Ross Lewin, *With the Thirty-Second in the Peninsula*, pp. 188–89.

109. Neale, *Letters*, p. 121.

110. Landmann, *Recollections*, II, p. 146; Bell, *Rough Notes*, I, p. 57. The woman described in this anecdote appears to have been made of stern stuff. Named Susannah, she had married her husband in 1804 and thereafter accompanied him constantly, even on campaign. The night before Salamanca she is supposed to have shared a blanket with him on the ground despite the thunderstorm that drenched the entire army and narrowly escaped death when a cavalry regiment's horses bolted, while the night that followed saw her combing the battlefield in search of him. *Cf.* J. Tomkinson (ed.), *The Diary of a Cavalry Officer in the Peninsular and Waterloo Campaigns* (London, 1894), p. 188; Page, *Women in Wellington's Army*, pp. 56–57. A slightly different case is afforded by the wife of the sub-prefect of French frontier district of Céret. Thus, having been much taken with a passing Swiss officer named Hyacinthe Clemenso, she appears to have fled across the frontier to join him at his station of Prats de Mollo. However, the account given of her by Clemenso is suggestive of a woman driven by something other than just love: 'Boldness, modesty, literary talent, the ability to make herself agreeable: all these were each and every one of them a part of her make-up . . . Instead of affecting airs and graces on account of her position, every Sunday after Vespers she joined with the women and young girls . . . in dances that took place in a vast open space outside the town . . . Accompanied by the sound of the tambourine . . . these dances often went on far into the night . . . Being barely thirty years old, Madame de Lacour was always the heroine of these amusements. Everybody loved her because she made no distinction between rich and poor.' *Cf.* H. Clemenso, *Souvenirs d'un officier valaisan au service de France*, ed. M. Zermastten (Paris, 1999), pp. 32–33.

111. Ross-Lewin, *With the Thirty-Second in the Peninsula*, p. 163; such journeys were hard enough even without the intervention of officious militiamen: one evening in November 1812, for example, Buckham came across the wife of a staff-surgeon who had become lost on the road accompanied only by her husband's soldier-servant, a maid and her infant child, the little party being both utterly famished and soaked to the skin from the pouring rain; *cf.* Buckham, *Personal Narrative*, pp. 77–78.

112. *Cit.* Third Earl of Malmesbury (ed.), *A Series of Letters of the First Earl of Malmesbury, his Family and Friends from 1745 to 1820* (London, 1870), II, pp. 231–32.

113. Larpent, *Private Journal*, p. 34; *cf.* Sabine, *Letters of Colonel Sir Augustus Simon Frazer*, p. 106.

114. *Cf.* Henegan, *Seven Years' Campaigning*, I, pp. 275–89.

115. This is not to say, of course, that campfollowers cornered by bandits or enemy marauders did not on occasion seek to defend themselves—it is, indeed, conceivable that some carried arms of some sort or other—but it has to be said that no such stories have come to light.

116. The one known exception is a woman called Virginie Ghesquière from the village of Deûlémont who took the place of one of her brothers when the latter was called up in 1806, and in this guise fought in the Peninsular War until the moment her sex was discovered after she was wounded in battle. This is an interesting case—as Ghesquière had never married and was thirty-eight when the subterfuge first took place, it is tempting to believe that she was sent off to war to rid her family of an unwanted burden—and one that there seems to be no refuting; but, for all that, it is difficult to see it as anything other than an exception. *Cf.* Hopkin, 'The world turned upside-down', p. 82.

117. Another such case is mentioned by Crowe. Thus: 'A lieutenant of French artillery came in this afternoon with his wife, a very beautiful Spanish lady disguised as a French hussar officer, who had induced him to desert his guns.' *Cf.* Glover, *An Eloquent Soldier*, pp. 84–85.

118. Henegan, *Seven Years' Campaigning*, I, pp. 321–22; Buckley, *Journal of Captain Thomas Henry Browne*, p. 213.

Chapter 4

1. Such at least is the account of the affair that is currently accepted by Spanish specialists; *cf.* M. P. Queralt, *Agustina de Aragón: la mujer y el mito* (2008), pp. 80–81; for a more dramatic version embellished with a variety of more-or-less plausible detail, *cf.* C. Cobo, *La ilustre heróina de Zaragoza o la celebre amazona en la Guerra de la Independencia: novela histórica* (Madrid, 1859), pp. 213–16 (NB. Cobo was none other than Domenech's daughter). It will be noted, however, that the narrative offered here is rather different from the standard version of events. In this last, the product, it appears, of some rather extravagant embroidery on the part of José Palafox, Domenech is not married to the absent Roca, but rather engaged to one of the men serving the battery, and, indeed, snatches up the linstock from his dying hands.

2. For a detailed account of this affair, which gradually became ever more exaggerated in the telling, not least by Jarret herself, the reader is referred to the 'Dictionary of Canadian Biography Online'. *Cf.* http://www.biographi.ca/009004-119.01-e.php?BioId=35540 (accessed 12 September 2011). There are many similar stories, meanwhile, from the American colonies; *cf.* T. Purvis, *Colonial America to 1763* (New York, 1999), pp. 231–32; De Pauw, *Battle Cries and Lullabies*, pp. 114–15.

3. The fact that the story was well-known is due to its inclusion in the best-selling history of New France published by Pierre de Charlevoix in 1744.

4. *Cf.* R. A. Koestler-Grack, *Molly Pitcher: Heroine of the War for Independence* (Philadelphia, 2006); E. Rodríguez Solis, *María Pita: defensa de La Coruna en 1589—narración histórica* (Madrid, 1898).

5. The author is not the first observer to have spotted the importance of Domenech's patronym, as witness Ucelay, 'Agustina, la dama de cañón', p. 194. So far as he knows, however, he is the first to link it with a deliberate campaign of manipulation. It would also be interesting to know, of course, whether Domenech was as beautiful as some of the iconography seems to suggest. As Ucelay points out, we do not have a trustworthy visual image. However, the testimony of a British officer who saw her at Cádiz is not very encouraging: 'A heroine of all people ought to be beautiful, and I really should have thought it incumbent upon me to fall in love with her. But nature has bestowed on her a visage so

much in opposition to my ideas of beauty that with all my previous determination I could not do it.' *Cf.* Fletcher, *For King and Country*, p. 62. Another observer is rather more positive, but the impression conveyed by his words is still that she was little more than 'homely': 'Her countenance is mild and feminine, her smile pleasing, and her face altogether the last I should have supposed to belong to a woman who had led troops through blood and slaughter.' *Cf.* W. Jacob, *Travels in the South of Spain in Letters written A.D. 1809 and 1810* (London, 1811), pp. 123–24.

6. The political background to the outbreak of the Peninsular War is a complex subject. For an explanation that gives considerable weight to the actions of Palafox and his fellow *fernandinos*, *cf.* C. J. Esdaile, *The Peninsular War: a New History* (London, 2002), pp. 15–61.

7. *Cf.* H. Lafoz, *Zaragoza, 1808: revolución y guerra* (Zaragoza, 2006), pp. 51–62.

8. For a comprehensive collection, *cf.* H. Lafoz (ed.), *Manifiestos y bandos de la Guerra de la Independencia en Aragón, I: los sitios de Zaragoza* (Zaragoza, 2005), pp. 51–110.

9. It is, perhaps, worth noting here that the initial account of the first siege published by the *Gazeta de Zaragoza* makes no mention of Domenech; *cf. Gazeta de Zaragoza,* 16 August 1808, pp. 683–85.

10. Curiously enough, Doyle did not mention Agustina in the various dispatches he penned from Zaragoza in the autumn of 1808, but he did take her under his wing when she turned up in Seville, providing her with financial suppott, championing her case with the authorities, and introducing her to a variety of influential British visitors. *Cf.* G. Iglesias Rogers, *British Liberators in the Age of Napoleon: Volunteering under the Spanish Flag in the Peninsular War* (London, 2013), pp. 125–28.

11. For the full text of the petition of 12 August 1809, *cf.* Queralt, *Agustina de Aragón,* pp. 163–66. This success was not achieved entirely unopposed. To quote Carr, 'There were many in Cádiz . . . who coldly called this young heroine "the artillerywoman", and observed that they should soon have nothing but battalions of women in the field instead of attending to their domestic concerns if every romantic female were rewarded and commissioned as Agustina had been.' *Cf.* Carr, *Descriptive Travels,* pp. 33.

12. *Cf.* Carr, *Descriptive Travels,* pp. 31–33.

13. Donaldson, *Recollections,* pp. 204–205. It is also clear that Domenech was at Tortosa, a justification of his conduct that was written by the governor in 1814 noting that she appeared in the city in November 1809 and (supposedly) served as an artillery officer during the siege. However, even her most assiduous biographers have not been able to find any firm evidence as to what took place between the fall of Tortosa in January 1811 and the battle of Vitoria in June 1813; *cf.* Queralt, *Agustina de Aragón,* pp. 121–23. With regard to Vitoria, Morillo later issued a certificate testifying to her presence, but there is, alas, considerable reason to doubt its veracity. For this document, *cf.* Coy, *Agustina Saragossa,* pp. 136–37.

14. *Cf.* Fernández García, *Mujeres,* pp. 59–63; Queralt, *Agustina de Aragón,* p. 183.

15. E.g., Vaughan, *Narrative,* pp. 28–29; L. F. Lejeune, *Los sitios de Zaragoza,* ed. P. Rújula (Zaragoza, 2009), p. 24; A. Alcaide, *Historia de los sitios que pusieron a Zaragoza en los años de 1808 y 1809 las tropas de Napoleón* (Madrid, 1830), pp. 65–68; circular of J. Palafox to the bishops of Spain and the Indies, n.d.,

cit. Lafoz, *Manifiestos y bandos,* p. 73; F. Casamayor, *Diario de los sitios de Zaragoza, 1808–1809,* ed. H. Lafoz (Zaragoza, 2000), pp. 41–43.

16. *Cf.* http://es.wikipedia.org/wiki/Casta_%C3%811varez (accessed 23 November 2011).

17. Proclamation of J. Palafox, 15 June 1808, *cit.* Lafoz, *Manifiestos y bandos,* p. 53.

18. Proclamation of J. Palafox, 30 January 1809, *cit. ibid.*, p. 103.

19. Fernández García, *Mujeres,* pp. 62–63.

20. *Cf. ibid.*, pp. 53–54, 63–64.

21. Lejeune, *Sitios de Zaragoza,* p. 35.

22. Swinburne, *Travels,* pp. 14–15. For some examples from the English Civil War, *cf.* C. Carlton, *Going to the Wars: the Experience of the English Civil Wars, 1638–1651* (London, 1992), pp. 161–67; A. Fraser, *The Weaker Vessel: Woman's Lot in Seventeenth-Century England* (London, 1984), pp. 197–223.

23. *Cf.* Lynn, *Women, Armies and Warfare,* pp. 202–208.

24. L. F. Lejeune, *Memoirs of Baron Lejeune, aide de camp to Marshals Berthier, Davout and Oudinot,* ed. N. Bell (London, 1897), I, pp. 120–21. *Cf.* also C. Doyle to W. Cooke, 30 November 1808, NA. W0.1/227, f. 567: 'Such was the spirit of the inhabitants that . . . there was not a moment's cessation of work during day or night, and every individual of every class was at work on the batteries . . . the ladies had enrolled themselves, and hundreds of women of the lower class, and formed companies in order to supply the different batteries with provisions, etc . . . At the head of these heroines is the Countess of Bureta, cousin to General Palafox, who set the same example during the late siege and whose conduct seemed to inspire the inhabitants with the greatest zeal and devotion to their country.'

25. *Cit.* F. Presa *et al.* (eds.), *Soldados polacos en España durante la Guerra de la Independencia Española, 1808–1814* (Madrid, 2004), p. 230; for mentions of female involvement in the fighting, *cf. ibid.*, p. 226; Lejeune, *Memoirs,* I, pp. 141, 160, 173–74.

26. One point that may be significant here is that Marbot—normally very much someone who was both eager to tell a good story and utterly unscrupulous in his respect for the truth—makes no mention of 'amazons' of any sort in his account of the second siege. *Cf.* M. de Marbot, *The Memoirs of Baron de Marbot* (London, 1892), I, pp. 359–67. Equally devoid of any such reference is the account of Heinrich von Brandt, a German officer of Prussian extraction who served in the Legion of the Vistula in Navarre and Aragón from 1808 to 1811; *cf.* North , *In the Legions of Napoleon,* pp. 51–61.

27. The most detailed modern account of the Dos de Mayo is constituted by A. García Fuertes, *Dos de mayo de 1808: grito de una nación* (Madrid, 2008). However, *cf.* also F. Díaz Plaza, *Dos de mayo de 1808* (Madrid, 1996) and J. C. Montón, *La revolución armada del dos de mayo en Madrid* (Madrid, 1983), while J. Pérez de Guzmán, *El Dos de Mayo en Madrid* (Madrid, 1908) remains a fundamental text. In all, seventy-nine women died in the fighting, though it is worth noting that many of the fallen are noted as having either been hit by stray bullets or killed in their own homes.

28. R. Fraser, *Napoleon's Cursed War: Popular Resistance in the Spanish Peninsular War* (London, 2008), p. 26.

29. For all this, *cf.* R. Herr, 'Good, evil and Spain's rising against Napoleon' in R. Herr and H. Parker (eds.), *Ideas in History* (Durham, North Carolina, 1965), pp. 157–81.

30. R. Carr, *Spain, 1808–1975* (Oxford, 1982), p. 85.

31. The Iberian uprising, of course, did not just extend to Spain, but also spread to Portugal. In so far as this development is concerned, the traditional explanation that is offered is very similar to the one that pertains in respect of Spain: i.e. that popular xenophobia combined with religious devotion and patriotic pride to produce a conflagration. This construct, however, seems just as open to challenge as the Spanish one, while Portugal was suffering stresses that in some ways were just as serious as those that affected Spain (of particular importance here were the deleterious social effects of some of the reforms of the Marques de Pombal) . The issue awaits its historian, but, for some preliminary expressions of doubt, *cf.* Esdaile, *Peninsular War,* pp. 90–91.

32. *Cf.* E. de Diego, *España, el infierno de Napoleón* (Madrid, 2008), p. 196.

33. *Cf.* Landmann, *Recollections,* II, pp. 34–35; I. Castells, G. Espigado and M. C. Romeo, 'Heroínas para la patria, madres para la nación: mujeres en pie de guerra', in Castells *et al., Heroínas y patríotas,* p. 23; Fraser, *Napoleon's Cursed War,* p. 99; H. Lafoz (ed.), *José de Palafox: memorias* (Zaragoza, 1994), p. 60. Interestingly, it is never pointed out that in one or two instances, as in Cádiz, where a Señora Strange was badly wounded trying to protect the Captain-General of Seville from the crowd that murdered him, women actually resisted the uprising; *cf.* Leslie, *Military Journal,* pp. 20–21.

34. For all this, *cf.* Hufton, *The Prospect before Her,* pp. 458–72.

35. *Cf.* E. Vasco, *Ocupación e incendio de Valdepeñas por las tropas francesas en 1808* (Valdepeñas, 1908).

36. J. J. de Naylies, *Mémoires sur la guerre d'Espagne pendant les années 1808, 1809, 1810 et 1811* (Paris, 1817), pp. 63–67.

37. *Ibid.,* pp. 107–108. *Cf.* also A. Pinto, 'A resistência no feminino—simbolismo e representação de uma crise social -"patriotas da retaguarda" no contexto da guerra peninsular', unpublished conference paper (?) accessed at http://www.iseg.utl.pt/aphes30/docs/progdocs/ANTONIOPINTODOFUNDO.pdf, 30 October 2011. In May 2009 a monument featuring this unknown Portuguese heroine was unveiled in Penafiel.

38. Fantin des Odoards, *Journal,* pp. 154, 165.

39. J. Mendoza y Rico, *Historia de Málaga durante la revolución santa que agita a España desde marzo de 1808,* ed. M. Olmedo (Málaga, 2003), pp. 107–108.

40. *Cf.* http://www.scribd.com/doc/27464846/La-Palma-Del-Condado (accessed 10 February 2010); whether there is any truth in this story is unknown, but at some point in the nineteenth century the street in which her tavern was situated was renamed the Calle Marimarcos in honour of the incident.

41. Anon., *Recuerdo de algunos medios poderosos sin duda para que por fin triunfe Cataluña no obstante la sensibilísima e inesperada perdida de Tarragona* (Palma de Mallorca, 1811), p. 14. Note, however, that there is no suggestion here of the women of Catalonia marching off to war: rather, they were to remain very much 'homefront-heroines'. Similarly, a triumphalist account of the defeat of a French column by Catalan irregulars at El Bruch on 4 June 1808 leaves the reader in no doubt that the women and children of the men concerned remained at home,

there even being some suggestion that they opposed their departure; *cf.* Anon., 'Batalla primera del Bruch ganada a los franceses en 6 de julio de 1808', *cit.* S. Delgado (ed.), *Guerra de la Independencia: proclamas, bandos y combatientes* (Madrid, 1979), pp. 152–59.

42. Gonneville, *Recollections,* II, pp. 46–47; *cf.* also C. Bourachot (ed.), *Sergent Lavaux: mémoires du campagne* (Paris, 2004), pp. 158–59.

43. Sturgis, *Boy in the Peninsular War,* p. 145. An echo of this incident may be found in an article in the *Diario de Granada* complaining at the rapid collapse of recruitment in Andalucía in 1808: 'Why, beloved compatriots, have so many heroic sentiments given way to such silence and lack of confidence? Why are there mothers who shed tears when sending their sons off to a just and holy war at a moment when the women of Spain in general are finding such joy and glory in seeing them die in the defence of a *patria* that is often just a miserable little village rather than the rich and powerful provinces that we can boast of?' *Cf. Diario de Granada,* 24 June 1808, n.p.

44. *Cf.* M. López Pérez, 'María Bellido, la heroína de Bailén', *Revista de Historia Militar,* XXIV, No. 49 (July, 1980), pp. 59–80; *ibid.,* XXV, No. 50 (January, 1981), pp. 61–88; *Elogio a las matronas valencianas por lo que contribuyeron a la defensa de la ciudad el dia 28 de junio [de 1808] atacada por el mariscal Moncey que comandaba 10,000 franceses* (n.p., n.d). For a critical analysis of the story of María Bellido, *cf.* F. Acosta, 'Mujeres en la campaña de Andalucía: María Bellido y la batalla de Bailén', in Castells *et al., Heroínas y patriotas,* pp. 57–79.

45. Henegan, *Seven Years' Campaigning,* I, 22. Similar scenes were witnessed by Schaumann in La Coruña: 'Everybody, young and old, rich and poor alike—aye, even the women and girls—are busy on the ramparts helping to throw up entrenchments. Whole troops of young and beautiful girls go in procession with baskets on their heads, carrying ammunition . . . to the batteries.' *Cf.* Ludovici, *On the Road with Wellington,* p. 135. Finally, George Jackson writes very similarly of the short-lived attempt to defend Madrid in December 1808. Thus: 'Well-dressed women were seen helping the populace in taking up the pavement and carrying the stones to the tops of houses, cutting trenches through the streets, etc., etc.' *Cit.* Lady Jackson (ed.), *The Diaries and Letters of Sir George Jackson, K.C.H., from the Peace of Amiens to the Battle of Talavera* (London, 1872), II, p. 312.

46. For all this, *cf.* E. Fernández García, 'Las mujeres en los sitios de Gerona: la Companía de Santa Bárbara' in Castells *et al., Heroínas y patriotas,* pp. 105–28; Zermastten, *Souvenirs d'un officier valaisan,* p. 29. The involvement of women with the defence of fortress cities did not end with Gerona, as witness, for example, the following *apologium* in respect of the Spanish loss of Badajoz in March 1811: 'As they have done on thousands of other occasions, the very women prepared enormous meals at their own cost, and took them to the troops guarding the walls.' *Cf.* J. M. Calatrava *et al., Contestación por la provincia de Extremadura al aviso publicado por el Coronel Don Rafael Hore en el numero 55 del Redactor General* (Cádiz, 1811), p. 9.

47. W. F. K.Thompson (ed.), *An Ensign in the Peninsular War: the Letters of John Aitchison* (London, 1981), p. 204. Note, however, the ambiguity of this scene: the women may be glad to be rid of the French, but the sceptical observer cannot but ask whether the women were being paid for their efforts. The image of patriotic heroines doing their duty that the reference conjures up is therefore easily substituted by one of desperate housewives engaging in menial casual labour to feed their families.

48. Henegan, *Seven Years' Campaigning,* I, p. 354.

49. M. Cantos, 'Las mujeres en la prensa entre la ilustración y el romanticismo', in M. Cantos *et al.* (eds.), *La guerra de pluma: estudios sobre la prensa de Cádiz en el tiempo de las cortes, 1810–1814* (Cádiz, 2008), pp. 182–83; P. Haythornthwaite (ed.), *In the Peninsula with a French Hussar* (London, 1990), pp. 133–34. It should be noted, however, first, that the Patriot forces in the Serranía de Ronda were essentially composed of village militias rather than guerrilla bands, and, second, that a British commissary who witnessed just such a skirmish as the one described by Rocca makes it very clear not only that the women were present in an essentially auxiliary capacity, but also that their contribution to the fighting was limited to finishing off the French wounded; *cf.* Henegan, *Seven Years' Campaigning,* I, pp. 196, 199–200.

50. Cantos, 'Mujeres en la prensa', pp. 182, 187–88; Fernández García, *Mujeres,* pp. 108–10. Although he remembered her neither as his daughter nor his aunt, but rather as his niece, the woman who rode with Toribio Bustamente was actually encountered by William Carr-Gomm. As he wrote in a letter to his father dated 5 November 1810: 'There was another character of a different cast . . . that I met with at Salvatierra, Romana's headquarters at that time. It was the famous Caracola [NB. Bustamente was known as 'Caracol'], whom you must have read so much about in the English papers. She is very young, scarcely twenty and very pretty. She had lost her nearest relations since the French entered Spain, and, determining upon active vengeance, she enlisted under the banners of her uncle (a man of some rank and then at the head of a band of guerrillas) and had fought by his side at the bridge of Almaraz and on many other occasions. She was once wounded in the shoulder by a sabre, and was made an officer in the Spanish service in consequence. In the course of her adventures she had always dressed in disguise. She was now in deep mourning for the loss of her uncle, who had been killed a short time before in an affair he had with the French, and she came to Romana for the purpose of obtaining some reward for the distinguished services she had been rendering her country . . . We were particularly in luck, for she no sooner heard there were Englishmen in the place than she instantly came, attended by her squire (another female), and . . . gave us the whole story of her misfortunes and adventures.' *Cit.* F. C. Carr-Gomm (ed.), *Letters and Journals of Field Marshal Sir William Maynard Carr-Gomm* (London, 1881), p. 197.

51. Sánchez Arreiseigor, 'Mujeres en la guerra', pp. 710–13.

52. *Cit.* Malmesbury, *A Series of Letters,* II, pp. 258–59. Still more interesting, perhaps, is Paul Thiébault's claim to have caught sight of 'two young amazons, splendid with embroidery, beautiful as angels, ferocious as demons' actually fighting in the ranks of a *guerrilla* band in the course of an action in La Rioja in 1809; *cf.* A. J. Butler (ed.), *The Memoirs of Baron Thiébault, late Lieutenant-General in the French Army* (London, 1896), II, p. 271.

53. *Cf.* A. Grasset, *Málaga: provincia francesa, 1811–1812,* ed. M. C. Toledano (Málaga, 1996), p. 530. In general, very few women were executed by the French. However, for a handful of other cases, *cf.* Cantos, 'Mujeres en la prensa', pp. 180–83. Of these, perhaps the saddest was one Francisca de Artiaga who was sentenced to death in Valladolid for stealing food from a French restaurateur.

54. Fraser, *Napoleon's Cursed War,* pp. 430–31. *Cf.* also Sánchez Arreiseigor, 'Mujeres en la guerra', pp. 704–708. In only one of these cases—that of a fourteen-year-old girl called María Josefa de Iturbe who was sentenced to six years' detention—is there any suggestion of actual involvement in violence.

55. Sánchez Arreiseigor, 'Mujeres en la guerra', p. 713; Fernández García, pp. 112–13.

56. Larpent, *Private Journal*, p. 175.

57. Less ambiguous, perhaps, is the case of Francisca Cerpa, a woman from the village of Salteras, west of Seville, who threw herself on the pity of the authorities having, or so she claimed, not only given seven sons to the *guerrilla* bands, but clothed and equipped them at her own expense, with the result that she was reduced to living as a beggar. Duly impressed, the *cortes* awarded her a pension, but it is impossible not to wonder whether evidence derived from such sources can ever entirely be relied upon. *Cf.* Decree of the Cortes Generales y Extraordinarias, 6 December 1812, *cit. Colección de los decretos y órdenes que han expedidos las cortes generales y extraordinarias desde 24 de mayo de 1812 hasta 24 de febrero de 1813* (Madrid, 1820), III, p. 176. I owe my knowledge of this document to my good friend, and colleague, Arsenio García Fuertes.

58. For a discussion of French views of the Peninsular War, *cf.* A. Forrest, 'The French armies and their perceptions of the war in Spain', in A. Moliner (ed.), *Occapació i resistència a la Guerra del Francès, 1808–1814* (Barcelona, 2007), pp. 19–27.

59. An exception here is afforded by a decree issued by the Junta of Seville in June 1808 which called for women either to make themselves available for work in the fields so as to free manpower for the army or to dedicate themselves to the task of producing items that would be of use for the care of the wounded such as thread, bandages, bolsters and palliasses; *cf.* decree of the Junta of Seville, 6 June 1808, *cit. Diario Mercantil de Cádiz*, 20 June 1808, pp. 683–84.

60. *Cit.* Fernández García, *Mujeres*, p. 83.

61. I owe my knowledge of this text to my good friend and colleague, Cesar Rina Simón, who at the time of writing is working on a Ph.D. at the University of Navarre.

62. 'Súplica que hacen al gobierno las mujeres de Cartagena', *Diario de Granada*, 8 June 1808, n.p.

63. In fairness, it should be reported that in 1810 a small group of Cuban women attempted to organise a company of 100 women soldiers for dispatch to the Peninsula. However, as there was never any further mention of this enterprise, one can only assume that it never prospered (if, that is, it was ever really intended to take it forward: given the timing, the idea seems likely to have been a ploy on the part of the Cuban plantocracy to secure the support of Cádiz against domestic insurrection). *Cf.* Cantos, 'Mujeres en la prensa', p. 183.

64. North, *In the Legions of Napoleon*, p. 87.

65. F. Whittingham (ed.), *A Memoir of the Services of Samuel Ford Whittingham* (London, 1868), pp. 39–40.

66. E.g., Thirion, *Souvenirs militaires*, pp. 87–91; Ducor, *Aventures d'un marin*, I, pp. 112–13, 116–24.

67. *Cf.*, proclamation of B. de Aranza, 8 May 1810, Archivo Histórico Nacional, Sección de Estado (hereafter AHN. Estado) *legajo* 2994.

68. M. Reder, 'Espionaje y represión en la Serranía de Ronda: María García, "La Tinajera", un ejemplo de coraje ante los franceses', in Castells *et al.*, *Heroínas y patriotas*, pp. 175–92; *Gazeta de Oficio del Gobierno de Vizcaya*, 27 April 1810, p. 3; sentence of the Junta Criminal de Alava, 19 June 1812, IHCM. CGEN.7343.229. In January 1811 two other women named Ana Gutiérrez and María de la Soledad were put on trial in Seville with a group of nineteen men on charges of espionage

and inciting men to enlist in the guerrillas. In the event, neither were found guilty, but with several of the men they were nevertheless kept in detention pending further investigation, whilst Ana Gutiérrez's husband, an embroiderer named Bernardo Palacio, was sentenced to death. *Cf.* 'Sentencia dada por la comisión militar especial creada en Sevilla en nombre del Emperador y del Rey', 8 January 1811, Biblióteca Nacional, Colección Gómez Imaz (hereafter BN. CGI). R60014/79.

69. *Cf.* Fernández García, *Mujeres,* pp. 98–99.

70. Gonneville, *Recollections,* I, p. 312.

71. Haythornthwaite, *In the Peninsula with a French Hussar,* p. 123.

72. Anon., 'Noticias de Sevilla' (ms.), n.d., AHN. Estado, *legajo* 2994, No. 4. A variant on this theme was the organization of rival social events: in Ronda, for example, one Jerónima López celebrated the arrival of the news of Allied victories by holding masked balls and distributing money to the poor; *cf.* A.M. Jiménez Bartolomé, '"Los otros combatientes en la Guerra de la Independencia': el papel femenino', in P. Castañeda (ed.), *Las guerras en el primer tercio del siglo XIX en España y América: XII jornadas nacionales de historia militar* (Seville, 2004), p. 363.

73. C. Oman (ed.), 'A prisoner of Albuera: the journal of Major William Brooke from 16 May to 28 September 1811', in C. Oman, *Studies in the Napoleonic Wars* (Oxford, 1929), pp. 185–86; *cf.* also Bell, *Rough Notes,* I, p. 46, Kincaid, *Random Shots,* pp. 75–76, T. Fernyhough (ed.), *Military Memoirs of Four Brothers* (London, 1829), p. 231, and Gleig, *Light Dragoon,* pp. 51–52. A particularly interesting case, meanwhile, is the wife of the Spanish general, Domingo Belesta, who is said to have hidden two British officers who had gone astray during the retreat of Sir John Moore in her home in La Coruña in 1809 at the very same time as she was perforce having to play hostess to the headquarters of Marshal Ney; *cf.* P. Beslay (ed.), *Un officier d'état-major sous le Premier Empire: souvenirs militaires d'Octave Levavasseur, officier d'artillerie, aide de camp du Maréchal Ney, 1802–1815* (Paris, 1914), p. 167. Note, however, that assistance to prisoners of war cannot necessarily be seen as a political act: after the battle of Bailén, for example, women occasionally also came to the help of French captives, while, according to Jean-David Maillefer, a Swiss officer serving in the Spanish royal guard in 1808 who had gone over to the French and been taken prisoner after being dispatched to Seville as a spy, a Spanish girl whom he had got to know during his stay in the city regularly brought him food during his imprisonment; *cf.* J. Roy, *Les français en Espagne: souvenirs des guerres de la Péninsule* (Tours, 1856), pp. 149–50, 152–53; Anon. (ed.), 'Un vaudois à l'Armée d'Espagne d'après les souvenirs inédits du Lieutenant Jean-David Maillefer, 1809–13', in Anon. (ed.), *Soldats suisses au service étranger* (Geneva, 1909), pp. 257–58.

74. A. Hayter (ed.), *The Backbone: Diaries of a Military Family in the Napoleonic Wars* (Edinburgh, 1993), p. 126. Slessor appears to have been something of a fire-eater: her diary being full of complaints in respect of the failure of the Portuguese to defend their country in 1807, not to mention spirited denunciations of Napoleon. However, in the wake of Napoleon's re-occupation of Madrid in December 1808, she evidently decided that Portugal was untenable and took ship for England. As is entirely understandable, the British community in Oporto and, with it, its women, welcomed the dispatch of British troops to Portugal in 1808 with open arms: the staff of General Ferguson, for example, was provided with generous supplies of food by a Mrs Archer; *cf.* Warre, *Letters from the Peninsula,* p. 23.

75. *Cf.* C. Desboeufs (ed.), *Les étapes d'un soldat de l'Empire, 1800–1815: souvenirs du Capitaine Desboeufs* (Paris, 1901), pp. 156–59.

76. Fernández García, *Mujeres,* pp. 101–104.

77. J. Yangas, *Diccionario histórico-político de Tudela* (Zaragoza, 1823), p. 283.

78. *Cit.* H. d'Ideville, *Memoirs of Colonel Bugeaud from his Private Correspondence and Original Documents, 1784–1815* (London, 1884), p. 96. Another officer who complains of this situation is a nephew of the Empress Josephine named Maurice du Tascher. Thus, 'At Pinto . . . the women took the smallest pleasantry as an attempted rape, and treated the French as heretics and excommunicants.' *Cit.* R. Brindle (ed.), *Campaigning for Napoleon: the Diary of a Napoleonic Cavalry Officer, 1806–14* (Barnsley, 2006), p. 58. However, as Tascher goes on to remark, no sooner had the officer in command of his chasseur regiment ordered his officers to attend mass regularly, than the women became 'more manageable'; *ibid.*

79. P. Haythornthwaite (ed.), *Life in Napoleon's Army: the Memoirs of Captain Elzéar Blaze* (London, 1995), pp. 114–15.

80. Ludovici, *On the Road with Wellington,* p. 337.

81. A. L. A. Fée, *Souvenirs de la Guerre d'Espagne, dite de l'Independance, 1809–1813* (Paris, 1856), p. 66.

82. *Cf.* W. Verner (ed.), *A British Rifleman: Journals and Correspondence during the Peninsular War and the Campaign of Waterloo* (London, 1899), pp. 100–103.

83. Fantin des Odoards, *Journal,* p. 191.

84. Leslie, *Military Journal,* pp. 25–26, 30.

85. J. Leach, *Rough Sketches in the Life of an Old Soldier* (London, 1831), p. 42.

86. Kincaid, *Adventures,* p. 8.

87. Liddell Hart, *Letters of Private Wheeler,* p. 91; Grattan, *Adventures,* II, p. 90; J. Page (ed.), *Intelligence Officer in the Peninsula: Letters and Diaries of Major the Honourable Charles Cocks, 1786–1812* (Tunbridge Wells, 1986), p. 191.

88. Henegan, *Seven Years' Campaigning,* I, p. 354.

89. R. Brindle (ed.), *Campaigning for Napoleon: the Diary of a Napoleonic Cavalry Officer, 1806–13* (Barnsley, 2006), p. 86.

90. Bell, *Rough Notes,* I, pp. 59–60.

91. Stothert, *Narrative,* p. 122.

92. *Ibid.*, II, pp. 35–36.

93. Bell, *Rough Notes,* I, p. 12. It may be assumed that it was for the same sort of reason that the performances put on by an amateur dramatic society got up at Coria by the officers of Bell's regiment in the winter of 1812 always attracted the attendance of 'some very handsome Spanish *señoras* who looked on and laughed through their bright eyes, but understood nothing.' *Ibid.*, p. 78.

94. Leslie, *Military Journal,* p. 197.

95. *Cf.* A. M. Jiménez Bartolomé. 'Las mujeres en la Guerra de la Independencia: propaganda y resistencia', in Moliner, *Occapació i resistència,* p. 253. It will be noted, however, that the donations were not wholly spontaneous; *cf. Diario de Granada,* 30 December 1808, n.p. A variant on the idea is to be found in offers such as that made in Granada in June 1808 by two women named María Pastor and María del Rosario Muela to make up uniforms for the Spanish army for free. *Cf. Suplemento al Diario de Granada,* 30 June 1808, n.p.

96. *Diario de Granada,* 10 June 1808, n.p; *Suplemento al Diario de Granada,* 3 September 1808, n.p; *Suplemento al Gazeta de Gobierno de Sevilla,* 27 January 1809, pp. 78–80; *Gazeta del Gobierno,* 17 February 1809, p. 128. All this pales into insig-

nificance beside the consignment of 5,000 shirts and 4,000 complete uniforms presented to the army by *las señoras de Cádiz* in October 1808, it therefore being very frustrating that we know nothing at all about how so large a quantity of clothing was produced or otherwise got together, nor, still less, how it was financed. *Cf.* *Diario de Granada,* 2 November 1808, n.p.

97. *Suplemento a la Gazeta del Gobierno,* 17 February 1809, pp. 139–44. Donations were also accepted in kind, four women handing in a pair of shoes, and six a pair of stockings. Yet the mere existence of such lists should not be taken as evidence of massive popular support for the Patriot cause: in a society as rigidly hierarchical as that of *ancien-régime* Seville, the pressure that could be brought to bear to support such appeals was overwhelming. Equally, if the women of Puerto Real presented the local junta with 149 shirts for the use of the army in January 1809, it is probably safe to assume that the impulse came from the propertied classes. *Cf. Gazeta del Gobierno,* 17 February 1809, p. 126.

98. Bell, *Rough Notes,* I, pp. 46, 71.

99. Blakiston, *Twelve Years' Military Adventure,* II, pp. 257–58.

100. Wood, *Subaltern Officer,* pp. 130–31. Another such woman, a 'poor Portuguese widow [who] had little to give except commiseration, and seemed to feel much for me in particular' was encountered by Joseph Donaldson when he was left behind by his regiment when he fell sick in the wake of the storm of Badajoz; so far as can be judged, in this particular instance compassion appears to have been the most important force in operation; *cf.* Donaldson, *Recollections,* p. 163. Finally, desperately sick, Sherer was, or so the lady in question claimed, literally prayed back to health by 'the old woman of my house, who had passed many an hour during my illness before the small shrine of the saint that adorned her bedroom'; *cf.* Sherer, *Recollections,* p. 74.

101. *Cit.* Verner, *British Rifleman,* p. 71. Temporarily ordered to retire towards the coast rather than prosecute their march southwards to join the forces of Sir John Moore at Salamanca, in another such incident the troops commanded by Sir David Baird were jeered by some women at Santiago who 'called out to them that they were not taking the right road to meet the French, and pointed to the one they had left as the fittest for them to [take]'. Ilchester, *Spanish Journal of Elizabeth, Lady Holland,* pp. 236–37.

102. In one instance, at least, this in effect became reality as witness the appearance in Cádiz in August 1811 of the anonymous pamphlet entitled *Representación de las damas españolas a Jorge 30, rey de Inglaterra, sobre los vagos rumores acerca de la conducta del gobierno inglés y de sus ejércitos en la Guerra de España,* the basic idea of its author being to use the feminine voice to shame the British government into taking a more active role in the war. Yet in all there is a twist, for the author was not a woman at all, but rather one Luis de Sosa, a guards officer who had headed the insurrection in León and had since turned to patriotic pamphleteering. *Cf.* O. González García, 'Luis de Sosa y Tovar: un notable leonés en la Andalucía revolucionaría', in J. M. Cuenca Toribio (ed.), *Andalucía en la Guerra de la Independencia* (Córdoba, 2009), pp. 41–83. Interestingly enough, meanwhile, the various responses which the pamphlet elicited all refused point-blank to accept that the author could have been female.

103. Sherer, *Recollections,* p. 69. Corroboration of this story may be found in Bell, *Rough Notes,* I, p. 126. Meanwhile, Mercedes de Santa Cruz retails a story

of a Spanish girl from Barcelona who managed to persuade her infantry-officer lover to repent and return to the fold after he had temporarily gone over to the French. *Cf.* Santa Cruz, *Memorias,* II, pp. 162–66.

104. *Cf. Gazeta de Madrid,* 21 February 1810, pp. 213–14. What is certainly the case is that Patriot propagandists sought to use the vulnerability of women to murder and sexual assault as a means of galvanising support for the war effort. For a good example, *cf.* Anon., *Religiosas víctimas inmoladas en el corazón de España por la restauración y felicidad de su perseguido monarca el Señor Don Fernando el VII (que Díos guarda)* (n.p., 1808).

105. Ducor, *Aventures d'un marin,* I, p. 173.

106. Larrea was not the only woman who turned patriotic pamphleteer. On the contrary, Cantos has identified at least nineteen patriotic harangues and anti-French diatribes that appeared in the course of the uprising of 1808 as having been written by women; *cf.* Cantos, 'Las mujeres en la prensa', pp. 209–12. To these, meanwhile, must be added a few others missed by Cantos such as a proclamation entitled 'Una dama mejícana a las de su sexo' that was reproduced in the Cádiz press: a ferocious denunciation of the uprising against Spanish rule that had broken out in Mexico in July 1810 as a dastardly French plot, this was in effect an appeal to the colony's women to make use of their influence in the home to keep their menfolk loyal to the mother country. *Cf. El Redactor General,* 21 June 1811, pp. 27–28.

107. R. Solis, *El Cádiz de las cortes* (Madrid, 1958), pp. 366–68. Larrea was not the only woman to preside over a *tertulia* in Cádiz: on the contrary, up until 1811 the most important political hostess in the city was Margarita López: wife of the pre-war governor of the city, Tomás de Morla, the English-educated López succeeded in maintaining her influence in spite of her husband's defection to the French in December 1808, and became a prominent sponsor of the liberal cause, only to cast all this aside by rejoining her husband in the wake of the French invasion of Andalucía. *Cf. ibid.,* pp. 365–66.

108. M. Cantos, 'Entre la tertulia y la imprenta: la palabra encendida de una patríota andaluza—Frasquita Larrea, 1775–1838', in Castells, *Heroínas y patríotas,* pp. 269–94; *cf.* also M. Fernández Poza, 'Diarios y escritos políticos de Frasquita Larrea Böhl de Faber: romanticismo y nacionalismo, 1808–1814', in Moliner, *Occapació i resistència,* pp. 211–21, and M. Cantos, 'Lectura feménina de la prensa política de las cortes de Cádiz' in M. C. García Tejera *et al.* (eds.), *Lecturas del pensamiento filosófico, estético y político: XIII encuentro de la ilustración al romanticismo, 1750–1850—Cádiz, América y Europa ante la modernidad* (Cádiz, 2007), pp. 205–10.

109. B. Sánchez Hita, 'María del Carmen Silva: una heroína y periodista en la Guerra de la Independencia', in Castells, *Heroinas y patríotas,* pp. 399–425. Silva was not the only woman who was an active supporter of the liberal cause. Thus, in Oviedo the sister of the Conde de Toreno, one of the leading lights in the liberal caucus that dominated the *cortes,* married the prominent guerrilla commander, Juan Díez Porlier, and is reported as having played a leading role in persuading him to support the liberal cause. *Cf.* Fernández García, *Mujeres,* pp. 329–30.

110. For the involvement of women in political, military and diplomatic debate in Patriot Spain, *cf.* Cantos, 'Mujeres en la prensa', pp. 212–16; according to this author, between five and ten percent of the 1,000 or more pamphlets of all sorts published in the course of the war may have had female authors.

111. *Cf.* 'Constitución de la Real Hermandad Patriótica de Señoras', n.d., BN. CGI. R62679.

112. G. Espigado, 'La Marquesa de Villafranca y la Junta de Damas de Fernando VII' in Castells, *Heroínas y patríotas,* pp. 317–42.

113. Accounts of the frivolity of the women of the propertied classes are legion; *cf.*, for example, Henegan, *Seven Years Campaigning,* I, pp. 160–61; P. P. Nevill, *Some Recollections in the Life of Colonel P. P. Nevill, late Major, Sixty-Third Regiment* (London, 1864), p. 3.

114. Manifesto of Junta de Damas Españolas de Fernando VII, n.d., BN. CGI. R61659.

Chapter 5

1. Ludovici, *On the Road with Wellington,* p. 105. Here, too, is Warre on the situation in central Portugal early in 1812: 'It is quite impossible to give people in England an adequate idea of the sufferings of these unhappy people. We even . . . saw many people and children absolutely starving and living upon nettles and herbs they gathered in the fields . . . Hunger and famine surround us in all directions.' *Cf.* Warre, *Letters from the Peninsula,* pp. 222, 249.

2. With respect to the situation of central Portugal in late 1812, Frazer wrote: 'It is necessary . . . to be much on your guard since marauders come down from the mountains and carry off saddles, bridles or any other article left carelessly about. Wood is abundant, but the transporting it to the towns is difficult, both from the want of people and of industry . . . I was assured today by the commandant that a whole estate of a countess of his acquaintance in the neighbourhood has been untilled last year for want of husbandmen, and that this want of men is severely felt all over the kingdom.' *Cit.* Sabine, *Letters of Colonel Sir Augustus Simon Frazer,* pp. 25–27.

3. Jacob, *Travels in the South of Spain,* pp. 66, 73.

4. Blayney, *Narrative of a Forced Journey,* I, pp. 57–58.

5. The absence of the male population became ever more marked as the war wore on. As Frazer wrote of Espinal, for example, 'Yesterday . . . was a kind of fair here. The town swarmed . . . with women selling . . . rice, peas, beans and bread. There were at least ten women to one man.' *Cit.* Sabine, *Letters of Colonel Sir Augustus Simon Frazer,* pp. 35–36. A particular problem in areas occupied by the French was imprisonment: as soon as Junot occupied northern Portugal in 1807, all the many British males resident in the area were interned. Although their families were left alone, their situation immediately became very difficult. To quote Harriet Slessor, 'These poor men . . . are deprived of the means of sustaining their despairing wives and children, as they have done till now, by their industry from one day to another.' *Cit.* Hayter, p. 127.

6. For a case study in the economic exploitation of conquest, *cf.* C. J. Esdaile, *Outpost of Empire: the Napoleonic Occupation of Andalucía, 1810–1812* (Norman, Oklahoma, 2012), pp. 234–38. However, it cannot be stressed too strongly that the requisitioning of foodstuffs, if not money, was engaged in by all the belligerents, and that the behaviour of the Spanish forces in particular was frequently just as bad in this respect as that of their French opponents, as witness, for example, the impassioned complaints voiced by an Extremaduran deputy in the *cortes* of Cádiz on 16 November 1810 in respect of the erstwhile Army of the Left's

treatment of the population of Extremadura in the course of 1810; *cf. Correo Político y Militar de la Ciudad de Córdoba,* 16 January 1811, pp. 2–7.

7. *Cf.* J. Fontana and R. Garrabou, *Guerra y hacienda: la hacienda del gobierno central en lo saños de la Guerra de la Independencia, 1808–1814* (Alicante, 1986), pp. 89–95.

8. E.g., Gleig, *Light Dragoon,* p. 445.

9. *Cit.* C. Almuina (ed.), *Valladolid: diarios curiosos, 1807–1841* (Valladolid, 1989), pp. 300–301. It did not help that the Iberian climate continued to be as harsh as ever: amongst a variety of natural disasters known to have assailed Spain and Portugal in the course of the Peninsular War was a terrible hail storm that destroyed many crops in La Mancha and even killed large numbers of livestock; *cf. El Redactor General,* 18 July 1811, p. 120.

10. C. O'Neill, *The Military Adventures of Charles O'Neill* (Worcester, Massachusetts, 1851), pp. 190–92.

11. T. Bunbury, *Reminiscences of a Veteran* (London, 1861), I, p. 181; Buckham, *Personal Narrative,* p. 106.

12. E.g., W. Hay, *Reminiscences 1808–1815 under Wellington,* ed. S. Wood (London, 1901), pp. 20, 83.

13. Costello, *Adventures,* pp. 111–12; Liddell Hart, *Letters of Private Wheeler,* pp. 115–17. For a particularly unpleasant case, *cf.* Anon., *Memoirs of a Sergeant Late in the Forty-Third Light Infantry,* pp. 129–30.

14. Hay, *Reminiscences,* pp. 69–71.

15. From these they were often slow to return: writing of the state of central Portugal in 1812, Hay observed that, while the common people 'were beginning, but slowly, to return to their houses and to collect in the different towns and villages', the more prosperous inhabitants, had 'but little inducement to come back to the miserable remains of their once comfortable dwellings'. *Cf. ibid.,* p. 65.

16. For a good example of these measures, *cf.* Proclamation of the Junta of Cádiz, 16 January 1809, BN. CGI, 60002–60004.

17. Fée, *Souvenirs,* p. 22.

18. Junot, *Mémoires,* II, p. 579.

19. Boutflower, *Journal of an Army Surgeon,* p. 143.

20. Anon., *A Short Description of Badajoz and the Surrounding Country with Extracts from the* London Gazette *explanatory of the Picture exhibiting in the Panorama, Leicester Square, representing the Siege in 1812* (London, 1813), pp. 4–5.

21. Sherer, *Recollections,* pp. 190–91.

22. Anon., *Memoirs of a Sergeant late in the Forty-Third Light Infantry Regiment,* p. 114.

23. For a variety of accounts of the famine of 1812, *cf.* C. J. Esdaile, *Peninsular Eyewitnesses: the Experience of War in Spain and Portugal, 1808–1814* (Barnsley, 2008), pp. 194–97.

24. It would be wrong to assume that all women were as vigorous and resourceful as the following passage might suggest. On the contrary, it is probable that the tableau painted by William Wheeler of the nightly routine of an all-female household—a mother, her three daughters and four maid servants—that he encountered in 1812 is more representative as a reaction to disaster than many observers would care to admit. Thus: 'Huddled together, each having their string

of beads and crosses to charm the devil from them, they relate some horrid tale of some friend slaughtered by the enemy, or of some headless ghost, till their fears are worked to such a pitch that the least noise frightens them out of what little sense they have. Then they count their beads, cross themselves and repeat their Ave Marias till their fears are lulled to rest.' *Cf.* Liddell Hart, *Letters of Private Wheeler,* pp. 71–72.

25. Bunbury, *Reminiscences,* I, pp. 188–96. For some further examples of such disturbances, *cf.* Glover, *Eloquent Soldier,* pp. 39–40.

26. *Gazeta del Gobierno,* 10 March 1809, p. 198; for full details of the riots, *cf.* Esdaile, *Outpost of Empire,* pp. 73–79.

27. Tomkinson, *Diary of a Cavalry Officer,* pp. 128–29. When pleading failed, women might also try bribery, Schaumann describing how, no sooner had one village or another been stripped of its resources than 'hundreds of old women [would] appear on the scene with bottles of brandy or wine concealed in their aprons . . . [and] bargain with the men for the return of their corn'. *Cf.* also Ludovici, *On the Road with Wellington,* p. 218.

28. Ludovici, *On the Road with Wellington,* p. 108; Neale, *Letters,* p. 293. Dobbs, *Recollections,* p. 9. Women could sometimes play the opposite role, however. Engaged in gathering forage in the town of Thomar in June 1809, Schaumann claims that his life was saved by a woman who at the last moment spoiled the aim of her husband, the latter having taken aim at him with a musket; Ludovici, *On the Road with Wellington,* p. 160.

29. *Cit.* Sabine, *Letters of Colonel Sir Augustus Simon Frazer,* p. 173.

30. J. C. Stepney, *Leaves from the Diary of an Officer of the Guards* (London, 1854), pp. 281–82.

31. Perhaps the saddest case to have been uncovered in this respect is that of one Melchora Fortuny. Seized along with her husband and young son by rioters in Lérida on 28 December 1808, she immediately penned a desperate appeal to the authorities in which she claimed that her husband, a senior judge, was innocent of all crime. In this case, however, it was a futile effort: just four days later the whole family was hacked to death. *Cf.* petition of Melchora Fortuny, 28 December 1808, Archivo de la Corona de Aragón, Papeles de la Junta Suprema de Cataluña, *legajo* 4; *Noticias de Lérida* (Lérida, 1809), n.p.

32. Mendoza, *Historia de Málaga,* p. 132. It was not just the authorities who realised this: riding into a small town near Talavera de la Reina on 25 July 1809, Schaumann was greeted by an old woman who 'believing . . . that we were French, and wishing to do the right thing, cried, 'Vivan, vivan los franceses! Viva Francia!'; *cf.* Ludovici, *On the Road with Wellington,* p. 178.

33. A. Bigarré, *Mémoires du Général Bigarré, aide-de-camp du Roi Joseph, 1775–1813* (Paris, 1903), pp. 272–73. Also worth noting here is Marcel's account of his experiences of the first appearance of French troops in Albacete: 'I was feted by a large number of the most charming women, and treated to endless compliments . . . indeed, were it not for the fact that I was an officer of *voltigeurs,* I would have blushed!' *Cf.* Var, *Campagnes du Capitaine Marcel,* p. 149.

34. *Diario Mercantil de Cádiz,* 27 June 1813, p. 675.

35. Petition of Leonarda Esparza, n.d., IHCM. CGEN. 7343.361; R. Santillán, *Memorias de Don Ramón Santillán, 1808–1856,* ed. A. Berazáluce (Madrid, 1996), p. 50. One man who certainly owed his life to such an intervention was a weaver

from Córdoba named Alfonso de Aguilar whose death sentence was commuted to eight day's imprisonment after his wife begged the governor of the city to spare him. *Cf. Correo politico y militar de la ciudad de Córdoba,* 13 May 1810, p. 8. For a pictorial depiction of such an incident, *cf.* Charles Lafond's 1810 canvas, 'Napoléon 1er accorde a Mademoiselle de Saint-Simon la grâce se son pere, officier émigré au service de l'Espagne en 1790, Madrid, décembre 1808'. http://www.similart.fr/taxonomy/term/1115/diaporama, accessed 1 April 2012.

36. Grasset, *Málaga,* pp. 544–45.

37. Neale, *Letters,* p. 133.

38. Archivo Histórico Nacional, Sección de Consejos (hereafter AHN. Consejos), *libro* 1741, ff. 130–33 *passim.*

39. *Ibid.*, ff. 138–49 *passim.*

40. *Ibid.*, ff. 221–24 *passim.*

41. H. C. Wylly (ed.), *A Cavalry Officer in the Corunna Campaign: the Journal of Captain Gordon of the Fifteenth Hussars* (London, 1913), p. 149.

42. Patterson, *Adventures,* pp. 158–60.

43. Ludovici, *On the Road with Wellington,* p. 177; for equally distressing accounts, *cf.* Leslie, *Military Journal,* p. 208; Fantin des Odoards, *Journal,* p. 175.

44. For a graphic account, *cf.* Leach, *Rough Sketches,* pp. 175–76. Also worth citing here is a letter from Lisbon that was picked up by the *afrancesado* press: 'The misery of the unfortunate Portuguese who every day abandon their homes without a bite to eat and scarcely anything with which to cover themselves is a spectacle which breaks one's heart. Yesterday I passed by the convent of San Roque. Some 2,000 women and children have been given shelter there. They had just been fed (if, that is, the stuff that they get deserves to be called food), and were sitting on the ground eating the bit of rice which is all their daily ration amounts to. To be frank, the . . . misery that is endured by these unfortunate refugees completely outstrips anything that I might say to you: they are absolutely dying of hunger, and perish by the dozen every day; indeed, death is a kindness to them.' *Cit. Gazeta Nacional de Zaragoza,* 28 April 1811, pp. 245–46.

45. Henegan, *Seven Years' Campaigning,* I, pp. 41–47. The child was fortunate not simply to be abandoned: in 1812 the foundling hospital at nearby Salamanca received 317 babies, while another 100 were taken in in the first five months of 1813 alone. *Cf.* Sabine, *Letters of Colonel Sir Augustus Simon Frazer,* pp. 125–26.

46. AHN. Consejos, *libro* 1741, f. 64. In what is often a rather depressing story, it is pleasing to report that, in response to these appeals, Laglé and Rivero were awarded 200 *reales* and Eguía 300; *cf.* Conde de Montarco to B. de Aranza, 25 March 1811, AHN. Consejos, *libro* 1742, f. 51. It should be noted that the wives of Spaniards who served the *josefino* cause were not always left to shift for themselves: when the commander of the Bourbon gendarmerie of Aragón was murdered by a gang of insurgents in January 1810, for example, his widow was immediately awarded the sum of 30,000 *reales,* this sum being levied from all the villages in the vicinity of the place where her husband was killed; *cf. Gazeta Nacional de Zaragoza,* 21 April 1811, pp. 238–39.

47. A variant on this theme was the impact of the epidemic of gambling that gripped a civilian population desperate for some alleviation of its circumstances. As one irate Madrid churchman lamented, 'On . . . all sides one heard of . . . merchants, artisans and men of every class repeatedly staking the very substance

of their loved ones on the turn of the wheel; and, finally, of many families who had not just been left with nothing but also been abandoned by husbands and fathers who sought in this fashion to escape from the effects of their stupidity'. *Cf.* C. Carnicero, *Historia razonada de los principales sucesos de la gloriosa revolución de España* (Madrid, 1814), III, pp. 94–99.

48. The price for escaping the draft, it should be noted, was often paid by women, Frazer noting that the female relatives of those who absconded were often arrested until they should reappear. *Cf.* Sabine, *Letters of Colonel Sir Augustus Simon Frazer*, p. 74.

49. The travails of Carmen Langton Dillon de Aranza can be studied in detail in the Langton papers in the Bath Record Office. To add insult to injury, when her father died in 1810, the Patriot government embargoed her share of the estate in reprisal for her husband's support of the French cause; *cf.*, especially, M. T. Langton to A. Butler, 2 February 1811, Bath Record Office, Langton Papers, 0770/1/3/23, accessed at http://www.batharchives.co.uk/pdf/0770_1_3_1_44.pdf, 12 June 2012.

50. AHN. Consejos, *libro* 1741, ff. 11, 16. These pleas did not, it seems, go unanswered: on 3 October 1811, for example, Montarco ordered that one third of the rents of a resident of Marchena named José María Ayllón who had on no pretext whatsoever disappeared from his home and had since neglected to send his wife any news of his whereabouts, should henceforward be made over to the unfortunate woman concerned; *ibid.*, f. 172.

51. Sturgis, *Boy in the Peninsular War*, pp. 314–15.

52. *Cf.* Sabine, *Letters of Colonel Sir Augustus Simon Frazer*, p. 179. In addition to on occasion acting as couriers, the women of the Basque provinces also engaged in such tasks as helping to unload ships in the harbour of Wellington's chief supply base of Pasajes; *cf. ibid.*, p. 195.

53. Ludovici, *On the Road with Wellington*, p. 355. As witness the numerous advertisements placed in the press of Cádiz and other cities, wet-nursing was also as common as ever. Thus: 'A young first-time mother, who has been in milk for fifteen days, married to a soldier in the army and can provide references from people who will vouch for her conduct, is offering her services to some decent household . . . Rosa Domínguez, a robust first-time mother who has been in milk for two months, is looking for a position in a respectable family.' *Cf. Diario Mercantil de Cádiz*, 12 December 1813, p. 304; *ibid.*, 10 February 1814, p. 164.

54. Patterson, *Adventures*, p. 252. A more enterprising variant on this theme was to follow the armies as a sutler. Here, for example, are Thomas Browne's memories of the Portuguese village of Fresnada: 'Fresnada . . . was a miserable village . . . The accommodations of every kind were as wretched as it was possible to conceive and supplies of every kind . . . very difficult to be obtained. One or two sutlers, it is true, established themselves there, but their stores of every kind were bad, and the charges for them enormous . . . Amongst them there was a woman named Antonia. She was a stout lusty person of rather a jolly countenance, dirty enough, but one who in the midst of her filth always wore a massy gold necklace . . . and a pair of long pendant ear-rings. This Antonia was the greatest cheat of the whole set, and amassed a considerable fortune by her attendance on headquarters, to which she was attached . . . for several years, her goods becoming worse and her prices more exorbitant each succeeding

campaign. There were several candidates for her hand among the gentlemen sutlers, but she steadily rejects the honour of any alliance with them.' *Cf.* Buckley, *Napoleonic-War Journal,* pp. 199–200.

55. A. Ramos, 'La vida cotidiana en el Cádiz de las Cortes: el recurso a la prensa como fuente para su estudio' in Cantos *et al., Guerra de pluma,* p. 75.

56. For the prevalence of female begging, *cf.* Carnicero Torribio, *Historia razonada,* III, pp. 121–22. As for prostitution, direct evidence is lacking, but consider, for example, comments such as the following: 'British officers were seen in all directions with Spanish ladies leaning on their arms, who were pointing outto them the different habitations of the grandees by the light of the lamps'. *Cf.* Buckley, *Napoleonic-War Journal,* p. 177. Something else that should be mentioned in this context is petty crime, and, in particular, fencing stolen goods. When a female resident of Elvas named Joana Silveira was robbed of some sheets and a tablecloth by a British soldier billetted in her house in the summer of 1811, for example, the missing ítems were sold to a woman at Borba for five dollars. *Cf.* Lord Wellington to the Juiz de Fora, Borba, 23 July 1811, *cit.* J. Gurwood, *The Dispatches of Field Marshal the Duke of Wellington during his Various Campaigns in India, Denmark, Portugal, Spain, the Low Countries and France from 1789 to 1815* (London, 1852), V, p. 178.

57. On occasion such relationships appear to have been encouraged by parents who were desperate either to provide a refuge for their daughters or to rid themselves of the financial burden they represented. One such case appears to have taken place in Aldeia da Serra in the winter of 1812–13 when one of the village girls forged a relationship with a Portuguese-speaking corporal called McMorran, the response of her family being not the anger found in other accounts, but rather the warmest approval. Sadly, however, the story did not have a happy ending: bored and lonely, McMorran's company commander, a lieutenant named Dickinson, had designs upon the same girl, and appears to have resolved to get rid of his rival by seizing the first possible opportunity to disgrace him and reduce him to the ranks. Realising what was going on, McMorran calmly shot Dickinson dead, ending his own days some days later on the gallows. *Cf.* R. Burnham, 'Murder in the Forty-Second', http://www.napoleon-series.org/military/organization/c_murder.html; Anon., *Personal Narrative of a Private Soldier who served in the Forty-Second Highlanders,* pp. 176–82.

58. Ludovici, *On the Road with Wellington,* pp. 142–43.

59. Donaldson, *Recollections,* p. 361.

60. *Cf.* Dallas, *Félix Alvarez,* III, p. 289. This figure is certainly an exaggeration, yet there can be no doubt that the cities of Andalucía witnessed levels of fraternization that were certainly conspicuous enough to enter the fabric of popular culture in the occupied zone. Thus, passing through Seville in the wake of its liberation in August 1812, Bunbury attended a play entitled *El papamosca* (roughly, *The Gull*), this being a farce that told the story of a young girl who had fallen in love with a French officer, but had the misfortune to have a father who was a fanatical supporter of the Patriot cause. *Cf.* Bunbury, *Reminiscences,* I, pp. 144–47.

61. Blaze, *Mémoires,* II, p. 254. Of course, many women had no option but to follow their soldier lovers. When one María Antonia Pinilla Sánchez was made pregnant at Campillos in March 1810 by a French doctor named Kessler, for example,

her family cut her off completely and refused to provide her with a dowry. Such was the anger of one father at the news that his daughter had fallen in love with a Frenchman that he even murdered the girl on the grounds that she was better dead than *afrancesada; cf.* Jiménez Bartolomé, '"Los otros combatientes"', pp. 358–59.

62. Bell, *Rough Notes,* I, p. 94. The presence of so many women at Vitoria was in part explained by the fact that the battle was fought in the context of the wholesale evacuation of France's dominions in central Spain. If most of the women were treated well enough, their experiences were still terrifying: 'Poor Madame Gazan, who had jumped out of her barouche and stuck fast in a field about a hundred yards on one side, had the mortification of seeing the whole of her wardrobe ransacked and dispersed in about ten minutes.' *Cit.* Malmesbury, *Letters of the first Earl of Malmesbury,* II, p. 353.

63. Captain Marenghien to J. M. Caffarelli, 2 March 1813, IHCM. CGEN. 7343.280; Fantin des Odoards, *Journal,* p. 181.

64. Blayney, *Narrative,* I, p. 157.

65. For the Thorp affair, *cf.* Grattan, *Adventures,* II, pp. 204–208. Meanwhile, for a full history of the Kelly affair, *cf.* http://historiasdaminhafamilia.blogspot .co.uk/2009/09/historia-da-minha-4-avo-ana-ludovina.html (accessed 8 June 2012), and J. W. Chambers, 'The elopement of Ana Ludovina Teixeira de Aguilar with Lieutenant William Waldron Kelly' in A. Berkeley (ed.), *New Lights on the Peninsular War: International Congress on the Iberian Peninsula, 1780–1840* (Lisbon, 1991), pp. 259–70. In brief, Kelly appears to have spotted the girl he ran away with—the youngest daughter of a Portuguese nobleman—when he attended Mass at her family's private chapel. Outraged by her behaviour, her father disinherited her, and, though she lived till 1883, the new Mrs Kelly never saw her family again. Kelly, meanwhile, was a somewhat colourful character who had already been court-martialled for seducing the wife of a private soldier named Noah Cooper, and then using violence against him when the latter tried to reclaim her; *cf. General Orders, Spain and Portugal, January 1st to December 31st 1811,* III, pp. 252–54. *Cf.* also Larpent, *Private Journal,* p. 80: 'We have a most furious Portuguese lady now here, the wife of a *hidalgo* of Portugal, whose daughter has run away with an English officer. Ld. W. told her that he would give her up to the laws of Portugal, but, as he has now married her, Ld. W. says he will not interfere at all. The woman swears she will get the officer who married them transported for life by their law, as well as the officer, and has, moreover, declared she will kill the daughter if she meets her!' A more unhappy story is that of a soldier of the Ninety-Fourth Foot who fell head over heels in love with a village girl at Fonte Arcada, but was denied permission to marry her on the grounds that he not only had nothing to offer her, but was a Protestant heretic. Nothing daunted, the young man sought to elope with her, but the attempt was frustrated and the girl torn shrieking from his arms and sent away from the village, leaving the soldier in a 'state of listless melancholy from which he did not recover for many months'. *Cf.* Donaldson, *Recollections,* pp. 187–99. Finally, still more disastrous was the case of Carlota Freda Fernández de Córdoba, the twenty-two-year-old daughter of an Extremaduran nobleman named the Marqués de Mirabel, who eloped with a major of the Fifty-Seventh Foot in May 1813 only to be forced to return home with her tail between her legs some months later and find herself facing incarceration in a convent at Plasencia; *cf.* L. Stampa Pineiro, *Pólvora, plata*

y boleros: memorias de testigos y combatientes en la Guerra de la Independencia (Madrid, 2011), pp. 290–99.

66. Fée, *Souvenirs,* pp. 68, 104–105. Meanwhile, the history of Juana María de los Dolores de León can best be followed in G. C. Moore-Smith (ed.), *The Autobiography of Sir Harry Smith, 1787–1819* (London, 1910); however, *cf.* also Kincaid, *Random Shots,* pp. 292–96. For the incident respecting the evacuation of Madrid, meanwhile, *cf.* J. H. Cooke, 'The personal narrative of Captain Cooke of the Forty-Third Regiment, Light Infantry' in Anon. (ed.), *Memoirs of the Late War* (London, 1837), I, p. 228.

67. Sturgis, *A Boy in the Peninsular War,* pp. 291–94; Hibbert, *Recollections of Rifleman Harris,* p. 47. For yet another story of an abortive liaison between a British soldier and a local girl, *cf.* Donaldson, *Recollections,* pp. 187–99.

68. Boutflower, *Journal of an Army Surgeon,* p. 28.

69. Glover, *Eloquent Soldier,* p. 81.

70. *Cf.* Ludovici, *On the Road with Wellington,* p. 257.

71. It is, of course, very far from being the case that all women who found themselves in the baggage train of one army or another had separated from their husbands. For example, throughout the war Wellington employed large numbers of Portuguese muleteers, and at least some of these were accompanied by their wives; *cf.* Porter, *Letters from Portugal and Spain,* p. 230. Nor should it be imagined, meanwhile, that they were necessarily devoid of patriotic feeling: for example, two ragged Portuguese campfollowers who Frazer encountered following Wellington's crossing of the Bidássoa responded with outrage when he mistakenly greeted them with a cheerful 'Bonjour, Mesdames!'. *Cf.* Sabine, *Letters of Colonel Sir Augustus Simon Frazer,* p. 297.

72. Proclamation of Francisco Javier Castaños, 27 June 1808, Archivo de los Condes de Bureta, Papeles de Palafox; *cf.* also Anon., *Pensamientos militares de un paisano* (Seville, 1809), pp. 21–23. Prostitutes or not, it should be pointed out that the women of the Spanish army were capable of just as much devotion as their British and French counterparts: when Valencia fell, for example, the garrison's campfollowers rejected offers of release and instead marched with their menfolk into captivity in France, often enduring the most terrible sufferings in the process; *cf.* Desboeufs, *Etapes d'un soldat,* p. 158. As a good example of one such woman, albeit one taken prisoner at Tarragona rather than Valencia, we may cite the case of María Ferrer, a twenty-nine-year-old from Reus who died in the large Spanish prisoner-of-war depot that had been established at Nancy on 2 May 1811. As Ferrer is recorded as having been unmarried, we may surmise that she was either a prostitute or, more probably, the mistress or common-law-wife of one of the prisoners. *Cf.* IHCM. Sección de Capellanes Castrenses, *libro* 1079, 'Libro de difuntos del campo de prisoneros de Nancy', f. 58. I owe this reference to the kindness of my friend and colleague, Arsenio García Fuertes.

73. We have no reference to the presence of such vendors with the Spanish army, but, as conditions gradually returned to a semblance of normality towards the end of the war, they certainly became a common sight in the camps of Wellington's forces; e.g., Larpent, *Private Journal,* p. 226; Kincaid, *Adventures,* p. 235.

74. The sexual overtones of this song are still stronger in Spanish: thus, the phrase 'a-perching on his lance' can also mean 'impaled on his lance'. 'Don Julián' meanwhile, was Julián Sánchez, the commander of a force of regular

cavalry that harassed the French in the vicinity of Ciudad Rodrigo. For the full lyrics, *cf.* http://www.1808-1814.org/poesia/cancion.html (accessed 11 February 2010). Interestingly, Schaumann records actually seeing one of Sánchez's men literally sweeping a Spanish girl off her feet; *cf.* Ludovici, *On the Road with Wellington,* pp. 318–26 *passim.*

75. Wylly, *Cavalry Officer in the Corunna Campaign,* p. 32. Passing through Villagarcía de Campos during the march to Sahagún, Gordon had an even more suggestive experience. Thus: 'María Antonia de Barbadillo y Castro, the daughter of a *hidalgo* at whose house I was quartered . . . a very beautiful and agreeable young woman . . . made me promise to write to her, and engaged to accompany me to England when we returned from driving the Gallic invaders out of Spain'. *Ibid.,* p. 91.

76. Oyon, *Campagnes et souvenirs militaires,* pp. 151–52.

77. Henegan, *Seven Years' Campaigning,* I, pp. 103–106.

78. Hayter, *The Backbone,* pp. 143–44; *cf.* also Neale, *Letters,* pp. 198–99.

79. *Cf.* Fraser, *Napoleon's Cursed War,* p. 320.

80. A. Salvá, *Burgos en la Guerra de la Independencia,* ed. C. Borreguero (Burgos, 2008), p. 107.

81. AHN. Consejos, *libro* 1741, ff. 134, 140, 241.

82. North, *In the Legions of Napoleon,* p. 87. Von Brandt's remark is to a certain extent borne out by the fact that several officers of the Polish unit in which he served, including a lieutenant, two captains and two colonels are known to have married Spanish women (I owe this last information to the kindness of my good friend and colleague, Jaroslaw Czubaty of the University of Warsaw). What is certainly the case, meanwhile, is that, over and over again, French accounts insist that, left to themselves, women showed no hostility to the invaders. 'In so far as the women were concerned', wrote an *aide-de-*camp of Marshal Ney named Octave Levavasseur, 'whenever we encountered them free of the presence of their menfolk, they conversed with us and smiled on our flattery. So long as they could avoid anyone suspecting them, meanwhile, they revealed that political differences were foreign to them: otherwise, the price of the liberties that we took would have been paid in daggers.' *Cf.* Beslay, *Souvenirs militaires d'Octave Levavasseur,* p. 131. *Cf.* also Naylies, *Mémoires,* pp. 258–59; Fée, *Souvenirs,* p. 16.

83. J. Grivel, *Mémoires du Vice-Amiral Baron Grivel* (Paris, 1914), pp. 239–40.

84. It is worth pointing out here that fraternization was not necessarily sexual. In Toro, for example, women are recorded as having earned a living by taking in washing and mending for the French; *cf.* R. Robledo, *Salamanca, ciudad de paso, ciudad ocupada: la Guerra de la Independencia* (Salamanca, 2003), p. 72.

85. The lengths to which memoir writers were prepared to go to deceive themselves in respect of their sexual relationships is perfectly illustrated by a passage in Schaumann's memoirs. Thus: 'Here in Téntugal [a village in the region of Coimbra in central Portugal] . . . I had another love affair with an exquisite child called Joaquina Cavaleira. Her excellent mother brought her round to me every evening, decked out like a bride, and then fetched her in the morning. It is no good worrying one's head about the customs of different countries!' *Cf.* Ludovici, *On the Road with Wellington,* p. 219.

86. Jones, *Napoleon's Army,* pp. 113–14, 121. For a similar story, *cf.* Haythornthwaite, *Life in Napoleon's Army,* pp. 112–14; in this instance, the woman concerned

was a bored wife with an aged husband. Finally, billeted at Ledesma in the winter of 1809, in the intervals of impregnating the *cantinière* we have already mentioned, Marcel had an affair with a forty-year-old widow named Rosa de Paz; *cf.* Var, *Campagnes du Capitaine Marcel,* p. 97.

87. Ludovici, *On the Road with Wellington,* p. 228. The author here stills what appears to be an attack of conscience by a transparent attempt to shift his guilt to other shoulders: "Unfortunately, with all her youth and ingenuousness, it was impossible to assume she was still innocent, for the owner of the palace where Colonel de Grey and Sir Granby Calcraft were quartered . . . shared with his brother the evil reputation of having deflowered all the girls of their large village the moment they grew up.' *Ibid.*

88. For all this, *cf.* L. Reyes, 'Los amores españoles de José 1', *Tiempo,* No. 1558, accessed at http://www.tiempodehoy.com/cultura/historia/los-amores-espanoles-del-rey-jose, 12 June 2012, and D. Gonçalves, 'Havana's aristocrats in the Spanish War of Independence, 1808–1814' in C. Belaubre, J. Dym and J. Savage (eds.), *Napoleon's Atlantic: the Impact of Napoleonic Empire in the Atlantic World* (Leiden, 2010), pp. 87–92.

89. *Ibid.* One French general who certainly secured a Spanish (or, to be precise, *criolla*) wife in this fashion was Christophe Merlin. Thus, in 1809 he married Mercedes de Santa Cruz y Montalvo. The niece of Joseph's Minister of War, General Gonzalo O'Farrill, Santa Cruz came from a prominent *afrancesado* family, and it is clear that the match was desired both by king and general alike. However, according to her memoirs at least, much attracted by the idea of marrying a gallant soldier and but little engaged in the politics of the war, Santa Cruz genuinely fell in love with Merlin and was thereafter happy enough to throw in her lot with him; *cf.* Santa Cruz, *Memorias,* I, pp. 260–72. How far Spanish and Portuguese women married foreign soldiers in normal fashion with the blessing of their families rather than running off with them is unclear, but the phenomenon was far from unknown. Thus, a clutch of officers from the Polish 'Legion of the Vistula' are known to have married women whom they met whilst in garrison at Zaragoza, whilst in January 1811 Samuel Whittingham, who had now become a general in the Spanish army, wed Magdalena de Creus y Jiménez, the daughter of a prominent Seville merchant who currently occupied a post in the military administration. *Cf.* Stampa, *Pólvora, plata y boleros,* pp. 286–88; Iglesias Rogers, *British Liberators,* p. 135.

90. *Gazeta de Oficio del Gobierno de Vizcaya,* 1 August 1810, p. 4; I. Soares de Abreu, 'Condesa de Ega, la *citoyenne* aristócrata', in I. Castells, G. Espigado, and M. C. Romeo (eds.), *Heroínas y patriotas: mujeres de 1808* (Madrid, 2009), pp. 427–50.

91. Where passion led, however, politics may have followed. Thus, to quote an entry from Swabey's diary for July 1812, 'A courier was intercepted with many letters written from ladies of the best families of Llerena begging their French lovers to drive us out of the town. These letters ridiculed us and our manners in the most contemptuous terms.' *Cf.* Whinyates, *Campaigns in the Peninsula,* pp. 102–103.

92. Surtees, *Twenty-Five Years in the Rifle Brigade,* p. 200.

93. Buckley, *Napoleonic War Journal,* p. 220.

94. Cooke, 'Personal narrative', in Anon., *Memoirs of the Late War,* I, p. 228.

95. *Cf.* also Lisbon, however. Thus, according to Porter, it took the coming of the French to generalise the sort of changes seen elsewhere. As he remarked, 'Since the French brought their own manners into this capital, less ceremony has been used, and the ancient custom of the ladies being so constantly kept *à la turc* is declining rapidly.' *Cf.* Porter, *Letters from Portugal and Spain,* p. 44.

96. Bunbury, *Reminiscences of a Veteran,* I, p. 86.

97. *Ibid.,* I, pp. 90–93.

98. Leslie, *Military Journal,* p. 234.

99. Glover, *Eloquent Soldier,* p. 41; for lively accounts of various other dances, including one in which the officers involved all dressed up as women, *cf.* Ludovici, *On the Road with Wellington,* pp. 337–39; Stepney, *Leaves from the Diary of an Officer of the Guards,* pp. 120–21, and Larpent, *Private Journal,* p. 55. On occasion, the entertainments were much grander, good examples being the balls staged by Wellington at Valladolid in September 1812 and Ciudad Rodrigo in February 1813; *cf.* G. Glover (ed.), *Wellington's Lieutenant, Napoleon's Gaoler: the Peninsula and St Helena Diaries and Letters of Sir George Rideout Bingham, 1809–21* (Barnsley, 2005), p. 149; Larpent, *Private Journal,* p. 73.

100. Kincaid, *Adventures,* p. 94.

101. Kincaid, *Random Shots,* pp. 266–67. The song referred to is 'Marlbruck s'en va t'en guerra', a French marching song dating from the War of the Spanish Succession which is the origin of 'For he's a jolly good fellow'.

102. *Cit.* Fletcher, *In the Service of the King,* p. 168. In a subsequent letter, Keep claims that three 'fine young women' with whom he was billeted in Fuenterrabía with two other officers after being wounded in the neck at the battle of St Pierre on 13 December 1813 took flirtation a stage further: 'The girls, you must know, come to bed when they think we are asleep and pin themselves into the bed-clothes, we being quite strangers to them.' *Cit. ibid.,* p. 199.

103. Whinyates, *Diary of Campaigns in the Peninsula,* p. 103.

104. What is certainly true is that, even if it did not initiate a sexual revolution, for at least some women the war brought an unprecedented degree of sexual liberation. Consider, for example, the case of María Rosa Barbosa, a girl from Castelo Branco who ran away with a commissary called Hughes, only for her, first, to forsake him for the thoroughly libidinous Schaumann, and then to forsake Schaumann for an officer named Baertling (not that this prevented her from returning to Schaumann's bed when opportunity offered on a later occasion). *Cf.* Ludovici, *On the Road with Wellington,* pp. 277, 310.

105. Anon., *Soldier of the Seventy-First,* p. 179.

106. *Cf.* E. Martín-Valdepeñas, 'Afrancesadas y patriotas: la Junta de Honor y Mérito de la Real Sociedad Económica Matritense de Amigos del País', in Castells, Espigado and Romeo, *Heroínas y patriotas: mujeres de 1808* (Madrid, 2009), pp. 343–70.

107. This is no place to embark on a discussion of the complexities of the Spanish system of landholding. However, in brief, the estates of the nobility and the Church alike were held in entail, which meant in effect that in ordinary circumstances they could not be bought, sold or partitioned in any way without special permission.

108. *Cf.* AHN. Consejos, *libro* 1741, ff. 165, 188.

109. *Cf. ibid., ff.* 135, 230, 237.

110. R. Martín Rodrigo, *La Guerra de la Independencia en la provincia de Salamanca* (Salamanca, 2012), p. 210.

111. For a very clear instance of this development, we may cite the case of a widow named María Bosch who we find approaching the authorities in the wake of her *afrancesado* husband's death for permission not just to sell her house in order to pay her many debts, but also to assume the responsibility for the care and education of her children. *Cf.* E. Mendoza, 'Percepción de la Guerra de la Independencia a través de la documentación notarial de Málaga', in Castañeda, *Guerras en el primer tercio del siglo XIX*, p. 111.

112. *Gazeta Nacional de Zaragoza*, 24 March 1811, pp. 151–52.

113. Whinyates, *Diary of Campaigns in the Peninsula*, p. 72.

114. Consider, for example, the case of the orphan-women of Burgos, all of them by regulation aged under thirty, who took part in a lottery organised by the French as part of the celebrations organised to celebrate Joseph Bonaparte's saint's day in March 1812, the prize being four dowries of 500 *reales* apiece. In theory, no Spanish woman should have taken part in such a lottery at all, but there was no shortage of participants, while the winners—María Pardo, María Reojo, Gertrudis García and Leandra Martín—were delighted to claim their winnings, though Reojo was later disqualified on the grounds that she had falsified her age. That said, however, the mere fact that the women concerned took the money can scarcely be taken to mean that that they were *afrancesadas*. *Cf.* C. Borreguero, *Burgos en la Guerra de la Independencia; enclave estrátegico y ciudad expoliada* (Burgos, 2007).

Chapter 6

1. For details of *The Miracle*, which was known in Spain as *Promesa Rota*, *cf.* Maroto, *Guerra de la Independencia: imagenes en cine y television*, pp. 246–47.

2. The fall in the numbers of Spain's nuns was in part the result of the great crisis of mortality of 1803–1804: the six nuns who died in the convent of Santa Eufemia at Antequera in 1804 represented the greatest single annual loss in the whole of its four-hundred-year history; *cf.* F. Leiva and J. M. Leiva, *El monasterio de monjas mínimas de Antequera* (Antequera, 2007), p. 19. Also important, meanwhile, was the soaring cost of convental dowries in relation to marital ones (see below).

3. For details of the situation in Spain, *cf.* G. Desdevises, *La España del antiguo regimen*, ed. A. Gónzalez Enciso (Madrid, 1989), pp. 43–44. Portugal, meanwhile, is examined in D. Higgs, 'The Portuguese Church', in W. J. Callahan and D. Higgs (eds.), *Church and Society in Catholic Europe of the Eighteenth Century* (Cambridge, 1979), pp. 54–55. The shortage of novices seen here is also reflected elsewhere: Boutflower writes of one community that he observed at worship in Badajoz that 'they were all very old women, not one of them appearing less than sixty'; *cf.* Boutflower, *Journal*, p. 20. Hence the fact that in Valladolid by 1810 the number of nuns had fallen to just 521; by contrast, however, the number of convents had gone down by just one. *Cf.* M. Álvarez García, *El clero de la diócesis de Valladolid durante la Guerra de la Independencia* (Valladolid, 1981), p. 158.

4. *Cf.* http://www.vilapoucadabeira.com/index.php?progoption=seccao&do=show&secid=2 (accessed 15 February 2012).

5. For the role of dowries in the conventual economy, *cf.* J. L. Sánchez Lora, *Mujeres, conventos y formas de la religiosidad barroca* (Madrid, 1988), pp. 114–38. The only postulants who were exempted from payment were girls who came from the families of founders of the convents they wished to enter or could prove real skill with respect to playing a musical instrument.

6. Menéndez González, *Barranco de las asturianas,* pp. 112–21.

7. Dalrymple, *Travels,* pp. 75–76.

8. For all this, *cf.* Hufton, *The Prospect Before Her,* pp. 379–90 *passim;* W. J. Callahan, *Church, Politics and Society in Spain, 1750–1874* (Cambridge, Mass., 1984), p. 27. The only exception to the general withdrawal into the cloister were the tiny handful of communities that ran the *de facto* prisons for prostitutes to which we have already referred. Also worth noting, however, are a few houses such as Madrid's Convento de la Visitacion which functioned as 'an institution for the education of the young female nobility'; *cf.* Fischer, *Picture of Madrid,* p. 28.

9. Higgs, 'The Portuguese Church', p. 63. For a general discussion of the widespread portrayal of the convent as a den of vice even amongst orthodox Catholics, *cf.* J. Caro Baroja, *Las formas complejas de la vida religiosa: religión, sociedad y carácter en la España de los siglos XVI y XVII* (Madrid, 1978), pp. 189–91.

10. For a particularly ridiculous example, *cf.* Twiss, *Travels,* p. 36. Other observers were less credulous. Bingham, for example, noted of one convent at Guarda that, although its members were 'said not to have the best of reputations', such were 'the gratings and bars with which they are secured' that it was was very hard to see how anything could have happened, and all the more so as most of the nuns were 'plain and old'; *cf.* Glover, *Wellington's Lieutenant, Napoleon's Gaoler,* p. 85. Indeed, as witness Patterson's description of a convent at the Portuguese town of Borba, even when access was obtained to a convent, there was no possibility of physical contact with the nuns themselves: 'From the courtyard [a] passage leads . . . to the visiting rooms to which strangers and friends of the imprisoned are admitted. In the centre of the thick and solid wall of this apartment is an opening about six feet square furnished with a solid iron grating separating the aforesaid room from another in which [the] Lady Abbess and her nuns may condescend to appear.' *Cf.* Patterson, *Adventures,* p. 155.

11. For an excellent analysis of a convent-based art collection, *cf.* M. C. de Carlos, 'Imagen y santidad en la España Moderna: el ejemplo de los Trinitarios Calzados de Madrid', doctoral thesis, Universidad Complutense de Madrid, November 2005. According to Twiss, meanwhile, the Dominican convent at the insignificant Castillian *pueblo* of Loeches had no fewer than ten works by Rubens; *cf.* Twiss, *Travels,* pp. 170–71.

12. Menéndez González, *Barranco de las asturianas,* p. 121. In 1786 one of the convents concerned—the house of the Benedictines at Oviedo—was visited by Townsend, the latter reporting that at that time its income amounted to almost £2,200 *per annum; cf.* Townsend, *Journey,* II, p. 22. In southern Spain, meanwhile, setting aside rents that were paid in kind, the convent of Santa Eufemia at Antequera had an annual income of 8,495 *reales; cf.* Leiva and Leiva, *Monasterio de monjas mínimas de Antequera,* p. 14.

13. For some examples of convent cuisine, *cf.* L. San Valentín, *La cocina de las monjas* (Madrid, 2002), and M. Serrano, *Dulces y postres de las monjas clarisas: 260 recetas tradicionales de 100 monasterios españoles* (Barcelona, 2011).

14. *Cf.* Hufton, *The Prospect Before Her,* pp. 367–68. For an interesting case study, *cf.* M. I. Lora, *La bótica de Sor Isabel: los remedios naturales de las monjas* (Barcelona, 2007). In fairness, it should be noted that literary interests, in particular, were generally pursued in a religious context: for example, if nuns wrote poems, they for the most part were based on religious themes. *Cf.* Palacios, 'Noticia sobre el panaso dramático femenino en el siglo XVIII', pp. 126–29.

15. *Cf.*, for example, A. Lavrin, 'Ecclesiastical reform of nunneries in New Spain in the eighteenth century', *The Americas,* XXII, No. 2 (October, 1965), pp. 182–203. In this respect, Dalrymple's discussion of the convent he visited at Salamanca is most revealing. Thus: 'The nuns . . . are subject to no other visitation than what is appointed by the king, and, on that occasion, he should appoint a knight of the Order of Santiago. They receive company in their own apartments and are allowed to keep as many servants as they please, but men must not be known to sleep in the convent all night.' *Cf.* Dalrymple, *Travels,* p. 76.

16. How far vocations were the product of *force majeure* is unclear. However, from the sixteenth century onwards, the Church itself had expressed numerous concerns that women from propertied families were being compelled to take the veil. *Cf.* Sánchez Lora, *Mujeres, conventos y formas de la religiosidad barroca,* pp. 139–47. Meanwhile, many convents included amongst their inmates lay sisters—to reiterate, unpaid drudges—whose fate was the product of circumstances beyond their control. Passing through Santiago de Compostela in December 1808, for example, the English traveller, Francis Darwin, was informed that there was a beautiful English girl in one of the local convents. Gaining access to her on the pretext that he was a relative, he discovered that her name was Charlotte Glasgow and that she had been forced to take refuge in the convent when she had eloped with a Spanish officer some five years before, only for the latter to fall ill and die, leaving her utterly destitute and bereft of friends and family alike. *Cf.* Darwin, *Travels,* p. 4.

17. S. Evangelisti, *Nuns: a History of Convent Life, 1450–1750* (Oxford, 2007), pp. 67–68. To prove the point, we can cite the example of Juana Inés Ramírez, a seventeenth-century Mexican noblewoman of a high level of intelligence and education alike, who chose to become a nun as the only means she had of devoting herself to the study which she so adored; *cf.* Arenal, 'The convent as catalyst', pp. 164–81. At the same time, of course, there was even the possibility of love: for example, the stress which Saint Teresa of Avila and other Church authorities placed on the need for nuns to avoid 'particular friendships' almost certainly had its roots in a desire to root out lesbianism; *cf.* S. M. Velasco, *Lesbians in Early-Modern Spain* (Nashville, Tennessee, 2011), pp. 90–132 *passim.*

18. Bunbury, *Reminiscences,* I, pp. 286–87.

19. Many British officers claimed to have seen nuns looking sad or to have found the sound of their singing melancholy: e.g., Hunt, *Charging against Napoleon,* pp. 76–77; Whinyates, *Diary of Campaigns in the Peninsula,* p. 16. However, this means nothing. The officers concerned invariably being staunchly Protestant and fiercely anti-Catholic, we may assume that they simply saw what they wanted to see and recorded it accordingly.

20. Bunbury, *Reminiscences,* I, pp. 268–69.

21. *Cf.* http://www.npg.org.uk/collections/search/portraitLarge/mw63006/Spanish-patriots-attacking-the-French-banditti-loyal-Britons-lending-a-lift (accessed 6 January 2012). Published as early as 15 August 1808, this cartoon

is almost certainly the very first visual depiction of the Peninsular War ever to have appeared in Britain, and is doubly interesting on account of the fact that, besides the nuns, it also features a woman loading a cannon in the style of Agustina Zaragoza.

22. The nearest that we have to a report of nuns becoming involved in combat comes from the French attack on Alcántara on 14 May 1809 in that the inmates of the convent of San Bénito are supposed to have assisted in the defence by making cartridges from the books and manuscripts housed in its library. As an amusing footnote to this story, it might be noted that the French dish, *perdrix à la mode d'Alcantara,* is believed to come from a recipe looted from the same convent by French troops after they entered the town.

23. Earl of Westmoreland, *Memoir of the Early Campaigns of the Duke of Wellington in Portugal and Spain* (London, 1820), pp. 126–27.

24. Anon., 'Fundación de las monjas carmelitas descalzas de San Jose de Zaragoza: trabajos que padecieron con heroísmo y servicios que hicieron', *cit.* J. Sanz (ed.), *Monjas en guerra, 1808–1814: testimonios de mujeres desde el claustro* (Madrid, 2010), p. 97.

25. R. Chambers, *The Book of Days: a Miscellany of Popular Antiquities in Connection with the Calendar* (London, 1832), I, pp. 105–106.

26. L. Galmés, *Real monasterio de Santa Inés, virgin y mártir: monjas domínicas de Zaragoza—ensayo histórico* (Zaragoza, n.d.), pp. 82–87. Of the twelve nuns left behind, four died of typhus, while the others were expelled from the city after its surrender and left to make shift for themselves as best they could.

27. For a good example of a community that fled for a few days only, *cf.* A. Laspra (ed.), *Las relaciones entre la Junta Central del Principado de Asturias y el Reino Unido en la Guerra de la Independencia: repertorio documental* (Oviedo, 1999), pp. 610–11.

28. *Cf.* Anon., 'Salida de la Comunidad de Carmelitas Descalzas de Burgos y trabajos que pasaron en la invasión francesa', *cit.* Sanz , *Monjas en guerra,* pp. 23–26. For a touching account of one of their many adventures en route, *cf.* Haythornthwaite, *In the Peninsula with a French Hussar,* pp. 30–31. The sudden appearance of large groups of strangers in times of dearth such as the ones that were currently being experienced could not but cause some tension. For years after 1814, for example, there were mutterings in the Barefoot-Carmelite convent of San José in Toledo at the manner in which it had bankrupted itself caring for nuns who had fled there from its sister community in nearby Talavera de la Reina. *Cf.* 'Relación de lo sucedido en nuestro convento del nuestro padre San José de Carmelitas Descalzas de la ciudad de Toledo en todo el tiempo de la invasión de los enemigos', *cit.* Sanz, *Monjas en guerra,* pp. 68–69.

29. The many convents which were evacuated at the behest of the Portuguese authorities in the course of the 'scorching' of Beira in the autumn of 1810 deserve a special mention here. In such instances, of course, though still traumatic enough, flight amounted to participation in the war effort. For a good description of the departure of one such community, *cf.* Boutflower, *Journal,* p. 52. In this particular instance, the nuns concerned may be presumed to have reached safety in Lisbon. However, some communities remained behind, and these may eventually have had to disperse for want of food and money; hence, perhaps, the alleged presence of a number of nuns among the thousands of

Portuguese women who rallied to Wellington's army; *cf.* Anon., *Adventures in the Peninsula,* pp. 226, 248–49; Ludovici, *On the Road with Wellington,* p. 281. At all events in the spring of 1811 parties of nuns tramping the roads of central Portugal in search of food and shelter were a common sight; *cf.* Buckley, *Napoleonic War Journal,* p. 138.

30. E.g., Anon., *Enérgica exhortación que hace una religiosa descalza al ejército español, vencedor de los que llaman invencibles, persuadiéndole que corone con sus heróicos triunfos, arrancado del poder del enemigo del honor y de la humanidad al pérfido Napoleón y colocando en su trono a nuestro amado rey, Fernando VII* (Madrid, n.d.); Anon., *Proclama de las religiosas del monasterio de la Santísima Faz, valerosos y católicos alicantinos* (Alicante, 1808). For the María Rosa de Jesus affair, *cf.* Solis, *Cádiz,* pp. 308–15. Interrogated by the religious authorities of the city, the nun in question was eventually (and quite rightly) declared to be a mere fantasist.

31. Leslie, *Military Journal,* p. 191; *Diario Mercantil de Cádiz,* 19 October 1813, p. 79.

32. *Diario de Granada,* various issues, May 1808; Galmés, *Real monasterio de Santa Inés,* p. 82; Álvarez García, *Clero de la diócesis de Valladolid,* p. 164.

33. Steevens, *Reminiscences,* p. 55; Stothert, *Narrative,* pp. 26, 144, 147; Leach, *Rough Sketches,* p. 73; Surtees, *Twenty-Five Years in the Rifle Brigade,* p. 161; Fletcher, *For King and Country,* pp. 160–61; Malmesbury, *Letters of the First Earl of Malmesbury,* II, p. 101; Glover, *Gentleman Volunteer,* p. 74; Monick, *Iberian and Waterloo Campaigns,* p. 93. There were, alas, rather less laudable ways of showing solidarity with the Allied war effort: in at least one convent in Seville, two French nuns who had taken refuge there in the wake of the French Revolution found themselves not just ostracised by their fellow sisters, but denied all food. *Cf.* AHN. Consejos, *libro* 1741, f. 180.

34. 'Relación de lo ocurrido en este convento de Carmelitas Descalzas de Sevilla', *cit.* Sanz, *Monjas en guerra,* p. 74.

35. *Cf.* Francisca Teresa del Espíritu Santo, 'Relación de los prodigios que durante la Guerra de los franceses hizo la intercesión de Nuestra Gloriosa madre, Santa Teresa de Jésus desde el año de 1808 hasta el de 1813 en este convento y villa de Alba de Tormes', *cit. ibid.,* pp. 11–21.

36. Elena de Nuestra Señora de la Consolación, 'Relación de lo ocurrido en este convento de Carmelitas Descalzas de Sevilla en la desgraciada época en que los franceses ocuparon nuestra España', *cit. ibid.,* pp. 73–87.

37. Blaze, *Mémoires,* II, p. 86.

38. For some unhappy memories of French occupation, *cf.* María Monica de Jesus, 'Historia de la Comunidad de Madres Agustinas Recoletas de Salamanca', *cit.* Sanz Hermida, *Monjas en guerra,* pp. 123–71; Anon., 'Historia de la fundación del real monasterio de Agustinas Recoletas de Santa Isabel de Madrid' *cit. ibid.,* pp. 113–18.

39. A. Salvá, *Burgos en la Guerra de la Independencia,* ed. C. Borreguero Beltrán (Burgos, 2008), p. 136.

40. Joaquina del Salvador, 'Razón de lo que pasó esta comunidad en tiempo de los franceses y varios lances que tuvimos con ellos desde el año de 1808 hasta el de 1813', *cit.* Sanz Hermida, *Monjas en guerra,* p. 61. More concrete evidence of the desperate straits to which many convents were reduced is provided by the numerous petitions that were sent to the Conde de Montarco by communities

anxious to sell off some of their property so as to raise funds or hopeful that he might be persuaded to relieve them of some of their obligations. *Cf.* AHN. Consejos, *libro* 1741, ff. 155, 164, 258. Meanwhile, for an affecting account of the misery to which one community in Salamanca was reduced, *cf.* Butler, *Memoirs of General Thiébault,* II, pp. 334–36.

41. Desboeufs, *Etapes d'un soldat,* p. 148.

42. *Cf.* Dallas, *Felix Alvarez,* III, pp. 154–55, 293. It is possible that this episode was based on nothing more than rumour, while a similar story that has been shown to have been invented altogether may be found in C. González Caizán (ed.), *El anónimo polaco: Zaragoza en el año de 1809: fragmento de las memorias todavía no publicadas* (Zaragoza, 2012), p. 54. Indeed, during the first attack on the city in the summer of 1808 the very *Gazeta de Zaragoza* was forced to recognise that various communities that were overrun were treated with perfect courtesy; *cf. Gazeta de Zaragoza,* 16 August 1808, p. 684. However, three Carmelite nuns were certainly amongst the sixty-nine civilians killed when French troops sacked Uclés following the defeat of the Army of the Centre outside that town on 13 January 1809; *cf. Gazeta de Gobierno,* 24 April 1809, pp. 389–92.

43. Fantin des Odoards, *Journal,* p. 143. If the nuns were not physically harmed, in typical fashion (see below), they were nonetheless subjected to repeated attempts on the part of amorous or inquisitive young officers to make their acquaintance. From these advances, they were seemingly kept well barricaded, but Fantin des Odoards still had no hesitation in claiming that, had his regiment stayed in León for any length of time, they would eventually have been 'humanised to advantage'.

44. *Cf.* AHN. Consejos, *libro* 1741, f. 235; Conde de Montarco to acting bishop of Seville, 29 January 1812, AHN. Consejos, *libro* 1743, f. 28.

45. Elena de Nuestra Señora de la Consolación, 'Relación de lo ocurrido en este convento de Carmelitas Descalzas de Sevilla', *cit.* Sanz, *Monjas en guerra,* p. 80; Álvarez García, *Clero de la diócesis de Valladolid,* p. 168. Conventual solidarity also proved very strong in other situations, as well. Thus, particularly in the wake of the French invasion of 1810–11, conditions in Portugal's convents reached a pitch of misery that was even worse than that experienced by their counterparts in Spain. However, when William Warre made arrangements to have a female relative transferred from a convent in a remote mountain village near Viseu to more comfortable quarters in Lisbon, to his considerable irritation, the nun in question refused point-blank to leave her friends; *cf.* Warre, *Letters from the Peninsula,* p. 136. The desperate situation to which many communities were reduced is, perhaps, exemplified by 'a convent containing about half a dozen miserable, wretched, dirty old nuns' that Bingham discovered near Sernancelhe early in 1812; *cf.* Glover, *Wellington's Lieutenant, Napoleon's Gaoler,* p. 99. It is difficult to believe, however, that, as the same author insinuates in respect of another house at Trancoso, any nuns resorted to prostitution in order to survive. *Cf. ibid.,* p. 102.

46. *Cf.* AHN. Consejos, *libro* 1741, ff. 136, 151, 249; Conde de Montarco to Joaquín María Sotelo, 6 November 1811, AHN. Consejos, *libro* 1745, f. 84; Conde de Montarco to sub-prefect of Ronda, 18 March 1812, AHN. Consejos, *libro* 1745, f. 118.

47. For a good example of a secularised nun who wished to return to the cloister, see AHN. Consejos, *libro* 1741, f. 198. Meanwhile, there are mentions of

campfollower nuns in Blaze, *Mémoires,* II, p. 85, and Bell, *Rough Notes,* I, p. 94, and a report of a nun turned informer in J. Orti, *Córdoba en la Guerra de la Independencía* (Córdoba, 1930), pp. 148–49.

48. In a few communities nuns appear to have been given leave to stay or go as they pleased, one such being the Recollective Augustinian community of Santa Isabel in Madrid. However, in this case at least, only four of the twenty members of which the household was made up opted to return to their homes, this being something that is worth noting as yet another instance of the emotional hold which communities had on their members (as is the fact that on their eventual return the four nuns found themselves stigmatised as cowards and traitors); *cf.* anon., 'Historia de la fundación del real monasterio Agustinas Recoletas de Santa Isabel de Madrid' *cit.* Sanz , *Monjas en Guerra,* pp. 113–14.

49. Leslie, *Military Journal,* p. 157.

50. Var, *Campagnes du Capiitaine Marcel,* pp. 61–63. According to the officer concerned, the nun paid a heavy price: having only embarked on the affair at the cost of a desperate struggle with her conscience, she was so remorseful that she ended up falling sick and dying of fever.

51. North, *In the Legions of Napoleon,* pp. 87–88, 91–99.

52. Desboeufs, *Etapes d'un soldat,* p. 149.

53. There is, of course, no proof at to what really happened. However, a French officer who was in garrison in Puente la Reina in the spring of 1813 makes some remarks that are the very least highly suggestive. Thus: 'Very charming as she was, the lady-abbess was more than capable of winning over any general, and in fact, our commander . . . spent many happy evenings in her convent . . . , in the course of which he was served preserves, pastries and iced milk, not to mention the inevitable chocolate.' *Cf.* Bourachot, *Souvenirs Militaires du Captaine Jean-Baptiste Lemonnier-Delafosse,* p. 115.

54. *Cf.* http://webs.ono.com/carrioncondes/leyendas.htm (accessed 14 January 2012); Álvarez García, *Clero de la diócesis de Valladolid,* p. 164.

55. Fantin des Odoards, *Journal,* p. 197.

56. *Cf.* AHN. Consejos, *libro* 1741, f. 191. That said, on occasion abbesses did essay a more direct approach; *cf. ibid.,* f. 262.

57. For a good example, *cf.* Nevill, *Some Recollections,* p. 15.

58. According to Porter, this is not quite true. Thus, quartered at Sahagún de Campos in December 1808, he claims to have come across the wife of a Portuguese muleteer reproaching three nuns who had been dispensing wine at the door of their convent on the useless nature of their way of life and telling them they should be out in the world doing their duty to their country by giving it sons! *Cf.* Porter, *Letters,* pp. 230–32.

59. Kincaid, *Adventures,* p. 63. It is also worth pointing out that Wellington's forces were just as capable of requisitioning convents for their own purposes as their French counterparts. E.g., Leslie, *Military Journal,* p. 166.

60. For some expressions of revulsion in respect of the convent, *cf.* Sherer, *Recollections,* pp. 170–71; Hunt, *Charging against Napoleon,* p. 136; Verner, *British Rifleman,* p. 49; Bell, *Rough Notes,* I, p. 22. With respect to the question of sexuality, the most explicit comments come from Thomas Bunbury. Thus: 'The unnatural state of a number of women huddled together . . . in a convent . . . does not always alter their temperament; rather, it is like a ship on fire with the

hatches battened down to exclude the air. The moment the hatches are opened, the flame bursts forth with uncontrollable energy, and ravages all within its influence.' *Cf.* Bunbury, *Reminiscences,* I, p. 212. Whether or not such views had any foundation scarcely matters: within months of the arrival of the first British troops in Portugal, the army was being swept by rumours of nuns so desperate for sex that they would solicit passing soldiers at the very doors of their convents. E.g., Porter, *Letters,* pp. 181–85; Neale, *Letters,* p. 231.

61. E.g., Patterson, *Adventures,* p. 154; Surtees, *Twenty-Five Years with the Rifle Brigade,* p. 197. *Cf. ibid.,* p. 155.

62. *Cf.* Bell, *Rough Notes,* I, p. 41. The doctor appears not just to have been drunk but unbalanced: within a few months his behaviour had become so violent and unpredictable that he had to be invalided home to Britain; *ibid.,* pp. 50–51. For a rather more subtle attempt to gain access, *cf.* Boutflower, *Journal,* pp. 47–48. Meanwhile, the extent to which fascination with nuns gripped at least some officers is suggested by the diary of Captain James Hughes: in three days in October 1808 he visited no fewer than four convents; *cf.* Hunt, *Charging against Napoleon,* p. 9. Such behaviour, of course, could not but attract the attention of the ecclesiastical authorities, the bishop of Viseu becoming so alarmed at the number of visits being paid to the town's Benedictine nunnery that he complained to the Mother Superior; *cf.* Stothert, *Narrative,* p. 155.

63. Hunt, *Charging against Napoleon,* p. 120; *cf.* Leach, *Rough Sketches,* p. 73; Kincaid, *Random Shots,* pp. 224–25; Sherer, *Recollections,* pp. 98–99.

64. Sherer, *Recollections,* p. 98. This method was also employed in the Ursuline convent in Salamanca in that, the Mother Superior obviously being convinced that in the case of her charges there was nothing to fear, British officers were permitted to attend the same thrice-weekly sessions at which the nuns received visits from their families. As the woman had clearly foreseen, the result was to shatter all possible sexual fantasy: 'Conceive . . . my disappointment when, on entering the convent, I beheld ten or twelve decrepit old women, wrapped up in woollen dresses, with . . . little of anything like feeling or sentiment in the lines of their wrinkled countenances.' *Cf.* Neale, *Letters,* p. 229.

65. Glover, *Eloquent Soldier,* pp. 34–35. It seems probable that the convent referred to here was the Convento do Desagravo, a house of the Order of Contemplative Dominicans that had been established in 1780.

66. *Cf.* also the short shrift meted out to a group of cavalry officers by the abbess of a convent at Olite in July 1813; *cf.* Hunt, *Charging against Napoleon,* pp. 114, 119.

67. Leach, *Rough Sketches,* pp. 78–79.

68. *Cf.* Hunt, *Charging against Napoleon,* p. 9.

69. Bunbury, *Reminiscences,* I, pp. 287–88. Bunbury does not appear to have been much abashed by this rebuke. However, other British officers were less insouciant. For example, a rabid evangelical, Boutflower was at first all too ready to fill his journal with stories of nuns behaving badly; *cf.* Boutflower, *Journal,* pp. 39, 46. Eventually, however, given regular access to a convent to treat a member of the community who had fallen ill, he was forced to admit that the sisters were 'most worthy people'; *cf. ibid.,* p. 52.

70. Álvarez García, *Clero en la diócesis de Valladolid,* p. 169. As Álvarez García admits, there is some doubt as to the extent this was a genuine ideological dis-

pute. This was how it was written up by the *josefino* authorities, but it seems probable that, serious though it was, the quarrel was founded much more on a mixture of petty jealousies and long-standing personal rivalries.

71. *Cf.* http://www.diariodenavarra.es/20080203/navarra/el-monasterio-tulebras.html?not=2008020303005685&dia=20080203&seccion=navarra&seccion2=sociedad&chnl=10 (accessed 24 January 2012). Meanwhile, there is also a story that marauding troops from Morillo's division sacked a convent in the Navarrese valley of the Baztán in the winter of 1813; *cf.* Henegan, *Seven Years' Campaigning,* II, pp. 193–94.

72. Elena de Nuestra Señora de la Consolación, 'Relación de lo ocurrido en este convento de Carmelitas Descalzas de Sevilla', *cit.* Sanz, *Monjas en guerra,* pp. 77–78.

73. *Ibid.,* pp. 78–79.

74. Anon., 'Fondación de las monjas carmelitas de San José de Zaragoza', pp. 97–105.

75. María Mónica de Jesus, 'Historia de la Comunidad de Madres Agustinas Recoletas de Salamanca', *cit.* Sanz, *Monjas en guerra,* pp. 149–50. According to a British eyewitness to the disaster, all the houses within 100 yards of the explosion were flattened by it, and between forty and fifty men, women and children killed by it. *Cf.* Glover, *Gentleman Volunteer,* p. 25. However, the final death toll was much higher, some accounts putting it at as much as 600.

76. Leach, *Rough Sketches,* p. 196. Also interesting is Swabey's account of the state in which he found the nuns of Trujillo's six convents when he passed through the town in the summer of 1812: 'The inhabitants . . . are now crowded into one house, and, having been robbed of all their riches and emoluments, subsist precariously by the sale of stockings and other work; they indeed kept a pastry-cook's shop during our stay.' *Cf.* Whinyates, *Diary of Campaigns in the Peninsula,* p. 121.

77. Anon., 'Historia de la fundación del real monasterio Agustinas Recoletas de Santa Isabel de Madrid', *cit.* Sanz, *Monjas en Guerra,* pp. 114–17.

78. Anon., 'Relación de algunos sucesos ocurridos en España y en esta comunidad desde el año de 1808 hasta el de 1910', *cit. ibid.,* p. 44.

79. If the recruitment situation was bad, Bingham's letters contain a hint that all was not lost. Thus, in April 1812 he came across a Portuguese family at Portalegre that was, with great reluctance, planning to send its eldest daughter into a convent because they no longer had the wherewithal to provide her with an adequate dowry (this in turn suggests, of course, that the need for fresh recruits had forced convents to reduce the dowries needed by fresh postulants). *Cf.* Glover, *Wellington's Lieutenant, Napoleon's Gaoler,* p. 117.

80. For the situation of the religious orders at the end of the war, *cf.* Callahan, *Church, Politics and Society,* pp. 104–16 *passim;* Higgs, 'The Portuguese Church', p. 55.

81. María Mónica de Jesus, 'Historia de la comunidad de Madres Agustinas Recoletas de Salamanca', *cit.* Sanz, *Monjas en guerra,* pp. 148–51.

82. A. Martínez Cuesta, 'Monjas augustinas recoletas: historia y espiritualidad', *Acta Ordinis,* No. 86 (January, 1992), p. 53. To take just one example of conventual debt, meanwhile, in 1814 the Franciscan convent of Santa Isabel reported that it owed 6,500 *reales* in respect of loans that it had obtained from various benefac-

tors. *Cf.* Martín Rodrigo, *Guerra de la Independencia en la provincia de Salamanca,* pp. 3–44.

Chapter 7

1. Bourgoing, *Modern State of Spain,* II, pp, 289–90; *cf.* also Laborde, *View of Spain,* V, pp. 267–68; Croker, *Travels,* p. 267. The only sour note in the general hymn of praise comes from such references as we have to the women of the lower classes. For example: 'Among the peasants and common females, you never see anything like beauty, and, in general, rather deformity of feature.' *Cf.* P. Thicknesse, *A Year's Journey through France and Part of Spain* (London, 1778), I, p. 283.

2. Bourgoing, *Modern State of Spain,* II, p. 293.

3. *Ibid.,* II, p. 294.

4. Thicknesse, *Journey through France and Part of Spain,* I, p. 284. The impact of the *fandango* appears to have been considerable. Writing after the Peninsular War, one private soldier remarked, 'This dance had a great effect upon us, but the Spaniards saw it without moving, and laughed at the quick breathing and amorous looks of our men.' Anon., *Journal of a Soldier of the Seventy-First,* p. 177.

5. Dalrymple, *Travels through Spain and Portugal,* pp. 18, 45.

6. Bourgoing, *Modern State of Spain,* II, p. 288.

7. Swinburne, *Travels through Spain,* pp. 47–48; *cf.* also Twiss, *Travels though Portugal and Spain,* p. 156.

8. Twiss, *Travels though Portugal and Spain,* p. 289.

9. Croker, *Travels,* pp. 233–34.

10. *Cit.* Fletcher, *In the Service of the King,* p. 90. For a hilarious account of Gil Blas on one young soldier, *cf.* Gleig, *Light Dragoon,* pp. 56–57.

11. Thirion, *Souvenirs militaires,* p. 61.

12. For the promotion of sexual aggression in the French army, *cf.* M. J. Hughes, *Forging Napoleon's Grande Armée: Motivation, Military Culture and Masculinity in the French Army, 1800–1808* (New York University Press, 2012), pp. 108–36. For a more general discussion of the ethos of Napoleon's army, *cf.* A. Forrest, 'The military culture of Napoleonic France', in P. Dwyer (ed.), *Napoleon and Europe* (London, 2001), pp. 43–59.

13. *Cit.* T. Moore, *Letters and Journals of Lord Byron with Notices of his Life* (Paris, 1830), p. 67.

14. *Cit.* L. A. Marchand (ed.), *Lord Byron: Selected Letters and Journals* (Newhaven, Connecticut, 1982), pp. 25–28.

15. Boutflower, *Journal,* p. 157; Glover, *Eloquent Soldier,* p. 78; H. d'Espinchal, *Souvenirs Militaires, 1792–1814,* ed. F. Masson and E. Boyer (Paris 1901). II, pp. 3–4; Gonneville, *Recollections,* II, p. 11; Leslie, *Military Journal,* pp. 29–30.

16. 'I was much amused, frequently', wrote Charles Crowe, 'at seeing an elegant young woman light a paper cigar.' *Cf.* Glover, *Eloquent Soldier,* p. 170. For a detailed discussion of the seductive effect of a habit whose health risks were as yet a very long way from being recognised, *cf.* Blaze, *Mémoires,* II, pp. 293–94.

17. *Cit.* Marchand, *Lord Byron,* pp. 25–28.

18. *Ibid.,* pp. 10–11.

19. Oyon, *Campagnes et souvenirs militaires,* pp. 119–20.

20. Saint Chamans, *Mémoires*, pp. 205–207. For a British counterpart to Saint Chamans, *cf.* Sherer, *Recollections*, pp. 58–59.

21. Fantin des Odoards, *Journal*, p. 186. For good measure, the same author repeats Bourgoing's claims in respect of the attitude of Spanish and Portuguese husbands: 'In no place are husbands more complacent, whilst the *dueñas* are more of an asset than an obstacle to anyone who would pursue the objects committed to their care.' *Cf. ibid.*, p. 187.

22. *Cit.* Verner, *British Rifleman*, pp. 14–15. *Cf.* also Porter, *Letters from Portugal and Spain*, pp. 52–54.

23. Leach, *Rough Sketches*, pp. 284–85.

24. Boutflower, *Journal of an Army Surgeon*, pp. 17–18.

25. Verner, *A British Rifleman*, p. 278. Swabey, meanwhile, is sharper still: 'Beauty in distress claims the tears of knight errantry, but I believe in most novels I have read it was generally accompanied by cleanliness and education.' *Cf.* Whinyates, *Diary of Campaigns in the Peninsula*, p. 35.

26. *Cit.* Hunt, *Charging against Napoleon*, p. 135.

27. Kincaid, *Adventures*, pp. 94–95.

28. Leslie, *Military Journal*, pp. 243–45.

29. Kincaid, *Adventures*, pp. 152–53. In the face of so much callousness, it is pleasant to record the case of a British infantryman who, having acquired a Spanish lover in the course of the Anglo-Portuguese army's occupation of Madrid in the summer of 1812, brought her away with him to Ciudad Rodrigo when it was forced to retreat, and then tried to enlist in the Spanish army rather than suffer her to be sent back to her home in the fashion which his commanding officer proceeded to demand. Though worthy of a happy ending, the story, alas, does not have one: apprehended by the provosts, he was promptly court-martialled and shot. Larpent, *Private Journal*, p. 44.

30. For a useful general discussion of the sexual *mores* of the British officer, *cf.* C. Kennedy, 'John Bull into battle: military masculinity and the British army officer during the Napoleonic Wars', in Hagemann *et al.*, *Gender, War and Politics*, pp. 127–46.

31. Surtees, *Twenty-Five Years in the Rifle Brigade*, pp. 110–11.

32. Ludovici, *On the Road with Wellington*, p. 29. Shortly after giving this account, Schaumann recalls he and a surgeon named Gordon simultaneously laying siege to 'a beautiful girl of sixteen' named Joaquina at the village of São Pedro de Penaferrim near Lisbon: 'The fair Joaquina sat between us . . . I had hold of one of her hands [while] the doctor held the other: it was touching to behold!' *Ibid.*, p. 32. As if this was not enough, by the time Schaumann had crossed the frontier into Spain in November, he had also attempted to seduce the wife of the man on whom he was billeted in Vilafranca and enjoyed a series of rather more innocent flirtations in Castelo Branco. *Ibid.*, pp. 53–54, 63.

33. Sturgis, *Boy in the Peninsular War*, pp. 285–86. This was very much a case of 'the biter bit'. Billeted in the winter of 1811 in the house of a Portuguese nobleman in Salgueiro, for example, Swabey and his brother officers thought it was a good joke to responding to the daughter of the house's appeals to teach her English by rendering 'Portuguese of which we were asked the English into all sorts of ridiculous expressions'. *Cf.* Swabey, *Diary*, p. 36.

34. Henegan, *Seven Years' Campaigning*, I, pp. 59–60. The author is distinctly disingenuous in his account of this affair, later admitting that, in the course of the evening that had caused so much trouble, he had himself flirted with 'a sweet pretty girl of fifteen' called Isabel, who, or so he claimed, several nights later appeared at his lodgings disguised as a boy, having fled her home to warn him that a plot was afoot to burn his convoy; *cf. ibid.*, pp. 75–80.

35. *Ibid.*, I, pp. 60–67.

36. *Ibid.*, I, p. 73.

37. Grattan, *Adventures*, II, p. 125.

38. Blayney, *Narrative*, I, p. 69.

39. Grattan, *Adventures*, II, pp. 95–96. For similar opinions, *cf.* Blakiston, *Twelve Years' Military Adventure*, II, p. 263, Sherer, *Recollections*, pp. 36–37, and Patterson, *Adventures*, p. 248. For once, we also have a feminine voice on the matter, albeit still openly a reported one. According to Bingham, then, some women at Fuente del Maestre were very candid in their views on the subject: 'We like you better than our own people, but we must confess we like the French better than you.' *Cf.* Glover, *Wellington's Lieutenant, Napoleon's Gaoler*, p. 110. On the other hand, if Frenchmen ranked higher than Britons, another Spanish woman can be found asserting that Britons ranked higher than Spaniards; *cf.* Ludovici, *On the Road with Wellington*, p. 300.

40. Var, *Campagnes du Capitaine Marcel*, pp. 100–101. There is something deeply disturbing about this particular episode. Thus: 'Not having any more doubt that my cause would triumph . . . I ended up introducing my young beloved to the most delectable pleasures of love, pleasures that I enjoyed to the full. Imagine: a pretty young girl of fourteen, with all the freshness that comes with that age, and a nascent bosom that was smooth as marble. Of all the women I knew in that period, she was the one who cost me most regrets when the time came for me to leave her.'

41. For an entertaining if doubtless semi-fictionalised account of Blaze's career as a philanderer, *cf.* Blaze, *Mémoires*, II, pp. 108–35. Note, however, the comparisons that can be made with the equally unrepentant Augustus Schaumann: in the course of a few days in October 1810, the latter claims to have had sexual relations with no fewer than three women: the Portuguese girl we have already mentioned, the mistress of a Portuguese officer, and a British campfollower whom he had engaged as a cook. *Cf.* Ludovici, *On the Road with Wellington*, pp. 257–67.

42. *Cf.* Dallas, *Felix Alvarez*, II, pp. 114–18, 257–58. This may just be a story, but there is something grimly matter-of-fact about Marcel's account of an incident that took place at the village of Mallo near Tamames in the summer of 1809: 'In our new cantonments we found . . . that all the young women had taken to the woods in the hope of saving their virtue. However, the soldiers . . . organised a round-up that brought in a good number of these divinities, the maidens among them having somehow just become women without contracting the sacrament of marriage at any altar.' *Cf.* Var, *Campagnes du Capitaine Marcel*, p. 102.

43. Bunbury, *Reminiscences*, I, p. 19; Hunt, *Charging against Napoleon*, p. 74. For a story involving just such an angry husband, *cf.* Ludovici, *On the Road with Wellington*, pp. 211–12.

44. *Cf.* Cadell, *Narrative,* p. 123; Patterson, *Adventures,* p. 340; Donaldson, *Recollections,* p. 205; Cassells, *Peninsular Portrait,* p. 120. Meanwhile, though they had been in all likelihood simply killed by bandits, it was popularly supposed that two men of the Tenth Light Dragoons who were murdered near Olite in June 1813 died because they had been seen flirting with a Spanish girl; *cf.* Ludovici, *On the Road with Wellington,* p. 385. Schaumann goes on to complain that an attempt was made to kill him as well for the same reason, not that this is entirely surprising given that he claims to have seduced no fewer than five different women in the course of his stay in the town; *ibid.,* p. 386.

45. Glover, *An Eloquent Soldier,* p. 150. A further act of what may well have been rape is hinted at by an officer of the Eighteenth Light Dragoons named James Hughes who hints that he committed such an act with 'a pretty and kind girl' whom he met in some woods near Hernani; *cf.* Hunt, *Charging against Napoleon,* pp. 148–49.

46. Beslay, *Souvenirs militaires d'Octave Levavasseur,* pp. 144–45.

47. As ever, there were beyond doubt many exceptions, the prime example being the rifle officer, Harry Smith, who, though in many respects an unsympathetic character, seems genuinely to have been devoted to the Spanish girl he married after the siege of Badajoz. At all events, there seems no reason to doubt the tribute he eventually paid her in his memoirs: 'The atrocities committed by our soldiers on the poor, innocent and defenceless inhabitants of the city, no words suffice to depict . . . Yet this scene of debauchery . . . has been the solace and whole happiness of my life for thirty-three years . . . If any reward is due to a soldier, never was one so honoured and distinguished as I have been . . . Thus, as good may come out of evil, this scene of devastation and spoil yielded to me a treasure invaluable . . . From that day to this she has been my guardian angel.' *Cf.* Haythornthwaite, *Autobiography of Sir Harry Smith,* pp. 68–73.

48. *Cf.* Martín Rodrigo, *Guerra de la Independencia en la provincia de Salamanca,* p. 73. Lamentably, women also seem in some instances to have been murdered quite casually by passing French troops: in December 1812 two women living in Aldeatejada named Ana Rodríguez and Francisca Martín are recorded as having died of injuries they had received after being tied up and beaten (one suspects that they were also raped but that the parish priest who recorded their deaths was reluctant to say as much in the parish register); *cf. ibid.,* p. 59.

49. Var, *Campagnes du Capitaine Marcel,* pp. 26–67.

50. *Ibid.,* pp. 40–41.

51. Baste's memoirs were originally published in A. de Beauchamp, *Collection des mémoires relatifs aux revolutions d'Espagne* (Paris, 1824). This translation, however, is that provided by T. Mahon as 'Recollections of Capitaine de Frégate Pierre Baste' at http://napoleon-series.org/military/battles/baste/c_baste1.htm.

52. Lavaux, *Mémoires,* pp. 152–53.

53. *Ibid.,* pp. 153–55. Lavaux, alas, is not exaggerating here: in 1814 the then parish priest compiled a list of no fewer than 239 victims, including a child just three days old; *cf.* F. L. Díaz Torrejón, *Guerrilla, contraguerrilla y delincuencia en la Andalucía napoleónica,1810–1812* (Granada, 2004), III, p. 163.

54. Lavaux, *Mémoires de campagne,* pp. 155–56.

55. Gonneville, *Reccollections,* I, p. 244.

56. 'Recollections of Capitaine de Frégate Pierre Baste'. For descriptions of the similar events that took place at Medina de Río Seco and Burgos, *cf.* Comtesse de Beaulaincourt-Marles (ed.), *Journal du Maréchal de Castellane, 1804–1862* (Paris, 1895–97), I, pp. 24, 32–33. Also good on Burgos are Fantin des Odoards, *Journal,* pp. 188–89, and A. Miot de Melito, *Mémoires du Comte Miot de Melito, ancien ministre, ambassadeur, conseilleur d'état et membre de l'institut* (Paris, 1858), III, p. 22. A somewhat different case is afforded by that of Salamanca which was brutally sacked by French troops on the night of 15 November 1812. In this instance, there was no pretext of any sort for such an event, the city having been abandoned without a fight. Rather, exhausted after a long and difficult campaign, the forces involved simply ran amok, though their behaviour was beyond doubt worsened by rumours that the populace had mistreated and even murdered the thousands of French wounded left in the town after the battle. Whatever the reason, the civilian populace suffered very severely. The day afterwards Marcel was confronted by a woman named Simporosa with whom he had a relationship whilst stationed in the city earlier in the war, and upbraided for having failed to seek her out and take her into his protection, the consequence being, she claimed, that she had been raped by fifteen or twenty dragoons and could scarcely walk. Marcel, alas, was unmoved, not least because he was currently enjoying the favours of a young girl he had already promised to protect, and turned her away, later quietening his conscience with the thought that she had always insisted that she hated the French and had once said that, if by killing him, she could kill every single Frenchman, he would be dead in an instant; *cf.* Var, *Campagnes du Capitaine Marcel,* pp. 182–83.

57. Var, *Campagnes du Capitaine Marcel,* p. 122.

58. L. N. Fririon, *Journal historique de la campagne de Portugal enterprise par les français sous les ordres du Maréchal Masséna, Prince d'Essling du 15 septembre 1810 au 12 mai 1811* (Paris, 1841), pp. 216–17; *cf.* also R. Brindle (ed.), *With Napoleon's Guns: the Military Memoirs of an Officer of the First Empire* (London, 2005), pp. 105–106.

59. For an exception, *cf.* Bourachot, *Souvenirs Militaires du Capitaine Jean-Baptiste Lemonnier-Delafosse,* pp. 57–58. Rape is not mentioned in this account, but it seems probable that it was a part of the proceedings. During the pursuit of Masséna's army as it fell back on the frontier, Donaldson was told of a man who 'had been hung up by some of the French soldiers because he would not . . . show them where he had hid his money', while his sisters 'had been first violated by the monsters and then cruelly used'. *Cf.* Donaldson, *Recollections,* p. 111.

60. *Cf.*, for example, Monick, *Iberian and Waterloo Campaigns,* pp. 5–6.

61. Verner, *British Rifleman,* pp. 137, 160–61.

62. *Ibid.*, pp. 151–52.

63. *Ibid.*, pp. 143–52 *passim.*

64. Hamilton, *Hamilton's Campaign,* p. 43; *cf.* also Wylly, *Cavalry Officer in the Corunna Campaign,* pp. 149–50.To misery was added anger and frustration. Here, then, is Augustus Schaumann: 'The English soldier, who was now quite well aware that he had been lured into this country . . . by false pretences, and had then been left in the lurch . . . set about burning everything out of revenge.' *Cf.* Ludovici, *On the Road with Wellington,* p. 93.

65. Henegan, *Seven Years' Campaigning,* I, pp. 70–73. For an example involving a woman who was shot dead by a marauding British soldier for no other reason than that she had denied him some onions, *cf.* Larpent, *Private Journal,* p. 59. Meanwhile, Boutflower recalls an incident in which a family near Guarda was butchered in horrific circumstances by, or so it was believed, British marauders fearful that their identity would be revealed; *cf.* Boutflower, *Journal of an Army Surgeon,* p. 50.

66. Coss argues very strongly that that British soldiers were fundamentally different in their approach to the civilian population in general, and the women of Spain and Portugal in particular, than their French counterparts in that, whereas the group culture of the British army was inclined to minimise the incidence of violence and rape amongst the common soldiers, that of the French one was inclined to promote it; *cf.* Coss, *All for the King's Shilling,* pp. 20–27. This claim seems a little disingenuous, however: one can certainly accept that the British soldier was by no means always the product of a criminal under-class, indeed, that, in practice he differed very little from his French counterpart in social terms. What Coss is inclined to ignore here, though, is the difference in the wars that the rival armies were experiencing: had the British been in the shoes of the French, then, it is probable that they would have exhibited the same capacity for violence, just as the French, in turn, would have displayed far less of a propensity for violence had they been playing the part of the British.

67. French troops, it should be observed, behaved no better on those occasions when they took Spanish and Portuguese towns by assault, good examples including Oporto, Lérida and Tarragona. Here, for example, is the description given by Bugeaud of the sack of Lérida: 'The soldiers, greedy for pillage, scatter themselves about among the houses; carnage ceases and gives place to scenes of quite another kind. The conquerors are everywhere to be seen in the arms of the vanquished: Carmelites . . . old women, young virgins, all experienced the transports of our grenadiers, and several of them are said to have cried out, 'Oh, if I had known that this would be all, we should not have been so afraid!' *Cit.* D'Ideville, *Memoirs of Colonel Bugeaud.* p. 124. In other accounts, however, the truth is not disguised with fantasy. Thus, writing of the storm of Tarragona, Gonneville is refreshingly honest: 'Tarragona was carried by assault on the 28th of June 1811, and became the scene of all the horrors that accompany such an event. Neither sex nor age protected the wretched inhabitants. The soldiers were exasperated by a resistance lasting three months that had cost us enormous losses.' *Cf.* Gonneville, *Recollections,* II, p. 6. Nor is Fantin des Odoards any less candid with respect to the fall of Oporto, though he is inclined to be more ready to excuse the French forces: 'Every street became a scene of massacre, while there followed all the calamities that take place whenever a town is taken by assault. And how could it be otherwise when our soldiers were harassed by shots fired at them from alleyways when they were already masters of the whole town.' *Cf.* Fantin des Odoards, *Journal,* p. 163 (also useful here is Naylies, *Mémoires,* pp. 99–100). Meanwhile, for a graphic account of injuries allegedly inflicted on two Portuguese women in the course of the sack of Oporto, *cf.* Henegan, *Seven Years' Campaigning,* I, p. 100. However, whilst it is worth noting that the French forces concerned in no case sustained the sort of casualties as those incurred at Ciudad Rodrigo, Badajoz and San Sebastián therefore had less excuse for their

behaviour, if only for the sake of balance the focus here will be on Wellington's forces.

68. *Cit.* Malmesbury, *Letters of the First Earl of Malmesbury*, II, pp. 268–69.

69. Sturgis, *Boy in the Peninsular War*, pp. 273–74.

70. Costello, *Adventures*, pp. 177–78.

71. An analysis carried out of the 577 general courts-martial conducted by the British army in Spain and Portugal between 1809 and 1814 by Oman seemingly revealed only a single case of rape. It being unlikely that the offence would have gone unpunished except in the wholly exceptional circumstances of a storm, and particularly not when directed against a member of the civilian populace, it can only be assumed that it was consistently hidden behind that of another—say, murder or robbery with violence—though it has to be said that offences committed by stragglers during such episodes as the retreat of Sir John Moore are unlikely ever to have reached the ears of the authorities. However, even the murder of civilians and robbery with violence do not figure that strongly, only fifty-seven such cases appearing in Oman's data. *Cf.* C. Oman, 'Courts martial in the Peninsular War, 1809–1814', *Journal of the Royal United Services Institution*, LXVI, No. 418, pp. 1699–1716.

72. Coss, *All for the King's Shilling*, pp. 50–85.

73. Buckley, *Napoleonic War Journal*, p. 198. Rather more thoughtful, perhaps, was Joseph Sherer who believed that, while the majority of British soldiers remained decent individuals throughout, they were 'often placed in situations which from their nature . . . give birth to an elevation of spirits it is difficult to control'. As he continued, 'I have seen common men distributed through a suite of rooms in the empty palace of a nobleman . . . surrounded by mirrors and marble, and I have observed in their countenances a jocular eagerness to smash and destroy them. But this does not arise out of cruelty. No: in such a case, a soldier feels himself lifted for a moment above his low and ordinary condition.' *Cf.* Sherer, *Recollections*, p. 131. As for marauding, meanwhile, Sherer believed that this, too, was the result of circumstance alone: 'When troops are neither fed, clothed or paid with regularity, they are tempted beyond their strength.' *Ibid.*

74. Donaldson, *Recollections*, p. 158. Donaldson claims that the excesses were the work of a minority. Thus: 'In justice to the army, I must say [the excesses] were not general, and in most cases perpetrated by cold-blooded villains who were backward enough in the attack.' *Ibid.*, p. 159. In this he is supported by another rank-and-file participant in the assault in the person of William Lawrence, the latter claiming that 'a great many of the more respectable' lamented what took place and did 'as much as lay in their power' to stop the disorder; *cf.* G. N. Bankes (ed.), *The Autobiography of Sergeant William Lawrence, a Hero of the Peninsular and Waterloo Campaigns* (London, 1886), p. 117. Such claims should certainly not be dismissed out of hand, but at the same time it is difficult to accept them in full.

75. *Cf.* Glover, *Gentleman Volunteer*, p. 17.

76. For reasons of space no attempt has been made to detail the events that took place at Ciudad Rodrigo and San Sebastián. However, whilst the former appears to have escaped comparatively lightly, the latter was possibly hit even harder than Badajoz. For a contemporary Spanish account which places particular emphasis on sexual violence, *cf. Manifiesto que el ayuntamiento constitucional,*

cabildo eclesiasástico, ilustre consulado y vecinos de la ciudad de San Sebastián presentan a la nación sobre la conducta de las tropas británicas y portuguesas en dicho plaza el 31 de agosto de 1813 y días sucésivos (San Sebastián, 1813). I owe my knowledge of this document to the kindness of Mrs Sarah Tuohy.

77. *Cf.* Costello, *Adventures,* p. 179.

78. How far a readiness even to contemplate such self-sacrifice went is unclear. Whilst some officers clearly did put their lives at risk trying to save women from rape, plenty chose rather to shrug their shoulders and retire to their tents; *cf.* Donaldson, *Recollections,* p. 159; Grattan, *Adventures,* II, pp. 3–9 *passim;* Kincaid, *Adventures,* p. 139.

79. It was not just foreign soldiers who engaged in violence against women. Amongst the bandits who infested Spain and Portugal, it was common for women caught in isolated farmsteads to be tortured so as to force them to reveal the whereabouts of any valuables that they might have hidden. *Cf.* A. Perich, 'Narració de los sis anys y quatre mesos que los francesos han estat en Catalunya, contant de los primers de febrer de 1808, fins al primers junys de 1814', ed. J. Pella, *Boletín de la Real Academía de Buenas Letras de Barcelona,* No. 49, p. 495.

Epilogue

1. Female attitudes to the war have never been explored and are probably unexplorable. However, the following passage from the memoirs of William Surtees is at the very least highly suggestive. 'One noble Spanish lady . . . when I was quartered at Cádiz . . . said she should rejoice to see all the French then in their country hung up in the intestines . . . of the English who had come to drive them out. Thus they should get rid of both.' *Cf.* Surtees, *Twenty-Five Years in the Rifle Brigade,* pp. 310–11.

2. E.g., *Diario Mercantil de Cádiz,* 1 November 1813, p. 132; *ibid.,* 14 February 1814, p. 180.

3. Buckham, *Personal Narrative,* pp. 13–14.

4. *Cf.* Ludovici, *On the Road with Wellington,* pp. 322–24; Smith, *Autobiography,* p. 90.

5. The presence of Spanish campfollowers in the Russian campaign is testified to by D. G. Chandler (ed.), *The Memoirs of Sergeant Bourgogne, 1812–1813* (London, 1979), pp. 4–5, 11–12.

6. In the French army, in theory only wives were allowed to travel with the army, but, if accounts of the scenes witnessed after the battle of Vitoria are to be believed, this was at best honoured in the breach, while the naval officer, Jean de Grivel, claims that in his company of Sailors of the Guard several women dressed themselves as soldiers so as to remain with their soldier-lovers and managed to remain undiscovered until they after they had got back to France. *Cf.* Grivel, *Mémoires,* p. 257. The French sources which are our chief source for such women would doubtless like to argue that none of them had any regrets, but Ross-Lewin has a story of one girl, who, having been captured along with her officer-lover, showed every sign of being delighted to have been thus presented with the chance of ditching him in favour of some alternative; *cf.* Ross-Lewin, *With the Thirty-Second in the Peninsula,* p. 228.

7. One woman who was certainly so favoured was Mercedes de Santa Cruz y Montalvo. A daughter of a powerful Cuban family, she had married the French general, Christophe Merlin, in 1809, and in 1813 followed him to France, where

she proceeded to enjoy a gilded existence as a prominent member of Parisian *salon* society until her death in 1852; *cf.* Martín-Valdepeñas, 'Afrancesadas y patriotas', p. 366.

8. *Cf.* Larreguy de Civrieux, *Souvenirs*, pp. 3–4, 56–68.

9. In fact, the provisions laid down by Wellington's headquarters did allow commanding officers a little latitude. Thus: 'There will be no objection to a few of those who have proved themselves useful and regular accompanying the soldiers to whom they are attached with a view to their being ultimately married.' *Cf.* circular letter of E. M. Packenham, 26 April 1814, *cit.* Page, *Following the Drum*, pp. 136–37.

10. Grattan, *Adventures*, pp. 202–203; Costello, *Adventures of a Soldier*, p. 186; Donaldson, *Recollections*, p. 232; Surtees, *Twenty-Five Years in the Rifle Brigade*, p. 317.

11. Fernández García, *Mujeres*, p. 326.

12. Gleig, *The Subaltern*, p. 167.

13. The couple survived until 1865 when, now aged eighty-two and sixty-nine, they died within two months of one another, and were laid together in a single grave that may still be seen in the graveyard of St Mary's church. It seems probable that this grave is the only known resting place of a campfollower from Wellington's army. I owe all this information to the great-granddaughter and great-great-great-grandson of Stephen and Maria, Mrs Olive Palmer and Mr Glenn Ivett, and it is with their kind permission that it is reproduced in this work. Interestingly, in mute testimony to the couple's limited command of Spanish orthography, the gravestone gives the name as 'Marear'.

14. *Cf.* http://javiersevillano.es/AbuelaInglesa.htm (accessed 2 October 2012). Touchingly, María de la Encarnación Delgado is still remembered by her descendents as *la abuela inglesa*—the English grandmother.

15. Haythornthwaite, *Redcoats*, pp. 119–20.

16. *Cit.* Sabine, *Letters of Colonel Sir Augustus Simon Frazer*, p. 86.

17. R. Woodhead, 'My family hero', *Who do you think you are?* (April, 2012), p. 98; further details accessed at http://www.vivientomlinson.com/batley/p197.htm, 4 September 2012. There is an extraordinary sequel to this story: evidently unable to work any longer, Exley was reduced to living in a single basement room in a state of near destitution, and at length resolved to attempt to make some money by writing her memoirs. These were eventually serialised in a local newspaper many years later, while, at the time of writing, efforts are afoot to have them published in book form.

18. It would be interesting to know how officers' wives intellectualised their experiences in Spain and Portugal. However, setting aside a collection of epic lays of little relevance to our topic—viz., Anon., *Poems founded on the Events of the War in the Peninsula by the Wife of an Officer* (London, 1819)—the only text that has been located in this respect is a brief memoir of a very impersonal nature that offers little in the way of personal experience. *Cf.* F. M. Fitzmaurice, *Recollections of a Rifleman's Wife at Home and Abroad* (London, 1851).

19. Henegan, *Seven Years' Campaigning*, I, pp. 230–31.

20. Bunbury, *Reminiscences of a Veteran*, I, pp. 296–98.

21. Order of the town council of Oporto, 13 July 1809, Biblioteca Municipal do Porto, MS. 1773.

22. In Andalucía the Polish officer, Kajetan Wojciechowski, noted seeing women who had been hung for the crime of dancing with a Frenchman; *cf.* K. Wojciechowski, *Mis Memorias de España*, ed. J.S. Ciechanowski *et al.* (Madrid,

2009), p. 106. Meanwhile, also from Andalucía comes a story of a prominent *afrancesada* who was captured while out riding with a group of French officers and given a severe birching; *cf.* Dallas, *Felix Alvarez,* II, pp. 217–20, 270.

23. In 1813, for example, a pamphlet appeared in Córdoba with the catchy title, *El día 8 de enero de 1812 dió muerte esta mujer a sus padres con solimán y veneno, a una hermana suya, y a una tía que asistía a la cocina, por esta resuelta y determinada irse con un oficial de la nación francesa que estaba alojado en su misma casa, y el día 12 de mayo de 1813 fue castigada para ejemplo e escarmiento de otras como vera el curioso lector en este lastimoso romance.* Essentially a penny-dreadful, this told the story of a young girl of sixteen who was so denatured by her love for a French soldier who was quartered in her house that she murdered her parents, her aunt and her sister so that she could escape with him. *Cf.* M. C. Simón, 'De heroínas a traidoras', in J. M. Cuenca Toribio (ed.), *Andalucía en la Guerra de la Independencia* (Córdoba, 2008), pp. 415–25.

24. *Cf.* Leslie, *Military Journal,* p. 270. However, if political persecution was limited, nothing could save women who had transgressed from the norms of the patriarchal society in which they lived: how many women were subjected to some form of punishment or ostracization by their families for having, for example, illegitimate babies, we shall never know.

25. E.g., Wylly, *Cavalry Officer in the Corunna Campaign,* p. 35; J. Catalina (ed.), *Diario de un Patriota Complutense en la Guerra de la Independencia* (Alcalá de Henares, 1894), pp. 82–83.

26. *Gazeta de la Junta Superior de la Mancha,* 23 May 1812, p. 73.

27. Note, for example, the manner in which the Patriot press seemingly never missed an opportunity to note the involvement of women in *la guerrilla; cf.* Cantos, 'Las mujeres en la prensa', pp. 181–83.

28. *Cf. Suplemento a la Gazeta de Gobierno,* 7 July 1809, pp. 692–93.

29. F. E. Castrillón, *El sermón sin frutas, o sea Josef Botellas en el ayuntamiento de Logroño: pieza jocosa en un acto* (Valencia, 1809), p. 2.

30. *Cit.* Lady Jackson (ed.), *The Diaries and Letters of Sir George Jackson, K.C.H., from the Peace of Amiens to the Battle of Talavera* (London, 1872), II, p. 386.

31. *Ibid.* The then Bishop of Durham, Shute Barrington, was a conservative evangelical who had won some notoriety by introducing a Bill designed to prevent divorced women from remarrying.

32. *Cf.* Sabine, *Letters of Colonel Sir Augustus Simon Frazer,* p. 36.

33. *Cf.* Herr, *Memorias del Cura Liberal Don Juan Antonio Posse,* p. 135.

Select Bibliography

Primary Sources

Alcaide, A., *Historia de los dos sitios que pusieron a Zaragoza en los años de 1808 y 1809 las tropas de Napoleón* (Burgos, 1830)

Alexander, B. (ed.), *The Journal of William Beckford in Portugal and Spain, 1787–1788* (London, 1954)

Almuina, C. (ed.), *Valladolid: diarios curiosos, 1807–1841* (Valladolid, 1989)

Anon., *Jottings from my Sabretache* (London, 1847)

———, *Journal of a Soldier of the Seventy-First, or Glasgow Regiment, Highland Light Infantry, from 1806 to 1815* (Edinburgh, 1819)

———, *Memoirs of a Sergeant late in the Forty-Third Light Infantry Regiment previously to and during the Peninsular War* (London, 1835)

———, *Personal Narrative of a Private Soldier who served in the Forty-Second Highlanders for Twelve Years during the Late War* (London, 1821)

——— (ed.), 'Un vaudois à l'Armée d'Espagne d'après les souvenirs inédits du Lieutenant Jean-David Maillefer, 1809–13', in Anon. (ed.), *Soldats suisses au service étranger* (Geneva, 1909), pp. 257–98

Anton, J., *Retrospect of a Military Life during the Most Eventful Periods of the Late War* (Edinburgh, 1841)

Bankes, G.N. (ed.), *The Autobiography of Sergeant William Lawrence, a Hero of the Peninsular and Waterloo Campaigns* (London, 1886)

Beaulaincourt-Marles, Comtesse de (ed.), *Journal du Maréchal de Castellane, 1804–1862* (Paris, 1895–97)

Bégos, L., 'Souvenirs de ses campagnes', in Anon. (ed.), *Soldats suisses au service étranger* (Geneva, 1909), pp. 112–233

Bell, G., *Rough Notes by an Old Soldier* (London, 1867)

Bell, N. (ed.), *Memoirs of Baron Lejeune, aide-de-camp to Marshals Berthier, Davout and Oudinot* (London, 1897)

Berazáluce, A. (ed.), *Recuerdos de la vida de Don Pedro Agustín Girón* (Pamplona, 1978)

Beslay, P. (ed.), *Un officier d'état-major sous le Premier Empire: souvenirs militaires d'Octave Levavasseur, officier d'artillerie, aide de camp du Maréchal Ney, 1802–1815* (Paris, 1914)

Bigarré, A., *Mémoires du Général Bigarré, aide-de-camp du Roi Joseph, 1775–1813* (Paris, 1903)

Blakiston, J., *Twelve Years' Military Adventure in Three Quarters of the Globe* (London, 1829)

Blaze, S., *Mémoires d'un apothicaire sur le guerre d'Espagne pendant les années 1808 à 1814* (Paris, 1828)

Blayney, A., *Narrative of a Forced Journey through France and Spain as a Prisoner of War in the Years 1810 to 1814* (London, 1814)

Boulart, J. F., *Mémoires militaries du Général Baron Boulart sur les guerres de la république et de l'empire* (Paris, n.d.)

Bourachot, C. (ed.), *Sergent Lavaux: mémoires du campagne* (Paris, 2004)

———, *Souvenirs militaires du Captaine Jean-Baptiste Lemonnier-Delafosse* (Paris, n.d.)

Bourgoing, J. F. de, *Modern State of Spain* (London, 1808)

Boutflower, C., *The Journal of an Army Surgeon during the Peninsular War* (London, 1912)

Brindle, R. (ed.), *Campaigning for Napoleon: the Diary of a Napoleonic Cavalry Officer, 1806–13* (Barnsley, 2006)

———, *With Napoleon's Guns: the Military Memoirs of an Officer of the First Empire* (London, 2005)

Buckham, E., *Personal Narrative of Adventures in the Peninsula during the War in 1812–13* (London, 1827)

Buckley, R. N. (ed.), *The Napoleonic War Journal of Captain Thomas Henry Browne, 1807–1816* (London, 1987)

Bunbury, T., *Reminiscences of a Veteran* (London, 1861)

Butler, A. J. (ed.), *The Memoirs of Baron Thiébault, late Lieutenant-General in the French Army* (London, 1896)

Cadell, C., *Narrative of the Campaigns of the Twenty-Eighth Regiment since their Return from Egypt in 1802* (London, 1835)

Carnicero, C., *Historia razonada de los principales sucesos de la gloriosa revolución de España* (Madrid, 1814)

Carr, J., *Descriptive Travels in the Southern and Eastern Parts of Spain and the Balearic Islands in the Year 1809* (London, 1811)

Carr-Gomm, F. C. (ed.), *Letters and Journals of Field Marshal Sir William Maynard Carr-Gomm* (London, 1881)

Casamayor, F., *Diario de los sitios de Zaragoza, 1808–1809*, ed. H. Lafoz Rabaza (Zaragoza, 2000)

Cassells, S. A. C. (ed.), *Peninsular Portrait, 1811–1814: the Letters of William Bragge, Third (King's Own) Dragoons* (London, 1963)

Catalina, J. (ed.), *Diario de un patriota complutense en la Guerra de la Independencia* (Alcalá de Henares, 1894)

Clemenso, H., *Souvenirs d'un officier valaisan au service de France*, ed. Zermastten, M. (Paris, 1999)

Costello, E., *Adventures of a Soldier* (London, 1852)

Croker, R., *Travels through Several Provinces of Spain and Portugal* (London, 1799)

Dallas, A., *Félix Alvarez* (London, 1818)

Dalrymple, W., *Travels through Spain and Portugal in 1774* (London, 1777)

Darwin, F. S., *Travels in Spain and the East, 1808–1810*, ed. Darwin, F. D. (Cambridge, 1927)

Desboeufs, C. (ed.), *Les étapes d'un soldat de l'Empire, 1800–1815: souvenirs du Capitaine Desboeufs* (Paris, 1901)

D'Espinchal, H. *Souvenirs militaires, 1792–1814,* ed. Masson, F., and Boyer, E. (Paris 1901)

D'Ideville, H. (ed.), *Memoirs of Colonel Bugeaud from his Private Correspondence and Original Documents, 1784–1815* (London, 1884)

Dillon, J. T., *Letters from an English Traveller in Spain in 1778* (London, 1781)

———, *Travels through Spain* (Dublin, 1781)

Dobbs, J., *Recollections of an Old Fifty-Second Man* (Waterford, 1863)

Donaldson, J., *Recollections in the Eventful Life of a Soldier* (Edinburgh, 1852)

Ducor, H., *Aventures d'un marin de la Garde Imperiale, prisonnier de guerre sur les pontons espagnols, dans l'ile de Cabrera et en Russie* (Paris, 1838)

Fantin des Odoards, L.F., *Journal du Général Fantin des Odoards: étapes d'un officier de la Grande Armée, 1800–1830* (Paris, 1895)

Fée, A.L.A, *Souvenirs de la Guerre d'Espagne, dite de l'Independance, 1809–1813* (Paris, 1856)

Fernyhough, T. (ed.), *Military Memoirs of Four Brothers* (London, 1829)

Fischer, C. *A Picture of Madrid taken on the Spot* (London, 1808)

Fitzmaurice, F. M. *Recollections of a Rifleman's Wife at Home and Abroad* (London, 1851)

Fletcher, I. (ed.), *For King and Country: the Letters and Diaries of John Mills, Coldstream Guards, 1811–14* (Staplehurst, 1995)

———, *In the Service of the King: the Letters of William Thornton Keep at Home, Walcheren and in the Peninsula* (Staplehurst, 1997)

García de León y Pizarro, J., *Memorias de la vida del Excmo. Señor D. José García de León y Pizarro escritas por el mismo,* ed. A. Alonso Castrillo (Madrid, 1894)

Girardin, L.S. de, *Journal et souvenirs, discours et opinions de S. Girardin* (Paris, 1828)

Glover, G. (ed.), *An Eloquent Soldier: the Peninsular War Journals of Lieutenant Charles Crowe of the Inniskillings, 1812–1814* (Barnsley, 2011)

———, *Wellington's Lieutenant, Napoleon's Gaoler: the Peninsula and St Helena Diaries and Letters of Sir George Rideout Bingham, 1809–21* (Barnsley, 2005)

Glover, M. (ed.), *A Gentleman Volunteer: the Letters of George Hennell from the Peninsular War, 1812–13* (London, 1979)

Gonneville, A. de, *Recollections of Colonel de Gonneville,* ed. C. Yonge (London, 1875)

Graham, W., *Travels through Portugal and Spain during the Peninsular War* (London, 1820)

Grattan, W., *Adventures of the Connaught Rangers from 1808 to 1814* (London, 1847)

Grivel, J., *Mémoires du Vice-Amiral Baron Grivel* (Paris, 1914)

Hamilton, A., *Hamilton's Campaign with Moore and Wellington during the Peninsular War* (Troy, New York, 1847)

Hay, W., *Reminiscences 1808–1815 under Wellington,* ed. S. Wood (London, 1901)

Haythornthwaite, P. (ed.), *In the Peninsula with a French Hussar* (London, 1990)

———, *Life in Napoleon's Army: the Memoirs of Captain Elzéar Blaze* (London, 1995)

Henegan, R., *Seven Years' Campaigning in the Peninsula and the Netherlands from 1808 to 1815* (London, 1846)

Herr, R., *Memorias del cura liberal Don Juan Antonio Posse con su discurso sobre la constitución de 1812* (Madrid, 1984)

Hibbert, C. (ed.), *The Recollections of Rifleman Harris as told to Henry Curling* (London, 1970)

Hunt, E. (ed.), *Charging against Napoleon: Diaries and Letters of Three Hussars, 1808–1815* (London, 2001)

Ilchester, Earl of (ed.), *The Spanish Journal of Elizabeth, Lady Holland* (London, 1910)

Jackson, Lady (ed.), *The Diaries and Letters of Sir George Jackson, K.C.H., from the Peace of Amiens to the Battle of Talavera* (London, 1872)

Jacob, W., *Travels in the South of Spain in Letters written A.D. 1809 and 1810* (London, 1811)

Jones, B. T. (ed.), *Military Memoirs of Charles Parquin* (London, 1987)

Junot, L., *Mémoires de Madame la Duchesse d'Abrantes* (Brussels 1837)

Kincaid, J., *Adventures in the Rifle Brigade* (London, 1830)

———, *Random Shots from a Rifleman* (London, 1835)

Laborde, A. de, *A View of Spain* (London, 1809)

Larpent, G. (ed.), *The Private Journal of Judge-Advocate Larpent attached to the Headquarters of Lord Wellington during the Peninsular War from 1812 to its Close* (London, 1854)

Larreguy de Civrieux, S., *Souvenirs d'un cadet, 1812–1823*, ed. Larreguy de Civrieux, L. (Paris, 1912)

Lavaux, F., *Mémoires de campagne, 1793–1814*, ed. C. Bourachot (Paris, 2004).

Leach, J., *Rough Services in the Life of an Old Soldier* (London, 1831)

Lejeune, L. F., *Los sitios de Zaragoza*, ed. Rújula, P. (Zaragoza, 2009)

Leslie, C., *Military Journal of Colonel Leslie, K.H., of Balquhain, whilst serving with the Twenty-Ninth Regiment in the Peninsula and the Sixtieth Rifles in Canada, etc., 1807 -1832* (Aberdeen, 1887)

Ludovici, A. (ed.), *On the Road with Wellington: the Diary of a War Commissary in the Peninsular Campaigns* (New York, 1925)

Malmesbury, Third Earl of (ed.), *A Series of Letters of the First Earl of Malmesbury, his Family and Friends from 1745 to 1820* (London, 1870)

Mämpel, J. C., *Adventures of a Young Rifleman in the French and English Armies during the War in Spain and Portugal from 1806 to 1816* (London, 1826)

Marbot, M. de, *The Memoirs of Baron de Marbot* (London, 1892)

Mendoza y Rico, J., *Historia de Málaga durante la revolución santa que agita a España desde marzo de 1808*, ed. M. Olmedo (Málaga, 2003)

Monick, S. (ed.), *Douglas' Tale of the Peninsula and Waterloo* (London, 1997)

———, *The Iberian and Waterloo Campaigns: the Letters of James Hope, Ninety- Second (Highland) Regiment, 1811–1815* (London, 2000)

Moore-Smith. G. C. (ed.), *The Autobiography of Sir Harry Smith, 1787–1819* (London, 1910)

Naylies, J. J. de, *Mémoires sur la guerre d'Espagne pendant les années 1808, 1809, 1810 et 1811* (Paris, 1817)

Neale, A., *Letters from Portugal and Spain* (London, 1809)

Nevill, P. P., *Some Recollections in the Life of Lieut.-Col. P.P. Nevill, late Major, 63rd Regiment* (London, 1864)

North, J. (ed.), *In the Legions of Napoleon: the Memoirs of a Polish Officer in Spain and Russia, 1808–1813* (London, 1999)

Oman, C. (ed.), 'A prisoner of Albuera: the journal of Major William Brooke from 16 May to 28 September 1811', in Oman, C., *Studies in the Napoleonic Wars* (Oxford, 1929), pp. 175–206

O'Neill, C., *The Military Adventures of Charles O'Neill* (Worcester, Massachusetts, 1851)

Ormsby, J.W., *An Account of the Operations of the British Army and of the State and Sentiments of the People of Portugal and Spain during the Campaigns of the Years 1808 and 1809* (London, 1809)

Oyon, J. A., *Campagnes et souvenirs militaires, 1805–1814* (Paris, 1997)

Page, J. (ed.), *Intelligence Officer in the Peninsula: Letters and Diaries of Major the Honourable Charles Somers Cocks, 1786–1812* (Tunbridge Wells, 1986)

Patterson, J., *The Adventures of Captain John Patterson* (London, 1837)

Peltier, J. G., *Campagne de Portugal en 1810 et 1811* (Paris, 1814)

Porter, R. K., *Letters from Portugal and Spain written during the March of the British Troops under Sir John Moore* (London, 1809)

Presa, F., *et al.* (eds.), *Soldados polacos en España durante la Guerra de la Independencia Española, 1808–1814* (Madrid, 2004)

Ross-Lewin, H., *With the Thirty-Second in the Peninsula and other Campaigns*, ed. J. Wardell (Dublin, 1904)

Rouillard, T. (ed.), *Rélations de la campagne d'Andalousie* (La Vouvre, 1999)

Roy, J., *Les français en Espagne: souvenirs des guerres de la péninsule* (Tours, 1856)

Sabine, E. (ed.), *Letters of Colonel Sir Augustus Simon Frazer, K.C.B.* (London, 1859)

Saint-Chamans, A. de, *Mémoires du Général Comte de Saint-Chamans, ancien aide-de-camp du Maréchal Soult, 1802–1832* (Paris, 1896)

Santa Cruz y Montalvo de Merlin, M. de, *Memorias y recuerdos de la Señora Condesa de Merlin* (Havana, 1853)

Santillán, R., *Memorias de Don Ramón Santillán, 1808–1856*, ed. A. Berazaluce (Madrid, 1996)

Sanz, J. (ed.), *Monjas en guerra, 1808–1814: testimonios de mujeres desde el claustro* (Madrid, 2010)

Steevens, C., *Reminiscences of my Military Life from 1795 to 1818* (Winchester, 1878)

Stepney, J. C., *Leaves from the Diary of an Officer of the Guards* (London, 1854)

Stothert, W., *A Narrative of the Principal Events of the Campaigns of 1809, 1810 and 1811 in Spain and Portugal* (London, 1812)

Sturgis, J. (ed.), *A Boy in the Peninsular War: the Services, Adventures and Experiences of Robert Blakeney, Subaltern in the Twenty-Eighth Regiment* (London, 1899)

Surtees, W., *Twenty-Five Years in the Rifle Brigade* (Edinburgh, 1833)

Swinburne, H., *Travels through Spain in the Years 1775 and 1776* (Dublin, 1779)

Thirion, A., *Souvenirs militaires* (Paris, 1892)

Thompson, W. F. K. (ed.), *An Ensign in the Peninsular War: the Letters of John Aitchison* (London, 1981)

Tomkinson, J. (ed.), *The Diary of a Cavalry Officer in the Peninsular and Waterloo Campaigns* (London, 1894)

Townsend, J., *A Journey through Spain in the Years 1786 and 1787* (London, 1791)

Twiss, R., *Travels through Portugal and Spain in 1772 and 1773* (London, 1775)

Var, L. (ed.), *Campagnes du Capitaine Marcel du 69e de Ligne en Espagne et Portugal, 1808–1814* (Paris, 1914)

Vaughan, C. R., *Narrative of the Siege of Zaragoza* (London, 1809)

Verner, W. (ed.), *A British Rifleman: Journals and Correspondence during the Peninsular War and the Campaign of Waterloo* (London, 1899)

Warre, E. (ed.), *Letters from the Peninsula, 1808–1812 by William Warre* (London, 1909)

Westmoreland, Earl of, *Memoir of the Early Campaigns of the Duke of Wellington in Portugal and Spain* (London, 1820)

Whinyates, F. (ed.), *Diary of Campaigns in the Peninsula for the Years 1811, 12 and 13 written by Lieutenant William Swabey, an Officer of E Troop (present E Battery), Royal Horse Artillery* (Woolwich, 1895)

Whittingham, F. (ed.), *A Memoir of the Services of Samuel Ford Whittingham* (London, 1868)

Wojciechowski, K., *Mis memorias de España,* ed. Ciechanowski, J.S., *et al.* (Madrid, 2009)

Wood, G., *The Subaltern Officer: a Memoir* (London, 1825)

Wylly, H. C. (ed.), *A Cavalry Officer in the Corunna Campaign: the Journal of Captain Gordon of the Fifteenth Hussars* (London, 1913)

Secondary Sources

Acosta, F., 'Mujeres en la campaña de Andalucía: María Bellido y la batalla de Bailén', in Castells, I., Espigado, G., and Romeo, M.C. (eds.), *Heroínas y patriotas: mujeres de 1808* (Madrid, 2009), pp. 57–79

Ansón, M. C., 'El papel de la mujer aragonesa en el proceso emigratorio aragonés a fines del siglo XVIII', in López-Cordón, M.V., and Carbonell, M. (eds.), *Historia de la mujer e historia de la familia* (Murcia, 1997), pp. 241–60

Antiguedad, M. D., 'Goya y la genesis de un nuevo modelo femenino en la Guerra de la Independencia', *Revista Historia Moderna y Contemporánea,* VIII (2010), pp. 8–24

Barbastro, L., 'Plan de la reforma de la iglesia española impulsado por Napoleón Bonaparte', *Hispania Sacra,* LX, No. 121 (January, 2008), pp. 267–95

Baz, M. J., 'Las mujeres en la Guerra de la Independencia en Galicia: una historia de omisión y anonimato', in Castells, I., Espigado, G., and Romeo, M. C. (eds.), *Heroínas y patriotas: mujeres de 1808* (Madrid, 2009), pp. 81–104

Bertrand, C., and Diéz López, A., 'Mujeres solas en la ciudad del siglo XVIII' in López-Cordón, M. V., and Carbonell, M. (eds.), *Historia de la mujer e historia de la familia* (Murcia, 1997), pp. 165–72

Blanco, C., *Historia social de la literatura española* (Madrid, 1978)

Bolufer, M., *Mujeres e ilustración: la construcción de la feminidad en la España del siglo XVIII* (Valencia, 1998)

———, 'Neither male nor female: rational equality in the early Spanish Enlightenment', in Knott, S., and Taylor, B. (eds.), *Women, Gender and Enlightenment* (Basingstoke, 2005), pp. 389–409

———, 'Women of letters in eighteenth-century Spain: between tradition and modernity', in Jaafe, C. M. and Lewis, E. F. (eds.), *Eve's Enlightenment:*

Women's Experience in Spain and Spanish America, 1726–1839 (Baton Rouge, 2009), pp. 17–32

Borreguero, C. *Burgos en la Guerra de la Independencia; enclave estratégico y ciudad expoliada* (Burgos, 2007)

Callahan, W. J., *Church, Politics and Society in Spain, 1750–1874* (Cambridge, Mass., 1984)

Câmara, M. E. da, 'A imagem da mulher na ficção literária anti-napoleónica', *Revista Historia Moderna y Contemporánea,* VIII (2010), pp. 25–32

Cantos, M., 'Entre la tertulia y la imprenta: la palabra encendida de una patriota andaluza—Frasquita Larrea, 1775–1838', in Castells, I., Espigado, G., and Romeo, M.C. (eds.), *Heroínas y patriotas: mujeres de 1808* (Madrid, 2009), pp. 269–94

———, 'La literatura femenina en la Guerra de la Independencia: a la ciudadanía por el patriotismo', *Revista Historia Moderna y Contemporánea,* VIII (2010), pp. 33–48

———, 'Las mujeres en la prensa entre la ilustración y el romanticismo', in Cantos, M., Durán F., and Romero, A. (eds.), *La guerra de pluma: estudios sobre la prensa de Cádiz en el tiempo de las cortes, 1810–1814* (Cádiz, 2008), pp. 161–336

Capel, R. M., 'La prostitución en España: notas para un estudio socio-histórico', in Capel, R. M. (ed.), *Mujer y sociedad en España, 1700–1975* (Madrid, 1982), pp. 47–108

Carasa, P., *Pauperismo y revolución burguesa: Burgos, 1750–1900* (Valladolid, 1987)

Cardoza, T., *Intrepid Women: Cantinières and Vivandières of the French Army* (Bloomington, Indiana, 2010)

Caro, J., *Las formas complejas de la vida religiosa: religion, sociedad y cáracter en la España de los siglos XVI y XVII* (Madrid, 1978)

Castells, I., Espigado, G., and Romeo, M.C., 'Heroínas para la patria, madres para la nación: mujeres en pie de guerra', in Castells, I., Espigado, G., and Romeo, M.C. (eds.), *Heroínas y patriotas: mujeres de 1808* (Madrid, 2009), pp. 15–54

Conner, S., '*Les femmes militaires:* women in the French army, 1792–1815', *CREP,* XII (1982), pp. 290–302

Coy, A., *Agustina Saragossa* [sic] *Domenech: heroína de los sitios de Zaragoza* (Ceuta, 1914)

Desdevises, G., *La España del antiguo régimen,* ed. González, A. (Madrid, 1989)

Díaz Plaja, F., *Dos de mayo de 1808* (Madrid, 1996)

Doumergue, L., 'Goya, las mujeres y la guerra contra Bonaparte', in Reder, M., and Mendoza, E. (eds.), *La Guerra de la Independencia en Málaga y su provincia, 1808–1814* (Málaga, 2005), pp. 231–48

Esdaile, C. J., 'Bullets, baggages and ballads: forgotten sources for the experience of British women in the Revolutionary and Napoleonic Wars, 1793–1815', in Duarte, M. D. (ed.), *Da Guerra Peninsular: retratos y representações* (Lisbon, 2011), pp. 13–37

Espigado, G., 'Armas de mujer: el patriotismo de las españolas en la Guerra de la Independencia', in Diego, E. de, and Martínez, J.L. (eds.), *El comienzo de la Guerra de la Independencia: congreso internacional del bicentenario* (Madrid, 2009), pp. 709–49

———, 'Europeas y españolas contra Napoleón: un estudio comparado', *Revista Historia Moderna y Contemporánea,* VIII (2010), pp. 49–64

———, 'La Marquesa de Villafranca y la Junta de Damas de Fernando VII', in Castells, I., Espigado, G., and Romeo, M. C. (eds.), *Heroínas y patriotas: mujeres de 1808* (Madrid, 2009), pp. 317–42

Evangelisti, S., *Nuns: a History of Convent Life, 1450–1750* (Oxford, 2007)

Fernández Álvarez, M., *Casadas, monjas, rameras y brujas: la olvidada historia de la mujer española en el Renacimiento* (Madrid, 2002)

Fernández García, E., 'El liberalismo, las mujeres y la Guerra de la Independencia', in Moliner, A. (ed.), *Occapació i resistència a la Guerra del Francès, 1808–1814* (Barcelona, 2007), pp. 203–10

———, 'Heroínas del cine', *Revista Historia Moderna y Contemporánea,* VIII (2010), pp. 64–78

———, 'Las mujeres en los sitios de Gerona: la Compañía de Santa Bárbara', in Castells, I., Espigado, G., and Romeo, M.C. (eds.), *Heroínas y patriotas: mujeres de 1808* (Madrid, 2009), pp. 105–28

———, *Mujeres en la Guerra de la Independencia* (Madrid, 2009)

———, 'Transgresión total y trangresión parcial en las defensoras de la Patria', *Mélanges de la Casa de Velasquez,* XXXVIII, No. 1 (January, 2008), pp. 135–54

Fernández Poza, M., 'Diarios y escritos políticos de Frasquita Larrea Böhl de Faber: romanticismo y nacionalismo, 1808–1814', in Moliner, A. (ed.), *Occapació i resistència a la Guerra del Francès, 1808–1814* (Barcelona, 2007), pp. 211–21

Fernández Vargas, V., 'Las españolas en la Guerra de la Independencia', in Ministerio de Defensa (ed.), *La Guerra de la Independencia, 1808–1814: el pueblo español, su ejército y sus aliados frente a la ocupación napoleónica* (Madrid, 2008), pp. 127–51

Flores, E. M., 'El gran teatro del mundo: el Cádiz de las cortes de Galdós', *Cuadernos de ilustración y romanticismo,* No. 10 (2002), pp. 45–58

Fraser, R., *Las dos guerras de Espana* (Madrid, 2012)

———, *Napoleon's Cursed War: Popular Resistance in the Spanish Peninsular War* (London, 2008)

García Carrión, M.G., '"Por qué me habeís hecho soldado si no podía dejar de ser mujer?" El mito de Agustina de Aragón en su primera recreación cinematográfica', in Castells, I., Espigado, G., and Romeo, M. C. (eds.), *Heroínas y patriotas: mujeres de 1808* (Madrid, 2009), pp. 129–53

García Fuertes, A., *Dos de mayo de 1808: grito de una nación* (Madrid, 2008)

García Hourcade, J. J., 'Asistidas, recogidas, corregidas: el lugar de la mujer en el sistema asistencial del siglo XVIII' in López-Cordón, M. V., and Carbonell, M. (eds.), *Historia de la mujer e historia de la familia* (Murcia, 1997), pp. 233–40

Gomes da Torre, M., 'A segunda invasão francesa em *The Sisters of the Douro*', in Machado, M. L. (ed.), *A Guerra Peninsular: perspectivas multidisciplinares* (Lisbon, 2007), I, pp. 541–49

Gomes Fernandes, A., 'Da baioneta à pena: as invasões francesas na obra de Arnaldo Gama', in Machado, M. L. (ed.), *A Guerra Peninsular: perspectivas multidisciplinares* (Lisbon, 2007), I, pp. 587–609

Gómez de Arteche, J., *La mujer en la Guerra de la Independencia* (Madrid, 1906)

Grant de Pauw, L., *Battle Cries and Lullabies: Women in War from Prehistory to Present* (Norman, Oklahoma, 1998)

Hacker, B. C., 'Women and military institutions in early-modern Europe: a reconnaissance', *Signs,* VI, No. 4 (Summer, 1981), pp. 643–71

Haidt, R., 'The wife, the maid and the woman in the street', in Jaafe, C. M. and Lewis, E. F. (eds.), *Eve's Enlightenment: Women's Experience in Spain and Spanish America, 1726–1839* (Baton Rouge, 2009), pp. 115–27

Higgs, D., 'The Portuguese Church', in Callahan, W. J., and Higgs, D. (eds.), *Church and Society in Catholic Europe of the Eighteenth Century* (Cambridge, 1979), pp. 51–65

Hopkin, D., 'The world turned upside-down: female soldiers in the French armies of the Revolutionary and Napoleonic Wars', in Forrest, A., *et al.* (eds.), *Soldiers, Citizens and Civilians: Experiences and Perceptions of the Revolutionary and Napoleonic Wars, 1790–1820* (Houndmills, 2009), pp. 77–95

Hufton, O., *The Prospect before Her: a History of Women in Western Europe, I: 1500–1800* (London, 1995)

Iglesias Rogers, G., *British Liberators in the Age of Napoleon: Volunteering under the Spanish Flag in the Peninsular War* (London, 2013)

Jiménez Bartolomé, A. M., 'Las mujeres en la Guerra de la Independencia: propaganda y resistencia', in Moliner, A. (ed.), *Occapació i resistència a la Guerra del Francès, 1808–1814* (Barcelona, 2007), pp. 247–56

———, '"Los otros combatientes en la Guerra de la Independencia": el papel femenino', in Castañeda, P. (ed.), *Las guerras en el primer tercio del siglo XIX en España y América: XII jornadas nacionales de historia militar* (Seville, 2004), pp. 347–64

Kitts, S. A., *The Debate on the Nature, Role and Influence of Women in Eighteenth-Century Spain* (Lewiston, New York, 1995)

Lavrin, A., 'Ecclesiastical reform of nunneries in New Spain in the eighteenth century', *The Americas,* XXII, No. 2 (October, 1965), pp. 182–203

López Barahona, V., *El cepo y el torneo: la reclusión femenina en el Madrid del siglo XVIII* (Madrid, 2009)

López-Cordón, M. V., *Condición femenina y razón ilustrada: Josefa Amar y Borbón* (Zaragoza, 2005)

———, 'La literatura religiosa y moral como conformadora de la mentalidad femenina, 1760–1860', in Folguera, P. (ed.), *La mujer en la historia de España (SS. XVI-XX): actas de las II Jornadas de Investigación Interdisciplinaria* (Madrid, 1990), pp. 59–69

———, 'La situación de la mujer a finales del Antiguo Régimen', in Capel, R. M. (ed.), *Mujer y Sociedad en España, 1700–1975* (Madrid, 1982), pp. 47–108

———, 'Women in society in eighteenth-century Spain: models of sociability' in Jaafe, C. M. and Lewis, E. F. (eds.), *Eve's Enlightenment: Women's Experience in Spain and Spanish America, 1726–1839* (Baton Rouge, 2009), pp. 103–14

López Pérez, M., 'María Bellido, la heroína de Bailén', *Revista de Historia Militar,* XXIV, No. 49 (July, 1980), pp. 59–80; *ibid.*, XXV, No. 50 (January, 1981), pp. 61–88

Lynn, J., *Women, Armies and Warfare in Early-Modern Europe* (Cambridge, 2008)

Marinho, M. F., 'A memoria e a ficçao da segunda invasão francesa', in Valente de Oliveira, L. (ed.), *O Porto e as invasões francesas, 1809–2009* (Oporto, 2009), IV, pp. 205–32

Maroto, J., *Guerra de la Independencia: imágenes en cine y televisión* (Madrid, 2007)

———, 'La Guerra de la Independencia en la novela del siglo XX', in Miranda, F. (ed.), *Guerra, sociedad y política, 1808–1814* (Pamplona, 2008), pp. 355–403

———, 'La Guerra de la Independencia en los tebeos', in Armillas, J. (ed.), *La Guerra de la Independencia: estudios* (Zaragoza, 2001), I, pp. 387–416

Martín Gaite, C., *Love Customs in Eighteenth-Century Spain* (Berkeley, California, 1991)

Martín Pozuelo, L., 'Quereís recordar el Dos de Mayo? Estampas populares de la Guerra de La Independencia' in Demange, C., *et al.* (eds.), *Sombras de mayo: mitos y memorias de la Guerra de la Independencia en España, 1808–1908* (Madrid, 2007), pp. 321–44

Martín Rodrigo, R., *La Guerra de la Independencia en la provincia de Salamanca* (Salamanca, 2012)

Martín-Valdepeñas, E., 'Afrancesadas y patriotas: la Junta de Honor y Mérito de la Real Sociedad Económica Matritense de Amigos del País', in Castells, I., Espigado, G., and Romeo, M.C. (eds.), *Heroínas y patriotas: mujeres de 1808* (Madrid, 2009), pp. 343–70

———, 'Mis señoras las traidoras: las afrancesadas, una historia olvidada', *Revista Historia Moderna y Contemporánea*, VIII (2010), pp. 79–108

Martínez Cuesta, A., 'Monjas augustinas recoletas: historia y espiritualidad', *Acta Ordinis*, No. 86 (January, 1992), pp. 49–60

Menéndez González, A., *El barranco de las asturianas: mujer y sociedad en el antiguo régimen* (Oviedo, 2006)

Montón, J.C., *La revolución armada del dos de mayo en Madrid* (Madrid, 1983)

Morant, I. (ed.), *Historia de la mujer en España y América Látina* (Madrid, 2006–11)

Orti, J., *Córdoba en la Guerra de la Independencía* (Córdoba, 1930)

Page, F. C. G., *Following the Drum: Women in Wellington's Wars* (London, 1986)

Pascua, M. J. de la, 'Las mujeres en la Andalucía de la Guerra de la Independencia', in Delgado, J. M., and López, M. A. (eds.), *Andalucía en Guerra, 1808–1814* (Jaén, 2010), pp. 209–18

———, 'Las mujeres en un mundo de transición: espacios de sociabilidad y conflictividad en España entre los siglos XVIII y XIX', in Acosta, F. (ed.), *Conflicto y sociedad civil—la mujer en la guerra: actas de las cuartas jornadas sobre la batalla de Bailén y la España contemporánea* (Jaén, 2003), pp. 105–32

———, 'Women alone in Enlightenment Spain', in Jaafe, C. M. and Lewis, E. F. (eds.), *Eve's Enlightenment: Women's Experience in Spain and Spanish America, 1726–1839* (Baton Rouge, 2009), pp. 129–41

Pérez de Guzmán, J., *El Dos de Mayo en Madrid* (Madrid, 1908)

Pérez Estévez, R. M., *El problema de los vagos en la España del siglo XVIII* (Madrid, 1976)

Pérez Molina, I., *et al.*, *Las mujeres en el antiguo régimen: imagen y realidad, SS. XVI-XVIII* (Barcelona, 1994)

Perry, M. E., *Gender and Disorder in Early-Modern Seville* (Princeton, New Jersey, 1990)

Peyrou, I., 'Manuela Malasaña: de joven costurero a mito madrileño', in Castells, I., Espigado, G., and Romeo, M. C. (eds.), *Heroínas y patriotas: mujeres de 1808* (Madrid, 2009), pp. 155–74

Queralt, M. P., *Agustina de Aragón: la mujer y el mito* (2008)

Ramos, A., 'La vida cotidiana en el Cádiz de las cortes: el recurso a la prensa como fuente para su estudio', in Cantos Casenave, M., Durán López, F., and Romero, A. (eds.), *La guerra de pluma: estudios sobre la prensa de Cádiz en el tiempo de las cortes, 1810–1814*, III, pp. 21–102

Reder, M., 'Espionaje y represión en la Serranía de Ronda: María García, "la Tinajera", in Castells, I., Espigado, G., and Romeo, M.C. (eds.), *Heroínas y patriotas: mujeres de 1808* (Madrid, 2009), pp. 175–91

Rial, S., *Las mujeres en la economía urbana del antiguo régimen: Santiago durante el siglo XVIII* (La Coruña, 1995)

Rodríguez Solis, E., *Los guerrilleros de 1808: historia popular de la Guerra de la Independencia* (Barcelona, 1895)

Ruiz Carnal, J., *Dependientes y esclavizadas: historia de la mujer sevillana, 1803–1805* (Seville, 1993)

Saint-Saëns, A. (ed.), *Historia silenciada de la mujer: la mujer española desde la época medieval hasta la contemporánea* (Madrid, 1996)

Salgues, M., 'La Guerra de la Independencia y el teatro: tentativa de creación y de recuperación de una epopeya popular, 1840–1868', in Demange, C., *et al.* (eds.), *Sombras de mayo: mitos y memorias de la Guerra de la Independencia en España, 1808–1908* (Madrid, 2007), pp. 267–87

Salvá, A., *Burgos en la Guerra de la Independencia*, ed. C. Borreguero (Burgos, 2008)

Sánchez Arreiseigor, J. J., 'Mujeres en la guerra', in F. Miranda (ed.), *Guerra, sociedad y política, 1808–1814* (Pamplona, 2008), I, pp. 691–722

Sánchez Hita, B., 'Las escritoras en la prensa de la Guerra de la Independencia vista por sus colegas: lucha de genero o política?', *Revista Historia Moderna y Contemporánea*, VIII (2010), pp. 117–40

———, 'María del Carmen Silva, la Robespierre española: una heroína y periodista en la Guerra de la Indepndencia', in Castells, I., Espigado, G., and Romeo, M. C. (eds.), *Heroínas y patriotas: mujeres de 1808* (Madrid, 2009), pp. 399–425

Sánchez Lora, J. L., *Mujeres, conventos y formas de la religiosidad barroca* (Madrid, 1988)

Sánchez Ortega, M. H., 'La mujer, el amor y la religión en el antiguo régimen', in Folguera, P. (ed.), *La mujer en la historia de España (SS. XVI-XX): actas de las II Jornadas de Investigación Interdisciplinaria* (Madrid, 1990), pp. 35–58

Simón, M. C., 'De heroínas a traidoras', in Cuenca, J.M. (ed.), *Andalucía en la Guerra de la Independencia* (Córdoba, 2008), pp. 415–25

Soares de Abreu, I., 'Condesa de Ega, la *citoyenne* aristócrata', in Castells, I., Espigado, G., and Romeo, M. C. (eds.), *Heroínas y patriotas: mujeres de 1808* (Madrid, 2009), pp. 427–50

Soares de Abreu, I., 'O ar do tempo: la moda "a francesa"', *Revista Historia Moderna y Contemporánea*, VIII (2010), pp. 141–55

Solduga, F. J., *Agustina Saragossa* [sic] *Domenech: la artillera del Portillo* (Barcelona, 2007)

Solis, R., *El Cádiz de las cortes* (Madrid, 1958)

Tomlinson, J. A., 'Mothers, *majas* and *marcialidad:* faces of enlightenment in Spain', in Jaafe, C. M. and Lewis, E. F. (eds.), *Eve's Enlightenment: Women's Experience in Spain and Spanish America, 1726–1839* (Baton Rouge, 2009), pp. 218–36

Tone, J. L., 'A dangerous Amazon: Agustina Zaragoza and the Spanish revolutionary war, 1808–1814', *European History Quarterly,* XXXVII, No. 4 (October, 2007), pp. 548–61

———, 'Spanish women and the resistance to Napoleon', in Enders, V. L. and Radcliff, P. B. (ed.), *Constructing Spanish Womanhood: Female Identity in Modern Spain* (New York, 1999), pp. 259–82

Triviño, L., 'Percepción e iconografía de la "heroicidad de género" en la Guerra de la Independencia' in Ramos, A., and Romero, A. (eds.), *1808–1812: los emblemas de la libertad* (Cádiz, 2009), pp. 541–58

Ucelay, E., 'Agustina, la dama de cañón: el *topos* de la mujer fálica y el invento del patriotismo', in Castells, I., Espigado, G., and Romeo, M.C. (eds.), *Heroínas y patriotas: mujeres de 1808* (Madrid, 2009), pp. 193–265

Valenzuela, F., *La sociedad de Jaén ante la invasión napoleónica, 1808* (Jaén, 2000)

Vasco, E., *Ocupación e incendio de Valdepeñas por las tropas francesas en 1808* (Valdepeñas, 1908)

Velasco, S. M., *Lesbians in Early-Modern Spain* (Nashville, Tennessee, 2011)

Venning, A., *Following the Drum: the Lives of Army Wives and Daughters* (London, 2005)

Vlachou, F., 'Painting the Battle of Porto, 29 March 1809: the *desastre da ponte das barcas* in its Portuguese and French context', *Revista de estudos anglo-portugueses,* XVIII (2009), pp. 49–68

Whitaker, D., 'A new voice: the rise of the enlightened woman in eighteenth-century Spain', in G. Adamson and E. Myers (eds.), *Continental, Latin-American and Francophone Women Writers: Selected Papers from the Wichita State University Conference on Foreign Literature, 1986–1987* (Lanham, Maryland, 1990), II, pp. 31–40

Yépez, D.,'Víctimas y participantes: la mujer española en la Peninsular War desde la óptica británica', *Revista Historia Moderna y Contemporania,* VIII (2010), pp. 156–78

Zorrozúa, M. P., *Escritoras de la ilustración española* (Deusto, 1999)

Index

CPSIA information can be obtained
at www.ICGtesting.com
Printed in the USA
LVHW041323160322
713506LV00005B/311

9 780806 185699